D1452027

The
Harvard University
Hymn Book
2007

The
Harvard University
Hymn Book

Fourth edition

Harvard University Press

Cambridge, Massachusetts
London, England
2007

The Harvard University Hymn Book
Fourth Edition

Peter J. Gomes
Matthew F. Burt
Carson P. Cooman
Harry Lyn Huff
Edward Elwyn Jones

Editorial Committee

The Memorial Church
Harvard University
One Harvard Yard
Cambridge, MA 02138-6500

ISBN 10: 0-674-02696-9
ISBN 13: 978-0-674-02696-4

Printed in the United States of America

Preface

This is the fourth hymn book designed for the use of the chapel in Harvard University, the first edition having appeared in 1895, issued at the direction of the Board of Preachers after nearly a decade of voluntary and non-denominational chapel services. In 1886, compulsory attendance at chapel was abolished, and it was agreed that in addition to good preaching shared among a board of distinguished ministers, good music was essential to the success of the new model for University worship. Each of the several preachers was invited to propose fifty hymns in which young men would find "masculine piety and honest aspiration," and the final selection was left to the Plummer Professor of Christian Morals, Dr. Francis Greenwood Peabody, with the tunes chosen by the University Organist and Choirmaster, Andrew Warren Locke.

The book excluded "hymns of a character foreign to the natural sentiments of young men," and as it was intended for use at the daily service of Morning Prayers and the principal service on Sunday evenings, it contained a large number of hymns for morning and evening worship. The theological context within which the College chapel conducted its worship, while self-consciously non-denominational, was essentially Unitarian and non-sacramental. Until 1909, when the Sunday service was moved from evening to morning, the choir was one of men and boys, who lead the singing from the organ gallery in the west end of Appleton Chapel. The first edition was mildly revised in 1905, and served until 1926, when the second edition of *The Harvard University Hymn Book* was published.

In his "Preface to the Hymns," in 1926, Edward Caldwell Moore, then chairman of the Board of Preachers, noted that the old book had served for thirty-seven years, and had witnessed many changes in the life of the Christian community. The experiment of voluntary chapel was now long a fixture of University life, the service had been transferred from the evening to the morning, and the choir of men and boys replaced by a choir of undergraduate men. Perhaps of greatest significance was the fact that the music was now in the charge of Archibald Thompson Davison, who even then was regarded as one of the greatest choral conductors and church musicians of his generation. "Doc" Davison, as he was known at Harvard and beyond, had already transformed the Harvard Glee Club into a serious choral ensemble of national reputation and, as the choir that sang in the chapel daily and on Sundays consisted of the best men of the Glee Club, that musical standard was upheld in the chapel services. In 1909, Davison and Moore developed the annual Carol Services, which proved immensely popular, partly due to the then novel introduction of women's voices from Radcliffe College to the choral sound of the Harvard chapel.

The Harvard University Hymn Book of 1926 would represent the best of musical scholarship then available. In Professor Moore's words, a book suitable for use in the University chapel

> "must be impartial and comprehensive...endeavoring to convey to worshippers a true sense of the long and varied past through which the Christian spirit has come down to us, and perhaps not less, of the types of Christian spirit which prevail in our own time. Those distinctions should have a place in the mind of an educated man."

Archibald Thompson Davison argued for a lean and superior book over one larger and less discriminating, as far as the tunes were concerned. With fewer tunes, it was suggested, the congregation would become more familiar with those available. Davison wrote:

> "The aim has not been to include as many good tunes as possible. We have preferred to use the best tunes a number of times. To be exact, there are one hundred and twenty-one melodies set to three hundred and four texts."

There is an amusing incident concerning one of the new tunes for the book, to wit, Dr. Davison wrote to his good friend, Ralph Vaughan Williams, who had served as music editor of the English Hymnal, asking for permission to include his tune SINE NOMINE, set to Bishop W.W. Howe's text, "For All the Saints," in the Harvard book. Up to that time, most of America had sung "For All the Saints" to Joseph Barnby's tune SARUM. Davison, noting the conservative nature of the Harvard congregation, asked if in the Harvard edition Vaughan Williams's tune, famous for starting on the second beat, could commence on a whole note. It does so at Hymn 83, in perhaps the only permitted alteration extant of that great tune.

That book would remain in use for thirty-eight years, and as the years passed there were many criticisms. In a letter to George A. Buttrick, appointed in 1955 the new Plummer Professor of Christian Morals and Preacher to the University, Dr. John Howard Lathrop, of the Church of the Saviour in Brooklyn, New York, wrote:

> "I wish you might be bold and bring about a change
> in the hymn book. If I remember correctly, E. C.
> Moore was largely responsible for the one now used
> and, to my way of thinking, no hymn book in cre-
> ation has more unsingable music."

Buttrick, former minister of New York City's Madison Avenue Presbyterian Church and used to a large denominational hymn book filled with familiar hymns, was tempted simply to replace the Harvard book with a new one, but in his distinguished but brief tenure of five years he never got around to doing it. In 1958 he did, however, appoint a new University Organist and Choirmaster, John R. Ferris, who succeeded George Wallace Woodworth. "Woody" had succeeded his mentor Dr. Davison in 1940, and played a significant part in the preparation of the 1926 book. Although Dr. Buttrick retired in 1960, and thus had no hand in the production of a new book, the consideration of one was taken up by Mr. Ferris who, upon his appointment, had transformed the University Choir from a male chorus to a four-part choir through the inclusion of female voices.

In 1959, the Board of Preachers asked President Pusey to appoint a committee to prepare a proposal for a new hymn book. The committee was chaired by Carlton Fuller, a local business executive, Harvard graduate, and member of the Sunday congregation. Joining him were Samuel H. Miller, dean of the Divinity School, Professors John Ward and Randall Thompson, of the Music Department, and John R. Ferris, who was appointed music editor.

After considerable study, the committee agreed that Harvard should prepare a new hymnal designed for use in The Memorial Church, which would take advantage of the nucleus of hymns taken from the then-new *Pilgrim Hymnal* and allow the addition of hymns desired for use in this church. The Harvard Corporation approved this proposal and agreed to pay for one-half the cost, provided that the other half be provided by friends of The Memorial Church. John Ferris was appointed music editor, and the texts were assigned to the review of Dean Miller. Professor Amos Niven Wilder, also of the Divinity School, was asked to prepare the responsive readings, to be selected from the Bible, the psalms in the King James translation, and the New Testament selections in the Revised Standard Version.

In September 1964 the new book was in the pews, and welcomed in a service of dedication composed by the new Preacher to the University, Dr. Charles P. Price, himself a musician and sympathetic to the project, although having had no part in it. In some sense this book was as conservative as its predecessors, seeking to be exemplary, and representative of the variety of traditions present in the worship of The Memorial Church. Mr. Ferris gave more attention to the inclusion of plainsong, Lutheran chorales, and Genevan psalm tunes; Victorian tunes and gospel songs were not included, while efforts were made to find New England psalm tunes and southern folk hymn tunes. Contemporary hymnody was a problem. This was, after all, in the 1960s, and John Ferris observed:

> "It is when we turn to the present that we encounter
> difficulty in finding new music as well as new texts.
> The styles of most serious contemporary composers
> are incompatible with the simplicity demanded of
> congregational song. Until the contemporary church
> finds a musical idiom in which it can express itself,
> we must continue to worship with the hymns of an
> earlier generation."

As a result, only one text and two tunes were commissioned for this book: Joseph Goodman's tune CRANMER; and the complete hymn, "Thy Book Falls Open, Lord," with text by Harvard poet David Thompson Watson McCord and music by Professor Randall Thompson—the tune NISI DOMINUS.

When in 1974 I became Plummer Professor of Christian Morals, the "new" book was just ten years old. With the 1968 Fisk organ, and the four-part University Choir, the hymn book formed part of a formidable musical trilogy created by John Ferris who, until his retirement in 1990 after thirty-two years of service, used all three to great advantage. The third *Harvard University Hymn Book* would enjoy a service of forty-three years, the longest tenure so far in Harvard's service.

Since 1964, the theological and liturgical world has changed in many ways, with liturgical reform the order in nearly every denomination, and the revision of hymnals following in almost every case. Although The Memorial Church is no more a denominational church than it, or its predecessor Appleton Chapel, ever has been, the worship of our community has not been immune to these changes. Not many years after I began my service, concerns were raised about the suitability of the hymn book, many of them over the vexed issue of gendered language. Images of the Divine were called into question, and as our University and congregation became increasingly diverse, the rather austere menu of hymnody appeared increasingly problematic. Music for singing at the celebrations of Holy Communion, for example, hardly an issue in any of the earlier editions of the hymn book, was found to be in short supply as the Communion service became more important in our liturgical life. Also, as more people were eager to find something of their own religious tradition represented in our worship, the hymn book, by excluding so much representative hymnody, gradually became removed from the religious experience of our congregation.

Two sharp criticisms were leveled at the previous edition. One morning, when one of our most distinguished professors was leafing through the hymn book seeking a hymn suitable for use with his Morning Prayer talk, he said to me in exasperation, "Your book is full of advice to God." Another comment, after a Sunday service, suggested that our book was truly "'democratic,' for it offends everyone." By the mid-nineteen-nineties it was clear that something should be done to provide a book more in sympathy with, and reflective of, our present worship needs.

This situation has argued for a book larger and more comprehensive than any of the earlier editions of the *Harvard University Hymn Book*. In order to provide one hundred more hymns than were in the 1964 book, we determined to remove the responsive readings and prepare a separate Psalter for use in the daily service of Morning Prayers. Since we read the psalms on Sunday mornings from the Bibles in the pews there is no longer any reason to provide responsive readings in the new hymnal, and thus, at just under four hundred hymns, this edition, while considerably larger than any of its predecessors, is still much smaller than most denominational books.

For this Fourth Edition we have accepted the principle of the liturgical year as one of our organizing standards, while elsewhere providing hymns reflective of important occasions in the life of the University, such as Armistice Day, Commencement, and Memorial Services. We have endeavored to make this book reflect the way in which we actually worship.

Furthermore, as Holy Communion, and the Office of Compline—popular with us in recent years—were less frequently observed in years past, we have made necessary provision for those services. While we haven't many Marian hymns in this book, we have more than we ever had before. We have also determined that hymns of personal piety and devotion are not inconsistent with the lively worship of a university congregation, and we do not share the aversion of our predecessors to hymns with gospel or evangelical associations. We have not hesitated, for example, to include Stuart K. Hine's 1953 hymn, "How Great Thou Art," or Robert Lowry's 1864 Victorian thumper, "Shall We Gather at the River." Here will also be found Thomas O. Chisholm's "Great is Thy Faithfulness," and John Newton's "Amazing Grace."

In recognizing that a variety of traditional ceremonial music is both important within our community and often requested by those leading worship in The Memorial Church, we have included two distinct examples: the Johnson brothers' "Lift Every Voice and Sing," adopted in 1920 by the NAACP as the Negro National Anthem; and William Blake's poem, "And Did Those Feet in Ancient Time," set to Sir Charles Hubert Hastings Parry's stately tune, JERUSALEM.

Provision has also been made for local usage in our Sunday and University services. As in 1964, for example, the first hymn in the book is OLD HUNDREDTH, in long meter to the text "All People That on Earth Do Dwell," with which we continue to open the Sunday service. In addition to ST. MARTIN'S, the text to which is the paraphrase of Psalm 78, "Give Ear, Ye Children to My Law," that has been sung at Commencement since at least 1806, we have included the revised version of Samuel Gilman's "Fair Harvard," and retained the University Hymn in Latin, "Deus omnium Creator," and David McCord's "Thy Book Falls Open, Lord," from the 1964 book. To these we have added Cyril Alington's affecting baccalaureate text, "Lord, You have Brought Us to Our Journey's End," set to Cyril Vincent Taylor's 1949 tune, SHELDONIAN. We have also included "Father of All, We Lift to Thee our Praise," a 1915 text by Lionel deJersey Harvard, the only known relative of John Harvard to attend Harvard College. We are also graced with a tune, MEMORIAL CHURCH, by our own Carson P. Cooman, which sets the text "Morning Glory, Starlit Sky," by W. H. Vanstone.

One of our tasks has been to include hymns long available in the wider church that for various reasons were not acceptable to our predecessors. We have also used hymns not available to them, such as "Mothering God, You Gave Me Birth," an adaptation of the writings of Julian of Norwich; and "Dear Mother God, Your Wings Are Warm Around Us," a text of Janet Wootton. We have included tunes by twentieth century composers such as Francis Jackson, Jane Marshall, Richard Wayne Dirksen, Peter Cutts, Calvin Hampton, and David Hurd; texts from Timothy Dudley-Smith, Brian Wren, Jeffrey Rowthorn, Christopher Idle, Carl P. Daw, Jr., and Thomas H. Troeger; and hymns from our own Harvard tradition, including one written by my predecessor, Charles P. Price.

What of language? I believe we were wise not to produce a hymnal in the 1980s, at the height of the debate about gender and inclusive language; here, rather, we have attempted something of a middle course. In the spirit of diversity we recognize that there are many ways of speaking of God, and those diverse ways are represented in this book. We have not therefore exercised a gratuitous excision of all male pronouns, especially where long and fond association would render such alterations unsympathetic to the integrity of the texts; where in old texts a judicious revision makes the hymn more sing-able by more people, however, we have made one. We have done our best to include many new texts that do not raise gender issues or give pride of place to the feminine; for instance, we have chosen not to tamper with Bishop Heber's Epiphany text, "Brightest and Best of the Sons of the Morning," while we felt at liberty to change Theodore Parker's text, "O Thou Great Friend to all the Sons of Men," to read "O Thou Great Friend to All of Us Below."

We have a healthy proportion of texts with "thee" and "thou," and a large number of texts without those archaic words, for in a book that seeks to cover a wide range of hymnic expression, it seemed to us wise to proceed in this way. Just as we have a large and diverse selection of styles in the tunes, so too have we a genuine pluralism represented in the texts.

Following the happy and useful precedents of the three earlier editions of this book we have included notes on the authors and com-posers, and we have a full compliment of indices so that this book can serve as well as its predecessors as a contribution to the study of hymnody, and prove useful and interesting to clergy, choir, and congregation. Unlike the editors of the previous Harvard books, we have decided to omit the once obligatory "Amen" at the close of each hymn, leaving its use to the discretion of the organist.

In the preparation of this book I am pleased to acknowledge the contributions of many individuals. Jeffrey Grossman is responsible for the visual design and layout, and, together with Marisa Green typeset the book's contents. John Christensen, of the Firefly Press, provided invaluable advice on typefaces. We are grateful for the hymnological counsel of Carl P. Daw, Jr., Executive Director of the Hymn Society in the United States and Canada; and we are grateful for the support and services of Lindsay Waters and John Walsh of the Harvard University Press. Philip McCosker generously edited the foreign language first lines, and supplied bibliographic assistance.

Above all, this hymn book would not have been possible without the work of the editorial committee. Matthew F. Burt has managed the project since 2001, and I am grateful for his constant superintendence; he and Carson P. Cooman, principal author of the notes on the hymns, have seen it through its many stages of production and finally into print. The counsel of Edward Elwyn Jones, current Gund University Organist and Choirmaster and Curator of the University Organs, and of Harry Lyn Huff, Assistant University Organist and Choirmaster, has been invaluable. I am honored to serve with them as this book enters into use in The Memorial Church.

In the preparation of such an ambitious task as a new hymn book for Harvard University, I am also both mindful of and grateful for the heroic work of my predecessors. It is my prayer that this Fourth Edition will be a worthy contribution to the lively inheritance that we share in this church; and for all of the musicians, clergy, and people who have sung and will continue to sing God's praises in this place, I give thanks to God.

Peter J. Gomes
Plummer Professor of Christian Morals and
Pusey Minister in The Memorial Church
Chairman, Editorial Committee

Sparks House
Cambridge, Massachusetts

October 2007

Contents

THE HYMNS

The Hymns

All People That on Earth Do Dwell

para. of Psalm 100
William Kethe, 1561, alt.

OLD HUNDREDTH   LM
Genevan Psalter, 1551

1 All peo-ple that on earth do dwell, sing
2 Know that the Lord is God in - deed; with -
3 O en - ter then his gates with praise, ap -
4 For why? The Lord our God is good, his

to the Lord with cheer - ful voice; him serve with mirth, his
out our aid he did us make; we are his folk, he
proach with joy his courts un - to; praise, laud, and bless his
mer - cy is for - ev - er sure; his truth at all times

praise forth tell, come ye be - fore him and re - joice.
doth us feed, and for his sheep he doth us take.
name al - ways, for it is seem - ly so to do.
firm - ly stood, and shall from age to age en - dure.

PRAISE

All Creatures of Our God and King

Cantico delle creature
Francis of Assisi (1182–1226)
trans. William H. Draper, 1931

LASST UNS ERFREUEN   88 44 88 with Refrain
Auserlesene Catholische Geistliche Kirchengesäng, 1623
adapt. Ralph Vaughan Williams, 1906

1 All crea-tures of our God and King, lift
2 Thou rush-ing wind that art so strong, ye
3 Thou flow-ing wa-ter, pure and clear, make
4 And now all ye of ten-der heart, for-
5 Let all things their cre-a-tor bless, and

up your voice and with us sing Al-le-
clouds that sail in heaven a-long, O
mu-sic for thy Lord to hear, Al-le-
giv-ing oth-ers, take your part, O
wor-ship him in hum-ble-ness, O

lu-ia! Al-le-lu-ia! Thou burn-ing sun with gold-en
praise him, Al-le-lu-ia! Thou ris-ing morn, in praise re-
lu-ia! Al-le-lu-ia! Thou fire so mas-ter-ful and
sing ye, Al-le-lu-ia! Ye who long pain and sor-row
praise him, Al-le-lu-ia! Praise, praise the Fa-ther, praise the

PRAISE

beam,   thou   sil - ver moon with   soft - er
joice,   ye   lights of   eve - ning, find   a
bright, that   giv - est us   both warmth and
bear,   praise God   and on   him   cast your
Son,   and   praise the Spir - it, Three in

gleam,
voice,
light,   O   praise him, O   praise him, Al - le -
care.
One.

lu - ia, Al - le - lu - ia, Al - le - lu - ia!

This music in D, 31.

PRAISE

3   Let the Whole Creation Cry

Stopford A. Brooke, 1881, alt.

LLANFAIR   77 77 with Alleluias
Robert Williams, 1817
harm. John Roberts, 1837

1 Let the whole cre - a - tion cry,
2 Praise your ma - ker, hosts a - bove,
3 Men and wom - en, young and old,
4 From the north to south - ern pole,

Al - le - lu - ia!

Glo - ry to our Lord on high!
Ev - er bright and fair in love;
Raise the an - them man - i - fold;
Let the might - y cho - rus roll:

Al - le - lu - ia!

Heaven and earth, a - wake and sing,
Sun and moon, up - lift your voice,
And let child - ren's hap - py hearts,
Ho - ly, ho - ly, ho - ly one,

Al - le - lu - ia!

unison

"God is good, and there - fore King."
Night and stars, in God re - joice!
In this wor - ship bear their parts.
Glo - ry be to God a - lone!

Al - le - lu - ia!

This music in G, 165.

PRAISE

For the Beauty of the Earth

Folliot Sandford Pierpoint, 1864, alt.

DIX 77 77 77
Conrad Kocher, 1838
adapt. William Henry Monk (1823–1889)
harm. The English Hymnal, 1906

1 For the beau-ty of the earth, for the beau-ty of the skies,
2 For the beau-ty of each hour of the day and of the night,
3 For the joy of ear and eye, for the heart and mind's de-light,
4 For the joy of hu-man love, bro-ther, sis-ter, par-ent, child,
5 For the Church which ev-er-more lift-eth ho-ly hands a-bove,

for the love which from our birth o-ver and a-round us lies,
hill and vale, and tree and flower, sun and moon, and stars of light,
for the mys-tic har-mo-ny link-ing sense to sound and sight,
friends on earth, and friends a-bove, for all gen-tle thoughts and mild,
of-fering up on ev-ery shore thy pure sac-ri-fice of love,

Christ our Lord, to thee we raise this our hymn of grate-ful praise.

PRAISE

5   Now Thank We All Our God

Nun danket alle Gott
Martin Rinckart, 1636?
trans. Catherine Winkworth, 1858, alt.

NUN DANKET ALLE GOTT   67 67 66 66
Johann Crüger, 1647
harm. Felix Mendelssohn, 1840, alt.

1 Now thank we all our God with heart and hands and voi - ces, who
2 O may this boun-teous God through all our life be near us, with
3 All praise and thanks to God the Fa - ther now be gi - ven, the

won - drous things hath done, in whom this world re - joi - ces, who,
ev - er joy - ful hearts and bless - ed peace to cheer us, and
Son, and him who reigns with them in high - est hea - ven, e -

from our pa - rents' arms, hath blessed us on our way with
keep us in his grace, and guide us when per - plexed, and
ter - nal, tri - une God, whom earth and heaven a - dore; for

count - less gifts of love, and still is ours to - day.
free us from all ills in this world and the next.
thus it was, is now, and shall be ev - er - more.

Albert F. Bayly, 1969, alt.

EVERTON 87 87 D
Henry Thomas Smart, 1867

1 When the morn-ing stars to-geth-er their cre-a-tor's glo-ry sang,
2 When in syn-a-gogue and tem-ple voic-es raised the psalm-ists' songs,
3 Voice and in-stru-ment in u-nion through the a-ges spoke your praise,
4 Lord, we bring our gift of mu-sic; touch our lips and fire our hearts,

and the an-gel host all shout-ed till with joy the heav-ens rang.
of-fer-ing the a-do-ra-tion which a-lone to you be-longs,
plain-song, tune-ful hymns, and an-thems told your faith-ful, gra-cious ways.
teach our minds and train our sens-es, fit us for these sa-cred arts.

Then your wis-dom and your great-ness their ex-ul-tant mu-sic told,
when the sing-ers and the cym-bals with the trum-pet made ac-cord,
Choir and or-ches-tra and or-gan each a sa-cred of-fering brought,
Then with skill and con-se-cra-tion we would serve you, Lord, and give

all the beau-ty and the splen-dor which your might-y works un-fold.
glo-ry filled the house of wor-ship, and all knew your pres-ence, Lord.
while, in-spired by your own Spi-rit, po-et and com-pos-er wrought.
all our powers to glo-ri-fy you, and in serv-ing ful-ly live.

PRAISE

7

O Be Joyful in the Lord

para. of Psalm 100
Curtis Beach, 1958, alt.

FINLAY 77 77 57 67
Harold W. Friedell, 1958

1 O be joy-ful in the Lord! Sing be-fore him, all the earth!
2 Know ye that the Lord is King! All his works his wis-dom prove!
3 En-ter now his ho-ly gate; let our bur-dened hearts be still;
4 For the Lord our God is kind, and his love shall con-stant be;

Praise him with a glad ac-cord and with lives of no-blest worth.
By his might the hea-vens ring; in his love we live and move.
in the sa-cred si-lence wait, as we seek to know his will.
in his will our peace we find; in his ser-vice, lib-er-ty.

Through-out ev-ery land, hum-bly now be-fore him stand!
By him we are made, so we trust him un-a-fraid.
Let our lives ex-press our a-bun-dant thank-ful-ness;
Yea, his law is sure; in his light we walk se-cure;

PRAISE

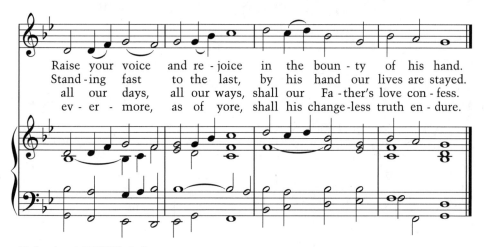

Raise your voice and re-joice in the boun-ty of his hand.
Stand-ing fast to the last, by his hand our lives are stayed.
all our days, all our ways, shall our Fa-ther's love con-fess.
ev-er-more, as of yore, shall his change-less truth en-dure.

Let Us, with a Gladsome Mind 8

para. of Psalm 136
John Milton, 1624, alt.

MONKLAND 77 77
Geistreiches Gesang-Buch, 1704
adapt. John Antes, c. 1790
adapt. John B. Wilkes, 1861

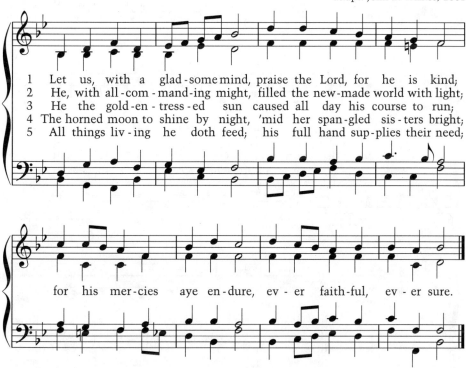

1 Let us, with a glad-some mind, praise the Lord, for he is kind;
2 He, with all-com-mand-ing might, filled the new-made world with light;
3 He the gold-en-tress-ed sun caused all day his course to run;
4 The horned moon to shine by night, 'mid her span-gled sis-ters bright;
5 All things liv-ing he doth feed; his full hand sup-plies their need;

for his mer-cies aye en-dure, ev-er faith-ful, ev-er sure.

PRAISE

Praise, My Soul, the King of Heaven

Henry Francis Lyte, 1834, alt.

LAUDA ANIMA   87 87 87
John Goss, 1869

1 Praise, my soul, the King of heav - en, to his feet thy
2 Praise him for his grace and fa - vor to his peo - ple
3 Fa - ther - like, he tends and spares us; well our fee - ble
4 An - gels, help us to a - dore him; ye be - hold him

trib - ute bring; ran - somed, healed, re - stored, for - giv - en,
in dis - tress; praise him still, the same for - ev - er,
frame he knows; in his hands he gen - tly bears us,
face to face; sun and moon, bow down be - fore him,

who, like me, his praise should sing? Al - le - lu - ia!
slow to chide, and swift to bless. Al - le - lu - ia!
res - cues us from all our foes. Al - le - lu - ia!
dwell - ers all in time and space. Al - le - lu - ia!

Al - le - lu - ia! Praise the ev - er - last - ing King!
Al - le - lu - ia! Glo - rious in his faith - ful - ness!
Al - le - lu - ia! Wide - ly as his mer - cy flows!
Al - le - lu - ia! Praise with us the God of grace!

PRAISE

Christopher Smart, 1763, alt.

MAGDALEN COLLEGE   886 886
William Hayes (1706–1777)

1 We sing of God, the might-y source of all things;
the stu-pen-dous force on which all strength de-pends; from
whose right arm, be-neath whose eyes, all pe-riod,
power, and en-ter-prise com-men-ces, reigns, and ends.

2 Tell them I AM, the Lord God said, to Mo-ses
while on earth in dread and smit-ten to the heart, at
once, a-bove, be-neath, a-round, all na-ture
with-out voice or sound re-plied, O Lord, thou art.

3 Glo-rious the sun in mid ca-reer; glo-rious the as-
sem-bled fires ap-pear; glo-rious the com-et's train: glo-
rious the trum-pet and a-larm; glo-rious the al-
might-y stretched-out arm; glo-rious the en-rap-tured main:

4 glo-rious, most glo-rious, is the crown of him that
brought sal-va-tion down by meek-ness, Ma-ry's Son; seers
that stu-pen-dous truth be-lieved, and now the
match-less deed's a-chieved, de-ter-mined, dared, and done.

11   Sing Praise to God Who Reigns Above

Sei Lob und Ehr' dem höchsten Gut
Johann Jakob Schütz, 1675
trans. Frances Elizabeth Cox, 1864, alt.

MIT FREUDEN ZART   87 87 887
Kirchengeseng darinnen die Heubtartickel
des Christlichen Glaubens gefasset, 1566

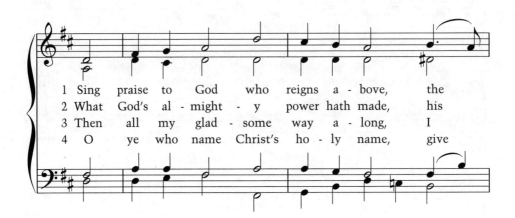

1 Sing praise to God who reigns a - bove, the
2 What God's al - might - y power hath made, his
3 Then all my glad - some way a - long, I
4 O ye who name Christ's ho - ly name, give

God of all cre - a - tion, the God of power, the
gra - cious mer - cy keep - eth; by morn - ing glow or
sing a - loud thy prais - es, that all may hear the
God all praise and glo - ry; all ye who own his

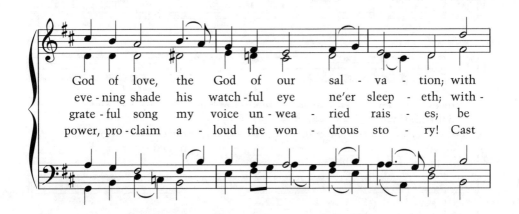

God of love, the God of our sal - va - tion; with
eve - ning shade his watch - ful eye ne'er sleep - eth; with -
grate - ful song my voice un - wea - ried rais - es; be
power, pro - claim a - loud the won - drous sto - ry! Cast

heal - ing	balm	my	soul	he	fills,	and	ev - ery	faith - less
in	the	king - dom	of	his	might,	lo!	all	is	just	and
joy - ful	in	the	Lord,	my	heart,	both	soul and bod - y
each	false	i - dol	from	his	throne,	the	Lord	is	God,	and

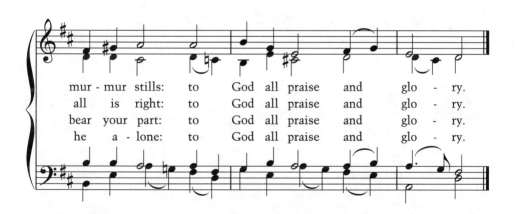

mur - mur stills:	to	God	all	praise	and	glo - ry.
all	is	right:	to	God	all	praise	and	glo - ry.
bear	your	part:	to	God	all	praise	and	glo - ry.
he	a - lone:	to	God	all	praise	and	glo - ry.

This music in D♭, 105.

The God of Abraham Praise

יִגְדַּל אֱלֹהִים חַי וְיִשְׁתַּבַּח

attrib. Daniel ben Judah (c.1400)
trans. Max Landsberg and Newton M. Mann, 1885, alt.

LEONI   66 84 D
Jewish melody
adapt. Meyer Lyon, c. 1770

1 The God of A-braham praise, all prais-ed be his name, who
2 His spir-it flow-eth free, high surg-ing where it will; in
3 He hath e-ter-nal life im-plant-ed in the soul; his

was, and is, and is to be, for aye the same! The
proph-et's word he spoke of old; he speak-eth still. Es-
love shall be our strength and stay, while a - ges roll. Praise

one e-ter-nal God, ere aught that now ap - pears; the
tab-lished is his law, and change-less it shall stand, deep
to the liv-ing God! All prais-ed be his name, who

first, the last: be - yond all thought his time-less years!
writ up-on the hu-man heart, on sea, or land.
was, and is, and is to be, for aye the same!

George Wither, 1641, alt.

SALZBURG 77 77 D
Jakob Hintze, 1678
harm. Johann Sebastian Bach (1685–1750)

1 Come, O come, in pi - ous lays sound we God Al-might-y's praise;
2 Come, ye heirs of hu - man race, in this cho - rus take a place;
3 So this huge wide orb we see shall one choir, one tem - ple be;

hith - er bring in one con - sent heart, and voice, and in - stru-ment.
and, a - mid the mor - tal throng, be you mas - ters of the song.
where-in such a praise - ful tone we will sing what God hath done,

Sound the trum - pet, touch the lute, let no tongue nor string be mute,
Let, in praise of God, the sound run a nev - er - end - ing round,
that our song shall ov - er - climb all the bounds of place and time;

nor a crea - ture dumb be found, that hath ei - ther voice or sound.
that our songs of praise may be sung with joy e - ter - nal - ly.
come, then, come, in pi - ous lays sound we God Al-might-y's praise.

PRAISE

God Is Love, Let Heaven Adore Him

Timothy Rees (1874–1939), alt.

ABBOT'S LEIGH   87 87 D
Cyril Vincent Taylor, 1941

1 God is Love, let heaven a - dore him; God is Love, let
2 God is Love; and love en - folds us, all the world in
3 God is Love; and though with blind-ness sin af - flicts all

earth re - joice; let cre - a - tion sing be - fore him
one em - brace: with un - fail - ing grasp God holds us,
hu - man life, God's e - ter - nal lov - ing - kind-ness

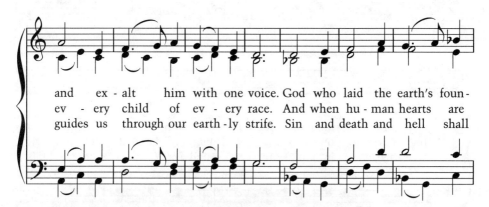

and ex - alt him with one voice. God who laid the earth's foun -
ev - ery child of ev - ery race. And when hu - man hearts are
guides us through our earth -ly strife. Sin and death and hell shall

PRAISE

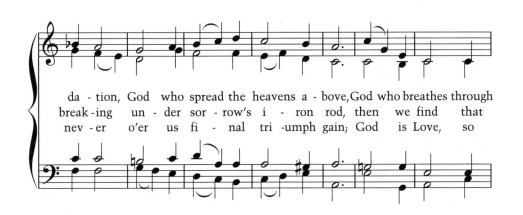

da - tion, God who spread the heavens a - bove, God who breathes through
break -ing un - der sor - row's i - ron rod, then we find that
nev - er o'er us fi - nal tri -umph gain; God is Love, so

all cre - a - tion: God is Love, e - ter - nal Love.
self - same ach -ing deep with - in the heart of God.
Love for ev - er o'er the u - ni - verse must reign.

15   Praise Our Great and Gracious Lord

Harriet Auber (1773–1862), alt.

MAOZ TSUR 77 77 67 67
Jewish melody, alt.

1 Praise our great and gra-cious Lord,   call up-on God's ho - ly name;
2 God has given the cloud by day,   given the mov-ing fire by night;

rais-ing hymns in glad ac-cord,   all his might-y acts pro-claim:
guid - ing Is - rael on its way   from the dark -ness in - to light.

how he leads his cho - sen   un - to Ca -naan's prom - ised land,
God it is who grants us   sure re-treat and ref - uge nigh;

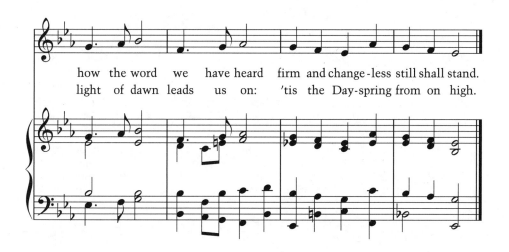

how the word we have heard firm and change-less still shall stand.
light of dawn leads us on: 'tis the Day-spring from on high.

O God, We Praise Thee and Confess 16

para. of Te Deum laudamus, *4th cent.*
A Supplement to the New Version of
the Psalms of David, 1698, alt.

TALLIS' ORDINAL CM
Thomas Tallis, c. 1567, alt.

1 O God, we praise thee, and con-fess that thou the on - ly
2 To thee all an - gels cry a - loud; to thee the powers on
3 O ho - ly, ho - ly, ho - ly Lord, whom heaven-ly hosts o -
4 The a-pos-tles' glo - rious com-pa-ny, and proph-ets crowned with
5 The ho - ly Church through-out the world, O Lord, con-fess - es

Lord and ev-er-last-ing Fa-ther art, by all the earth a - dored.
high, both cher-u-bim and ser-a-phim, con-tin-ual-ly do cry:
bey, the world is with the glo-ry filled of thy ma - jes-tic sway!
light, with all the mar-tyrs' no-ble host, thy con-stant praise re-cite.
thee, that thou e-ter-nal Fa-ther art, of bound-less maj-es-ty.

Another harmonization, 190.

PRAISE

Ye Holy Angels Bright

Richard Baxter, 1672
adapt. John Hampden Gurney, 1838

DARWALL 148   66 66 44 44
John Darwall, 1770

1 Ye ho - ly an - gels bright, who wait at God's right hand, or through the realms of light fly at your Lord's com - mand, as - sist our song, for else the theme too high doth seem for mor - tal tongue.

2 Ye bless - ed souls at rest, who ran this earth - ly race, and now, from sin re - leased, be - hold the Sav - ior's face, God's prais - es sound, as in his light with sweet de - light ye do a - bound.

3 Ye saints who toil be - low, a - dore your heaven - ly King, and on - ward as ye go some joy - ful an - them sing; take what he gives and praise him still, through good and ill, who - ev - er lives.

4 My soul, bear thou thy part, tri - umph in God a - bove, and with a well - tuned heart sing thou the songs of love. Let all thy days till life shall end, what - e'er he send, be filled with praise.

PRAISE

King of Glory, King of Peace

George Herbert (1593–1632)

GWALCHMAI 74 74 D
Joseph D. Jones, 1868

1 King of glo-ry, King of peace, I will love thee;
2 Where-fore with my ut-most art I will sing thee,
3 Seven whole days, not one in seven, I will praise thee;

and, that love may ne-ver cease, I will move thee.
and the cream of all my heart I will bring thee.
in my heart, though not in heaven, I can raise thee.

Thou has grant-ed my re-quest, thou hast heard me;
Though my sins a-gainst me cried, thou didst clear me,
Small it is, in this poor sort to en-roll thee:

thou didst note my work-ing breast, thou hast spared me.
and a-lone, when they re-plied, thou didst hear me.
e'en e-ter-ni-ty's too short to ex-tol thee.

PRAISE

19   O Praise Ye the Lord! Sing Praise in the Height

para. of Psalm 150   LAUDATE DOMINUM   10 10 11 11
Henry W. Baker, 1875, alt.   *Charles Hubert Hastings Parry, 1894*

1 O praise ye the Lord! Sing praise in the height; re-
2 O praise ye the Lord! Sing praise up - on earth, in
3 O praise ye the Lord! All things that give sound; each
4 O praise ye the Lord! Thanks - giv - ing and song to

joice in his word, ye an - gels of light; ye
tune - ful ac - cord, all ye of new birth; O
ju - bi - lant chord, re - ech - o a - round; loud
him be out - poured all a - ges a - long; for

heav - ens, a - dore him by whom ye were made, and
praise him who brought you his grace from a - bove; O
or - gans, his glo - ry forth tell in deep tone, and
love in cre - a - tion, for heav - en re - stored, for

wor - ship be - fore him, in bright - ness ar - rayed.
praise him who taught you to sing of his love.
sweet harp, the sto - ry of what he hath done.
grace of sal - va - tion, O praise ye the Lord!

PRAISE

Francis Pott, 1861, alt.

ANGEL VOICES   85 85 843
Edwin George Monk, 1861

1 An - gel - voic - es   ev - er sing - ing round thy throne of   light,
2 Thou who art   be - yond the farth - est mor - tal   eye can   see,
3 Yea, we know that   thou re - joic - est o'er each work of   thine;
4 In thy house, great God, we of - fer of thine own to   thee;
5 Ho - nor, glo - ry,   might, and mer - it thine shall ev - er   be,

an - gel - harps for - ev - er ring - ing rest not day or night;
can it be that   thou re - gard - est our poor hym - no - dy?
thou didst ears and hands and voic - es for thy praise de - sign;
and for thine ac - cep - tance prof - fer all un - wor - thi - ly
Fa - ther, Son, and Ho - ly Spi - rit, bless - ed Tri - ni - ty.

thou - sands on - ly live to bless thee and con - fess thee Lord of might.
Can we know that thou art near us, and wilt hear us? Yea,   can we.
art - ist's craft and mu - sic's mea - sure for thy plea - sure all com - bine.
hearts and minds and hands and voic - es in our choi - cest psal - mo - dy.
Of   the best that thou hast giv - en earth and hea - ven ren - der thee.

Holy God, We Praise Thy Name

para. of Te Deum laudamus, *4th cent.*
Ignaz Franz, *c. 1774*
trans. Clarence A. Walworth, 1853

GROSSER GOTT 78 78 77
Katholisches Gesangbuch, c. 1686
harm. Conrad Kocher (1786–1872)
adapt. Charles Winfred Douglas (1867–1944), alt.

1 Ho - ly God, we praise thy name; Lord of all, we
2 Hark, the glad ce - les - tial hymn an - gel choirs a -
3 Ho - ly Fa - ther, ho - ly Son, Ho - ly Spir - it:

bow be - fore thee; all on earth thy scep - ter claim,
bove are rais - ing; cher - u - bim and ser - a - phim,
Three we name thee, though in es - sence on - ly One;

all in heaven a - bove a - dore thee. In - fi - nite thy
in un - ceas - ing cho - rus prais - ing, fill the heavens with
un - di - vid - ed God we claim thee, and a - dor - ing

vast do - main, ev - er - last - ing is thy reign.
sweet ac - cord: ho - ly, ho - ly, ho - ly Lord.
bend the knee while we own the mys - te - ry.

O Worship the King, All Glorious Above   22

para. of Psalm 104
Robert Grant, 1833

HANOVER   10 10 11 11
attrib. William Croft, 1708

1 O   wor - ship the   King,   all   glo - rious   a - bove,   O
2 O   tell   of   his   might,   O   sing   of   his   grace,   whose
3 The   earth with   its   store   of   won - ders   un - told,   Al -
4 Thy   boun - ti - ful   care,   what tongue can   re - cite?   It
5 Frail   chil - dren   of   dust,   and   fee - ble   as   frail,   in

grate - ful - ly   sing   his   power   and   his   love;   our
robe   is   the   light,   whose   can - o - py   space;   his
might - y,   thy   power   hath   found - ed   of   old,   hath
breathes   in   the   air,   it   shines   in   the   light;   it
thee   do   we   trust,   nor   find   thee   to   fail;   thy

shield   and   de - fend - er,   the   An - cient   of   Days,   pa -
char - iots   of   wrath   the   deep   thun - der - clouds   form,   and
stab - lished   it   fast   by   a   change - less   de - cree,   and
streams from   the   hills,   it   de - scends   to   the   plain,   and
mer - cies   how   ten - der,   how   firm   to   the   end,   our

vil - ioned   in   splen - dor,   and   gird - ed   with   praise.
dark   is   his   path   on   the   wings   of   the   storm.
round   it   hath   cast,   like   a   man - tle,   the   sea.
sweet - ly   dis - tills   in   the   dew   and   the   rain.
mak - er,   de - fend - er,   re - deem - er,   and   friend!

PRAISE

Joyful, Joyful, We Adore Thee

Henry J. Van Dyke, 1907

HYMN TO JOY 87 87 D
Ludwig van Beethoven, 1824
adapt. Edward Hodges, 1824, alt.

1 Joy-ful, joy-ful, we a-dore thee, God of glo-ry, Lord of love;
2 All thy works with joy sur-round thee, earth and heaven re-flect thy rays,
3 Thou art giv-ing and for-giv-ing, ev-er bless-ing, ev-er blest,

hearts un-fold like flowers be-fore thee, prais-ing thee, their sun a-bove.
stars and an-gels sing a-round thee, cen-ter of un-bro-ken praise.
well-spring of the joy of liv-ing, o-cean depth of hap-py rest!

Melt the clouds of sin and sad-ness; drive the dark of doubt a-way; giv-
Field and for-est, vale and moun-tain, bloom-ing mea-dow, flash-ing sea, chant
Thou our Fa-ther, Christ our Bro-ther: all who live in love are thine; teach

-er of im-mor-tal glad-ness, fill us with the light of day.
-ing bird and flow-ing foun-tain, call us to re-joice in thee.
us how to love each o-ther, lift us to the joy di-vine.

PRAISE

John Henry Newman, 1865, alt.

GERONTIUS CM
John Bacchus Dykes, 1868

1 Praise to the Ho - liest in the height, and in the
2 O lov - ing wis - dom of our God! When all was
3 O wis - est love! that flesh and blood, which did in
4 and that the high - est gift of grace should flesh and
5 Praise to the Ho - liest in the height, and in the

depth be praise; in all his words most
sin and shame, a sec - ond Ad - am
Ad - am fail, should strive a - fresh a -
blood re - fine: God's pres - ence and his
depth be praise; in all his words most

won - der - ful, most sure in all his ways!
to the fight and to the res - cue came.
gainst the foe, should strive, and should pre - vail;
ve - ry self, and es - sence all di - vine.
won - der - ful, most sure in all his ways!

PRAISE

When in Our Music God Is Glorified

Fred Pratt Green, 1971

ENGELBERG   10 10 10 with Alleluias
Charles Villiers Stanford, 1904

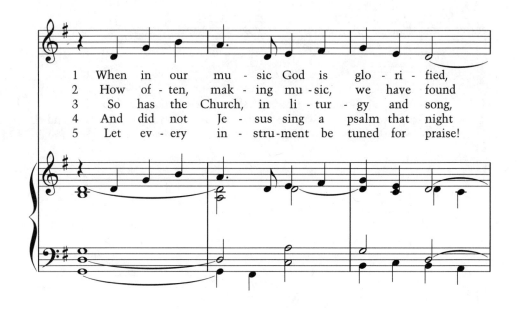

1 When in our mu - sic God is glo - ri - fied,
2 How of - ten, mak - ing mu - sic, we have found
3 So has the Church, in li - tur - gy and song,
4 And did not Je - sus sing a psalm that night
5 Let ev - ery in - stru - ment be tuned for praise!

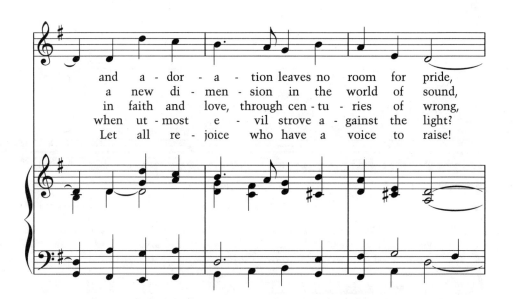

and a - dor - a - tion leaves no room for pride,
a new di - men - sion in the world of sound,
in faith and love, through cen - tu - ries of wrong,
when ut - most e - vil strove a - gainst the light?
Let all re - joice who have a voice to raise!

PRAISE

it is as though the whole cre - a - tion cried
as wor -ship moved us to a more pro -found
borne wit - ness to the truth in ev - ery tongue,
Then let us sing, for whom he won the fight,
And may God give us faith to sing al - ways:

1.2.3.4. 5.

Al - le - lu - ia! Al - le -

lu - ia! A - - men.

This music in F, 166.

Before Jehovah's Aweful Throne

para. of Psalm 100
Isaac Watts, 1719
alt. John Wesley, 1737, alt.

WINCHESTER NEW   LM
Musicalisch Hand-Buch, 1690
harm. William Henry Monk, 1847, alt.

1 Be - fore Je - ho - vah's awe - ful throne, ye
2 His sov - ereign power with - out our aid, made
3 We are his peo - ple, we his care, our
4 We'll crowd thy gates with thank - ful songs, high
5 Wide as the world is thy com - mand, vast

na - tions bow with sa - cred joy; know that the Lord is
us of clay, and formed us all; and when, like wan - dering
souls, and all our mor - tal frame; what last - ing hon - ors
as the heavens our voic - es raise; and earth, with her ten
as e - ter - ni - ty thy love; firm as a rock thy

God a - lone, he can cre - ate, and he de - stroy.
sheep, we strayed, the Shep - herd an - swered with his call.
shall we rear, Al - might - y Mak - er, to thy name?
thou - sand tongues, shall fill thy courts with sound - ing praise.
truth must stand, when roll - ing years shall cease to move.

PRAISE

Wilt heden nu treden voor God den Heere
Nederlandisch Gedenckclanck, 1626
trans. Theodore Baker, 1917

KREMSER   12 11 12 11
Nederlandisch Gedenckclanck, 1626
adapt. Eduard Kremser, 1877

1 We gath - er to - geth - er to ask the Lord's bless ing. He chas-tens and
2 Be - side us to guide us, our God with us join - ing, or - dain - ing, main
3 We all do ex - tol thee, thou lead - er tri - um-phant, and pray that thou

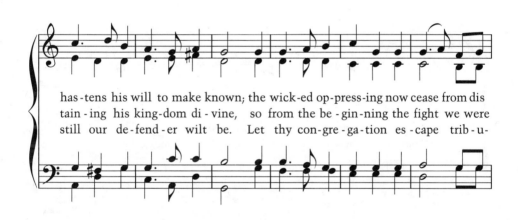

has-tens his will to make known; the wick-ed op-press-ing now cease from dis
tain - ing his king-dom di - vine, so from the be - gin-ning the fight we were
still our de-fend - er wilt be. Let thy con-gre-ga-tion es -cape trib-u-

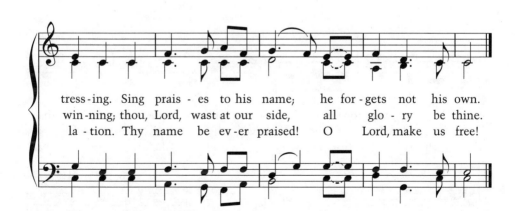

tress-ing. Sing prais - es to his name; he for - gets not his own.
win-ning; thou, Lord, wast at our side, all glo - ry be thine.
la - tion. Thy name be ev - er praised! O Lord, make us free!

PRAISE

28   **To God Be the Glory**

Fanny J. Crosby, 1875

TO GOD BE THE GLORY   11 11 11 11 with Refrain
William H. Doane, 1875

1 To God be the glory, great things he has done! So
2 O per - fect re - demp - tion, the pur - chase of blood! To
3 Great things he has taught us, great things he has done, and

loved he the world that he gave us his Son, who yield - ed his
ev - ery be - liev - er the pro - mise of God! The vi - lest of-
great our re - joic - ing through Je - sus the Son; but pu - rer and

life an a - tone - ment for sin and o - pened the life - gate that
fend - er who tru - ly be - lieves, that mo - ment from Je - sus for-
high - er and great - er will be our won - der, our rap - ture, when

PRAISE

all may go in.
give-ness re-ceives. Praise the Lord! Praise the Lord! Let the
Je-sus we see.

earth hear his voice! Praise the Lord! Praise the Lord! Let the peo-ple re-

joice! O come to the Fa-ther, through Je-sus the

Son, and give him the glo-ry! Great things he has done!

This Is My Song, O God of All the Nations

Lloyd Stone, 1934

FINLANDIA   11 10 11 10 11 10
Jean Sibelius, 1899
adapt. The Hymnal, 1933

1 This is my song, O God of all the na-tions, a song of
2 My coun-try's skies are blu-er than the o-cean, and sun-light

peace for lands a-far and mine. This is my home, the
beams on clo-ver-leaf and pine; but oth-er lands have

coun-try where my heart is; here are my hopes, my dreams, my ho-ly
sun-light too, and clo-ver, and skies are ev-ery-where as blue as

shrine; but oth-er hearts in oth-er lands are beat-ing
mine. O hear my song, thou God of all the na-tions,

with hopes and dreams　as　true and high　as mine.
a　song　of　peace　for　their land and　for mine.

To God with Gladness Sing 　　30

para. of Psalm 95　　　　　　　　　　　HAREWOOD　66 66 44 44
James Quinn, 1969　　　　　　　　Samuel Sebastian Wesley, 1839

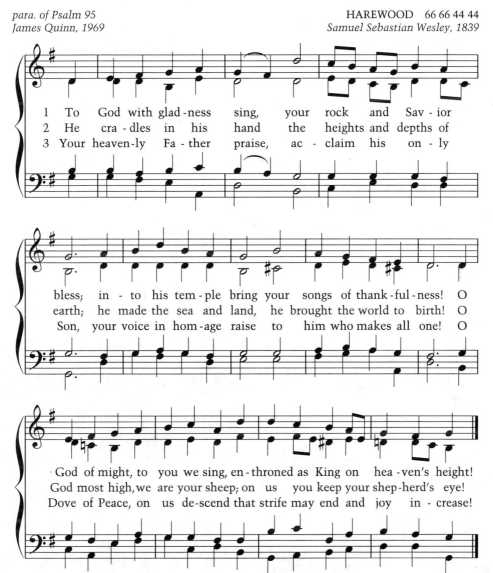

1 To　God with glad-ness　sing,　your　rock　and　Sav-ior
2 He　cra-dles in his　hand　the　heights and depths of
3 Your heaven-ly Fa-ther　praise,　ac-claim　his　on-ly

bless; in-to his tem-ple bring your songs of thank-ful-ness! O
earth; he made the sea and land, he brought the world to birth! O
Son, your voice in hom-age raise to him who makes all one! O

·God of might, to you we sing, en-throned as King on hea-ven's height!
God most high, we are your sheep; on us you keep your shep-herd's eye!
Dove of Peace, on us de-scend that strife may end and joy in-crease!

31 Ye Watchers and Ye Holy Ones

Athelstan Laurie Riley, 1906

LASST UNS ERFREUEN   88 44 88 with Refrain
Auserlesene Catholische Geistliche Kirchengesäng, 1623
adapt. Ralph Vaughan Williams, 1906

1 Ye watch-ers and ye ho-ly ones, bright
2 O high-er than the cher-u-bim, more
3 Re-spond, ye souls in end-less rest, ye
4 O friends, in glad-ness let us sing, su-

ser-aphs, cher-u-bim and thrones, raise the glad strain, Al-le-
glo-rious than the ser-a-phim, lead their prais-es, Al-le-
pa-tri-archs and proph-ets blest, Al-le-lu-ia, Al-le-
per-nal an-thems ech-o-ing, Al-le-lu-ia, Al-le-

lu-ia! Cry out, do-min-ions, prince-doms,
lu-ia! Thou bear-er of the e-ter-nal
lu-ia! Ye ho-ly twelve, ye mar-tyrs
lu-ia! To God the Fa-ther, God the

PRAISE

powers,   vir - tues, arch - an - gels, an - gels'
word,   most   gra - cious, mag - ni - fy the
strong,   all   saints tri - um - phant, raise the
Son,   and   God the Spir - it, Three in

choirs,
Lord,   Al - le - lu - ia, Al - le - lu - ia, Al - le -
song,
One,

lu - ia, Al - le - lu - ia, Al - le - lu - ia!

God, Beyond All Human Praises

Charles P. Price, 1993, alt.

DOMINUS REGNAVIT   87 87 with Refrain
Richard Wayne Dirksen, 1993

1 God,   be-yond all   hu - man prais - es,   wings of cher - u -
2 God   of har - mo - ny   and beau - ty,   God of floods   by
3 God   of his-tory's plan   un - fold - ing,   jus - tice as   its
4 Lead   us on - ward   to   your king - dom   on the way   your

bim   your   throne,   hid   by light's en - gulf - ing splen - dor,
tem - pest   blown,   God   of na - ture's   jea - lous or - der,
goal   and   crown;   God   of free - dom,   God   of mys - tery,
Love makes known.   God,   our joy,   our   peace, our glo - ry,

rule   in heaven as   God   a - lone.   You are the   Ho - ly One.
rule   on earth as   God   a - lone.   You are the   Ho - ly One.
rule through time as   God   a - lone.   You are the   Ho - ly One.
Ho - ly Love, you   rule   a - lone.   You are the   Ho - ly One.

PRAISE

Praise to the Lord, the Almighty

Lobe den Herren, den mächtigen König der Ehren
Joachim Neander, 1680
trans. Catherine Winkworth, 1863, alt.

LOBE DEN HERREN   14 14 4 7 8
Erneuerten Gesangbuch, 1665
harm. Johann Sebastian Bach, 1725

1 Praise to the Lord, the Al - might - y, the King of cre -
2 Praise to the Lord, who o'er all things so won - drous - ly
3 Praise to the Lord, who doth pros - per thy work and de -
4 Praise to the Lord! O let all that is in me a -

a - tion! O my soul, praise him, for he is thy
reign - eth, shel - ters thee un - der his wings, yea, so
fend thee; sure - ly his good - ness and mer - cy here
dore him! All that hath life and breath, come now with

health and sal - va - tion! All ye who hear, now to his
gen - tly sus - tain - eth! Hast thou not seen? All that is
dai - ly at - tend thee. Pon - der a - new what the Al -
prais - es be - fore him. Let the A - men sound from his

tem - ple draw near, join - ing in glad ad - o - ra - tion!
need - ful hath been grant - ed in what he or - dain - eth.
might - y can do, if with his love he be - friend thee.
peo - ple a - gain: glad - ly for aye we a - dore him.

PRAISE

Let All the World in Every Corner Sing

George Herbert (1593–1632)

LUCKINGTON   66 66 with Refrain
Basil Harwood, 1908

1 Let all the world in ev-ery cor-ner sing, my God and
2 Let all the world in ev-ery cor-ner sing, my God and

King! The heavens are not too high, his praise may thith - er
King! The Church with psalms must shout, no door can keep them

fly: the earth is not too low, his prais-es there may grow. Let
out: but, a - bove all, the heart must bear the long-est part. Let

all the world in ev-ery cor-ner sing, my God and King!
all the world in ev-ery cor-ner sing, my God and King!

God of the Morning, at Whose Voice

Isaac Watts, 1707, alt.

PARIS LM
William Billings, 1779

1 God of the morn - ing, at whose voice the cheer - ful
2 From the fair cham - bers of the east the cir - cuit
3 O like the sun, may I ful - fill the ap -point - ed
4 But I shall rove and lose the race if God, my
5 Lord! thy com - mands are clean and pure, en - light -ening

sun makes haste to rise, and like a gi - ant
of its race be - gins; and, with - out wea - ri -
du - ties of the day, with read - y mind and
sun, should dis - ap -pear, and leave me in this
our be - cloud - ed eyes; thy threat-enings just, thy

doth re - joice to run its jour - ney through the skies!
ness or rest, round the whole earth it flies and shines.
ac - tive will march on, and keep my heaven - ly way!
world's wide maze to fol -low ev - ery wan - dering star.
prom - ise sure; thy gos -pel makes the sim - ple wise.

MORNING

36 My Soul, Awake and Render

Wach auf, mein Herz, und singe
Paul Gerhardt, 1647
trans. John Christian Jacobi, 1720, alt.

WACH AUF, MEIN HERZ   77 77
Nikolaus Selnecker, 1587
harm. Johann Sebastian Bach, 1723

1 My soul, a - wake and ren - der to God, thy
2 Be thou my on - ly trea - sure, ful - fill in
3 Thy love, which once did find me, to thee shall

great de - fend - er, the God of all the liv -
me thy plea - sure, thy word my spir - it feed -
ev - er bind me; my life to thee be tend -

ing, thy prayer and thy thanks - giv - ing.
ing, thy light still on - ward lead - ing.
ing, be - gin - ning, mid - dle, end - ing.

Alternate harmonization, 170.

Father, We Praise Thee, Now the Night Is Over 37

Nocte surgentes vigilemus omnes
Latin, 9th cent.?
trans. Percy Dearmer, 1906

CHRISTE SANCTORUM   11 11 11 5
Paris Antiphoner, 1681
harm. Ralph Vaughan Williams, 1906

1 Fa - ther, we praise thee, now the night is o - ver; ac - tive and
2 Mon - arch of all things, fit us for thy man - sions; ban - ish our
3 All - ho - ly Fa - ther, Son, and e - qual Spir - it, Trin - i - ty

watch - ful, stand we all be - fore thee; sing - ing, we of - fer
weak - ness, health and whole - ness send - ing; bring us to hea - ven,
bless - ed, send us thy sal - va - tion; thine is the glo - ry,

prayer and med - i - ta - tion; thus we a - dore thee.
where thy saints u - ni - ted joy with - out end - ing.
gleam - ing and re - sound - ing through all cre - a - tion.

MORNING

Once More the Daylight Shines Abroad

Es geht daher des Tages Schein
Michael Weisse, 1531
trans. Catherine Winkworth, 1858, alt.

DAS WALT' GOTT VATER LM
attrib. Daniel Vetter, 1713
harm. Johann Sebastian Bach (1685–1750), alt.

1 Once more the day-light shines a-broad; with
2 E-ter-nal God, al-might-y friend, whose
3 now send us from thy heaven-ly throne thy
4 We of-fer up our-selves to thee, that

glad-ness, let us praise the Lord, whose grace and mer-cy
deep com-pas-sions have no end, whose nev-er-fail-ing
grace and help, through Christ thy Son, that with thy strength our
heart, and word, and deed may be in all things guid-ed

thus have kept the night-ly watch while we have slept.
strength and might have kept us safe-ly through the night:
hearts may glow, and fear not a-ny earth-ly foe.
by thy mind, and in thine eyes ac-cep-tance find.

Francis Turner Palgrave, 1862, alt.

CORNISH LM
M. Lee Suitor, 1975

1 Lord God of morn - ing and of night, we thank thee
2 Yet whilst thy will we would pur - sue, oft what we
3 O Lord of light, 'tis thou a - lone canst make our
4 To thee our ma - ker and our friend we sing through

for thy gift of light; as in the dawn the
would we can - not do; the sun may stand in
dark - ened hearts thine own; though this new day with
time till time shall end; till psalms and song thy

shad - ows fly, we seem to find thee now more nigh.
ze - nith skies, but on the soul thick mid - night lies.
joy we see, great dawn of God, we cry for thee.
name a - dore in heaven's great day of ev - er - more.

MORNING

Morning Has Broken

Eleanor Farjeon, 1931, alt.

BUNESSAN 55 54 D
Gaelic melody
harm. Alec Wyton, 1984

1 Morn-ing has bro - ken like the first morn - ing, black-bird has spo - ken like the first bird.
2 Sweet the rain's new fall sun-lit from heav - en, like the first dew - fall on the first grass.
3 Mine is the sun - light! Mine is the morn - ing born of the one light E - den saw play!

Praise for the sing - ing! Praise for the morn - ing! Praise for them spring - ing fresh from the word!
Praise for the sweet - ness of the wet gar - den, sprung in com - plete - ness where God's feet pass.
Praise with e - la - tion, praise ev - ery morn - ing, God's re - cre - a - tion of the new day!

Music © 1985 The Church Pension Fund.

MORNING

Charles Wesley, 1740

RATISBON   77 77 77
Geystliche gesangk Buchleyn, 1524
adapt. William Henry Havergal, 1861, alt.

1 Christ, whose glo - ry fills the skies, Christ, the true, the on - ly light,
2 Dark and cheer-less is the morn un - ac - com - pa - nied by thee;
3 Vis - it, then, this soul of mine; pierce the gloom of sin and grief;

Sun of Right-eous-ness, a - rise, tri-umph o'er the shades of night;
joy - less is the day's re - turn, till thy mer - cy's beams I see,
fill me, Ra - dian - cy di - vine, scat - ter all my un - be - lief;

Day-spring from on high, be near; Day-star, in my heart ap - pear.
till they in - ward light im - part, glad my eyes, and warm my heart.
more and more thy - self dis - play, shin - ing to the per - fect day.

MORNING

42   Each Morning Brings Us Fresh Outpoured

All' Morgen ist ganz frisch und neu
Johannes Zwick (c.1496–1542)
trans. Margaret Barclay, 1951

A MORNING HYMN   LM
Jeremiah Clarke, 1701

1 Each morn - ing brings us fresh out-poured the lov - ing kind -ness
2 O God, thou star of dawn -ing day, give us that light for
3 The dark - ness in us, Lord, dis - pel; from bit - ter -ness, O
4 To walk as by the light of day, that we may ev - er,

of the Lord. It ends not as the day goes past, but
which we pray; make thou thy flame in us to glow, that
shield us well, from ill de - sires, from cloud - ed sight; and
come what may, in our strong faith un - wav - ering be, a -

gives us strength while life shall last.
we no lack of grace may know.
do thou lead us, day and night.
bid - ing, stead - fast, one with thee.

MORNING

Awake, My Soul, and with the Sun

43

Thomas Ken, 1707

BROMLEY LM
Josef Haydn (1732–1809)

1 A - wake, my soul, and with the sun thy dai - ly
2 Thy pre - cious time mis - spent, re - deem; each pres - ent
3 Lord, I my vows to thee re - new; dis - perse my
4 Di - rect, con - trol, sug - gest, this day, all I de-
5 Praise God from whom all bless - ings flow; praise him, all

stage of du - ty run; shake off dull sloth, and
day thy last es - teem; im - prove thy tal - ent
sins as morn - ing dew; guard my first springs of
sign, or do, or say, that all my powers, with
crea - tures here be - low; praise him a - bove, ye

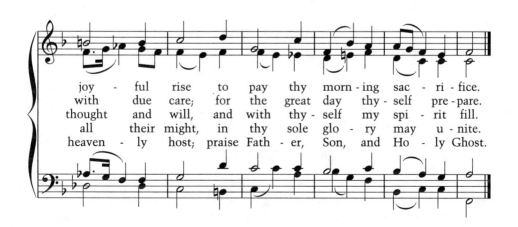

joy - ful rise to pay thy morn - ing sac - ri - fice.
with due care; for the great day thy - self pre - pare.
thought and will, and with thy - self my spi - rit fill.
all their might, in thy sole glo - ry may u - nite.
heaven - ly host; praise Fath - er, Son, and Ho - ly Ghost.

MORNING

When Morning Gilds the Skies

Beim frühen Morgenlicht
Katholisches Gesanguch, c. 1744
trans. Edward Caswall, 1854

LAUDES DOMINI 666 666
Joseph Barnby, 1868

1 When morn - ing gilds the skies, my heart a - wak - ing
2 When - e'er the sweet church bell peals o - ver hill and
3 My tongue shall nev - er tire of chant - ing with the
4 Be this, while life is mine, my can - ti - cle di -

cries, may Je - sus Christ be praised: a - like at work and
dell, may Je - sus Christ be praised: O hark to what it
choir, may Je - sus Christ be praised: this song of sac - red
vine, may Je - sus Christ be praised: be this the e - ter - nal

prayer to Je - sus I re - pair; may
sings, as joy - ous - ly it rings, may
joy, it nev - er seems to cloy, may
song through a - ges all a - long, may

MORNING

Je - sus Christ be praised.
Je - sus Christ be praised.
Je - sus Christ be praised.
Je - sus Christ be praised.

Heaven and Earth, and Sea and Air 45

Himmel, Erde, Luft und Meer
Joachim Neander, 1680
trans. Catherine Winkworth, 1858, alt.

GOTT SEI DANK 77 77
Geistreiches Gesang-Buch, 1704
adapt. Johann Stötzel, 1744

1 Heaven and earth, and sea and air, all their mak - er's praise de - clare;
2 See the glo - rious orb of day break - ing through the clouds its way;
3 See how God hath ev - ery - where made this earth so rich and fair;
4 Lord, great won - ders work - est thou! To thy sway all crea - tures bow;

wake, my soul, a - wake and sing; now thy grate - ful prais - es bring.
moon and stars with sil - very light prais - ing through the si - lent night.
hill and vale and fruit - ful land, all things liv - ing, show his hand.
write thou deep - ly in my heart what I am, and what thou art.

MORNING

Awake, Awake to Love and Work

Geoffrey A. Studdert-Kennedy, 1921

SHELTERED DALE   86 86 86
German melody
adapt. British Methodist Conference, 20th cent.

1 A-wake, a-wake to love and work, the lark is in the
2 Come, let thy voice be one with theirs, shout with their shout of
3 to give, and give, and give a-gain what God hath giv-en

sky,   the fields are wet with dia-mond dew, the
praise;   see how the gi-ant sun soars up, great
thee;   to spend thy-self nor count the cost, to

worlds a-wake to cry   their bless-ings on the
Lord of years and days!   So let the love of
serve right glo-rious-ly   the God who gave all

Lord   of   life,   as   he   goes meek-ly   by.
Je-   sus   come   and   set   thy soul a-   blaze:
worlds   that   are,   and   all   that   are   to   be.

MORNING

John Keble, 1822, alt.

MELCOMBE LM
Samuel Webbe, 1782

1 New ev-ery morn-ing is the love our wak-ening and up-
2 If on our dai-ly course our mind be set to hal-low
3 The triv-ial round, the com-mon task, will fur-nish all we
4 We pray thee, Lord, in thy dear love, pre-pare us for the

ris-ing prove; through sleep and dark-ness safe-ly brought, re-
all we find, new trea-sures still, of count-less price, God
ought to ask; room to de-ny our-selves— a road to
rest a-bove; and help us, this and ev-ery day, to

stored to life and power and thought.
will pro-vide for sac-ri-fice.
bring us dai-ly near-er God.
live more near-ly as we pray.

MORNING

48   Come, My Soul, Thou Must Be Waking

Seele, du musst munter werden
Friedrich von Canitz (1654–1699)
trans. Henry J. Buckoll, 1838

RICHTER   847 847
Geistreiches Gesang-Buch, 1704

1 Come, my soul, thou must be wak-ing. Now is break ing o'er the earth an-
2 Glad-ly hail the sun re-turn-ing, read-y burn-ing be the in-cense
3 Pray that he may pros-per ev-er each en-deav-or, when thine aim is
4 On-ly God's free gifts a-buse not, light re-fuse not, but his Spir-it's

oth - er day: come, to him who made this splen-dor
of thy powers; for the night is safe-ly end-ed,
good and true; but that he may ev-er thwart thee,
voice o-bey; thou with him shalt dwell, be-hold-ing

see thou ren-der all thy fee-ble strength can pay.
God hath tend-ed with his care thy help-less hours.
and con-vert thee, when thou e-vil wouldst pur-sue.
light en-fold-ing all things in un-cloud-ed day.

MORNING

Abide with Me, Fast Falls the Eventide 49

Henry Francis Lyte, 1847

EVENTIDE   10 10 10 10
William Henry Monk, 1861

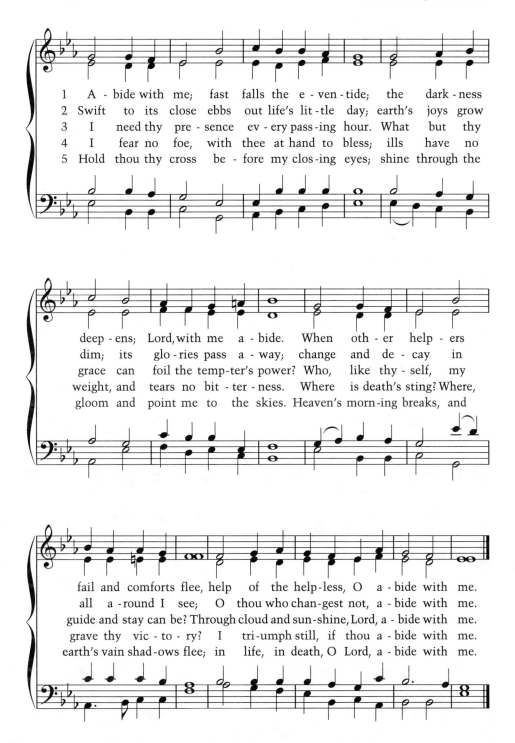

1 A - bide with me; fast falls the e - ven - tide; the dark - ness
2 Swift to its close ebbs out life's lit - tle day; earth's joys grow
3 I need thy pre - sence ev - ery pass - ing hour. What but thy
4 I fear no foe, with thee at hand to bless; ills have no
5 Hold thou thy cross be - fore my clos - ing eyes; shine through the

deep - ens; Lord, with me a - bide. When oth - er help - ers
dim; its glo - ries pass a - way; change and de - cay in
grace can foil the temp - ter's power? Who, like thy - self, my
weight, and tears no bit - ter - ness. Where is death's sting? Where,
gloom and point me to the skies. Heaven's morn - ing breaks, and

fail and comforts flee, help of the help - less, O a - bide with me.
all a - round I see; O thou who chan - gest not, a - bide with me.
guide and stay can be? Through cloud and sun - shine, Lord, a - bide with me.
grave thy vic - to - ry? I tri - umph still, if thou a - bide with me.
earth's vain shad - ows flee; in life, in death, O Lord, a - bide with me.

EVENING

O Gladsome Light, O Grace

φῶς ἱλαρὸν ἀγίας δόξης
Greek, 3rd cent.
trans. Robert Seymour Bridges, 1899, alt.

LE CANTIQUE DE SIMÉON   667 667
Louis Bourgeois, 1547
harm. Claude Goudimel, 1551

1 O   glad-some Light,   O   grace   of   our cre - a - tor's face,
2 Now,   ere   day   fad - eth   quite,   we   see the eve-ning light,
3 To   thee   of   right   be - longs   all   praise of ho - ly songs,

the e - ter - nal splen-dor wear - ing;   cel - les - tial, ho - ly,   blest,
our   wont-ed hymn out-pour - ing;   Fa - ther   of might un - known,
O   Son of God, life - giv - er;   thee,   there-fore, O Most High,

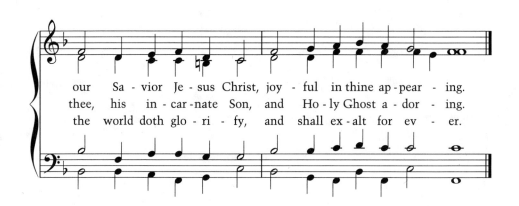

our   Sa - vior Je - sus Christ, joy - ful   in thine ap-pear - ing.
thee,   his   in - car - nate Son,   and   Ho - ly Ghost a - dor - ing.
the   world doth glo - ri - fy,   and   shall ex - alt for ev - er.

The Duteous Day Now Closeth 51

Nun ruhen alle Wälder
Paul Gerhardt, 1647
trans. Robert Seymour Bridges, 1899, alt.

O WELT, ICH MUSS DICH LASSEN 776 778
attrib. Heinrich Isaak, 1539
harm. Johann Sebastian Bach, 1729

1 The du-teous day now clos-eth, each flower and tree re-
2 Now all the heaven-ly splen-dor breaks forth in star-light
3 A-while our mor-tal blind-ness may miss God's lov-ing-

pos-eth, shade creeps o'er wild and wood. Let
ten-der from myr-iad worlds un-known, and
kind-ness, and grope in faith-less strife, but

us, as night is fall-ing, on God, our mak-er,
we, the mar-vel see-ing, for-get our self-ish
when life's day is o-ver shall death's fair night dis-

call-ing, give thanks to him, the giv-er good.
be-ing, for joy of beau-ty not our own.
cov-er the fields of ev-er-last-ing life.

EVENING

52 Christ, Mighty Savior, Light of All Creation

Christe lux mundi salus et potestas
Mozarabic rite, 10th cent.
trans. Anne K. LeCroy, 1982

CHRISTE LUX MUNDI   11 11 11 5
Plainsong, Mode 7
Freiburg manuscript, 14th cent.
accomp. Richard Proulx, 1982

1 Christ, might-y Savior, light of all cre-a-tion, you make the
2 Now comes the day's end as the sun is set-ting: mir-ror of
3 There-fore we come now, eve-ning rites to of-fer, joy-ful-ly
4 Give heed, we pray you, to our sup-pli-ca-tion: that you may
5 Though bo-dies slum-ber, hearts shall keep their vi-gil, for ev-er

day-time ra-diant with the sun-light and to the night give
day-break, pledge of re-sur-rec-tion; while in the hea-vens
chant-ing ho-ly hymns to praise you, with all cre-a-tion
grant us par-don for of-fens-es, strength for our weak hearts,
rest-ing in the peace of Je-sus, in light or dark-ness

glit-ter-ing a-dorn-ment, stars in the hea-vens.
choirs of stars ap-pear-ing hal-low the night-fall.
join-ing hearts and voic-es sing-ing your glo-ry.
rest for ach-ing bo-dies, sooth-ing the wear-y.
wor-ship-ing our Sa-vior now and for ev-er.

EVENING

Again, as Evening's Shadow Falls

Samuel Longfellow, 1859

ILLSLEY LM
John Bishop, 1711

1 A-gain as eve-ning's shad-ow falls, we gath-er in these hal-lowed walls, and ves-per hymn and ves-per prayer rise ming-ling on the ho-ly air.

2 May strug-gling hearts that seek re-lease here find the rest of God's own peace, and, strength-ened here by hymn and prayer, lay down the bur-den and the care.

3 O God, our Light, to thee we bow; with-in all shad-ows stand-est thou; give deep-er calm than night can bring; give sweet-er songs than lips can sing.

4 Life's tu-mult we must meet a-gain; we can-not at the shrine re-main; but in the Spir-it's se-cret cell may hymn and prayer for-ev-er dwell.

EVENING

54   O Strength and Stay Upholding All Creation

Rerum Deus tenax vigor
Ambrose of Milan (c.339–397)
trans. John Ellerton and Fenton J. A. Hort, 1871

STRENGTH AND STAY   11 10 11 10
John Bacchus Dykes, 1875

1 O strength and stay up-hold-ing all cre-a-tion,
2 grant to life's day a calm un-cloud-ed end-ing,
3 Hear us, O Fa-ther, gra-cious and for-giv-ing,

who ev-er dost thy-self un-moved a-bide,
an eve un-touched by shad-ows of de-cay,
through Je-sus Christ thy co-e-ter-nal Word,

yet day by day the light in due gra-da-tion
the bright-ness of a ho-ly death-bed blend-ing
who with the Ho-ly Ghost by all things liv-ing

from hour to hour through all its chang-es guide;
with dawn-ing glor-ies of the e-ter-nal day.
now and to end-less a-ges art a-dored.

The Day Thou Gavest, Lord, Is Ended 55

John Ellerton, 1870, alt.

ST. CLEMENT 98 98
Clement Cotterill Scholefield, 1874

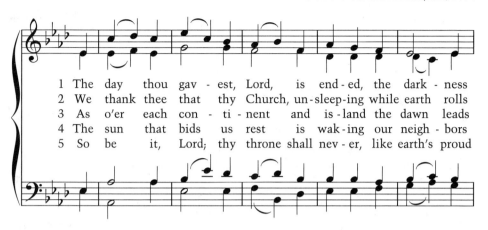

1 The day thou gav - est, Lord, is end - ed, the dark - ness
2 We thank thee that thy Church, un - sleep - ing while earth rolls
3 As o'er each con - ti - nent and is - land the dawn leads
4 The sun that bids us rest is wak - ing our neigh - bors
5 So be it, Lord; thy throne shall nev - er, like earth's proud

falls at thy be - hest; to thee our morn - ing hymns as -
on - ward in - to light, through all the world her watch is
on an - oth - er day, the voice of prayer is nev - er
'neath the west - ern sky, and hour by hour fresh lips are
em - pires, pass a - way; thy king - dom stands, and grows for -

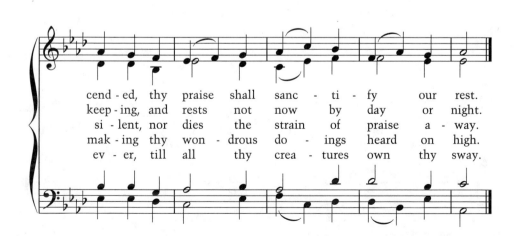

cend - ed, thy praise shall sanc - ti - fy our rest.
keep - ing, and rests not now by day or night.
si - lent, nor dies the strain of praise a - way.
mak - ing thy won - drous do - ings heard on high.
ev - er, till all thy crea - tures own thy sway.

EVENING

Creator of the Earth and Sky

Deus Creator omnium
Ambrose of Milan (c.339–397)
trans. Charles Bigg, 1906, alt.

UFFINGHAM LM
Jeremiah Clarke, 1701

1 Cre - a - tor of the earth and sky, rul - ing the
2 day sinks; we thank thee for thy gift; night comes; and
3 that when the dark - ness clos - es day, and shad - ows
4 Pray we the Fa - ther and the Son, and Ho - ly

fir - ma - ment on high, cloth - ing the day with robes of
once a - gain we lift our prayer and vows and hymns that
thick - en round our way, faith may no dark - ness know, and
Ghost: O Three in One, blest Trin - i - ty, whom all o -

light, bless - ing with gra - cious sleep the night:
we a - gainst all ills may shield - ed be,
night from faith's clear beam may bor - row light.
bey, guard thou thy sheep by night and day.

This music in E, 193.

All Praise to Thee, My God, This Night 57

Thomas Ken, 1707, alt.

TALLIS' CANON LM
Thomas Tallis, c. 1567

1 All praise to thee, my God, this night, for all the bless-ings
2 For-give me, Lord, for thy dear Son, the ill that I this
3 O may my soul on thee re-pose, and with sweet sleep mine
4 Praise God, from whom all bless-ings flow; praise him, all crea-tures

of the light! Keep me, O keep me,
day have done, that with the world, my -
eye - lids close, sleep that may me more
here be - low; praise him a - bove, ye

King of kings, be-neath thine own al-might-y wings!
self, and thee, I, ere I sleep, at peace may be.
vig-orous make to serve my God when I a - wake.
heaven-ly host; praise Fa-ther, Son, and Ho-ly Ghost.

EVENING

58 Savior, Again to Thy Dear Name We Raise

John Ellerton, 1866

ELLERS 10 10 10 10
Edward J. Hopkins, 1869, alt.

1 Sav - ior, a - gain to thy dear name we raise
2 Grant us thy peace up - on our home-ward way;
3 Grant us thy peace, Lord, through the com - ing night;
4 Grant us thy peace through - out our earth - ly life,

with one ac - cord our part - ing hymn of praise;
with thee be - gan, with thee shall end the day;
turn thou for us its dark - ness in - to light;
our balm in sor - row, and our stay in strife;

we stand to bless thee ere our wor - ship cease,
guard thou the lips from sin, the hearts from shame,
from harm and dan - ger keep thy chil - dren free,
then, when thy voice shall bid our con - flict cease,

then, low - ly kneel - ing, wait thy word of peace.
that in this house have called up - on thy name.
for dark and light are both a - like to thee.
call us, O Lord, to thine e - ter - nal peace.

EVENING

To You Before the Close of Day 59

Te lucis ante terminum
Latin, 6th cent.
stanzas 1-3: trans. Hymnal 1982
stanza 4: trans. James Waring McCrady, 1982

TE LUCIS ANTE TERMINUM LM
Plainsong, Mode 8
Antiphonale Sarisburiense, 13th cent.
accomp. Gerald Farrell (b. 1919)

1 To you be-fore the close of day, Cre-a-tor
2 Save us from trou-bled, rest-less sleep, from all ill
3 A health-y life we ask of you, the fire of
4 Al-might-y Fa-ther, hear our cry through Je-sus

of all things, we pray that in your con - stant
dreams your child-ren keep; so calm our minds that
love in us re-new, and when the dawn new
Christ, our Lord most high, whom with the Spi - rit

clem-en-cy our guard and keep-er you would be.
fears may cease and rest-ed bo-dies wake in peace.
light will bring your praise and glo-ry we shall sing.
we a-dore for ev-er and for ev-er-more.

EVENING

God, That Madest Earth and Heaven

stanza 1: Reginald Heber, 1827
stanza 2: Richard Whately, 1838, alt.

AR HYD Y NOS   84 84 88 84
Welsh melody
harm. Eton College Hymn Book, 1995, alt.

1 God, that mad-est earth and heav-en, dark - ness and light;
2 Guard us wak-ing, guard us sleep-ing, and, when we die,

who the day for toil hast giv-en, for rest the night;
may we in thy might - y keep-ing all peace - ful lie:

may thine an-gel guards de-fend us, slum-ber sweet thy mer - cy send us,
when the last dread call shall wake us, do not thou our God for-sake us,

ho - ly dreams and hopes at-tend us, this live - long night.
but to reign in glo - ry take us with thee on high.

EVENING

From Glory to Glory Advancing

para. of Liturgy of St. James, 4th cent.
Charles William Humphreys, 1906

SHEEN   14 14 14 15
Gustav Holst (1874–1934), alt.

61

1 From glo-ry to glo-ry ad-vanc-ing, we praise thee, O
2 Thanks-giv-ing and glo-ry and wor-ship and bless-ing and

Lord; thy name with the Fa-ther and Spi-rit be e-ver a-
love, one heart and one song have the saints up-on earth and a-

dored. From strength un-to strength we go for-ward on Si-on's high-
bove. Ev-er-more, O Lord, to thy serv-ants thy pres-ence be

way, to ap-pear be-fore God in the ci-ty of in-fin-ite day.
nigh; ev-er fit us by serv-ice on earth for thy serv-ice on high.

COMMUNION

62   And Now, O Father, Mindful of the Love

William Bright, 1874, alt.

UNDE ET MEMORES   10 10 10 10 10 10
William Henry Monk, 1875

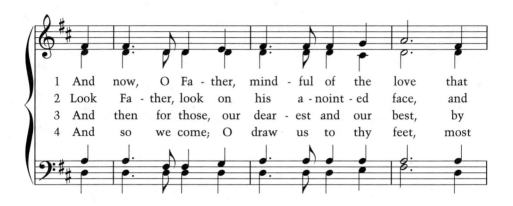

1 And now, O Fa - ther, mind - ful of the love that
2 Look Fa - ther, look on his a - noint - ed face, and
3 And then for those, our dear - est and our best, by
4 And so we come; O draw us to thy feet, most

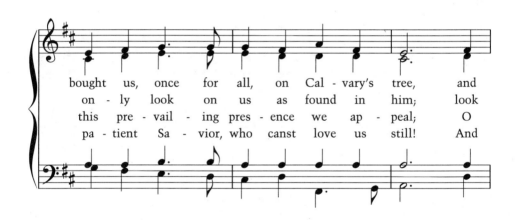

bought us, once for all, on Cal - vary's tree, and
on - ly look on us as found in him; look
this pre - vail - ing pres - ence we ap - peal; O
pa - tient Sa - vior, who canst love us still! And

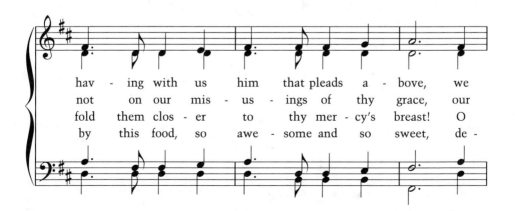

hav - ing with us him that pleads a - bove, we
not on our mis - us - ings of thy grace, our
fold them clos - er to thy mer - cy's breast! O
by this food, so awe - some and so sweet, de -

COMMUNION

here pre - sent, we here spread forth to thee, that
prayer so lan - guid, and our faith so dim: for
do thine ut - most for their souls' true weal! From
liv – er us from ev - ery touch of ill: in

on - ly of - fering per - fect in thine eyes, the
lo! be - tween our sins and their re - ward, we
taint - ing mis - chief keep them pure and clear, and
thine own ser - vice make us glad and free, and

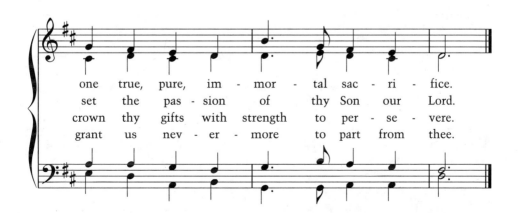

one true, pure, im - mor - tal sac - ri - fice.
set the pas - sion of thy Son our Lord.
crown thy gifts with strength to per - se - vere.
grant us nev - er - more to part from thee.

63   Draw Nigh and Take the Body of the Lord

Sancti venite corpus Christi sumite
Latin, 7th cent.
trans. John Mason Neale, 1851, alt.

EDINGTON   10 10 10 10
Peter J. Gomes, 2001

1 Draw nigh and take the bo - dy of the Lord, and
2 Sal - va-tion's giv - er, Christ, the on - ly Son, by
3 Ap - proach ye then with faith - ful hearts sin - cere, and
4 with heav-enly bread makes them that hun - ger whole, gives

drink the ho - ly blood for you out - poured. Saved
his dear cross and blood the vic - tory won. Of -
take the safe - guard of sal - va - tion here. He
liv - ing wa - ters to the thirst - ing soul. Al -

by that bo - dy and that pre - cious blood, with
fered was he for great - est and for least, him -
that in this world rules his saints and shields, to
pha and O - me - ga, to whom shall bow all

COMMUNION

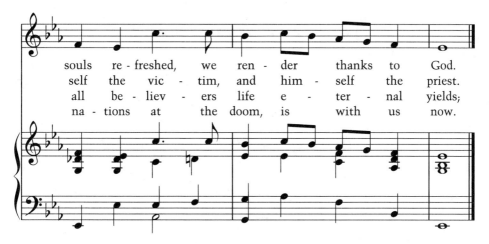

souls re - freshed, we ren - der thanks to God.
self the vic - tim, and him - self the priest.
all be - liev - ers life e - ter - nal yields;
na - tions at the doom, is with us now.

Music © 2007 Peter J. Gomes.

All for Jesus, All for Jesus 64

William J. Sparrow-Simpson, 1887

ALL FOR JESUS   87 87
John Stainer, 1887

1 All for Je - sus, all for Je - sus, this our song shall ev - er be;
2 All for Je - sus, thou wilt give us strength to serve thee, hour by hour;
3 All for Je - sus, at thine al - tar thou wilt give us sweet con - tent;
4 All for Je - sus, thou hast loved us; all for Je - sus, thou hast died;
5 All for Je - sus, all for Je - sus, this the Chur - ch's song must be,

for we have no hope, nor Sav - ior, if we have not hope in thee.
none can move us from thy pres - ence while we trust thy love and power.
there, dear Lord, we shall re - ceive thee in the so - lemn sac - ra - ment.
all for Je - sus, thou art with us; all for Je - sus cru - ci - fied.
till, at last, we all are ga - thered one in love and one in thee.

COMMUNION

Let Us Break Bread Together

African American

LET US BREAK BREAD   10 10 with Refrain
African American melody
harm. Harry Lyn Huff, 2006

1 Let us break bread to-geth-er on our knees; (on our knees) let us break bread to-ge-ther on our knees; (our knees) when I fall on my knees, with my face to the ris-ing sun, O Lord, have mer-cy on me. (on me)

2 Let us drink wine to-geth-er on our knees; (on our knees) let us drink wine to-ge-ther on our knees; (our knees)

Music © 2007 Harry Lyn Huff.

COMMUNION

3 Let us praise God to-ge-ther on our knees; (on our knees) let us praise God to-ge-ther on our knees; (our knees) when I fall on my knees with my face to the ris-ing sun, O Lord, have mer-cy on me. (on me)

COMMUNION

66   Here, O My Lord, I See Thee Face to Face

Horatius Bonar, 1855

NYACK   10 10 10 10
Warren Michel Swenson, 1970

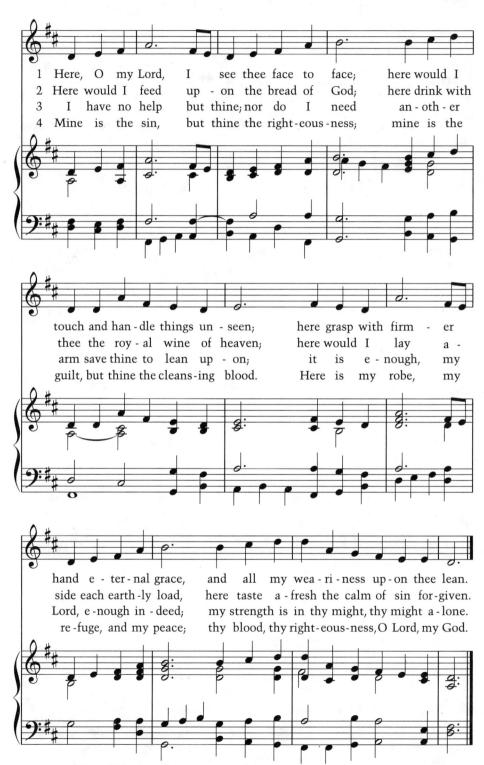

1 Here, O my Lord, I see thee face to face;
    here would I touch and han - dle things un - seen;
    here grasp with firm - er hand e - ter - nal grace,
    and all my wea - ri - ness up - on thee lean.

2 Here would I feed up - on the bread of God;
    here drink with thee the roy - al wine of heaven;
    here would I lay a - side each earth - ly load,
    here taste a - fresh the calm of sin for - given.

3 I have no help but thine; nor do I need
    an - oth - er arm save thine to lean up - on;
    it is e - nough, my Lord, e - nough in - deed;
    my strength is in thy might, thy might a - lone.

4 Mine is the sin, but thine the right - eous - ness;
    mine is the guilt, but thine the cleans - ing blood.
    Here is my robe, my re - fuge, and my peace;
    thy blood, thy right - eous - ness, O Lord, my God.

COMMUNION

Just As I Am, without One Plea

Charlotte Elliott, 1835

WOODWORTH LM
William B. Bradbury, 1849

1 Just as I am, with-out one plea, but that thy
2 Just as I am, though tossed a-bout with man-y a
3 Just as I am, poor, wretch-ed, blind; sight, rich-es,
4 Just as I am, thou wilt re-ceive; wilt wel-come,

blood was shed for me, and that thou bidd'st me
con-flict, man-y a doubt; fight-ings and fears with-
heal-ing of the mind, yea, all I need, in
par-don, cleanse, re-lieve, be-cause thy prom-ise

come to thee, O Lamb of God, I come, I come.
in, with-out, O Lamb of God, I come, I come.
thee to find, O Lamb of God, I come, I come.
I be-lieve, O Lamb of God, I come, I come.

5 Just as I am, thy love unknown
has broken every barrier down;
now to be thine, yea, thine alone,
O Lamb of God, I come, I come.

6 Just as I am, of thy great love
the breadth, length, depth, and height to prove,
here for a season, then above:
O Lamb of God, I come, I come.

COMMUNION

68   Lord, Enthroned in Heavenly Splendor

George H. Bourne, 1874

ST. HELEN   87 87 87
George C. Martin, 1881

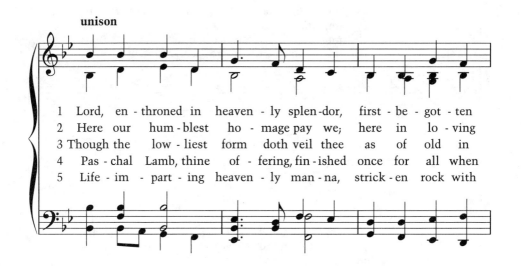

unison

1 Lord, en - throned in heaven - ly splen-dor, first - be - got - ten
2 Here our hum - blest ho - mage pay we; here in lo - ving
3 Though the low - liest form doth veil thee as of old in
4 Pas - chal Lamb, thine of - fering, fin - ished once for all when
5 Life - im - part - ing heaven - ly man - na, strick - en rock with

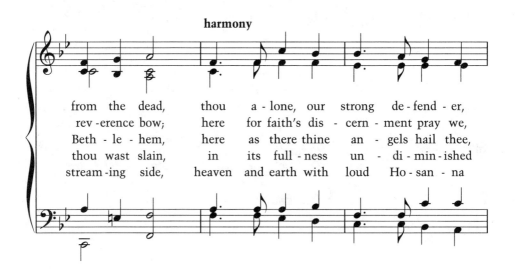

harmony

from the dead, thou a - lone, our strong de - fend - er,
rev - erence bow; here for faith's dis - cern - ment pray we,
Beth - le - hem, here as there thine an - gels hail thee,
thou wast slain, in its full - ness un - di - min - ished
stream - ing side, heaven and earth with loud Ho - san - na

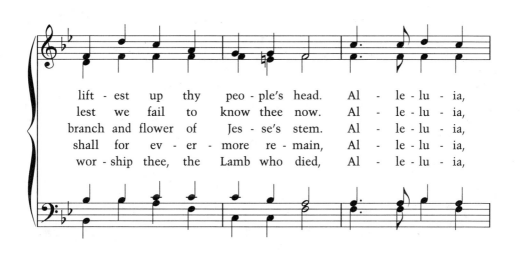

lift - est up thy peo - ple's head. Al - le - lu - ia,
lest we fail to know thee now. Al - le - lu - ia,
branch and flower of Jes - se's stem. Al - le - lu - ia,
shall for ev - er - more re - main, Al - le - lu - ia,
wor - ship thee, the Lamb who died, Al - le - lu - ia,

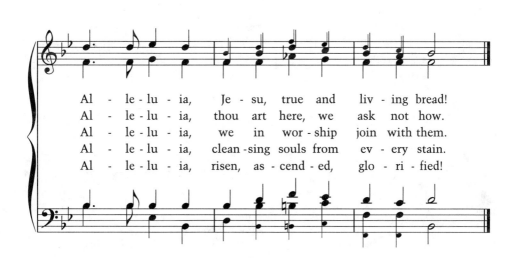

Al - le - lu - ia, Je - su, true and liv - ing bread!
Al - le - lu - ia, thou art here, we ask not how.
Al - le - lu - ia, we in wor - ship join with them.
Al - le - lu - ia, clean - sing souls from ev - ery stain.
Al - le - lu - ia, risen, as - cend - ed, glo - ri - fied!

69 Deck Thyself, My Soul, with Gladness

Schmücke dich, o liebe Seele
Johann Franck, 1649
trans. Catherine Winkworth, 1863, alt.

SCHMÜCKE DICH LMD
Johann Crüger, 1649
harm. Johann Sebastian Bach, 1724

1 Deck thy - self, my soul with glad - ness, leave the
2 Sun, who all my life dost bright - en; light, who
3 Je - sus, bread of life, I pray thee, let me

gloom - y haunts of sad - ness, come in - to the
dost my soul en - light - en; joy, the best that
glad - ly here o - bey thee; nev - er to my

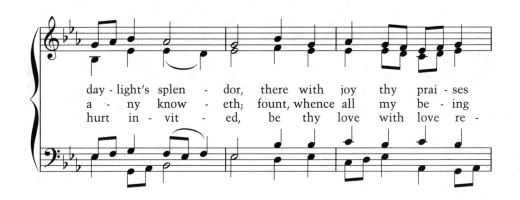

day - light's splen - dor, there with joy thy prai - ses
a - ny know - eth; fount, whence all my be - ing
hurt in - vit - ed, be thy love with love re -

ren - der un - to him whose grace un - bound -
flow - eth: at thy feet I cry, my Mak -
quit - ed; from this ban - quet let me mea -

ded hath this won - drous ban - quet
er, let me be a fit par -
sure, Lord, how vast and deep its

found - ed; high o'er all the heavens he reign - eth,
tak - er of this bless - ed food from heav - en,
trea - sure; through the gifts thou here dost give me,

yet to dwell with thee he deign - eth.
for our good, thy glo - ry, giv - en.
as thy guest in heaven re - ceive me.

COMMUNION

70   Thou, Who at Thy First Eucharist Didst Pray

William Harry Turton, 1881

SONG 1   10 10 10 10 10 10
Orlando Gibbons (1583–1625)
adapt. Ralph Vaughan Williams (1872–1958), alt.

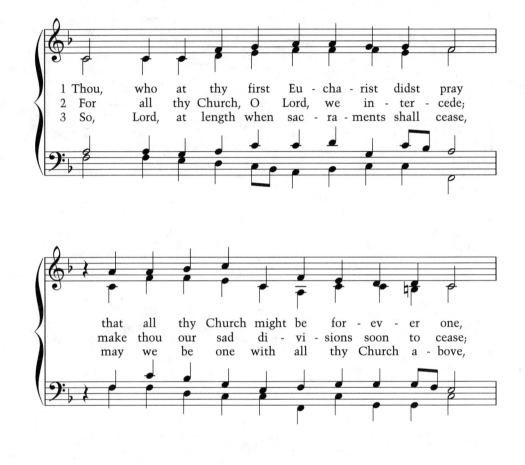

1 Thou, who at thy first Eu - cha - rist didst pray
2 For all thy Church, O Lord, we in - ter - cede;
3 So, Lord, at length when sac - ra - ments shall cease,

that all thy Church might be for - ev - er one,
make thou our sad di - vi - sions soon to cease;
may we be one with all thy Church a - bove,

grant us at ev - ery Eu - cha - rist to say
draw us the near - er each to each, we plead,
one with thy saints in one un - bro - ken peace,

COMMUNION

with long-ing heart and soul, "Thy will be done."
by draw-ing all to thee, O Prince of Peace;
one with thy saints in one un-bound-ed love;

O may we all one bread, one bo-dy be,
thus may we all one bread, one bo-dy be,
more bless-ed still, in peace and love to be

through this blest sac-ra-ment of u-ni-ty.
through this blest sac-ra-ment of u-ni-ty.
one with the Trin-i-ty in U-ni-ty.

71 O Day of Rest and Gladness

Christopher Wordsworth, 1862, alt.

ES FLOG EIN KLEINS WALDVÖGELEIN   76 76 D
German melody, 17th cent.
harm. H. Walford Davies, 1923

1 O day of rest and glad - ness, O day of joy and light, O
2 On thee, at the cre - a - tion, the light first had its birth; on
3 To - day on wea - ry na - tions the heaven - ly man - na falls; to
4 New grac - es ev - er gain - ing from this our day of rest, we

balm of care and sad - ness, most beau - ti - ful, most bright; on
thee for our sal - va - tion Christ rose from depths of earth; on
ho - ly con - vo - ca - tions the sil - ver trum - pet calls, where
reach the rest re - main - ing to spir - its of the blest. To

thee the high and low - ly, through a - ges joined in
thee our Lord vic - to - rious the Spir - it sent from
gos - pel light is glow - ing with pure and ra - diant
Ho - ly Ghost be prais - es, to Fa - ther, and to

tune, sing, Ho - ly, Ho - ly, Ho - ly, to the great God tri - une.
heaven, and thus on thee most glo - rious a tri - ple light was given.
beams, and liv - ing wa - ter flow - ing with soul - re - fresh - ing streams.
Son; the Church her voice up - rais - es to thee, blest Three in One.

We the Lord's People, Heart and Voice Uniting 72

John E. Bowers (b. 1923)

DECATUR PLACE   11 11 11 5
Richard Wayne Dirksen, 1984

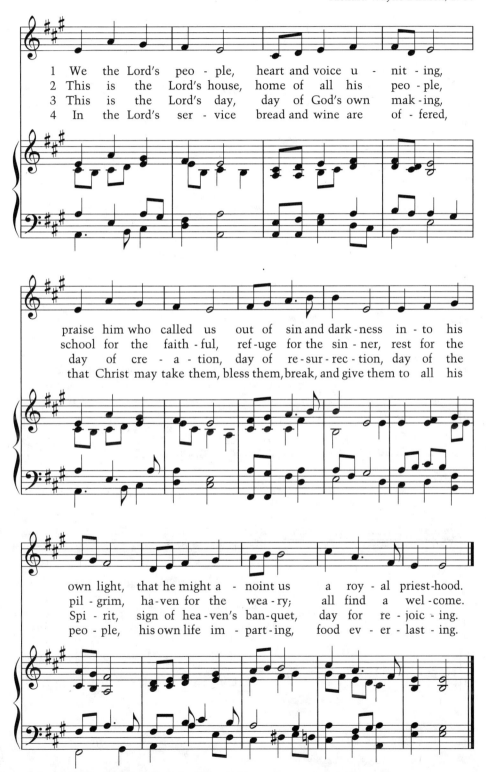

1 We the Lord's peo-ple, heart and voice u-nit-ing,
2 This is the Lord's house, home of all his peo-ple,
3 This is the Lord's day, day of God's own mak-ing,
4 In the Lord's ser-vice bread and wine are of-fered,

praise him who called us out of sin and dark-ness in-to his
school for the faith-ful, ref-uge for the sin-ner, rest for the
day of cre-a-tion, day of re-sur-rec-tion, day of the
that Christ may take them, bless them, break, and give them to all his

own light, that he might a-noint us a roy-al priest-hood.
pil-grim, ha-ven for the wea-ry; all find a wel-come.
Spi-rit, sign of hea-ven's ban-quet, day for re-joic-ing.
peo-ple, his own life im-part-ing, food ev-er-last-ing.

TIMES AND SEASONS

73   Great God, We Sing That Mighty Hand

Philip Doddridge (1702–1751)

WAREHAM LM
William Knapp, 1738

1 Great God, we sing that might-y hand by which sup-
2 By day, by night, at home, a-broad, still are we
3 With grate-ful hearts the past we own; the fu-ture,
4 In scenes ex-alt-ed or de-pressed, thou art our

port-ed still we stand; the o-pening year thy mer-cy
guard-ed by our God; by his in-ces-sant boun-ty
all to us un-known, we to thy guard-ian care com-
joy, and thou our rest; thy good-ness all our hopes shall

shows, that mer-cy crowns it till it close.
fed, by his un-err-ing coun-sel led.
mit, and, peace-ful, leave be-fore thy feet.
raise, a-dored through all our chang-ing days.

Praise to God, Immortal Praise

Anna Laetitia A. Barbauld, 1772

ORIENTIS PARTIBUS   77 77
attrib. Pierre de Corbeil (d. 1222)
harm. Harvard University Hymn Book, 1964

1 Praise to God, im-mor-tal praise, for the love that
2 All that spring with boun-teous hand scat-ters o'er the
3 these to thee, my God, we owe, source whence all our
4 Should thine al-tered hand re-strain the ear-ly and the
5 yet to thee my soul should raise grate-ful vows and

crowns our days! Boun-teous source of ev-ery
smil-ing land; all that lib-eral au-tumn
bless-ings flow; and for these my soul shall
lat-ter rain, blast each o-pening bud of
sol-emn praise, and, when ev-ery bless-ing's

joy, let thy praise our tongues em-ploy!
pours from her rich o'er-flow-ing stores,
raise grate-ful vows and sol-emn praise.
joy and the ris-ing year de-stroy—
flown, love thee for thy-self a-lone.

TIMES AND SEASONS

75

Lord, for the Years

Timothy Dudley-Smith, 1969

RUNCIE   11 10 11 10
Peter J. Gomes, 2001

1 Lord, for the years, your love has kept and
2 Lord, for that word, the word of life which
3 Lord, for our land, in this our gen - er -
4 Lord, for our world; when we dis - own and
5 Lord, for our - selves; in liv - ing power re -

guid - ed, urged and in - spired us,
fires us, speaks to our hearts and
a - tion, spir - its op - pressed by
doubt him, love - less in strength, and
make us, self on the cross and

cheered us on our way, sought us and
sets our souls a - blaze, teach - es and
plea - sure, wealth, and care; for young and
com - fort - less in pain; hun - gry and
Christ up - on the throne; past put be -

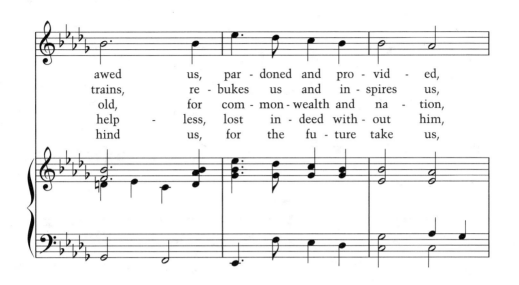

awed us, par - doned and pro - vid - ed,
trains, re - bukes us and in - spires us,
old, for com - mon - wealth and na - tion,
help - less, lost in - deed with - out him,
hind us, for the fu - ture take us,

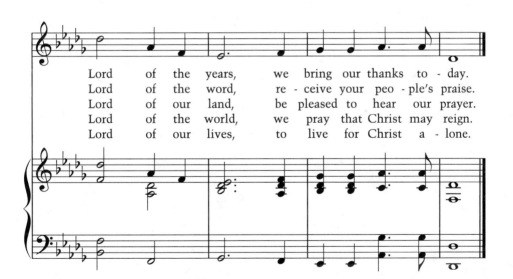

Lord of the years, we bring our thanks to - day.
Lord of the word, re - ceive your peo - ple's praise.
Lord of our land, be pleased to hear our prayer.
Lord of the world, we pray that Christ may reign.
Lord of our lives, to live for Christ a - lone.

TIMES AND SEASONS

Great Is Thy Faithfulness

Thomas O. Chisolm, 1923

FAITHFULNESS   11 10 11 10 with Refrain
William M. Runyan, 1923

1 Great is thy faith-ful-ness, O God my Fa-ther,
2 Sum-mer and win-ter, and spring-time and har-vest,
3 Par-don for sin and a peace that en-du-reth,

there is no sha-dow of turn-ing with thee; thou chang-est
sun, moon and stars in their cours-es a-bove, join with all
thy own dear pres-ence to cheer and to guide; strength for to-

not, thy com-pas-sions they fail not; as thou hast
na-ture in man-i-fold wit-ness to thy great
day and bright hope for to-mor-row, bless-ings all

been thou for-ev-er wilt be: Great is thy
faith-ful-ness, mer-cy, and love: Great is thy
mine, with ten thou-sand be-side!

TIMES AND SEASONS

faith-ful-ness! Great is thy faith-ful-ness! Morn-ing by morn-ing new

mer-cies I see; all I have need-ed thy hand has pro-

vi-ded, great is thy faith-ful-ness, Lord, un-to me.

TIMES AND SEASONS

Come, Ye Thankful People, Come

Henry Alford, 1844, alt.

ST. GEORGE'S WINDSOR 77 77 D
George J. Elvey, 1858

1 Come, ye thank-ful peo-ple, come, raise the song of har-vest home;
2 All the world is God's own field, fruit un-to his praise to yield;
3 For the Lord our God shall come, and shall take his har-vest home;
4 E-ven so, Lord, quick-ly come to thy fi-nal har-vest home;

all is safe-ly gath-ered in, ere the win-ter storms be-gin;
wheat and tares to-geth-er sown, un-to joy or sor-row grown;
from his field shall in that day all of-fens-es purge a-way,
gath-er thou thy peo-ple in, free from sor-row, free from sin;

God, our mak-er, doth pro-vide for our wants to be sup-plied;
first the blade, and then the ear, then the full corn shall ap-pear;
give his an-gels charge at last in the fire the tares to cast,
there for-ev-er pu-ri-fied, in thy pres-ence to a-bide;

come to God's own tem-ple, come, raise the song of har-vest home.
Lord of har-vest, grant that we whole-some grain and pure may be.
but the fruit-ful ears to store in his gar-ner ev-er-more.
come, with all thine an-gels, come, raise the glo-rious har-vest home.

TIMES AND SEASONS

Fred Pratt Green, 1970, alt.

EAST ACKLAM 84 84 88 84
Francis Jackson, 1957

1 For the fruit of all cre - a - tion, thanks be to God;
2 In the just re - ward of la - bor, God's will is done;
3 For the har - vests of the Spi - rit, thanks be to God;

gifts be - stowed on ev - ery na - tion, thanks be to God;
in the help we give our neigh - bor, God's will is done;
for the good we all in - her - it, thanks be to God;

for the plow - ing, sow - ing, reap - ing, si - lent growth while we are sleep - ing,
in our world - wide task of car - ing for the hun - gry and de - spair - ing,
for the won - ders that as - tound us, for the truths that still con - found us,

fu - ture needs in earth's safe - keep - ing, thanks be to God.
in the har - vests we are shar - ing, God's will is done.
most of all, that love has found us, thanks be to God.

TIMES AND SEASONS

79   We Plow the Fields and Scatter

Wir pflügen und wir streuen   WIR PFLÜGEN   76 76 D with Refrain
Matthias Claudius, 1782   *Johann A. P. Schulz, 1800*
trans. Jane Montgomery Campbell, 1861

1 We plow the fields, and scat - ter the good seed on the
2 He on - ly is the ma - ker of all things near and
3 We thank thee, then, O Fa - ther, for all things bright and

land, but it is fed and wa - tered by
far; he paints the way - side flow - er, he
good, the seed - time and the har - vest, our

God's al - might - y hand; he sends the snow in
lights the eve - ning star; the winds and waves o -
life, our health, our food: the gifts we have to

win - ter, the warmth to swell the grain, the
bey him, by him the birds are fed; much
of - fer are what thy love im - parts, but

TIMES AND SEASONS

breez - es and the sun - shine, and soft re - fresh - ing rain.
more to us, his chil - dren, he gives our dai - ly bread.
chief - ly thou de - sir - est our hum - ble, thank - ful hearts.

All good gifts a - round us are sent from heaven a - bove; then

thank the Lord, O thank the Lord for all his love.

80 Sing to the Lord of Harvest

John S. B. Monsell, 1866, alt.

WIE LIEBLICH IST DER MAIEN 76 76 D
Johann Steurlein, 1575
harm. Healey Willan, 1954

1 Sing to the Lord of har - vest, sing songs of love and
2 God makes the clouds drop fat - ness, the des - erts bloom and
3 Bring to this sa - cred al - tar all things God's good-ness

praise, with joy - ful hearts and voi - ces your
spring, the hills leap up in glad - ness, the
gave, the gold - en sheaves of har - vest, the

hal - le - lu - jahs raise; by whom the roll - ing
val - leys laugh and sing. God fills them all with
souls Christ died to save: your hearts lay down be -

TIMES AND SEASONS

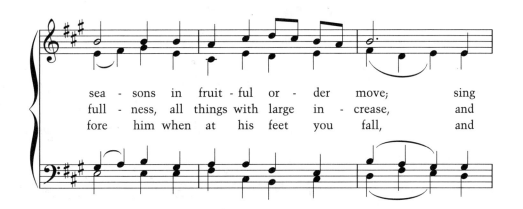

sea - sons in fruit - ful or - der move; sing
full - ness, all things with large in - crease, and
fore him when at his feet you fall, and

to the Lord of har - vest a joy - ful song of love.
crowns the year with good - ness, with plen - ty and with peace.
with your lives a - dore him who gave his life for all.

81 Lord of All Hopefulness, Lord of All Joy

Jan Struther, 1931

SLANE 10 11 11 12
Irish melody
harm. Hymnal 1982

1 Lord of all hope-ful-ness, Lord of all joy, whose
2 Lord of all ea-ger-ness, Lord of all faith, whose
3 Lord of all kind-li-ness, Lord of all grace, your
4 Lord of all gen-tle-ness, Lord of all calm, whose

trust, ev-er child-like, no cares could de-stroy, be
strong hands were skilled at the plane and the lathe, be
hands swift to wel-come, your arms to em-brace, be
voice is con-tent-ment, whose pres-ence is balm, be

there at our wak-ing, and give us, we pray, your
there at our la-bors, and give us, we pray, your
there at our hom-ing, and give us, we pray, your
there at our sleep-ing, and give us, we pray, your

bliss in our hearts, Lord, at the break of the day.
strength in our hearts, Lord, at the noon of the day.
love in our hearts, Lord, at the eve of the day.
peace in our hearts, Lord, at the end of the day.

TIMES AND SEASONS

In Our Day of Thanksgiving

William H. Draper, 1894, alt.

ST. CATHERINE'S COURT   12 11 12 11
Richard Strutt, 1925

1 In our day of thanks - giv - ing one psalm let us of - fer for the
2 In the morn - ing of life, and at noon, and at ev - en, he
3 These stones that have ech -oed their prais - es are ho - ly, and
4 Sing prais - es for all who here sought peace and found it, whose

saints who be - fore us have found their re - ward; when the
called them a - way from our wor - ship be - low; but
dear is the ground where their feet have once trod; yet
jour - ney is end - ed, whose per - ils are past: they be -

sha - dow of death fell up - on them, we sor -rowed, but
not till his love, at the font and the al - tar, had
here they con -fessed they were strang-ers and pil-grims, and
lieved in the light; and its glo - ry is round them, where the

now we re - joice that they rest in the Lord.
girt them with grace for the way they should go.
still they were seek - ing the ci - ty of God.
clouds of earth's sor - row are lift - ed at last.

TIMES AND SEASONS

83   For All the Saints

William Walsham How, 1864

SINE NOMINE   10 10 10 with Alleluias
Ralph Vaughan Williams, 1906

1 For all the saints, who from their la-bors rest, who
2 Thou wast their rock, their for-tress, and their might:
3 O may thy sol - diers, faith-ful, true, and bold,
6 From earth's wide bounds, from o-cean's far-thest coast, through

thee by faith be - fore the world con - fessed, thy
thou, Lord, their cap - tain in the well-fought fight;
fight as the saints who no-bly fought of old, and
gates of pearl streams in the count-less host,

name, O Je - sus, be for-ev - er blest. Al -
thou, in the dark - ness drear, the one true light. Al -
win, with them, the vic-tor's crown of gold. Al -
sing - ing to Fa - ther, Son, and Ho - ly Ghost, Al -

Music © 1906 Oxford University Press.

TIMES AND SEASONS

-le-lu - ia, Al - le-lu - ia!

harmony

4 O blest com-mun-ion, fel-low-ship di-vine! We fee-bly strug-gle,
5 And when the strife is fierce, the war-fare long, steals on the ear the

they in glo-ry shine; yet all are one in thee, for all are
dis-tant tri-umph song, and hearts are brave a-gain, and arms are

D. C.
for stanza 6

thine. Al - le-lu - ia, Al - le-lu - ia!
strong. Al - le-lu - ia, Al - le-lu - ia!

TIMES AND SEASONS

84   Give Us the Wings of Faith to Rise

Isaac Watts (1674–1748), alt.

SAN ROCCO   CM
Derek Williams, 1968

1 Give us the wings of faith to rise with - in the veil, and
2 We ask them whence their vic-tory came; they, with u - ni - ted
3 They marked the foot-steps that he trod, his zeal in-spired their
4 Our glo - rious lead - er claims our praise for his own pat - tern

see the saints a - bove, how great their joys, how
breath, as - cribe their con - quest to the Lamb, their
quest, and fol - lowing their in - car - nate God, they
given; while the long cloud of wit - ness - es show

1.2.3.

bright their glo - ries be.
tri - umph to his death.
reached the prom - ised rest.
the same path to (heaven.)

4.

heaven.

TIMES AND SEASONS

Carl P. Daw, Jr., 1994

KINGSFOLD CMD
English melody
harm. Ralph Vaughan Williams, 1906

1 We sing for all the un-sung saints, that count-less, name-less throng, who
2 Though un-in-scribed with date or place, with ti-tle, rank, or name, as
3 So we take heart from un-known saints be-reft of earth-ly fame, those

kept the faith and passed it on, with hope stead-fast and strong, through
liv-ing stones their sto-ries join to form a hal-lowed frame a-
faith-ful ones who have re-ceived a more en-dur-ing name: for

all the dai-ly griefs and joys no chron-i-cles re-cord, for-
round the mys-tery in their midst: the Lamb once sac-ri-ficed, the
they re-veal true bless-ing comes when we our pride ef-face and

get-ful of their lack of fame, but mind-ful of their Lord.
Love that wrest-ed life from death, the wound-ed, ris-en Christ.
of-fer back our lives to be the ves-sels of God's grace.

TIMES AND SEASONS

86   Who Are These Like Stars Appearing

Wer sind die vor Gottes Throne
Theobald Heinrich Schenk, 1719
trans. Frances Elizabeth Cox, 1864, alt.

ZEUCH MICH, ZEUCH MICH   87 87 77
Geistreiches Gesang-Buch, Darmstadt, 1698
harm. William Henry Monk (1823–1889), alt.

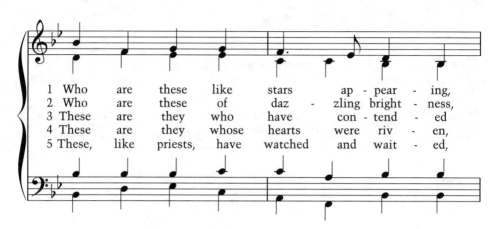

1 Who are these like stars ap - pear - ing,
2 Who are these of daz - zling bright - ness,
3 These are they who have con - tend - ed,
4 These are they whose hearts were riv - en,
5 These, like priests, have watched and wait - ed,

these, be - fore God's throne who stand?
these in God's own truth ar - rayed,
for their Sa - vior's hon - or long,
sore with woe and an - guish tried,
of - fering up to Christ their will,

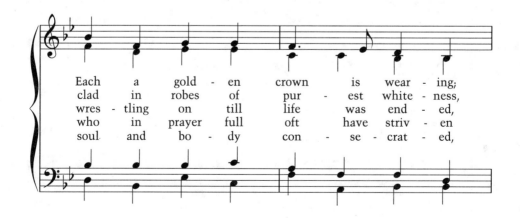

Each a gold - en crown is wear - ing;
clad in robes of pur - est white - ness,
wres - tling on till life was end - ed,
who in prayer full oft have striv - en,
soul and bo - dy con - se - crat - ed,

who   are   all   this   glo - rious   band?
robes   whose   lus - ter   ne'er   shall   fade,
fol - lowing   not   the   sin - ful   throng;
with   the   God   they   glo - ri - fied;
day   and   night   in   serv - ice   still.

Al - le - lu - ia!   hark,   they   sing,
ne'er   be   touched   by   time's   rude   hand?
these,   who   well   the   fight   sus - tained,
now,   their   pain - ful   con - flict   o'er,
Now   in   God's   most   ho - ly   place,

prais - ing   loud   their   heaven - ly   King.
Whence   comes   all   this   glo - rious   band?
tri - umph   by   the   Lamb   have   gained.
God   has   bid   them   weep   no   more.
blest   they   stand   be - fore   his   face.

87 I Sing a Song of the Saints of God

Lesbia Scott, 1929, alt.

GRAND ISLE   IRREGULAR
John Henry Hopkins, 1940

1 I sing a song of the saints of God, pa-tient and brave and
2 They loved their Lord so dear, so dear, and his love made them
3 They lived not on-ly in a - ges past: there are hun-dreds of thou-sands

true, who toiled and fought and lived and died for the
strong; and they fol-lowed the right, for Je - sus' sake, the
still. The world is bright with the joy - ous saints who

Lord they loved and knew. And one was a doc - tor, and
whole of their good lives long. And one was a sol - dier, and
love to do Je - sus' will. You can meet them in school, or in

one was a queen, and   one was a shep-her-dess on   the green: they were
one was a priest, and   one   was slain by   a fierce wild beast: and there's
lanes, or at sea, in   church, or in trains, or in shops, or at tea: for   the

all of them saints of   God, and I mean, God help-ing, to be one   too.
not a - ny   rea - son,   no, not the least, why I should-n't be one   too.
saints   of   God are just folk like me, and   I   mean to be one   too.

88 O Lord of Life, Whose Power Sustains

John Russell Darbyshire (1880–1948)

ARMISTICE 88 88 88
Peter J. Gomes, 2002

1 O Lord of Life, whose power sus-
2 As nature's heal - ing through the
3 Not names en - graved in mar - ble
4 O help us in the si - lence,

tains the world un - seen no less than this— one
years re -clothes the strick - en bat - tle -fields; so
make the best me - mor - ials of the dead, but
Lord, to hear the whis - pered call of love, and

fam - i - ly in him who reigns, tri - umph - ant o - ver
mer - cy gives us joy for tears, and grief to proud re -
bur - dens shoul -dered for their sake and tasks com - ple - ted
day by day thy strength af - ford our work to do, our

Music © 2007 Peter J. Gomes.

TIMES AND SEASONS

death, in bliss; to thee with thank - ful-ness we
mem-brance yields, and mind - ful hearts are glad to
in their stead; a brav - er faith and strong-er
faith to prove. So be thy bless - ing rich - ly

pray for all our val-iant dead to - day.
keep a tryst of love with them that sleep.
prayers, de - vout - er wor-ship, no - bler cares.
shed on our com-mun-ion with our dead.

89   Christ the Victorious, Give to Your Servants

Carl P. Daw, Jr., 1982

RUSSIAN HYMN   11 10 11 9
Alexis F. Lvov, 1833

1 Christ the vic - to - ri - ous, give to your ser - vants
2 On - ly im - mor - tal one, might - y cre - a - tor!
3 God - spok - en pro - phe - cy, word at cre - a - tion:
4 Christ the vic - to - ri - ous, give to your ser - vants

rest with your saints in the re - gions of light.
We are your crea - tures and chil - dren of earth.
"You came from dust and to dust shall re - turn."
rest with your saints in the re - gions of light.

Grief and pain end - ed, and sigh - ing no long - er,
From earth you formed us, both glo - rious and mor - tal,
Yet at the grave shall we raise up our glad song:
Grief and pain end - ed, and sigh - ing no long - er,

there may they find ev - er - last - ing life.
and to the earth shall we all re - turn.
"Al - le - lu - ia, Al - le - lu - ia!"
there may they find ev - er - last - ing life.

Another harmonization (in D), 327.

TIMES AND SEASONS

God Be with You Till We Meet Again

Jeremiah E. Rankin, 1880

RANDOLPH 98 89
Ralph Vaughan Williams, 1906

unison · harmony

1 God be with you till we meet a - gain; by his coun - sels
2 God be with you till we meet a - gain; 'neath his wings pro -
3 God be with you till we meet a - gain; when life's per - ils
4 God be with you till we meet a - gain; keep love's ban - ner

guide, up - hold you, with his sheep se -
tect - ing hide you, dai - ly man - na
thick con - found you, put his arm un -
float - ing o'er you, smite death's threat - ening

unison

cure - ly fold you: God be with you till we meet a - gain.
still pro - vide you: God be with you till we meet a - gain.
fail - ing round you: God be with you till we meet a - gain.
wave be - fore you: God be with you till we meet a - gain.

TIMES AND SEASONS

91   O Come, O Come, Emmanuel

Veni veni Emmanuel
Latin, 8th cent.
stanzas 1, 2: John Mason Neale, 1851, alt.
stanzas 3, 4: Henry Sloane Coffin, 1916

VENI EMMANUEL   88 88 88
Plainsong, Mode 1
Processionale, 15th cent.
adapt. Thomas Helmore, 1854

unison

1 O come, O come, Em - man - u - el, and ran - som cap - tive
2 O come, thou Day - spring, now ap - pear and cheer us by thine
3 O come, thou Wis - dom from on high, and or - der all things,
4 O come, De - sire of na - tions, bind all peo - ples in one

Is - ra - el, that mourns in lone - ly ex - ile
ad - vent here; dis - perse the gloom - y clouds of
far and nigh; to us the path of knowl - edge
heart and mind; bid en - vy, strife, and quar - rels

harmony

here, un - til the Son of God ap - pear.
night, and death's dark shad - ows put to flight. Re -
show, and cause us in her ways to go.
cease; and fill the world with heav - en's peace.

joice! Re - joice! Em - man - u - el shall come to thee, O Is - ra - el!

ADVENT

Creator of the Stars of Night

Conditor alme siderum
Latin, 9th cent.
trans. John Mason Neale, 1851, alt.

CONDITOR ALME SIDERUM LM
Plainsong, Mode 4
Sarum rite
accomp. J. H. Arnold, 1925

1 Cre - a - tor of the stars of night, thy peo - ple's ev - er -
2 To thee the trav - ail deep was known that made the whole cre -
3 When the old world drew on toward night, thou cam - est, not in
4 At thy great name ex - alt - ed now all knees must bend, all

last - ing light, O Christ, thou Sav - ior of us all,
a - tion groan, till thou, Re - deem - er, should - est free
splen - dor bright as mon - arch, but the hum - ble child
hearts must bow; and things ce - les - tial thee shall own,

we pray thee, hear us when we call.
thine own in glo - rious lib - er - ty.
of Mar - y, blame - less moth - er mild.
and things ter - res - trial, Lord a - lone. A - men.

ADVENT

93 Wake, Awake, for Night Is Flying

Wachet auf, ruft uns die Stimme
Philipp Nicolai, 1599
trans. Catherine Winkworth, 1858, alt.

WACHET AUF   898 898 664 88
Philipp Nicolai, 1599
harm. Johann Sebastian Bach, 1731

1 Wake, a-wake, for night is fly - ing; the watch-men on the
2 Zi-on hears the watch-men sing - ing; her heart with deep de-
3 Now let all the heavens a-dore thee, and sing in full-est

heights are cry - ing, a-wake, Je - ru - sa - lem, a - rise!
light is spring - ing, she wakes, she ris - es from her gloom,
voice be - fore thee, with harp and cym - bal's clear est tone;

Mid-night hears the wel-come voic - es, and at the thrill-ing
for her Lord comes down all glo - rious, in grace ar - rayed, by
of one pearl each shin-ing por - tal, where we shall join the

cry re-joic — es; he comes! O Church, lift up thine eyes! Rise
truth vic-to — rious; her star is risen, her light is come! Ah,
choirs im-mor — tal in prais-es round thy glo-rious throne; no

up, with will-ing feet go forth, the Bride-groom
come thou bless-ed One, God's own be-lov-ed
vi — sion ev-er brought, no ear hath ev-er

meet: Hal-le-lu — jah! Lo, great and small, we
Son, Hal-le-lu — jah! We haste a-long, an
caught such great glo — ry! There-fore will we, e —

an-swer all; we fol-low where thy voice shall call.
ea — ger throng, and glad-ly join the ad-vent song.
ter-nal-ly, sing hymns of joy and praise to thee.

94   Comfort, Comfort Ye My People

Tröstet, tröstet meine Lieben
Johannes G. Olearius, 1671
trans. Catherine Winkworth, 1863, alt.

GENEVAN 42   87 87 77 88
Claude Goudimel (1514–1572)

1 Com-fort, com-fort ye my peo-ple, speak ye peace, thus saith our God;
2 Hark, the voice of one that cri-eth in the des-ert far and near,
3 Make ye straight what long was crook-ed, make the rough-er pla-ces plain;

com-fort those who sit in dark-ness, mourn-ing 'neath their sor-rows' load.
call-ing us to new re-pent-ance since the king-dom now is here.
let your hearts be true and hum-ble, as be-fits his ho-ly reign.

Speak ye to Je-ru-sa-lem of the peace that waits for them;
Oh, that warn-ing cry o-bey! Now pre-pare for God a way;
For the glo-ry of the Lord now o'er earth is shed a-broad;

tell her that her sins I cov-er, and her war-fare now is o-ver.
let the val-leys rise to meet him and the hills bow down to greet him.
and all flesh shall see the to-ken that his word is ne-ver bro-ken.

ADVENT

Watchman, Tell Us of the Night

John Bowring, 1825

ABERYSTWYTH   77 77 D
Joseph Parry, 1879

1 Watch-man, tell us of the night, what its signs of prom-ise are.
2 Watch-man, tell us of the night, high-er yet that star as-cends.
3 Watch-man, tell us of the night, for the morn-ing seems to dawn.

Trav-eler, o'er yon moun-tain's height, see that glo-ry-beam-ing star.
Trav-eler, bless-ed-ness and light, peace and truth its course por tends.
Trav-eler, dark-ness takes its flight, doubt and ter-ror are with-drawn.

Watch-man, does its beau-teous ray aught of joy or hope fore-tell?
Watch-man, will its beams a-lone gild the spot that gave them birth?
Watch-man, let thy wan-derings cease; hie thee to thy qui-et home.

Trav-eler, yes; it brings the day, prom-ised day of Is-ra-el.
Trav-eler, a-ges are its own; see, it bursts o'er all the earth.
Trav-eler, lo, the Prince of Peace, lo, the Son of God is come.

ADVENT

On Jordan's Bank the Baptist's Cry

Jordanis oras prævia
Charles Coffin, 1736
trans. John Chandler, 1837, alt.

WINCHESTER NEW   LM
Musicalisch Hand-Buch, 1690
harm. William Henry Monk, 1847, alt.

1 On Jor - dan's bank the bap - tist's cry an -
2 Then cleansed be ev - ery breast from sin; make
3 For thou art our sal - va - tion, Lord, our
4 All praise, e - ter - nal Son, to thee, whose

nounc - es that the Lord is nigh; a - wake and heark - en,
straight the way for God with - in! Yea, let us each our
ref - uge and our great re - ward; once more up - on thy
ad - vent sets thy peo - ple free; whom with the Fa - ther

for he brings glad tid - ings from the King of kings.
hearts pre - pare for Christ to come and en - ter there.
peo - ple shine and fill the world with love di - vine.
we a - dore and Ho - ly Ghost for ev - er - more.

ADVENT

Birjina gaztettobat zegoen
Basque
trans. *Sabine Baring-Gould (1834–1924)*

GABRIEL'S MESSAGE 10 10 12 10
Basque melody
harm. *Edgar Pettman (1865–1943)*

1 The an - gel Ga - bri - el from hea - ven came, his
2 "For known a bless - ed mo - ther thou shalt be, all
3 Then gen - tle Ma - ry meek - ly bowed her head, "To
4 Of her, Em - man - u - el, the Christ, was born in

wings as drift - ed snow, his eyes as flame; "All
gen - er - a - tions laud and hon - or thee, thy
me be as it pleas - eth God," she said, "my
Beth - le - hem, all on a Christ - mas morn, and

hail," said he, "thou low - ly maid - en Ma - ry, most
Son shall be Em - man - u - el, by seers fore - told, most
soul shall laud and mag - ni - fy his ho - ly name." Most
Chris - tian folk through - out the world will ev - er say "Most

high - ly fa - vored la - dy." *Glo* - - *ri - a!*
high - ly fa - vored la - dy." *Glo* - - *ri - a!*
high - ly fa - vored la - dy! *Glo* - - *ri - a!*
high - ly fa - vored la - dy." *Glo* - - *ri - a!*

ADVENT

98   The Lord Will Come and Not Be Slow

John Milton, 1648, alt.

YORK CM
Scottish Psalter, 1615
harm. John Milton, Sr., 1621

1 The Lord will come and not be slow, his
2 Truth from the earth, like to a flower, shall
3 Rise, God, judge thou the earth in might, this
4 The na - tions all whom thou hast made shall
5 For great thou art, and won - ders great by

foot - steps can - not err; be - fore him right - eous -
blos - som on that day; and jus - tice, from her
wick - ed earth re - dress; for thou art he who
come, and all shall frame to bow them low be -
thy strong hand are done: thou in thy ev - er -

ness shall go, his roy - al har - bin - ger.
heaven - ly bower, shine down in bright ar - ray.
shalt by right the na - tions all pos - sess.
fore thee, Lord, and glo - ri - fy thy name.
last - ing seat re - main - est God a - lone.

ADVENT

Vox clara ecce intonat
Latin, 10th cent.
trans. Edward Caswall, 1849, alt.

MERTON 87 87
William Henry Monk, 1850

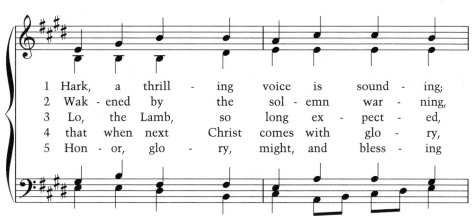

1 Hark, a thrill - ing voice is sound - ing;
2 Wak - ened by the sol - emn warn - ing,
3 Lo, the Lamb, so long ex - pect - ed,
4 that when next Christ comes with glo - ry,
5 Hon - or, glo - ry, might, and bless - ing

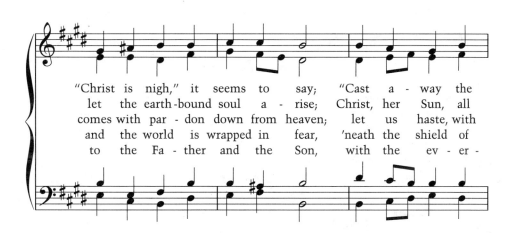

"Christ is nigh," it seems to say; "Cast a - way the
let the earth-bound soul a - rise; Christ, her Sun, all
comes with par - don down from heaven; let us haste, with
and the world is wrapped in fear, 'neath the shield of
to the Fa - ther and the Son, with the ev - er -

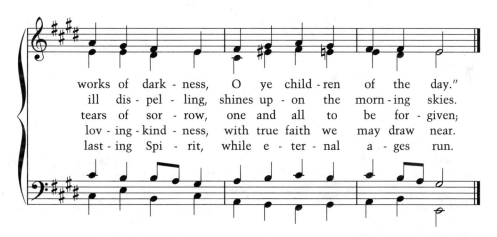

works of dark - ness, O ye child - ren of the day."
ill dis - pel - ling, shines up - on the morn - ing skies.
tears of sor - row, one and all to be for - given;
lov - ing-kind - ness, with true faith we may draw near.
last - ing Spi - rit, while e - ter - nal a - ges run.

ADVENT

100   Lo! He Comes, with Clouds Descending

Charles Wesley, 1758, alt.

HELMSLEY   87 87 87 47
melody Augustine Arne (1710–1778)
harm. Thomas Olivers, 1765

1 Lo!   he   comes, with   clouds   de - scend - ing,
2 Ev - ery   eye   shall   now   be - hold   him,
3 Those   dear   to - kens   of   his   pas - sion
4 Yea,   A - men!   Let   all   a - dore   thee,

once   for   our   sal - va - tion   slain;   thou - sand
robed   in   dread - ful   ma - jes - ty;   those   who
still   his   daz - zling   bo - dy   bears,   cause   of
high   on   thine   e - ter - nal   throne;   Sa - vior,

thou - sand   saints   at - tend - ing   swell   the
set   at   nought   and   sold   him,   pierced,   and
end - less   ex - ul - ta - tion   to   his
take   the   power   and   glo - ry;   claim   the

tri - umph of his train: Al - le -
nailed him to the tree, deep - ly
ran - somed wor - ship - ers: with what
king - dom for thine own: Al - le -

lu - ia, Al - le - lu - ia, Al - le -
wail - ing, deep - ly wail - ing, deep - ly
rap - ture, with what rap - ture, with what
lu - ia, Al - le - lu - ia, Al - le -

lu - ia! Christ the Lord re - turns to reign.
wail - ing, shall the true Mes - si - ah see.
rap - ture gaze we on those glo - rious scars!
lu - ia! Thou shalt reign, and thou a - lone.

101 Lift Up Your Heads, Ye Mighty Gates

Macht hoch die Tür, die Tor' macht weit
Georg Weissel, 1642
trans. Catherine Winkworth, 1855, alt.

MACHT HOCH DIE TÜR   88 88 88 66
Geistreiches Gesang-Buch, 1704

1 Lift up your heads, ye might-y gates; be-hold the King of
2 Fling wide the por-tals of your heart; make it a tem-ple,
3 Re-deem-er, come! I o-pen wide my heart to thee; here,

glo-ry waits. The King of kings is draw-ing near; the
set a-part from earth-ly use for heaven's em-ploy, a-
Lord, a-bide. Let me thy in-ner pres-ence feel, thy

Sav-ior of the world is here. For us sal-va-tion
dorned with prayer and love and joy. So let your Sov-ereign
grace and love in me re-veal; thy Ho-ly Spir-it

he doth bring, so let us all re-joice and sing: we
en-ter in, and new and no-bler life be-gin: to
guide us on un-til our glo-rious goal is won. E-

ADVENT

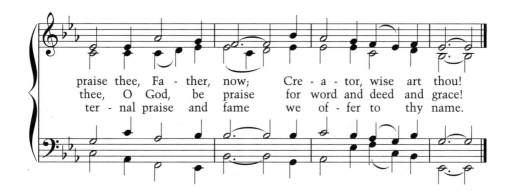

praise thee, Fa - ther, now; Cre - a - tor, wise art thou!
thee, O God, be praise for word and deed and grace!
ter - nal praise and fame we of - fer to thy name.

Savior of the Nations, Come 102

Veni Redemptor gentium
Ambrose of Milan (c.339–397)
trans. Martin Luther, 1524
trans. William M. Reynolds, 1860, alt.

NUN KOMM, DER HEIDEN HEILAND 77 77
Erfurt Enchiridia, 1524
harm. Seth Calvisius, 1594

1 Sa - vior of the na - tions, come, Vir - gin's Son, make here thy home.
2 From the Fa - ther forth he came, and re - turn - eth to the same,
3 Thou, the Fa - ther's on - ly Son, hast o'er sin the vic - tory won.
4 Bright - ly doth thy man - ger shine; glo - rious is its light di - vine.

Mar - vel now, O heaven and earth, that the Lord chose such a birth.
cap - tive lead - ing death and hell: high the song of tri - umph swell!
Bound - less shall thy king - dom be; when shall we its glo - ries see?
Let not sin o'er - cloud this light; ev - er be our faith thus bright.

103   Let All Mortal Flesh Keep Silence

σιγησάτω πᾶσα σὰρξ βροτεία
Liturgy of St. James, 4th cent.
trans. Gerald Moultrie, 1864

PICARDY   87 87 87
French melody, 17th cent.
accomp. The English Hymnal, 1906

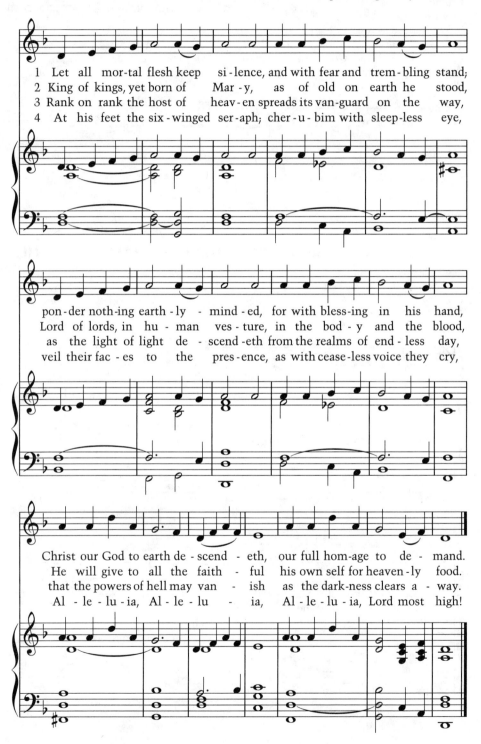

1 Let all mor-tal flesh keep si-lence, and with fear and trem-bling stand;
2 King of kings, yet born of Mar-y, as of old on earth he stood,
3 Rank on rank the host of heav-en spreads its van-guard on the way,
4 At his feet the six-winged ser-aph; cher-u-bim with sleep-less eye,

pon-der noth-ing earth-ly - mind-ed, for with bless-ing in his hand,
Lord of lords, in hu-man ves-ture, in the bod-y and the blood,
as the light of light de-scend-eth from the realms of end-less day,
veil their fac-es to the pres-ence, as with cease-less voice they cry,

Christ our God to earth de-scend-eth, our full hom-age to de-mand.
He will give to all the faith-ful his own self for heaven-ly food.
that the powers of hell may van-ish as the dark-ness clears a-way.
Al-le-lu-ia, Al-le-lu-ia, Al-le-lu-ia, Lord most high!

ADVENT

Hark, What a Sound, and Too Divine for Hearing 104

Frederick W. H. Myers, 1867

HIGHWOOD 11 10 11 10
Richard Runciman Terry (1865–1938)

1 Hark, what a sound, and too div-ine for hear - ing,
2 Sure - ly he com - eth, and a thou-sand voic - es
3 This hath he done, and shall we not a - dore him?
4 Yea, through life, death, through sor-row and through sin - ning,

stirs on the earth and trem-bles in the air!
shout to the saints, and to the deaf are dumb;
This shall he do, and can we still des - pair?
he shall suf - fice me, for he hath suf - ficed:

Is it the thun - der of the Lord's ap - pear - ing?
sure - ly he com - eth, and the earth re - joic - es,
Come, let us quick - ly fling our - selves be - fore him,
Christ is the end, for Christ was the be - gin - ning,

Is it the mu - sic of his peo - ple's prayer?
glad in his com - ing who hath sworn: I come!
cast at his feet the bur - den of our care.
Christ the be - gin - ning, for the end is Christ.

ADVENT

105 Lord Christ, When First Thou Cam'st to Earth

Walter Russell Bowie, 1928, alt.

MIT FREUDEN ZART 87 87 887
*Kirchengeseng darinnen die Heubtartickel
des Christlichen Glaubens gefasset, 1566*

1 Lord Christ, when first thou cam'st to earth, up - on a cross they
2 O awe - ful love, which found no room in life where sin de -
3 New ad - vent of the love of Christ, shall we a - gain re -
4 O wound-ed hands of Je - sus, build in us thy new cre -

bound thee, and mocked thy sav - ing king-ship then by
nied thee, and, doomed to death, must bring to doom the
fuse thee, till in the night of hate and war we
a - tion; our pride is dust; our vaunt is stilled: we

thorns with which they crowned thee; and still our wrongs may
powers which cru - ci - fied thee, till not a stone was
per - ish as we lose thee? From old un - faith our
wait thy rev - e - la - tion. O love that tri - umphs

weave thee now new thorns to pierce that
left on stone, and all those na - tions'
souls re - lease to seek the king - dom
o - ver loss, we bring our hearts be -

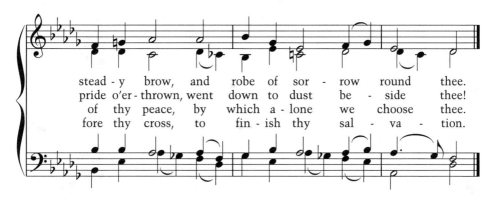

steady brow, and robe of sorrow round thee.
pride o'er-thrown, went down to dust beside thee!
of thy peace, by which alone we choose thee.
fore thy cross, to finish thy salvation.

This music in D, 11.

Come, Thou Long-Expected Jesus 106

Charles Wesley, 1744, alt.

STUTTGART 87 87
Christian F. Witt, 1715
adapt. Hymns Ancient and Modern, 1861

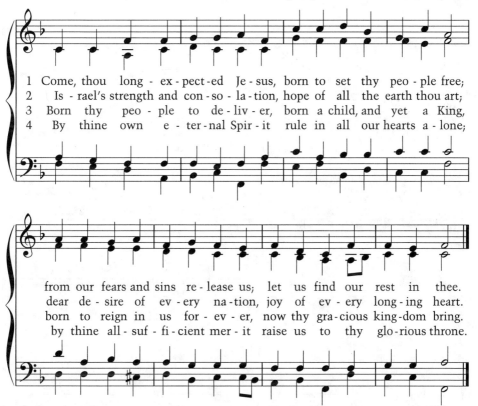

1 Come, thou long-expected Jesus, born to set thy people free;
2 Israel's strength and consolation, hope of all the earth thou art;
3 Born thy people to deliver, born a child, and yet a King,
4 By thine own eternal Spirit rule in all our hearts alone;

from our fears and sins release us; let us find our rest in thee.
dear desire of every nation, joy of every longing heart.
born to reign in us forever, now thy gracious kingdom bring.
by thine all-sufficient merit raise us to thy glorious throne.

107 I Want to Walk as a Child of the Light

Kathleen Thomerson, 1966

HOUSTON 10 7 10 8 with Refrain
Kathleen Thomerson, 1966

1 I want to walk as a child of the light.
2 I want to see the bright-ness of God.
3 I'm look-ing for the com-ing of Christ.

I want to fol-low Je - sus.
I want to look at Je - sus.
I want to be with Je - sus.

God set the stars to give light to the world. The
Clear Sun of Right-eous-ness shine on my path, and
When we have run with pa-tience the race, we

star of my life is Je - sus.
show me the way to the Fa - ther.
shall know the joy of Je - sus

ADVENT

In him there is no dark-ness at all. The night and the day are both a - like. The Lamb is the light of the cit - y of God. Shine in my heart, Lord Je - sus.

108   **Hail to the Lord's Anointed**

para. of Psalm 72
James Montgomery, 1821, alt.

JESUS CHRIST, UNSER HERRE   76 76 D
attrib. Bartholomäus Gesius, 1605
harm. Johann Sebastian Bach (1685–1750)

1 Hail to the Lord's A - noint - ed, great Da - vid's great - er
2 He comes with suc - cor speed - y to those who suf - fer
3 He shall come down like show - ers up - on the fruit - ful
4 O'er ev - ery foe vic - to - rious, he on his throne shall

Son! Hail, in the time ap - point - ed, his
wrong; to help the poor and need - y, and
earth; and love, joy, hope, like flow - ers, spring
rest, from age to age more glo - rious, all -

reign on earth be - gun! He comes to break op -
bid the weak be strong; to give them songs for
in his path to birth; be - fore him on the
bless - ing and all - blest: the tide of time shall

pres - sion, to set the cap - tive free, to
sigh - ing, their dark - ness turn to light, whose
moun - tains shall peace, the her - ald, go; and
nev - er his cov - e - nant re - move; his

take a - way trans - gres - sion, and rule in eq - ui - ty.
souls, con-demned and dy - ing, were pre-cious in his sight.
right-eous-ness, in foun - tains, from hill to val - ley flow.
name shall stand for - ev - er: that name to us is Love.

109 People, Look East, the Time Is Near

Eleanor Farjeon, 1928, alt.

BESANÇON 87 98 87
French melody
harm. Barry Rose, 1986

1 Peo - ple, look east, the time is near of the
2 Fur - rows, be glad. Though earth is bare, one more
3 Birds, though you long have ceased to build, guard the
4 Stars, keep the watch. When night is dim, one more
5 An - gels, an - nounce with shouts of mirth Christ who

crown - ing of the year. Make your house fair as you are
seed is plant - ed there. Give up your strength the seed to
nest that must be filled. E - ven the hour when wings are
light the bowl shall brim, shin - ing be - yond the frost - y
brings new life to earth. Set ev - ery peak and val - ley

a - ble, trim the hearth and set the ta - ble. Peo-ple, look
nour - ish, that in course the flower may flou - rish. Peo-ple, look
froz - en now for fledg - ing time is chos - en. Peo-ple, look
weath - er, bright as sun and moon to - geth - er. Peo-ple, look
hum - ming with the word, the Lord is com - ing. Peo-ple, look

east, and sing to - day: Love, the guest, is on the way.
east, and sing to - day: Love, the rose, is on the way.
east, and sing to - day: Love, the bird, is on the way.
east, and sing to - day: Love, the star, is on the way.
east, and sing to - day: Love, the Lord, is on the way.

ADVENT

Joy to the World! The Lord Is Come 110

Isaac Watts, 1719, alt.

ANTIOCH CM
adapt. Lowell Mason, 1836

1 Joy to the world! the Lord is come: let earth re-ceive her King; let ev-ery heart pre-pare him room, and heaven and na-ture sing, and heaven and na-ture sing, and heaven, and heaven and na-ture sing.

2 Joy to the earth! the Sav-ior reigns: let us our songs em-ploy; while fields and floods, rocks, hills, and plains re-peat the sound-ing joy, re-peat the sound-ing joy, re-peat, re-peat the sound-ing joy.

3 No more let sins and sor-rows grow, nor thorns in-fest the ground; he comes to make his bless-ings flow far as the curse is found, far as the curse is found, far as, far as the curse is found.

4 He rules the world with truth and grace, and makes the na-tions prove the glo-ries of his right-eous-ness, and won-ders of his love, and won-ders of his love, and won-ders, won-ders of his love.

CHRISTMAS

It Came upon the Midnight Clear

Edmund Hamilton Sears, 1849, alt.

CAROL CMD
Richard Storrs Willis, 1850

1 It came up-on the mid-night clear, that glo-rious song of
2 Still through the clov-en skies they come, with peace-ful wings un-
3 Yet with the woes of sin and strife the world has suf-fered
4 For lo! the days are haste-ning on, by pro-phets seen of

old, from an-gels bend-ing near the earth to
furled, and still their heaven-ly mu-sic floats o'er
long; be-neath the heaven-ly hymn have rolled two
old, when with the ev-er-cir-cling years shall

touch their harps of gold: "Good-will to all, and
all the wea-ry world; a-bove its sad and
thou-sand years of wrong; and war-ring hu-man-
come the time fore-told, when peace shall o-ver

peace on earth, from heaven's all-gra-cious King." The
low-ly plains they bend on hov-ering wing, and
kind hears not the tid-ings which they bring; O
all the earth its an-cient splen-dors fling, and

CHRISTMAS

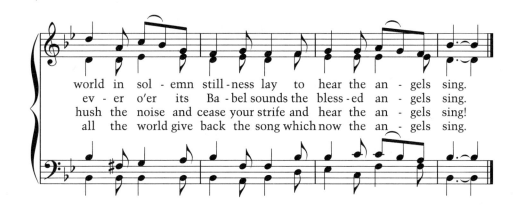

world in sol - emn still - ness lay to hear the an - gels sing.
ev - er o'er its Ba - bel sounds the bless - ed an - gels sing.
hush the noise and cease your strife and hear the an - gels sing!
all the world give back the song which now the an - gels sing.

All My Heart This Night Rejoices 112

Fröhlich soll mein Herze springen
Paul Gerhardt, 1653
trans. Catherine Winkworth, 1858

WARUM SOLLT' ICH MICH DENN GRÄMEN 8336 D
Johann Georg Ebeling, 1666

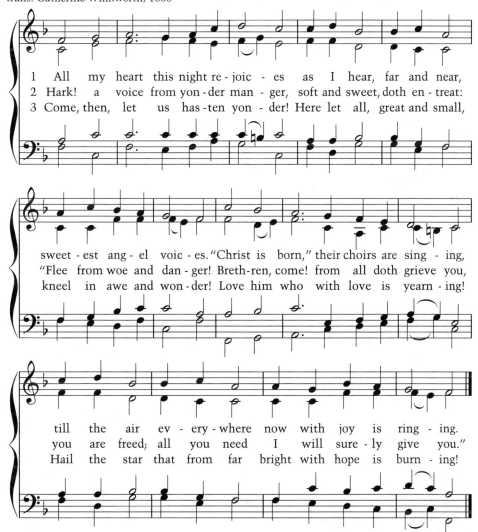

1 All my heart this night re - joic - es as I hear, far and near,
2 Hark! a voice from yon - der man - ger, soft and sweet, doth en - treat:
3 Come, then, let us has - ten yon - der! Here let all, great and small,

sweet - est ang - el voic - es. "Christ is born," their choirs are sing - ing,
"Flee from woe and dan - ger! Breth - ren, come! from all doth grieve you,
kneel in awe and won - der! Love him who with love is yearn - ing!

till the air ev - ery - where now with joy is ring - ing.
you are freed; all you need I will sure - ly give you."
Hail the star that from far bright with hope is burn - ing!

113 O Little Town of Bethlehem

Phillips Brooks, 1876, alt.

ST. LOUIS   CMD
Lewis H. Redner, 1868

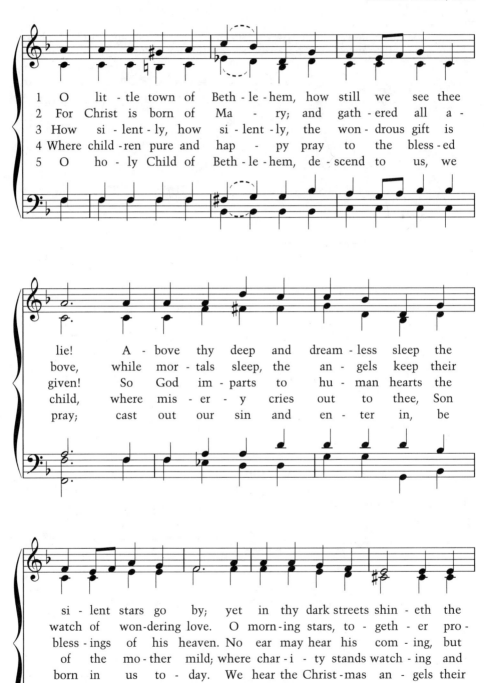

1 O lit-tle town of Beth-le-hem, how still we see thee
2 For Christ is born of Ma - ry; and gath-ered all a-
3 How si-lent-ly, how si-lent-ly, the won-drous gift is
4 Where child-ren pure and hap - py pray to the bless-ed
5 O ho-ly Child of Beth-le-hem, de-scend to us, we

lie! A - bove thy deep and dream-less sleep the
bove, while mor-tals sleep, the an - gels keep their
given! So God im-parts to hu - man hearts the
child, where mis-er - y cries out to thee, Son
pray; cast out our sin and en - ter in, be

si - lent stars go by; yet in thy dark streets shin - eth the
watch of won-dering love. O morn-ing stars, to - geth - er pro-
bless-ings of his heaven. No ear may hear his com - ing, but
of the mo-ther mild; where char-i - ty stands watch-ing and
born in us to - day. We hear the Christ-mas an - gels their

ev - er - last - ing light; the hopes and fears of
claim the ho - ly birth! and prais - es sing to
in this world of sin, where meek souls will re -
faith holds wide the door, the dark night wakes, the
great glad tid - ings tell: O come to us, a -

all the years are met in thee to - night.
God the King, and peace to those on earth.
ceive him, still the dear Christ en - ters in.
glo - ry breaks, and Christ - mas comes once more.
bide with us, our Lord Em - man - u - el!

114   Stille Nacht! Heilige Nacht!

Josef Mohr, 1818

STILLE NACHT   IRREGULAR
Franz Xaver Gruber, 1818

1 Stil - le Nacht! Heil - i - ge Nacht! Al - les schläft; ein - sam wacht
2 Stil - le Nacht! Heil - i - ge Nacht! Hir - ten erst kund - ge - macht
3 Stil - le Nacht! Heil - i - ge Nacht! Got - tes Sohn, o wie lacht

nur das trau - te heil - i - ge Paar. Hol - der Knab' im lock - ig - ten Haar,
durch der Eng - el Al - le - lu - ja, tönt es laut bei Fer - ne und Nah:
Lieb' aus dei - nem gött - li - chen Mund, da uns schlägt die ret - ten - de Stund'.

Schlaf' in himm - li - scher Ruh!   Schlaf' in himm - li - scher Ruh!
"Christ der Ret - ter ist da!   Christ der Ret - ter ist da!"
Christ in dei - ner Ge - burt!   Christ in dei - ner Ge - burt!

CHRISTMAS

Silent Night, Holy Night

115

Stille Nacht! Heilige Nacht!
Josef Mohr, 1818
trans. John Freeman Young, 1863

STILLE NACHT   IRREGULAR
Franz Xaver Gruber, 1818

1 Si - lent night, ho - ly night, all is calm, all is bright
2 Si - lent night, ho - ly night, shep-herds quake at the sight,
3 Si - lent night, ho - ly night, Son of God, Love's pure light,

round yon Vir - gin Mo - ther and child. Ho - ly in - fant, so
glo - ries stream from heav - en a - far, heaven - ly hosts sing
ra - diant beams from thy ho - ly face, with the dawn of re -

ten - der and mild, sleep in heav - en - ly peace, sleep in heav - en - ly peace.
al - le - lu - ia; Christ, the Sa - vior, is born! Christ, the Sav - ior is born.
deem - ing grace, Je - sus, Lord at thy birth, Je - sus, Lord at thy birth.

CHRISTMAS

Calm, on the Listening Ear of Night

Edmund Hamilton Sears, 1834, alt. NUN DANKET ALL' UND BRINGET EHR' CM
Johann Crüger, 1653

1 Calm, on the list - ening ear of night, come heaven's me-
2 Ce - les - tial choirs, from courts a - bove, shed sa - cred
3 The an - swering hills of Pal - es - tine send back the
4 O'er the blue depths of Gal - i - lee there comes a

lo - dious strains, where wild Ju - de - a
glo - ries there; and an - gels, with their
glad re - ply; and greet, from all their
ho - lier calm; and Shar - on waves, in

stretch - es far her sil - ver - man - tled plains.
spark - ling lyres, make mu - sic on the air.
ho - ly heights, the Day - spring from on high.
so - lemn praise, her si - lent groves of palm.

5 "Glory to God!" the sounding skies
loud with their anthems ring;
"Peace and goodwill, to those on earth,
from heaven's eternal King!"

6 Light on thy hills, Jerusalem!
The Savior now is born!
And bright, on Bethlehem's joyous plains,
breaks the first Christmas morn.

CHRISTMAS

See, Amid the Winter's Snow

Edward Caswall, 1858

HUMILITY   77 77 with Refrain
John Goss, 1871

117

unison

1 See, a-mid the win-ter's snow, born for us on earth be-low,
2 Lo, with-in a man-ger lies he who built the star-ry skies,
3 Say, ye ho-ly shep-herds, say, what your joy-ful news to-day;
4 "As we watched at dead of night, lo, we saw a won-drous light;
5 Sa-cred In-fant, all di-vine, what a ten-der love was thine,

see, the Lamb of God ap-pears, prom-ised from e-ter-nal years!
he who, throned in height sub-lime, sits a-mid the che-ru-bim!
where-fore have ye left your sheep on the lone-ly moun-tain steep?
an-gels, sing-ing 'Peace on earth,' told us of the Sa-vior's birth."
thus to come from high-est bliss down to such a world as this!

harmony

Hail, thou ev-er-bless-ed morn! Hail, re-demp-tion's hap-py dawn!

Sing through all Je-ru-sa-lem: Christ is born in Beth-le-hem!

CHRISTMAS

118   Christians, Awake, Salute the Happy Morn

John Byrom, 1745, alt.

YORKSHIRE   10 10 10 10 10 10
John Wainwright, 1750

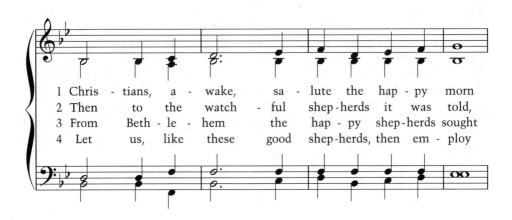

1 Chris - tians, a - wake,   sa - lute the hap - py morn
2 Then   to the watch - ful shep-herds it was told,
3 From   Beth - le - hem the hap - py shep-herds sought
4 Let   us, like these   good shep-herds, then em - ploy

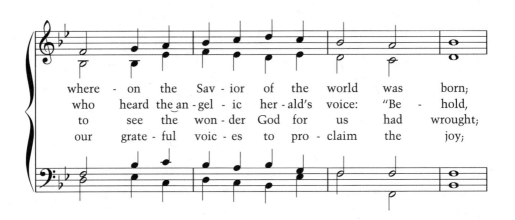

where - on the Sav - ior of the world was born;
who heard the an-gel - ic her - ald's voice: "Be - hold,
to see the won - der God for us had wrought;
our grate - ful voic - es to pro - claim the joy;

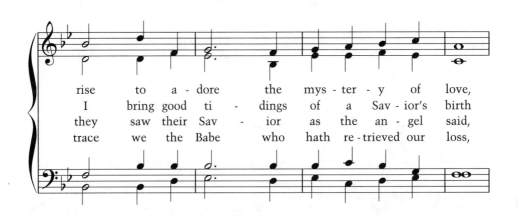

rise to a - dore the mys - ter - y of love,
I bring good ti - dings of a Sav - ior's birth
they saw their Sav - ior as the an - gel said,
trace we the Babe who hath re - trieved our loss,

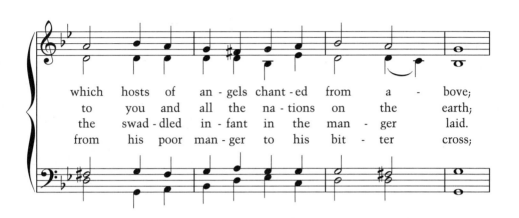

which hosts of an-gels chant-ed from a - bove;
to you and all the na-tions on the earth;
the swad-dled in-fant in the man - ger laid.
from his poor man-ger to his bit - ter cross;

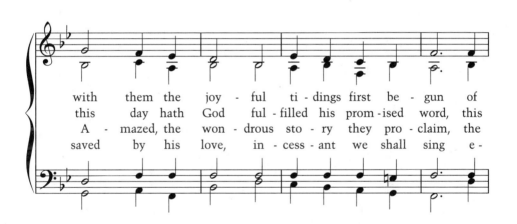

with them the joy - ful ti-dings first be - gun of
this day hath God ful-filled his prom-ised word, this
A - mazed, the won-drous sto-ry they pro-claim, the
saved by his love, in-cess-ant we shall sing e-

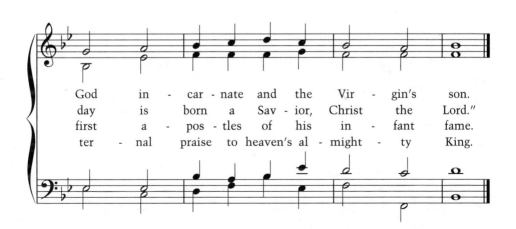

God in - car-nate and the Vir - gin's son.
day is born a Sav-ior, Christ the Lord."
first a - pos-tles of his in - fant fame.
ter - nal praise to heaven's al - might - ty King.

119   **Adeste fideles**

attrib. John Francis Wade (c.1711–1786)

ADESTE FIDELES   IRREGULAR
attrib. John Francis Wade (c.1711–1786)

1 A - des - te, fi - de - les, læ - ti tri - um -
2 De - um de De - o, lu - men de
3 Can - tet nunc i - o cho - rus an - ge -
4 Pro no - bis e - ge - num, et fœ - no cu -
5 Er - go qui na - tus Di - e ho - di -

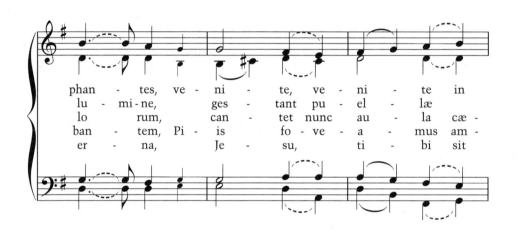

phan - tes, ve - ni - te, ve - ni - te in
lu - mi - ne, ges - tant pu - el - læ
lo - rum, can - tet nunc au - la cæ -
ban - tem, Pi - is fo - ve - a - mus am -
er - na, Je - su, ti - bi sit

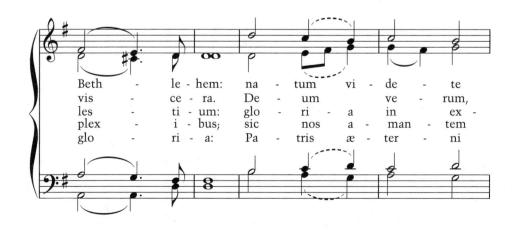

Beth - le - hem: na - tum vi - de - te
vis - ce - ra. De - um ve - rum,
les - ti - um: glo - ri - a in ex -
plex - i - bus; sic nos a - man - tem
glo - ri - a: Pa - tris æ - ter - ni

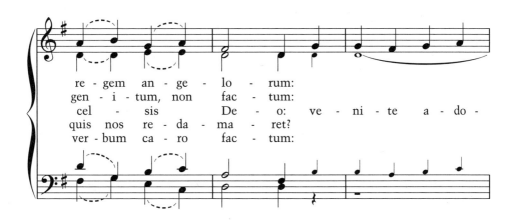

re - gem an - ge - lo - rum:
gen - i - tum, non fac - tum:
cel - sis De - o: ve - ni - te a - do -
quis nos re - da - ma - ret?
ver - bum ca - ro fac - tum:

re - mus, ve - ni - te a - do - re - mus, ve -

ni - te a - do - re - mus Do - mi - num.

120   O Come, All Ye Faithful

Adeste fideles læti triumphantes
attrib. John Francis Wade (c.1711–1786)
trans. Frederick Oakeley, 1841, alt.

ADESTE FIDELES   IRREGULAR
attrib. John Francis Wade (c.1711–1786)

1 O come, all ye faith - ful, joy - ful and tri -
2 God from God, light from light e -
3 Sing, choirs of an - gels, sing in ex - ul -
4 Child, for us sin - ners poor and in the
5 Yea, Lord, we greet thee, born this hap - py

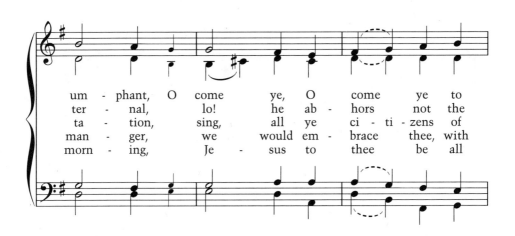

um - phant, O come ye, O come ye to
ter - nal, lo! he ab - hors not the
ta - tion, sing, all ye ci - ti - zens of
man - ger, we would em - brace thee, with
morn - ing, Je - sus to thee be all

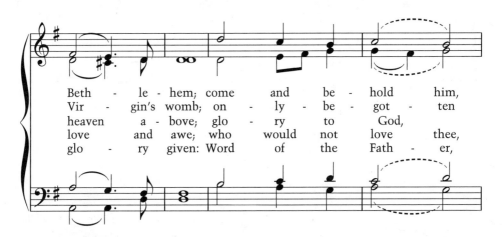

Beth - le - hem; come and be - hold him,
Vir - gin's womb; on - ly - be - got - ten
heaven a - bove; glo - ry to God,
love and awe; who would not love thee,
glo - ry given: Word of the Fath - er,

CHRISTMAS

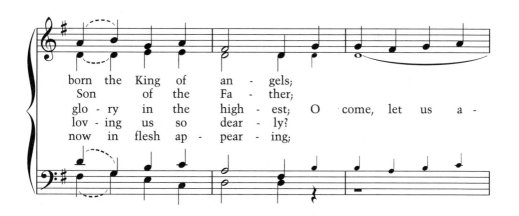

born the King of an - gels;
Son of the Fa - ther;
glo - ry in the high - est; O come, let us a -
lov - ing us so dear - ly?
now in flesh ap - pear - ing;

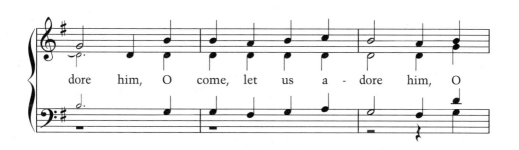

dore him, O come, let us a - dore him, O

come, let us a - dore him, Christ, the Lord!

Hark! the Herald Angels Sing

Charles Wesley, 1739
adapt. George Whitefield, 1753, alt.

MENDELSSOHN 77 77 D
Felix Mendelssohn, 1840
adapt. William H. Cummings, 1856

1 Hark! the her-ald an-gels sing, "Glo-ry to the new-born King;
2 Christ, by high-est heaven a-dored; Christ, the ev-er-last-ing Lord!
3 Hail the heaven-born Prince of Peace! Hail the Sun of Right-eous-ness!

peace on earth, and mer-cy mild, God and sin-ners rec-on-ciled!"
Late in time be-hold him come, off-spring of the Vir-gin's womb.
Light and life to all he brings, risen with heal-ing in his wings,

Joy-ful, all ye na-tions, rise, join the tri-umph of the skies;
Veiled in flesh the God-head see; hail the in-car-nate de-i-ty,
mild he lays his glo-ry by, born that we no more may die,

with the an-gel-ic host pro-claim, "Christ is born in Beth-le-hem!"
pleased as man with us to dwell, Je-sus, our Em-man-u-el.
born to raise us from the earth, born to give us sec-ond birth.

CHRISTMAS

Hark! the her-ald an-gels sing, "Glo-ry to the new-born King!"

Shepherds Came, Their Praises Bringing 122

Quem pastores laudavere
Hohenfurth manuscript, 1410
trans. George Bradford Caird, 1944

QUEM PASTORES LAUDAVERE   88 87
German melody, 14th cent.
harm. Ralph Vaughan Williams, 1906

1 Shep-herds came, their prais-es bring-ing, who had
2 Sag-es, whom a star had guid-ed, in-cense,
3 Je-sus, born the King of heav-en, un-to

heard the an-gels sing-ing, "Far from you be
gold, and myrrh pro-vid-ed, made their sac-ri-
us in mer-cy giv-en, be un-to thy

fear un-rul-y, Christ is King of glo-ry born."
fic-es du-ly to the King of glo-ry born.
mer-it tru-ly hon-or, praise, and glo-ry done.

CHRISTMAS

Angels We Have Heard On High

Les anges dans nos campagnes
French
James Chadwick (1813–1882), alt.

GLORIA   77 77 with Refrain
French melody
harm. Edward Shippen Barnes (1887–1958), alt.

1 An-gels we have heard on high, sing-ing sweet-ly through the night,
2 Shep-herds, why this ju - bi - lee? Why these songs of hap - py cheer?
3 Come to Beth - le - hem and see him whose birth the an - gels sing;
4 See him in a man - ger laid whom the an - gels praise a - bove;

and the moun-tains in re - ply ech - o - ing their brave de - light.
What great bright-ness did you see? What glad tid - ings did you hear?
come, a - dore on bend - ed knee Christ, the Lord, the new - born King.
Ma - ry, Jo - seph, lend your aid, while we raise our hearts in love.

Glo - - - - - - ri - a

in ex - cel - sis De - o. Glo - - - -

CHRISTMAS

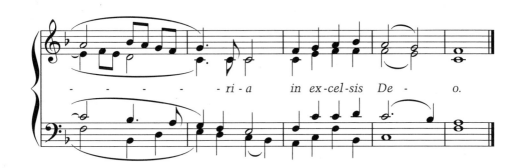

- - - - - ri-a   in ex-cel-sis De -   o.

While Shepherds Watched Their Flocks   124

Nahum Tate, 1700, alt.

WINCHESTER OLD   CM
*The Whole Booke of Psalmes, 1592
harm. Hymns Ancient and Modern, 1922*

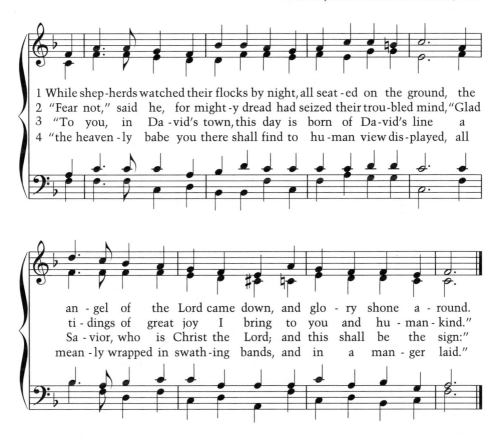

1 While shep-herds watched their flocks by night, all seat-ed on the ground, the
2 "Fear not," said he, for might-y dread had seized their trou-bled mind, "Glad
3 "To you, in Da-vid's town, this day is born of Da-vid's line   a
4 "the heaven-ly babe you there shall find to hu-man view dis-played, all

an - gel of the Lord came down, and glo - ry shone a - round.
ti - dings of great joy I bring to you and hu - man - kind."
Sa - vior, who is Christ the Lord; and this shall be the sign:"
mean - ly wrapped in swath-ing bands, and in a man - ger laid."

5 Thus spake the seraph; and forthwith
   appeared a shining throng
   of angels praising God, who thus
   addressed their joyful song:

6 "All glory be to God on high,
   and peace to all the earth.
   Goodwill is brought to humankind
   through this, the Savior's birth."

125 Personent hodie

Piæ cantiones, 1582

PERSONENT HODIE   666 66 66 66
Piæ cantiones, 1582
adapt. Gustav Holst, 1924

1 Per-so-nent ho-di-e
2 In mun-do nas-ci-tur,
3 Ma-gi tres ve-ne-runt,
4 Om-nes cle-ri-cu-li,

vo-ces pu-er-u-læ, lau-dan-tes iu-cun-de
pan-nis in-vol-vi-tur, præ-se-pi po-ni-tur
par-vu-lum in-qui-runt, Beth-le-hem a-de-unt,
par-i-ter pu-e-ri, can-tent ut an-ge-li:

qui no-bis est na-tus, sum-mo De-o da-tus,
sta-bu-lo bru-to-rum, rec-tor su-per-no-rum.
stel-lu-lam se-quen-do, ip-sum a-do-ran-do,
ad-ven-is-ti mun-do, lau-des ti-bi fun-do.

CHRISTMAS

et de vir-　vir-　vir,　et de vir-　vir-　vir,
Per - di - dit,　dit,　dit,　per - di - dit,　dit,　dit,
au-rum,thus,　thus,　thus,　au-rum thus,　thus,　thus,
Id - e - o,　-o,　-o,　id - e - o,　-o,　-o

et de vir - gi - ne - o　ven-tre pro-cre - a - tus.
per - di - dit　spo - li - a　prin-ceps in - fer - no - rum.
au -rum, thus,　et myrr-ham　e - i of - fe - ren - do.
id - e - o　glo - ri - a　in ex-cel-sis De - o!

126   **Once in Royal David's City**

stanzas 1, 2, 4-6: Cecil Frances Alexander, 1848, alt.   IRBY   87 87 77
stanza 3: James Waring McCrady, 1982   *Henry J. Gauntlett, 1849*
                                        harm. Arthur Henry Mason (1850–1929)

1 Once in roy - al Da - vid's ci - ty stood a
2 He came down to earth from hea - ven, who is
3 We, like Ma - ry, rest con - found - ed that a
4 For he is our life - long pat - tern; dai - ly,

low - ly cat - tle shed, where a mo - ther laid her
God and Lord of all, and his shel - ter was a
sta - ble should dis play hea - ven's Word, the world's cre -
when on earth he grew, he was tempt - ed, scorned, re -

ba - by in a man - ger for his bed: Ma - ry
sta - ble, and his cra - dle was a stall; with the
a - tor, cra - dled there on Christ - mas Day; yet this
ject - ed, tears and smiles like us he knew. Thus he

CHRISTMAS

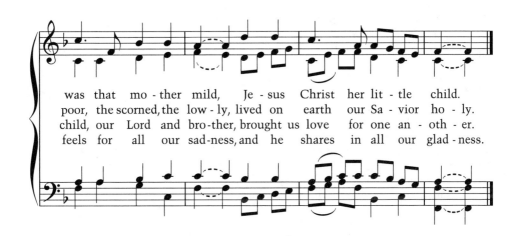

was that mo - ther mild, Je - sus Christ her lit - tle child.
poor, the scorned, the low - ly, lived on earth our Sa - vior ho - ly.
child, our Lord and bro - ther, brought us love for one an - oth - er.
feels for all our sad - ness, and he shares in all our glad - ness.

5 And our eyes at last shall see him,
through his own redeeming love;
for that child who seemed so helpless
is our Lord in heaven above;
and he leads his children on
to the place where he is gone.

6 Not in that poor lowly stable,
with the oxen standing round,
we shall see him; but in heaven,
where his saints his throne surround:
Christ, revealed to faithful eye,
set at God's right hand on high.

Stanza 3 © 1982 James Waring McCrady.
Music © 1957 Novello and Co., Ltd.

CHRISTMAS

127   In dulci jubilo

German, 14th cent.
trans. Percy Dearmer, 1928

IN DULCI JUBILO   Irregular
German melody, 14th cent.
harm. Bartholoäus Gesius, 1601

1 *In dul - ci ju - bi - lo*   now sing with hearts a - glow!
2 *O Je - su par - vu - le,*   for thee I long al - way;
3 *O Pa - tris ca - ri - tas!*   *O Na - ti le - ni - tas!*
4 *U - bi sunt gau - di - a*   in an - y place but there?

Our de - light and plea - sure lies *in prae - se - pi - o,*   like
com - fort my heart's blind - ness, *O pu - er op - ti - me,*   with
Deep - ly were we stain - ed *per nos - tra cri - mi - na;*   but
There are an - gels sing - ing, *No - va can - ti - ca,*   and

sun - shine is our trea - sure *ma - tris in gre - mi - o.*
all thy lov - ing - kind - ness, *O Prin - ceps glo - ri - æ.*
thou for us hast gain - ed *coe - lo - rum gau - di - a.*
there the bells are ring - ing *in Re - gis cu - ri - a.*

Al - pha es et O!   *Al - pha es et O!*
Tra - he me post te!   *Tra - he me post te!*
O that we were there!   O that we were there!
O that we were there!   O that we were there!

CHRISTMAS

Lo, How a Rose E'er Blooming

Es ist ein Ros entsprungen
stanzas 1, 2: German, 15th cent.,
trans. Theodore Baker, 1894, alt.
stanza 3: Friedrich Layritz (1808–1859),
trans. Harriett Reynolds Krauth Spaeth, 1875

ES IST EIN ROS   87 87 D
Alte Catholische Geistliche Kirchengesäng, 1599
harm. Michael Praetorius, 1609

1 Lo, how a Rose e'er bloom-ing from ten-der stem hath sprung!
2 I - sa - iah 'twas fore-told it, the Rose I have in mind,
3 O Flower, whose fra-grance ten-der with sweet-ness fills the air,

Of Jes-se's lin-eage com-ing as seers of old have sung.
with Ma-ry we be-hold it, the Vir-gin Mo - ther kind.
dis - pel in glo-rious splen-dor the dark-ness ev - ery-where;

It came, a blos-som bright, a - mid the cold of win - ter,
To show God's love a - right, she bore to us a Sa - vior,
true man, yet ve - ry God, from sin and death now save us,

when half spent was the night.
when half spent was the night.
and share our ev - ery load.

CHRISTMAS

129   **Of the Father's Love Begotten**

Corde natus ex Parentis
Marcus Aurelius Prudentius Clemens (348–c.410)
trans. John Mason Neale, 1854
adapt. Henry W. Baker, 1859

DIVINUM MYSTERIUM   87 87 877
Plainsong, Mode 5
Sanctus trope, 11th cent.
harm. Charles Winfred Douglas, 1940

1   Of the Fa-ther's love be-got - ten,   ere the worlds be-gan   to be,
2   O ye heights of heaven a-dore him;   an-gel hosts, his prais - es sing;
3 Christ, to thee with God the Fa - ther,   and, O Ho - ly Ghost, to thee,

he is Al - pha and O - me - ga,   he the source, the end - ing he;
powers, do-min-ions, bow be - fore him, and ex - tol our God   and King;
hymn and chant and high thanks-giv-ing, and un - wea-ried prais - es be:

of   the things that are,   that   have   been,   and that
let   no tongue on earth   be   si   -   -   lent,   ev - ery
hon - or,   glo - ry,   and   do - min   -   -   ion,   and   e -

fu - ture years shall see, ev - er - more and ev - er - more!
voice in con - cert ring, ev - er - more and ev - er - more!
ter - nal vic - to - ry, ev - er - more and ev - er - more!   A - men.

130   Angels, from the Realms of Glory

James Montgomery, 1816, alt.

REGENT SQUARE   87 87 87
Henry Thomas Smart, 1867

1 An - gels, from the realms of glo - ry, wing your flight o'er all the earth;
2 Shep-herds, in the fields a - bid - ing, watch-ing o'er your flocks by night,
3 Sag - es, leave your con-tem -pla - tions, bright - er vi - sions beam a - far;
4 Saints be -fore the al - tar bend-ing, watch-ing long in hope and fear,

ye who sang cre - a -tion's sto - ry, now pro-claim Mes - si -ah's birth:
God with us is now re - sid - ing, yon-der shines the in-fant light:
seek the great de - sire of na-tions, ye have seen his na - tal star:
sud - den - ly the Lord, de -scend-ing, in his tem - ple shall ap-pear:

come and wor-ship, come and wor-ship, wor-ship Christ, the new-born King.

CHRISTMAS

Jesus, the Light of the World

Charles Wesley, 1739, alt.
adapt. George Elderkin, 1895

WE'LL WALK IN THE LIGHT   77 77 with Refrain
George D. Elderkin, 1895

1 Hark! the her-ald an-gels sing, Je-sus, the light of the world;
2 Joy-ful, all you na-tions, rise, Je-sus, the light of the world;
3 Christ, by high-est heaven a-dored, Je-sus, the light of the world;
4 Hail the heaven-born Prince of Peace! Je-sus, the light of the world;

"Glo-ry to the new-born King," Je-sus, the light of the world.
join the tri-umph of the skies; Je-sus, the light of the world.
Christ, the ev-er-last-ing Lord! Je-sus, the light of the world.
hail the Sun of right-eous-ness! Je-sus, the light of the world.

We'll

walk in the light, beau-ti-ful light, come where the dew-drops of mer-cy are bright.

Shine all a-round us by day and by night, Je-sus, the light of the world.

CHRISTMAS

132　The First Nowell

English, 18th cent.

THE FIRST NOWELL　IRREGULAR with Refrain
English melody, 17th cent.
harm. John Stainer, 1871

1 The first No - well, the an - gel did
2 They look - ed up and saw a
3 And by the light of that same
4 This star drew nigh to the north -

say, was to cer - tain poor shep - herds in fields as they
star shin - ing in the east, be - yond them
star three wise men came from coun - try
west, o'er Beth - le - hem it took its

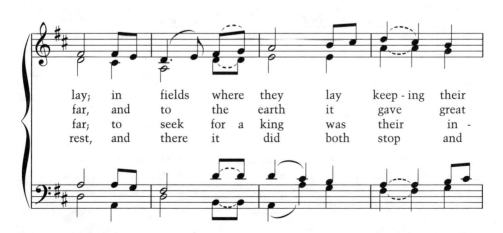

lay; in fields where they lay keep - ing their
far, and to the earth it gave great
far; to seek for a king was their in -
rest, and there it did both stop and

CHRISTMAS

5   Then entered in those wise men three,
     full reverently upon their knee,
     and offered there, in his presence,
     their gold and myrrh and frankincense.

          Nowell, Nowell, Nowell, Nowell,
          born is the King of Israel.

6   Then let us all with one accord
     sing praises to our heavenly Lord;
     that hath made heaven and earth of nought,
     and with his blood our life hath bought.

          Nowell, Nowell, Nowell, Nowell,
          born is the King of Israel.

133 How Brightly Shines the Morning Star!

Wie schön leuchtet der Morgenstern
Phillip Nicolai, 1597
trans. William Mercer (1811–1873), alt.

WIE SCHÖN LEUCHTET   887 887 48 48
Philipp Nicolai, 1599
harm. Johann Sebastian Bach (1685–1750)

1 How bright-ly shines the morn-ing star! The na-tions see and
2 Though cir-cled by the hosts on high, he deigns to cast a
3 Re-joice, ye heavens; thou earth, re-ply; with praise, ye sin-ners,

hail a-far the light in Ju-dah shin-ing. Thou Da-vid's son of
pit-ying eye up-on his help-less crea-ture; the whole cre-a-tion's
fill the sky, for this his in-car-na-tion. In-car-nate God, put

Ja-cob's race, the Bride-groom, and the King of Grace, for
head and Lord, by high-est ser-a-phim a-dored, as-
forth thy power, ride on, ride on, great Con-que-ror, till

thee our hearts are pin - ing! Low - ly, ho - ly,
sumes our ve - ry na - ture. Je - su, grant us,
all know thy sal - va - tion. A - men, A - men!

great and glo - rious, thou vic - to - rious Prince of Gra - ces,
through thy me - rit, to in - he - rit thy sal - va - tion;
Al - le - lu - ia, Al - le - lu - ia! Praise be gi - ven

fil - ling all the heaven - ly plac - es!
hear, O hear our sup - pli - ca - tion.
ev - er - more by earth and hea - ven.

EPIPHANY

134   What Star Is This, with Beams So Bright

Quæ stella sole pulchrior
Charles Coffin, 1736
trans. John Chandler, 1837

PUER NOBIS   LM
German melody, 15th cent.
adapt. Michael Praetorius, 1609
harm. Cowley Carol Book, 1902

1 What star is this, with beams so bright, more
2 True spake the pro - phet from a - far who
3 The guid - ing star a - bove is bright; with -
4 O Je - sus, while the star of grace im -
5 To God the Fa - ther, heaven - ly light, to

beau - teous than the noon - day light? It shines to her - ald
told the rise of Ja - cob's star; and east - ern sa - ges
in them shines a clear - er light, and leads them on with
pels us on to seek thy face, let not our sloth - ful
Christ, re - vealed in earth - ly night, to God the Ho - ly

forth the King, and gen - tiles to his crib to bring.
with a - maze up - on the won - drous to - ken gaze.
power be - nign to seek the Giv - er of the sign.
hearts re - fuse the guid - ance of thy light to use.
Ghost we raise our e - qual and un - ceas - ing praise.

EPIPHANY

As with Gladness Men of Old 135

William Chatterton Dix, 1860

DIX 77 77 77
Conrad Kocher, 1838
adapt. William Henry Monk (1823–1889)
harm. The English Hymnal, 1906

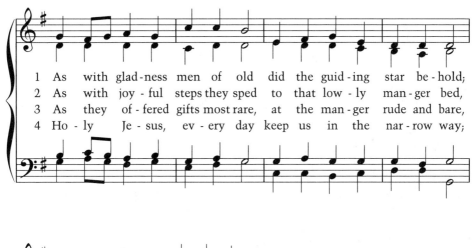

1 As with glad-ness men of old did the guid-ing star be-hold;
2 As with joy-ful steps they sped to that low-ly man-ger bed,
3 As they of-fered gifts most rare, at the man-ger rude and bare,
4 Ho-ly Je-sus, ev-ery day keep us in the nar-row way;

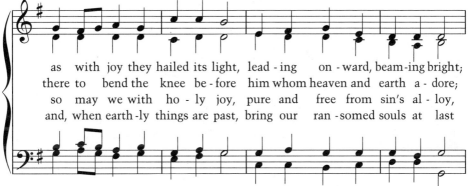

as with joy they hailed its light, lead-ing on-ward, beam-ing bright;
there to bend the knee be-fore him whom heaven and earth a-dore;
so may we with ho-ly joy, pure and free from sin's al-loy,
and, when earth-ly things are past, bring our ran-somed souls at last

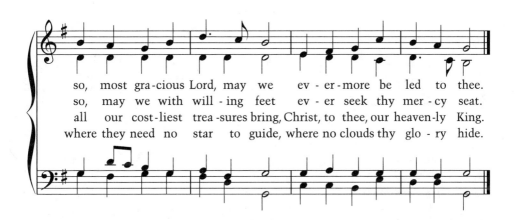

so, most gra-cious Lord, may we ev-er-more be led to thee.
so, may we with will-ing feet ev-er seek thy mer-cy seat.
all our cost-liest trea-sures bring, Christ, to thee, our heaven-ly King.
where they need no star to guide, where no clouds thy glo-ry hide.

EPIGHANY

We Three Kings

John Henry Hopkins, Jr., 1857, alt.

KINGS OF ORIENT   IRREGULAR with Refrain
John Henry Hopkins, Jr., 1857

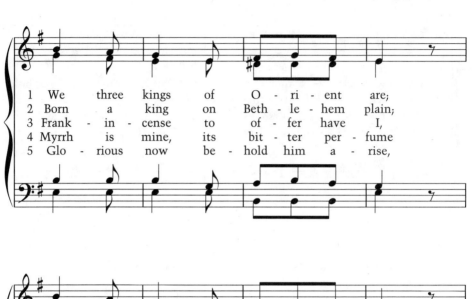

1 We three kings of O - ri - ent are;
2 Born a king on Beth - le - hem plain;
3 Frank - in - cense to of - fer have I,
4 Myrrh is mine, its bit - ter per - fume
5 Glo - rious now be - hold him a - rise,

bear - ing gifts we trav - erse a - far;
gold I bring, to crown him a - gain,
in - cense owns a de - i - ty nigh,
breathes a life of gath - er - ing gloom;
King and God and sac - ri - fice;

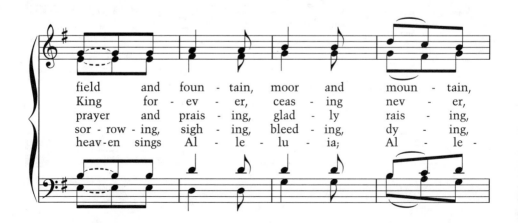

field and foun - tain, moor and moun - tain,
King for - ev - er, ceas - ing nev - er,
prayer and prais - ing, glad - ly rais - ing,
sor - row - ing, sigh - ing, bleed - ing, dy - ing,
heav-en sings Al - le - lu - ia; Al - le -

EPIPHANY

fol - low - ing   yon - der   star.
o - ver   us   all   to   reign.
wor - ship   him,   God   most   high.   O
sealed   in   the   stone   cold   tomb.
lu - ia   the   earth   re - plies.

star   of   won - der,   star   of   night,   star   with   roy - al

beau - ty   bright,   west - ward   lead - ing,   still   pro -

ceed - ing,   guide   us   to   thy   per - fect   light.

EPIPHANY

Brightest and Best

Reginald Heber, 1811, alt.

MORNING STAR   11 10 11 10
James Proctor Harding, 1892

1 Bright - est and best of the sons of the
2 Cold on his cra - dle the dew - drops are
3 Shall we then yield him, in cost - ly de -
4 Vain - ly we of - fer each am - ple o -
5 Bright - est and best of the sons of the

morn - ing, dawn on our dark - ness, and
shin - ing, low lies his head with the
vo - tion, o - dors of E - dom, and
bla - tion, vain - ly with gifts would his
morn - ing, dawn on our dark - ness, and

lend us thine aid; star of the
beasts of the stall; an - gels a -
of - ferings di - vine, gems of the
fa - vor se - cure; rich - er by
lend us thine aid; star of the

EPIPHANY

east,   the   hor - i - zon a - dorn - ing,
dore   him   in   slum - ber re - clin - ing,
moun - tain, and   pearls   of   the   o - cean,
far   is   the   heart's a - dor - a - tion,
east,   the   hor - i - zon a - dorn - ing,

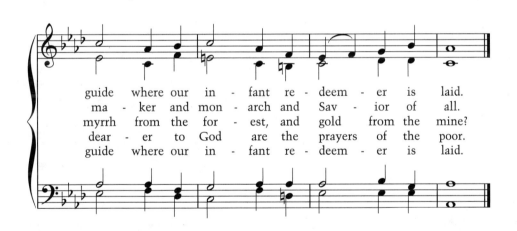

guide where our in - fant re - deem - er is laid.
ma - ker and mon - arch and Sav - ior of all.
myrrh from the for - est, and gold from the mine?
dear - er to God   are the prayers of the poor.
guide where our in - fant re - deem - er is laid.

138   Worship the Lord in the Beauty of Holiness

John S. B. Monsell, 1863, alt.

WAS LEBET   IRREGULAR
Choral-Buch vor Johann Heinrich Reinhardt, 1754
harm. Ralph Vaughan Williams, 1906

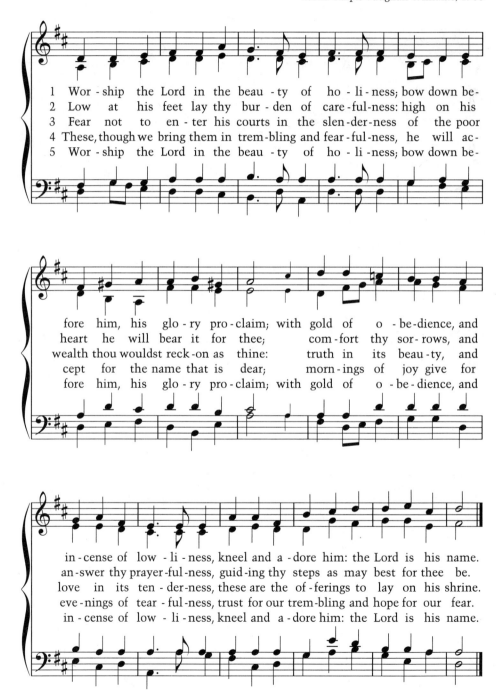

1 Wor - ship the Lord in the beau - ty of ho - li - ness; bow down be-
2 Low at his feet lay thy bur - den of care - ful - ness: high on his
3 Fear not to en - ter his courts in the slen - der - ness of the poor
4 These, though we bring them in trem - bling and fear - ful - ness, he will ac-
5 Wor - ship the Lord in the beau - ty of ho - li - ness; bow down be-

fore him, his glo - ry pro - claim; with gold of o - be - dience, and
heart he will bear it for thee; com - fort thy sor - rows, and
wealth thou wouldst reck - on as thine: truth in its beau - ty, and
cept for the name that is dear; morn - ings of joy give for
fore him, his glo - ry pro - claim; with gold of o - be - dience, and

in - cense of low - li - ness, kneel and a - dore him: the Lord is his name.
an - swer thy prayer - ful - ness, guid - ing thy steps as may best for thee be.
love in its ten - der - ness, these are the of - ferings to lay on his shrine.
eve - nings of tear - ful - ness, trust for our trem - bling and hope for our fear.
in - cense of low - li - ness, kneel and a - dore him: the Lord is his name.

Music © 1906 Oxford University Press.

EPIPHANY

Jesus, on the Mountain Peak

Brian Wren, 1962, rev. 1988

MOWSLEY 78 78 4
Cyril Vincent Taylor (1907–1991)

1 Je - sus, on the moun-tain peak, stands a - lone in
2 Trem-bling at his feet we saw Mo - ses and E -
3 Swift the cloud of glo - ry came, God pro-claim-ing,
4 This is God's be - lov - ed Son! Law and proph - ets

glo - ry blaz-ing; let us, if we dare to speak,
li - jah speak-ing. All the proph - ets and the law
in its thun - der, Je - sus as the Son by name!
sing be - fore him, first and last and on - ly one,

join the saints and an - gels prais-ing. Al - le - lu - ia!
shout through them their joy - ful greet-ing: Al - le - lu - ia!
Na - tions, cry a - loud in won - der: Al - le - lu - ia!
all cre - a - tion shall a - dore him! Al - le - lu - ia!

EPIPHANY

140 Songs of Thankfulness and Praise

stanzas 1-3: Christopher Wordsworth, 1862
stanza 4: F. Bland Tucker, 1982

SALZBURG 77 77 D
Jakob Hintze, 1678
harm. Johann Sebastian Bach (1685–1750)

1 Songs of thank-ful-ness and praise, Je-sus, Lord to thee we raise,
2 Man-i-fest at Jor-dan's stream, pro-phet, priest, and King su-preme;
3 Man-i-fest in mak-ing whole pal-sied limbs and faint-ing soul;
4 Man-i-fest on moun-tain height, shin-ing in re-splen-dent light,

man-i-fest-ed by the star to the sag-es from a-far;
and at Ca-na, wed-ding-guest, in thy God-head man-i-fest;
man-i-fest in val-iant fight, quell-ing all the dev-il's might;
where dis-ci-ples filled with awe thy trans-fi-gured glo-ry saw.

branch of roy-al Da-vid's stem, in thy birth at Beth-le-hem;
man-i-fest in power di-vine, chang-ing wat-er in-to wine;
man-i-fest in gra-cious will, ev-er bring-ing good from ill;
When from there thou led-dest them stead-fast to Je-ru-sa-lem,

an-thems be to thee ad-dressed, God in man made man-i-fest.
an-thems be to thee ad-dressed, God in man made man-i-fest.
an-thems be to thee ad-dressed, God in man made man-i-fest.
cross and Eas-ter Day at-test God in man made man-i-fest.

Clarum decus jejunii
Latin, 10th cent.
trans. Maurice F. Bell, 1906, alt.

ERHALT UNS, HERR   LM
Geistliche Lieder, Wittenberg, 1543
harm. Johann Sebastian Bach (1685–1750)

1 The glo - ry of these for - ty days we cel - e - brate with songs of praise; for Christ, through whom all things were made, him - self has fast - ed and has prayed.

2 A - lone and fast - ing Mo - ses saw the lov - ing God who gave the law; and to E - li - jah, fast - ing, came the steeds and char - i - ots of flame.

3 So Dan - iel trained his mys - tic sight, de - liv - ered from the li - ons' might; and John, the Bride - groom's friend, be - came the her - ald of Mes - si - ah's name.

4 Then grant us, Lord, like them to be full oft in fast and prayer with thee; our spi - rits strength - en with thy grace, and give us joy to see thy face.

5 O Fa - ther, Son, and Spi - rit blest, to thee be ev - ery prayer ad - dressed, who art in three - fold name a - dored, from age to age, the on - ly Lord.

LENT

Eternal Lord of Love, Behold Your Church

Thomas H. Cain, 1982

OLD 124TH 10 10 10 10 10
Pseaumes octante trois de David, 1531
harm. Charles Winfred Douglas, 1940

1 E - ter - nal Lord of love, be - hold your Church walk - ing once
2 So dai - ly dy - ing to the way of self, so dai - ly
3 If dead in you, so in you we a - rise, you the first-

more the pil - grim way of Lent, led by your cloud by
liv - ing to your way of love, we walk the road, Lord
born of all the faith - ful dead; and, as through ston - y

day, by night your fire, moved by your love and toward your pres-ence
Je - sus, that you trod, know - ing our - selves bap - tized in - to your
ground the green shoots break, glo - rious in spring - time dress of leaf and

bent: far off yet here— the goal of all de - sire.
death: so we are dead and live with you in God.
flower, so in the Fa - ther's glo - ry shall we wake.

LENT

Forty Days and Forty Nights

George H. Smyttan, 1856, alt.

AUS DER TIEFE   77 77
attrib. Martin Herbst, 1676
harm. William Henry Monk (1823–1889)

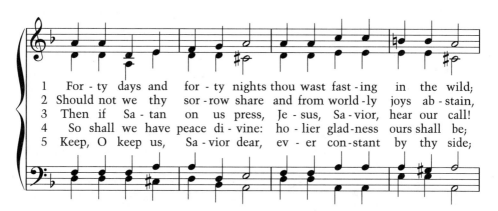

1 For - ty days and for - ty nights thou wast fast - ing in the wild;
2 Should not we thy sor - row share and from world - ly joys ab - stain,
3 Then if Sa - tan on us press, Je - sus, Sa - vior, hear our call!
4 So shall we have peace di - vine: ho - lier glad - ness ours shall be;
5 Keep, O keep us, Sa - vior dear, ev - er con - stant by thy side;

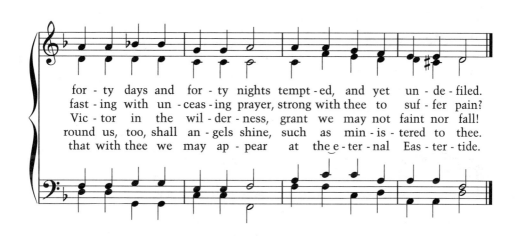

for - ty days and for - ty nights tempt - ed, and yet un - de - filed.
fast - ing with un - ceas - ing prayer, strong with thee to suf - fer pain?
Vic - tor in the wil - der - ness, grant we may not faint nor fall!
round us, too, shall an - gels shine, such as min - is - tered to thee.
that with thee we may ap - pear at the e - ter - nal Eas - ter - tide.

LENT

144   Now Let Us All with One Accord

Ex more docti mystico
attrib. Gregory the Great (c.540–604)
trans. James Quinn, 1972, alt.

GONFALON ROYAL   LM
Percy Carter Buck, 1919

1 Now let us all with one ac - cord, in com - pa -
2 The cov - e - nant, so long re - vealed to those of
3 Your love, O Lord, our sin - ful race has not re -
4 Re - mem - ber, Lord, though frail we be, in your own
5 There - fore, we pray you, Lord, for - give; so when our

ny with a - ges past, keep vig - il with our heaven-ly Lord in
faith in for - mer time, Christ by his own ex-am-ple sealed, the
turned, but fal - si - fied; Au - thor of mer - cy, turn your face and
im - age were we made; help us, lest in anx - i - e - ty, we
wan-derings here shall cease, we may with you for ev - er live, in

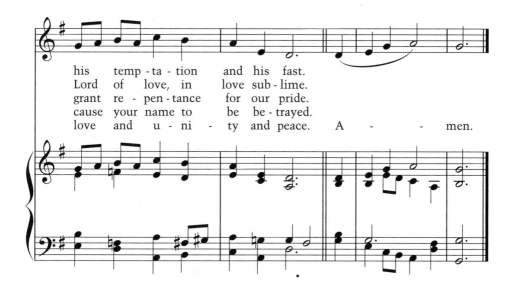

his temp-ta-tion and his fast.
Lord of love, in love sub-lime.
grant re-pen-tance for our pride.
cause your name to be be-trayed.
love and u-ni-ty and peace. A - - men.

Lord, Who Throughout These Forty Days   145

Claudia F. Hernaman, 1873

ST. FLAVIAN CM
English Psalter, 1562
adapt. Richard Redhead, 1853

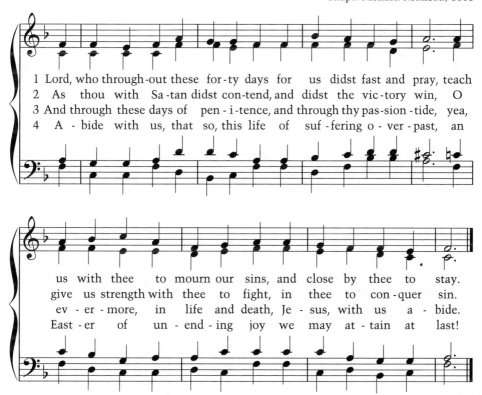

1 Lord, who through-out these for-ty days for us didst fast and pray, teach
2 As thou with Sa-tan didst con-tend, and didst the vic-tory win, O
3 And through these days of pen-i-tence, and through thy pas-sion-tide, yea,
4 A-bide with us, that so, this life of suf-fering o-ver-past, an

us with thee to mourn our sins, and close by thee to stay.
give us strength with thee to fight, in thee to con-quer sin.
ev-er-more, in life and death, Je - sus, with us a-bide.
East-er of un-end-ing joy we may at-tain at last!

LENT

146   Jesus, Who This Our Lententide

Jesu quadragenariæ
Latin, 10th cent.
trans. Walter Howard Frere, 1932

ROCKINGHAM LM
Second Supplement to Psalmody in Miniature, c. 1780
adapt. Edward Miller, 1790

1 Je - sus, who this our Len - ten - tide, of ab - sti -
2 And as thou dost, for - give the past, thy shel - tering
3 Make, Lord, this Lent - en dis - ci - pline an ex - pi -

nence, hast sanc - ti - fied, be with thy Church in
arms ar - ound us cast that we may in thy
a - tion for our sin; and through these days our -

sav - ing power, in this her pen - i - ten - tial hour.
grace re - main, and fall not back to sins a - gain.
selves pre - pare the joys of Eas - ter - tide to share.

LENT

Ride On, Ride On in Majesty

147

Henry Hart Millman, 1827, alt.

THE KING'S MAJESTY   LM
Graham George, 1940

1 Ride on, ride on in maj - es - ty! Hark! all the
2 Ride on, ride on in maj - es - ty! In low - ly
3 Ride on, ride on in maj - es - ty! The wing - ed
4 Ride on, ride on in maj - es - ty! Thy last and

tribes Ho - san - na cry; thy hum - ble beast pur - sues his
pomp ride on to die; O Christ, thy tri - umphs now be -
squad - rons of the sky look down with sad and won - dering
fierc - est strife is nigh; bow thy meek head to mor - tal

road with palms and scat - tered gar - ments strowed.
gin o'er cap - tive death and con - quered sin.
eyes to see the ap - proach - ing sac - ri - fice.
pain, then take, O Christ, thy power, and reign.

LENT

All Glory, Laud, and Honor

Gloria laus et honor
Theodulph of Orleans, c. 820
trans. John Mason Neale, 1851

ST. THEODULPH   76 76 D
Melchior Teschner, 1615
harm. William Henry Monk, 1861

All glo-ry, laud, and hon - or to thee, Re-deem-er, King! to

whom the lips of chil - dren made sweet ho-san-nas ring.

1 Thou art the King of Is - ra - el, thou
2 The com - pa - ny of an - gels is
3 The peo - ple of the He - brews with
4 To thee be - fore thy pas - sion they
5 Thou didst ac - cept their prais - es; ac -

Da - vid's roy - al Son, who in the Lord's name
prais - ing thee on high; and we with all cre -
palms be - fore thee went; our praise and prayers and
sang their hymns of praise; to thee, now high ex -
cept the prayers we bring, who in all good de -

LENT

com - est, the King and bless - ed One.
a - tion in cho - rus make re - ply.
an - thems be - fore thee we pre - sent.
alt - ed, our mel - o - dy we raise.
light - est, thou good and gra - cious King.

Alone Thou Goest Forth, O Lord 149

Solus ad victimam procedis Domine
Peter Abelard (1079–1142)
trans. F. Bland Tucker, 1938

BANGOR CM
William Tans'ur, 1735

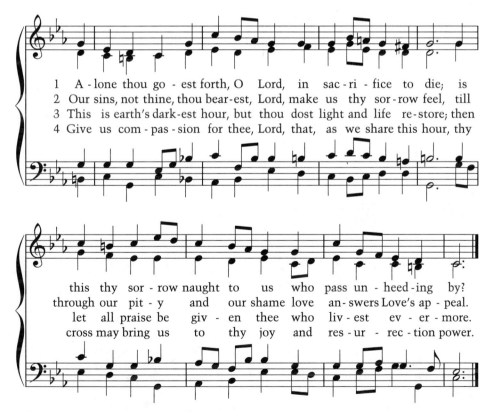

1 A - lone thou go - est forth, O Lord, in sac - ri - fice to die; is
2 Our sins, not thine, thou bear-est, Lord, make us thy sor - row feel, till
3 This is earth's dark-est hour, but thou dost light and life re-store; then
4 Give us com - pas - sion for thee, Lord, that, as we share this hour, thy

this thy sor - row naught to us who pass un - heed-ing by?
through our pit - y and our shame love an - swers Love's ap - peal.
let all praise be giv - en thee who liv - est ev - er - more.
cross may bring us to thy joy and res - ur - rec - tion power.

LENT

150   My Song Is Love Unknown

Samuel Crossman, 1664, alt.

LOVE UNKNOWN   66 66 44 44
John Ireland, 1918

1 My song is love unknown, my Sav-ior's love to
2 He came from his blest throne, sal - va - tion to be-
3 Some-times they strew his way, and his sweet prais - es
4 Why, what hath my Lord done? What makes this rage and
5 Here might I stay and sing, no sto - ry so di-

me, love to the love - less shown, that they might
stow; but hearts were turned and none the longed - for
sing; re - sound - ing all the day ho - san - nas
spite? He made the lame to run, he gave the
vine; there ne'er was love, dear King, and nev - er

love - ly be. O who am I, that
Christ would know. But O, my friend, my
to their King. Then "Cru - ci - fy!" is
blind their sight. Sweet in - ju - ries! yet
grief like thine. This is my friend, in

for my sake my Lord should take frail flesh, and die.
friend in - deed, who at my need his life did spend.
all their breath, and for his death they thirst and cry.
they at these them - selves dis - please, and 'gainst him rise.
whose sweet praise I all my days could gai - ly spend.

LENT

Go to Dark Gethsemane

James Montgomery, 1820

PETRA   77 77 77
Richard Redhead, 1853

1 Go to dark Geth - se - ma - ne, ye that feel the tempt-er's power;
2 Fol - low to the judg - ment hall; view the Lord of life ar-raigned;
3 Cal-vary's mourn-ful moun-tain climb; there, a - dor-ing at his feet,

your re-deem-er's con-flict see, watch with him one bit - ter hour;
O the worm wood and the gall! O the pangs his soul sus-tained!
mark the mir - a - cle of time, God's own sac - ri - fice com-plete;

turn not from his griefs a - way, learn of Je - sus Christ to pray.
Shun not suf-fering, shame, or loss; learn of him to bear the cross.
"It is fi -nished!" hear him cry; learn of Je - sus Christ to die.

LENT

152

To Mock Your Reign

Fred Pratt Green, 1973

THE THIRD TUNE   CMD
Thomas Tallis, c. 1567

1 To mock your reign, O dear-est Lord, they made a crown of thorns,
2 In mock ac-claim, O gra-cious Lord, they snatched a pur-ple cloak,
3 A scep-tered reed, O pa-tient Lord, they thrust in-to your hand,

set you with taunts a-long that road from which no one re-turns.
your pas-sion turned, for all they cared, in-to a sol-dier's joke.
and ac-ted out their grim cha-rade to its ap-poin-ted end.

They did not know, as we do now, that glo-rious is your crown;
They did not know, as we do now, that though we mer-it blame
They did not know, as we do now, though em-pires rise and fall,

that thorns would flower up-on your brow, your sor-rows heal our own.
you will your robe of mer-cy throw a-round our na-ked shame.
your king-dom shall not cease to grow till love em-bra-ces all.

LENT

Ah, Holy Jesus, How Hast Thou Offended 153

Herzliebster Jesu, was hast du verbrochen
Johann Heermann, 1630
trans. Robert Seymour Bridges, 1899, alt.

HERZLIEBSTER JESU   11 11 11 5
Johann Crüger, 1640

1 Ah, ho-ly Je-sus, how hast thou of-fend-ed,
2 Who was the guilt-y? Who brought this up-on thee?
3 For me, kind Je-sus, was thy in-car-na-tion,
4 There-fore, kind Je-sus, since I can-not pay thee,

that mor-tal judg-ment hath on thee de-scend-ed?
A-las, my trea-son, Je-sus, hath un-done thee!
thy mor-tal sor-row, and thy life's ob-la-tion;
I do a-dore thee, and will ev-er pray thee,

By foes de-rid-ed, by thine own re-ject-ed, O most af-flict-ed!
'Twas I, Lord Je-sus, I it was de-nied thee; I cru-ci-fied thee.
thy death of an-guish and thy bit-ter pas-sion, for my sal-va-tion.
think on thy pit-y and thy love un-swerv-ing, not my de-serv-ing.

LENT

154 Cross of Jesus, Cross of Sorrow

William J. Sparrow-Simpson, 1887

CROSS OF JESUS 87 87
John Stainer, 1887

1 Cross of Je-sus, cross of sor-row, where the blood of Christ was shed,
2 Here the King of all the a-ges, throned in light ere worlds could be,
3 O mys-ter-ious con-de-scend-ing! O a-ban-don-ment sub-lime!
4 Cross of Je-sus, cross of sor-row, where the blood of Christ was shed,

per-fect man on thee did suf-fer, per-fect God on thee has bled!
robed in mor-tal flesh is dy-ing, cru-ci-fied by sin for me.
Ve-ry God him-self is bear-ing all the suf-fer-ings of time!
per-fect man on thee did suf-fer, per-fect God on thee has bled!

My Faith Looks up to Thee

Ray Palmer, 1830

OLIVET   664 6664
Lowell Mason, 1830

155

1 My faith looks up to thee, thou Lamb of Cal - va - ry,
2 May thy rich grace im -part strength to my faint - ing heart,
3 While life's dark maze I tread, and griefs a - round me spread,

Sa - vior di - vine! Now hear me while I pray, take all my
my zeal in - spire; as thou hast died for me, O may my
be thou my guide; bid dark -ness turn to day, wipe sor - row's

guilt a - way; O let me from this day be whol - ly thine.
love to thee pure, warm, and change -less be, a liv - ing fire.
tears a - way, nor let me ev - er stray from thee a - side.

LENT

156   Sing, My Tongue, the Glorious Battle

Pange lingua gloriosi prœlium certaminis
Venantius Honorius Fortunatus (c.530–c.610)
stanza 1: trans. Percy Dearmer, 1906, alt.
stanzas 2, 3: trans. John Mason Neale, 1851

PANGE LINGUA   87 87 87
Plainsong, Mode 3
Sarum rite
accomp. J. H. Arnold, 1933
adapt. Harvard University Hymn Book, 1964

1 Sing, my tongue, the glo-rious bat - tle, sing the win-ning of the fray;
2 He en-dured the nails, the spit - ting, vin - e - gar, and spear, and reed;
3 Faith-ful cross! a-bove all oth - er, one and on - ly no - ble tree!

now a-bove the cross, the tro-phy, sound the high tri-um-phal lay: tell how
from that ho -ly bod - y bro-ken blood and wa-ter forth pro-ceed: earth, and
None in fo -liage, none in blos-som, none in fruit thy peer may be: sweet-est

Christ, the world's re-deem-er, as a vic-tim won the day.
stars, and sky, and o-cean, by that flood from stain are freed.
wood, and sweet-est i -ron! sweet-est weight is hung on thee. A - men.

LENT

Beneath the Cross of Jesus

Elizabeth C. Clephane, 1868, alt.

ST. CHRISTOPHER   76 86 86 86
Frederick C. Maker, 1881

1 Be -neath the cross of Je - sus I fain would take my stand, the
2 Up - on that cross of Je - sus mine eye at times can see the
3 I take, O cross, thy shad - ow, for my a - bid-ing place; I

shad - ow of a might-y rock with - in a wear-y land; a
ve - ry dy-ing form of one who suf -fered there for me; and
ask no oth-er sun-shine than the sun-shine of his face; con-

home with-in a wil - der - ness, a rest up-on the way, from
from my smit-ten heart, with tears, two won-ders I con - fess: the
tent to let the world go by, to know no gain or loss; my

burn - ing of the noon-tide heat, and bur - den of the day.
won - ders of his glo-rious love, and my own worth-less-ness.
sin - ful self my on - ly shame, my glo - ry all the cross.

LENT

158 Were You There When They Crucified My Lord?

African American

WERE YOU THERE   IRREGULAR
African American melody
harm. Melva Wilson Costen, 1987

1 Were you there   when they cru - ci - fied   my Lord?
2 Were you there   when they nailed him to   the tree!
3 Were you there   when the   sun re - fused   to shine?   (Were you
4 Were you there   when they pierced him in   the side?
5 Were you there   when they laid him in   the tomb?

Were you   there   when they cru - ci - fied   my Lord?
Were you   there   when they nailed him to   the tree?
there?)   Were you   there   when the   sun re - fused   to shine?
Were you   there   when they pierced him in   the side?
Were you   there   when they laid him in   the tomb?

Oh!   some - times   it   caus - es me to

trem - ble,   trem - ble,   trem - ble.   Were   you
Were   you
Were   you
Were   you
Were   you

LENT

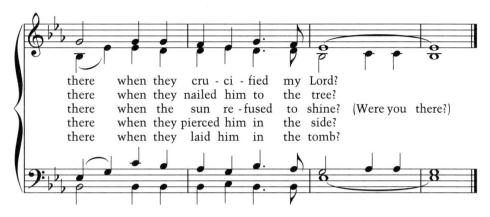

there   when they cru - ci - fied my Lord?
there   when they nailed him to   the tree?
there   when the sun re - fused to shine? (Were you there?)
there   when they pierced him in   the side?
there   when they laid him in   the tomb?

Music © Melva Wilson Costen.

There Is a Green Hill Far Away   159

Cecil Frances Alexander, 1847

HORSLEY CM
William Horsley, 1844

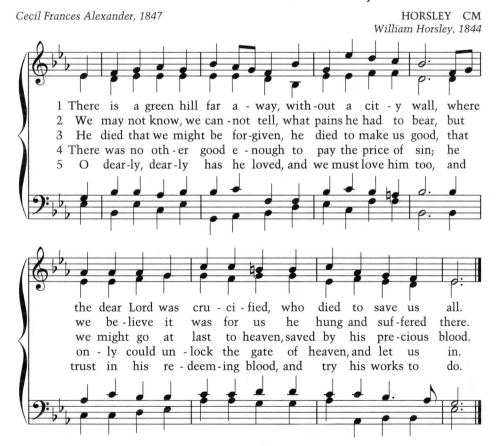

1 There is   a green hill far a - way, with -out a cit - y wall, where
2 We may not know, we can - not tell, what pains he had to bear, but
3 He died that we might be for-given, he died to make us good, that
4 There was no oth - er good e - nough to pay the price of sin; he
5 O dear-ly, dear-ly has he loved, and we must love him too, and

the dear Lord was cru - ci - fied, who died to save us   all.
we be - lieve it   was for us he hung and suf - fered there.
we might go at   last to heaven, saved by his pre - cious blood.
on - ly could un - lock the gate of heaven, and let us   in.
trust in his re - deem - ing blood, and try his works to   do.

LENT

160 When I Survey the Wondrous Cross

Isaac Watts, 1707, alt.

HAMBURG LM
Lowell Mason, 1824

1 When I sur - vey the won - drous cross on which the
2 For - bid it, Lord, that I should boast, save in the
3 See, from his head, his hands, his feet, sor - row and
4 His dy - ing crim - son, like a robe spreads o'er his
5 Were the whole realm of na - ture mine, that were an

Prince of Glo - ry died, my rich - est gain I
cross of Christ, my God: all the vain things that
love flow min - gled down! Did e'er such love and
bo - dy on the tree; then am I dead to
of - fering far too small; love so a - maz - ing,

count but loss, and pour con - tempt on all my pride.
charm me most, I sac - ri - fice them to his blood.
sor - row meet, or thorns com - pose so rich a crown?
all the globe, and all the globe is dead to me.
so di - vine, de - mands my soul, my life, my all.

LENT

We Sing the Praise of Him Who Died 161

Thomas Kelly, 1815

ONEONTA LM
William Henry Hall, 1918

1 We sing the praise of him who died, of
2 In - scribed up - on the cross we see in
3 The cross: it takes our guilt a - way, and
4 It makes the cow - ard spi - rit brave, and
5 The balm of life, the cure of woe, the

him who died up - on the cross; the sin - ner's hope let
shin - ing let - ters, God is Love: he bears our sins up -
holds the faint - ing spi - rit up; it cheers with hope the
nerves the fee - ble arm for fight; it takes its ter - ror
mea - sure and the pledge of love, the sin - ner's ref - uge

sin de - ride; for this we count the world but loss.
on the tree; he brings us mer - cy from a - bove.
gloom - y day, and sweet - ens ev - ery bit - ter cup.
from the grave, and gilds the bed of death with light.
here be - low, the an - gel's theme in heaven a - bove.

LENT

162   In the Cross of Christ I Glory

John Bowring, 1825

RATHBUN   87 87
Ithamar D. Conkey, 1849

1 In the cross of Christ I glo - ry, tower - ing o'er the wrecks of time; all the light of sa - cred sto - ry gath - ers round its head sub - lime.

2 When the woes of life o'er - take me, hopes de - ceive, and fears an - noy, nev - er shall the cross for - sake me: lo, it glows with peace and joy.

3 When the sun of bliss is beam - ing light and love up - on my way, from the cross the ra - diance stream - ing adds new lus - ter to the day.

4 Bane and bless - ing, pain and plea - sure, by the cross are sanc - ti - fied; peace is there that knows no mea - sure, joys that through all time a - bide.

5 In the cross of Christ I glo - ry, tower - ing o'er the wrecks of time; all the light of sa - cred sto - ry gath - ers round its head sub - lime.

LENT

O Sacred Head, Now Wounded

Salve caput cruentatum
Latin, 13th cent.?
trans. Paul Gerhardt, 1656
trans. James W. Alexander, 1830

HERZLICH TUT MICH VERLANGEN   76 76 D
Hans Leo Hassler, 1601
harm. Johann Sebastian Bach, 1729

1 O   sa-cred head, now wound-ed, with grief and shame laid down, now
2 What thou, my Lord, hast suf-fered was all   for sin-ners' gain; mine,
3 What lan-guage shall I   bor-row to thank thee, dear-est friend; for

scorn-ful-ly   sur-round-ed with thorns, thy on-ly   crown, how
mine was the   trans-gres-sion, but thine the dead-ly   pain. Lo,
this thy dy-ing   sor-row, thy pit-y   with-out end?   O

art   thou pale with   an-guish, with sore a-buse and scorn! How
here   I   fall, my Sav-ior! 'Tis I   de-serve thy   place; look
make me thine for-ev-er;   and, should I   faint-ing   be, Lord,

does that vis-age   lan-guish which once was bright as   morn!
on   me with thy   fa-vor, vouch-safe to   me thy   grace.
let   me nev-er,   nev-er out-live my love to   thee!

LENT

164 Come, Ye Faithful, Raise the Strain

ἄισωμεν πάντες λαοί
John of Damascus (8th cent.)
trans. John Mason Neale, 1859, alt.

ST. KEVIN   76 76 D
Arthur Seymour Sullivan, 1872

1 Come, ye faith-ful, raise the strain of tri-um-phant glad-ness;
2 'Tis the spring of souls to-day; Christ hath burst his pris-on,
3 Now the queen of sea-sons, bright with the day of splen-dor,
4 Nei-ther might the gates of death, nor the tomb's dark por-tal,
5 Al-le-lu-ia, now we cry to our King im-mor-tal,

God hath brought his Is-ra-el in-to joy from sad-ness;
and from three days' sleep in death as a sun hath ris-en;
with the roy-al feast of feasts, comes its joy to ren-der;
nor the watch-ers, nor the seal hold thee as a mor-tal:
who tri-um-phant burst the bars of the tomb's dark por-tal;

loosed from Pha-raoh's bit-ter yoke Ja-cob's sons and daugh-ters;
all the win-ter of our sins, long and dark, is fly-ing
comes to glad Je-ru-sa-lem, who with true af-fec-tion,
but to-day a-midst thine own thou didst stand be-stow-ing
Al-le-lu-ia, with the Son, God the Fath-er prais-ing;

led them with un-moist-ened foot through the Red Sea wa-ters.
from his light, to whom we give laud and praise un-dy-ing.
wel-comes in un-wea-ried strains Je-sus' res-ur-rec-tion.
that thy peace which ev-er-more pass-eth hu-man know-ing.
Al-le-lu-ia, yet a-gain to the Spi-rit rais-ing.

EASTER

Christ the Lord Is Risen Again **165**

Christus ist erstanden
Michael Weisse, 1531
trans. Catherine Winkworth, 1858, alt.

LLANFAIR 77 77 with Alleluias
Robert Williams, 1817
harm. John Roberts, 1837

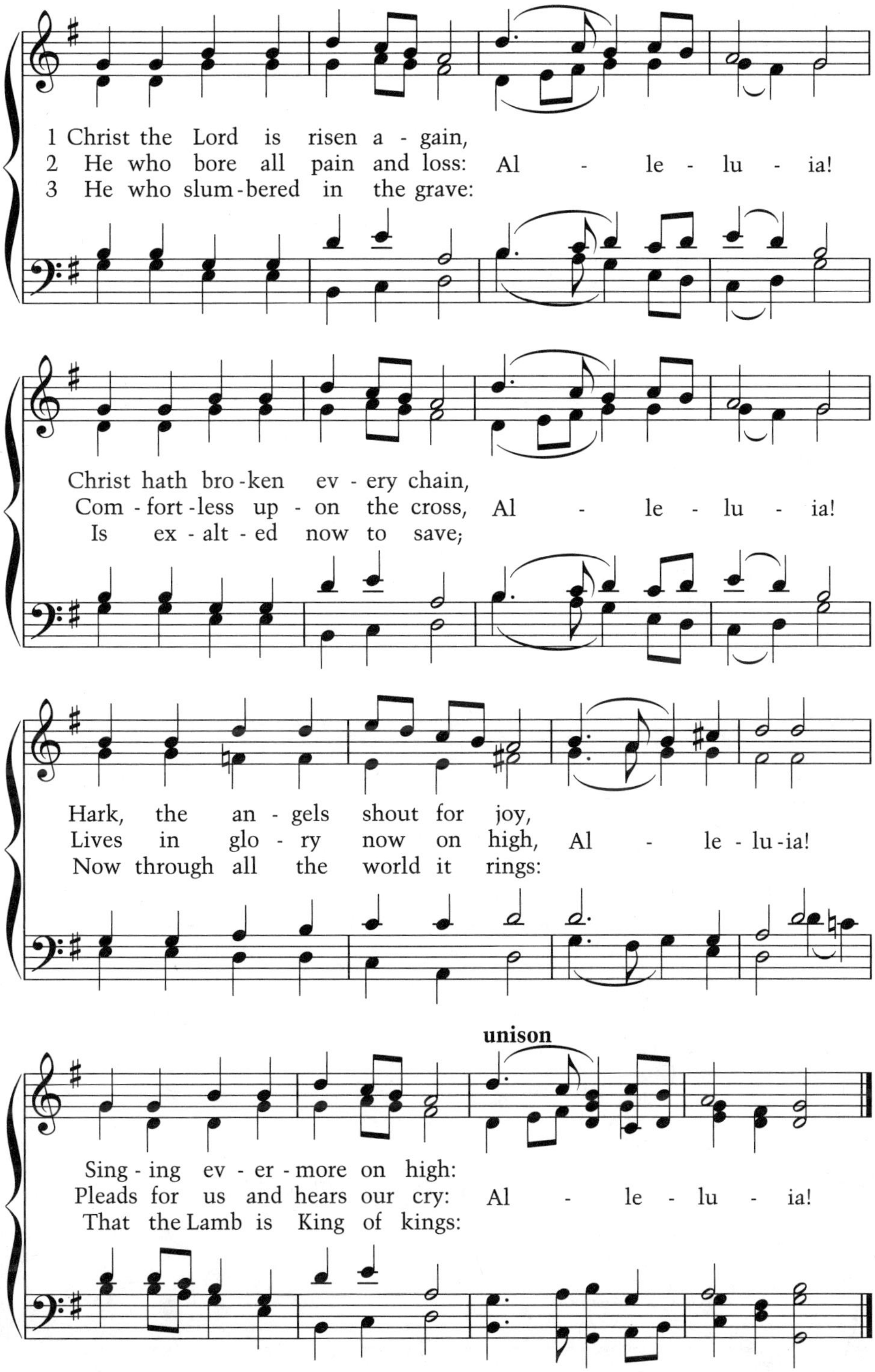

1 Christ the Lord is risen a - gain,
2 He who bore all pain and loss: Al - le - lu - ia!
3 He who slum-bered in the grave:
Christ hath bro-ken ev - ery chain,
Com - fort-less up - on the cross, Al - le - lu - ia!
Is ex - alt - ed now to save;
Hark, the an - gels shout for joy,
Lives in glo - ry now on high, Al - le - lu-ia!
Now through all the world it rings:
unison
Sing - ing ev - er - more on high:
Pleads for us and hears our cry: Al - le - lu - ia!
That the Lamb is King of kings:

This music in F, 3.

We Know That Christ Is Raised

John Brownlow Geyer, 1967

ENGELBERG   10 10 10 with Alleluias
Charles Villiers Stanford, 1904

1 We know that Christ is raised and dies no more.   Em-braced by
2 We share by wa-ter in his sav-ing death.   Re-born we
3 The Fa-ther's splen-dor clothes the Son with life.   The Spi-rit's
4 A new cre-a-tion comes to life and grows   as Christ's new

death, he broke its fear-ful hold;   and our des-pair he turned to
share with him an Eas-ter life   as liv-ing mem-bers of a
pow-er shakes the Church of God.   Bap-tized we live with God the
bo-dy takes on flesh and blood.   The u-ni-verse re-stored and

1.2.3.

blaz-ing joy.
liv-ing Christ.   Al - le - lu - ia!
Three in One.
whole will sing:

EASTER

Al - le - lu - ia! A - men.

Words © 1969 John Brownlow Geyer.

This music in G, 25.

Love's Redeeming Work Is Done   167

Charles Wesley, 1739

SAVANNAH 77 77
Moravian melody, c. 1730
harm. Foundery Collection, 1742

1 Love's re-deem-ing work is done; fought the fight, the bat-tle won:
2 Vain the stone, the watch, the seal; Christ has burst the gates of hell;
3 Lives a-gain our glo-rious King; where, O death, is now thy sting?
4 Soar we now where Christ has led, fol-low-ing our ex-alt-ed head;
5 Hail the Lord of earth and heaven! Praise to thee by both be given:

lo, our Sun's e-clipse is o'er, lo, he sets in blood no more.
death in vain for-bids his rise; Christ has o-pened pa-ra-dise.
dy-ing once, he all doth save; where thy vic-to-ry, O grave?
made like him, like him we rise; ours the cross, the grave, the skies.
thee we greet tri-um-phant now; hail, the Re-sur-rec-tion thou!

168   O Sons and Daughters, Let Us Sing

O filii et filiæ
attrib. Jean Tisserand (d. 1494)
trans. John Mason Neale, 1851, alt.

O FILII ET FILIAE   888 with Alleluias
French melody
Airs sur les hymnes sacrez, odes et noëls, 1623
adapt. Harvard University Hymn Book, 1964

Antiphon (sung at beginning and end)

Al - le - lu - ia!   Al - le - lu - ia!   Al - le - lu - ia!

1 O sons and daugh - ters, let us sing! The
2 That East - er morn at break of day, the
3 An an - gel clad in white they see, who
4 How blest are they who have not seen, and
5 On this most ho - ly day of days, our

King of heaven, the glo - rious King, o'er
faith - ful wom - en went their way to
sat and spake un - to the three, "Your
yet whose faith hath con - stant been; for
hearts and voic - es, Lord, we raise to

unison

death to - day rose tri - umph - ing,
seek the tomb where Je - sus lay,
Lord doth go to Gal - i - lee," Al - le - lu - ia!
they e - ter - nal life shall win,
thee, in ju - bi - lee and praise,

EASTER

Brian Wren, 1969, rev. 1995

TRURO LM
Psalmodia Evangelica, 1789, alt.

1 Christ is a-live! Let Christ-ians sing. The
2 Christ is a-live! No long-er bound to
3 In ev-ery in-sult, rift and war, where
4 Wom-en and men, in age and youth, can
5 Christ is a-live, and comes to bring good

cross stands emp-ty to the sky. Let streets and homes with
dis-tant years in Pal-es-tine, but sav-ing, heal-ing,
co-lor, scorn or wealth di-vide, Christ suf-fers still, yet
feel the Spi-rit, hear the call, and find the way, the
news to this and ev-ery age, till earth and sky and

prais-es ring. Love, drowned in death, shall nev-er die.
here and now, and touch-ing ev-ery place and time.
loves the more, and lives, where ev-en hope has died.
life, the truth, re-vealed in Je-sus, freed for all.
o-cean ring with joy, with just-ice, love and praise.

EASTER

A Brighter Dawn Is Breaking

Percy Dearmer, 1906

WACH AUF, MEIN HERZ   77 77
Nikolaus Selnecker, 1587

1 A bright - er dawn is break - ing, and
2 and thou hast come vic - tor - ious, with
3 O free the world from blind - ness, and
4 In sick - ness give us heal - ing, in

earth with praise is wak - ing; for thou, O King most
ris - en bo - dy glo - rious, who now for - ev - er
fill the world with kind - ness, give sin - ners re - sur -
doubt thy clear re - veal - ing, that praise to thee be

high - est, the power of death de - fi - est;
liv - est, and life a - bun - dant giv - est.
rec - tion, bring striv - ing to per - fec - tion.
giv - en in earth as in thy heav - en.

Alternate harmonization, 36.

EASTER

Alleluia! Alleluia! Hearts to Heaven 171

Christopher Wordsworth, 1872, alt.

LUX EOI   87 87 D
Arthur Seymour Sullivan, 1874

1 Al - le - lu - ia!   Al - le - lu - ia!   Hearts to heaven and voic - es raise;
2 Christ is ris - en, Christ the first fruits of the ho - ly harv - est field,
3 Christ is ris - en, we are ris - en; shed up - on us heaven - ly grace,
4 Al - le - lu - ia!   Al - le - lu - ia!   Glo - ry be to God on high;

sing to God a hymn of glad - ness, sing to God a hymn of praise:
which will all its full a - bun - dance at his sec - ond com - ing yield;
rain, and dew, and gleams of glo - ry from the bright - ness of thy face;
Al - le - lu - ia to the Sav - ior, who has gained the vic - to - ry;

he who on the cross a vic - tim for the world's sal - va - tion bled,
then the gold - en ears of harv - est will their heads be - fore him wave,
that we, with our hearts in heav - en, here on earth may fruit - ful be,
Al - le - lu - ia to the Spi - rit, fount of love and sanc - ti - ty;

Je - sus Christ, the King of glo - ry, now is ris - en from the dead.
rip - ened by his glo - rious sun - shine, from the fur - rows of the grave.
and by an - gel - hands be gath - ered, and be ev - er, Lord, with thee.
Al - le - lu - ia!   Al - le - lu - ia!   to the Tri - une Maj - es - ty.

EASTER

172   Christ the Lord Is Risen Today

Charles Wesley, 1739, alt.

EASTER HYMN   77 77 with Alleluias
Lyra Davidica, 1707
adapt. Complete Psalmodist, 1750

1 Christ the Lord is risen to-day,   Al - le lu - ia!
2 Lives a - gain our glo - rious King,
3 Love's re - deem - ing work is done,
4 Soar we now where Christ has led,
5 Sing we to our God a - bove:

Our tri - um -phant ho - ly day,   Al - le - lu - ia!
Where, O death, is now thy sting?
Fought the fight, the bat - tle won,
Fol-lowing our ex - alt - ed Head,
Praise e - ter - nal as his love,

Raise your joys and tri -umphs high,   Al - le - lu - ia!
Dy - ing once, he all doth save,
Death in vain for - bids him rise,
Made like him, like him we rise,
Praise him, all ye heaven - ly host,

Sing, ye heavens, and earth re - ply: Al - le - lu - ia!
Where thy vic - to - ry, O grave?
Christ has o - pened Par - a - dise,
Ours the cross, the grave, the skies,
Fa - ther, Son, and Ho - ly Ghost.

EASTER

The Strife Is O'er, the Battle Done

173

Finita jam sunt prœlia
Latin, 1695
trans. Francis Pott, 1861

VICTORY   888 with Alleluias
Giovanni Pierluigi da Palestrina, 1591
adapt. William Henry Monk, 1861

Antiphon (sung at beginning and end)

Al - le - lu - ia, Al - le - lu - ia, Al - le - lu - ia!

1 The strife is o'er, the bat - tle done, the vic - to -
2 The powers of death have done their worst, but Christ their
3 The three sad days are quick - ly sped, he ris - es
4 He closed the yawn - ing gates of hell, the bars from
5 Lord! by the stripes which wound - ed thee, from death's dread

ry of life is won; the song of tri - umph
le - gions hath dis - persed: let shouts of ho - ly
glo - rious from the dead: all glo - ry to our
heaven's high por - tals fell; let hymns of praise his
sting thy serv - ants free, that we may live and

has be - gun.   Al - le - lu - ia!
joy out - burst.   Al - le - lu - ia!
ris - en head!   Al - le - lu - ia!
tri - umphs tell! Al - le - lu - ia!
sing to thee.   Al - le - lu - ia!

EASTER

174   Thine Be the Glory, Risen, Conquering Son

À toi la gloire, O Ressuscité!
Edmond L. Budry, 1884
trans. Richard B. Hoyle, 1923

MACCABAEUS   10 11 11 11 with Refrain
George Frideric Handel, 1747

1 Thine be the glo - ry, ris - en, con-quering Son,
2 Lo, Je - sus meets us, ris - en from the tomb;
3 No more we doubt thee, glo - rious Prince of Life;

end - less is the vic - tory thou o'er death hast won;
lov - ing - ly he greets us, scat - ters fear and gloom;
life is nought with - out thee: aid us in our strife.

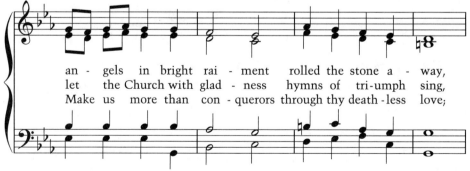

an - gels in bright rai - ment rolled the stone a - way,
let the Church with glad - ness hymns of tri - umph sing,
Make us more than con - querors through thy death - less love;

EASTER

kept the fold - ed grave -clothes where thy bo - dy lay.
for her Lord now liv - eth, death hath lost its sting:
bring us safe through Jor - dan to thy home a - bove.

Thine be the glo - ry, ris - en, con-quering Son,

end - less is the vic - tory thou o'er death hast won.

175 Jesus Lives! Thy Terrors Now

Jesus lebt, mit ihm auch ich
Christian Fürchtegott Gellert, 1751
trans. Frances Elizabeth Cox, 1841

ST. ALBINUS   78 78 with Alleluias
Henry J. Gauntlett, 1852

1 Je - sus lives! Thy ter - rors now can no long -er, death, ap -
2 Je - sus lives! For us he died; then, a - lone to Je - sus
3 Je - sus lives! Our hearts know well nought from us his love shall
4 Je - sus lives! To him the throne o - ver all the world is

pall us; Je - sus lives! by this we know thou, O
liv - ing, pure in heart may we a - bide, glo - ry
sev - er; life, nor death, nor powers of hell tear us
giv - en: may we go where he has gone, rest and

grave, canst not en - thrall us. Al - le - lu - ia!
to our Sa - vior giv - ing. Al - le - lu - ia!
from his keep - ing ev - er. Al - le - lu - ia!
reign with him in hea - ven. Al - le - lu - ia!

The Day of Resurrection

ἀναστάσεως ἡμέρα

John of Damascus (8th cent.)
trans. John Mason Neale, 1862, alt.

ELLACOMBE   76 76 D
Gesangbuch, 1784, alt.

1 The day of re-sur-rec-tion! Earth, tell it out a-broad; the
2 Our hearts be pure from e-vil, that we may see a-right the
3 Now let the heavens be joy-ful, let earth her song be-gin, the

Pass-o-ver of glad-ness, the Pass-o-ver of God. From
Lord in rays e-ter-nal of re-sur-rec-tion light; and,
round world keep high tri-umph, and all that is there-in; let

death to life e-ter-nal, from earth un-to the sky, our
lis-tening to his ac-cents, may hear so calm and plain his
all things seen and un-seen their notes in glad-ness blend, for

Christ hath brought us o-ver with hymns of vic-to-ry.
own "All hail!" and, hear-ing, may raise the vic-tor strain.
Christ the Lord is ris-en, our joy that hath no end.

EASTER

177

Now Is Eternal Life

G. W. Briggs (1875–1959), alt.

CHRISTCHURCH   66 66 88
Charles Steggall (1826–1905)

1 Now is e-ter-nal life, if risen with Christ we stand, in
2 God, yea, the liv-ing God, stooped down to our es-tate; by
3 Un-fath-omed love di-vine, reign thou with-in my heart; from

him to life re-born, and hold-en in his hand; no
death de-stroy-ing death, Christ o-pened wide life's gate. He
thee nor depth nor height, nor life nor death can part; my

more we fear death's an-cient dread, in Christ a-ris-en from the dead.
lives, who died; he reigns on high; who lives in him shall nev-er die.
life is hid in God with thee, now and through all e-ter-ni-ty.

Ye Choirs of New Jerusalem

178

Chorus novæ Jerusalem
Fulbert of Chartres (c.970–1028)
trans. Robert Campbell, 1850

ST. FULBERT   CM
Henry J. Gauntlett, 1849

1 Ye choirs of new Je - ru - sa - lem, your
2 How Ju - dah's Li - on burst his chains, and
3 Tri - um - phant in his glo - ry now his
4 While joy - ful thus his praise we sing, his
5 All glo - ry to the Fa - ther be, all

sweet - est notes em - ploy, the Pas - chal vic - to -
crushed the ser - pent's head; and brought with him, from
scep - ter ru - leth all, earth, heaven, and hell be -
mer - cy we im - plore, in - to his pal - ace
glo - ry to the Son, all glo - ry, Ho - ly

ry to hymn in strains of ho - ly joy.
death's do - mains, the long - im - pri - soned dead.
fore him bow, and at his foot - stool fall.
bright to bring and keep us ev - er - more.
Ghost, to thee, while end - less a - ges run.

EASTER

179   Christ Jesus Lay in Death's Strong Bands

Christ lag in Todesbanden   CHRIST LAG IN TODESBANDEN   87 87 787 with Alleluias
Martin Luther, 1524   *Geystliche gesangk Buchleyn, 1524*
trans. Richard Massie, 1854, alt.   *adapt. Harvard University Hymn Book, 2007*

1 Christ Je - sus lay in death's strong bands for our of - fens - es
2 It was a strange and dread - ful strife when life and death con -
3 So let us keep the fes - ti - val where - to the Lord in -
4 Then let us feast this Eas - ter day on the true bread of

giv - en; but now at God's right hand he stands and brings us life from
tend - ed; the vic - to - ry re - mained with life, the reign of death was
vites us; Christ is him - self the joy of all, the sun that warms and
heav - en. The word of grace hath purged a - way the old and wick - ed

heav - en: where - fore let us joy - ful be, and sing to God right
end - ed: stripped of power, no more he reigns, an emp - ty form a -
lights us; by his grace he doth im - part e - ter - nal sun - shine
leav - en; Christ a - lone our souls will feed, he is our meat and

thank - ful - ly loud songs of Al - le - lu - ia! Al - le - lu - ia!
lone re - mains; his sting is lost for - ev - er. Al - le - lu - ia!
to the heart; the night of sin is end - ed. Al - le - lu - ia!
drink in - deed, faith lives up - on no oth - er. Al - le - lu - ia!

Now the Green Blade Riseth

180

John MacLeod Campbell Crum, 1928, alt.

NOËL NOUVELET   11 10 10 11
French melody
harm. Martin Fallas Shaw, 1928, alt.

1 Now the green blade ris - eth from the bur - ied grain,
2 In the grave they laid him, Love whom hate had slain,
3 Forth he came at East - er, like the ris - en grain,
4 When our hearts are win - try, griev - ing, or in pain,

wheat that in the dark earth ma - ny days has 'lain;
think - ing that he nev - er would a - wake a - gain,
Je - sus who for three days in a grave had lain,
Je - sus' touch can call us back to life a - gain,

love lives a - gain, that with the dead has been:
laid in the earth like grain that sleeps un - seen:
quick from the dead my ris - en Lord is seen:
fields of our hearts that dead and bare have been:

Love is come a - gain, like wheat that spring - eth green.

EASTER

181   God Is Gone Up on High

Charles Wesley, 1746, alt.

DARWALL 148   66 66 88
John Darwall, 1770

1 God is gone up on high, with a tri - um -phant noise: the
2 God in the flesh be - low, for us he reigns a - bove: let
3 Till all the earth, re - newed in right-eous -ness di - vine, with

clar -ions of the sky pro-claim the an - gel - ic joys:
all the na -tions know our Je - su's con - quering love: re -
all the hosts of God in one great cho - rus join:

joice and sing! re -joice and sing; a - scrib-ing glo -ry to our King.

Hail Thee, Festival Day!

Salve festa dies toto venerabilis ævo
Venantius Honorius Fortunatus (c.530–c.610)
trans. Maurice Bell, 1906

SALVE FESTA DIES   79 77 with Refrain
Ralph Vaughan Williams, 1906

Verses on following pages.

ASCENSION

1 He who was nailed to the cross is
3 God the Cre - a - tor, the Lord who
5 Spi - rit of life and of power, now

Lord and the ru - ler of na - ture; all things cre -
rul - est the earth and the hea - vens, guard us from
flow in us, fount of our be - ing, light that dost

D.C.

a - ted on earth sing to the glo - ry of God:
harm with - out, cleanse us from e - vil with - in:
light - en all, life that in all dost a - bide:

ASCENSION

2 Dai - ly the love - li - ness grows, a - dorned with the
4 Je - sus the health of the world, en - light - en our
6 Praise to the Giv - er of good! Thou Love who art

glo - ry of blos - som; hea - ven her gates un -
minds, thou Re - deem - er, Son of the Fa - ther su -
au - thor of con - cord, pour out thy balm on our

D.C.

bars, fling - ing her in - crease of light:
preme, on - ly - be - got - ten of God:
souls, or - der our ways in thy peace:

ASCENSION

183 # Christ, Above All Glory Seated

Æterne Rex altissime
Latin, 10th cent.
trans. *James R. Woodford, 1852*

IN BABILONE 87 87 D
Oude en nieuwe Hollantse Boerenlities en Contradanseu, c. 1710
harm. *Julius Röntgen, 1906*

1 Christ, a - bove all glo - ry seat - ed! King e - ter - nal, strong to save!
2 There thy king - doms all a - dore thee, heaven a - bove and earth be - low,
3 So when thou a - gain in glo - ry on the clouds of heaven shalt shine,

Dy - ing, thou hast death de - feat - ed, bur - ied, thou hast spoiled the grave.
while the depths of hell be - fore thee, trem - bling and de - feat - ed bow.
we, thy flock, may stand be - fore thee, owned for ev - er - more as thine.

Thou art gone, where now is giv - en what no mor - tal might could gain:
We, O Lord! with hearts a - dor - ing, fol - low thee a - bove the sky:
Hail! all hail! in thee con - fid - ing, Je - sus, thee shall all a - dore,

on the e - ter - nal throne of heav - en, in thy Fa - ther's power to reign.
hear our prayers thy grace im - plor - ing, lift our souls to thee on high.
in thy Fa - ther's might a - bid - ing with one Spir - it ev - er - more!

ASCENSION

Hail the Day That Sees Him Rise

Charles Wesley, 1742, alt.

ORIENTIS PARTIBUS 77 77
attrib. Pierre de Corbeil (d. 1222)
harm. Harvard University Hymn Book, 1964

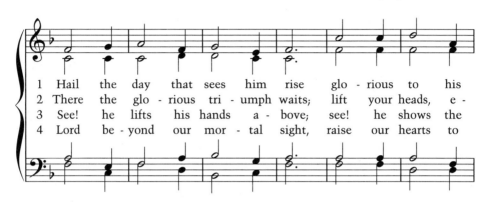

1 Hail the day that sees him rise glo - rious to his
2 There the glo - rious tri - umph waits; lift your heads, e -
3 See! he lifts his hands a - bove; see! he shows the
4 Lord be - yond our mor - tal sight, raise our hearts to

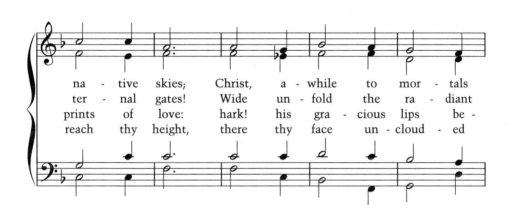

na - tive skies; Christ, a - while to mor - tals
ter - nal gates! Wide un - fold the ra - diant
prints of love: hark! his gra - cious lips be -
reach thy height, there thy face un - cloud - ed

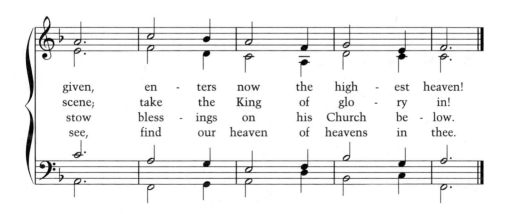

given, en - ters now the high - est heaven!
scene; take the King of glo - ry in!
stow bless - ings on his Church be - low.
see, find our heaven of heavens in thee.

ASCENSION

185 The Head That Once Was Crowned with Thorns

Thomas Kelly, 1820, alt.

ST. MAGNUS CM
attrib. Jeremiah Clarke, 1707
harm. William Henry Monk, 1868

1 The head that once was crowned with thorns is
2 The high - est place that heaven af - fords is
3 the joy of all who dwell a - bove, the
4 To them the cross with all its shame, with
5 They suf - fer with their Lord be - low, they

crowned with glo - ry now; a roy - al di - a -
Christ's a - lone by right, the King of kings, and
joy of all be - low, to whom he man - i -
all its grace is given; their name, an ev - er -
reign with him a - bove, their prof - it and their

dem a - dorns the might - y vic - tor's brow.
Lord of lords, and heaven's e - ter - nal light;
fests his love and grants his name to know.
last - ing name; their joy, the joy of heaven.
joy to know the mys - tery of his love.

And Have the Bright Immensities

Howard Chandler Robbins, 1932

HALIFAX CMD
George Frideric Handel, 1748
adapt. Charles Winfred Douglas, 1941

1 And have the bright im-men-si-ties re-ceived our ris-en Lord, where
2 The heaven that hides him from our sight knows nei-ther near nor far: an

light-years frame the Plei - a-des and point O - ri-on's sword? Do
al - tar can-dle sheds its light as sure-ly as a star; and

flam - ing suns his foot-steps trace through cor-ri - dors sub-
where his lov - ing peo - ple meet to share the gift di -

unison

lime, the Lord of in - ter - stel-lar space and con-quer-or of time?
vine, there stands he with un-hur-rying feet; there heaven-ly splen-dors shine.

ASCENSION

187   The Spacious Firmament on High

para. of Psalm 19
Joseph Addison, 1712

CREATION   LMD
Josef Haydn, 1798
adapt. The Choral, 1845

1 The spa-cious fir-ma-ment on high, with all the blue e-the-real sky, and span-gled heavens, a shin-ing frame, their great o-rig-i-nal pro-claim. The un-wea-ried sun, from

2 Soon as the eve-ning shades pre-vail, the moon takes up the won-drous tale; and night-ly, to the lis-tening earth, re-peats the sto-ry of her birth; whilst all the stars that

3 What though, in sol-emn si-lence, all move round the dark ter-res-trial ball? What though no re-al voice nor sound a-midst their ra-diant orbs be found? In rea-son's ear they

day to day, does his cre - a - tor's power dis-
round her burn, and all the plan - ets in their
all re - joice, and ut - ter forth a glo - rious

play, and pub - lish - es to ev - ery
turn, con - firm the ti - dings as they
voice; for - ev - er sing - ing, as they

land the work of an al - might - y hand.
roll, and spread the truth from pole to pole.
shine, "The hand that made us is di - vine."

188   I Sing the Mighty Power of God

Isaac Watts, 1715, alt.

ELLACOMBE   CMD
Gesangbuch, 1784, alt.

1   I   sing the might-y power of God, that made the moun-tains rise, that
2   I   sing the good-ness of the Lord, that filled the earth with food;   he
3 There's not a   plant or flower be-low, but makes thy glo-ries known; and

spread the flow-ing seas a-broad, and built the loft - y skies. I
formed the crea-tures with   a word, and then pro-nounced them good. Lord,
clouds a - rise, and tem-pests blow, by   or - der   from thy throne. While

sing the wis-dom that or - dained the   sun   to rule the   day;   the
how thy won-ders   are dis - played, wher - e'er   I   turn my   eye: if
all that bor-rows life from thee   is   ev - er   in   thy   care, and

moon shines full at God's com-mand, and all   the   stars o - bey.
I   sur - vey the ground I   tread, or   gaze up - on the   sky!
ev - ery-where that   I could be, thou, God, art   pres-ent there.

stanza 1: Maltbie D. Babcock, 1901, alt.
stanza 2: Mary Babcock Crawford, 1972, alt.

TERRA BEATA SMD
English melody
adapt. Franklin L. Sheppard, 1915
harm. Edward Shippen Barnes, 1933

1 This is our Fa-ther's world, and to my lis-tening ears all
2 This is our Mo-ther's world, O, let us not for - get that

na - ture sings and round me rings the mu - sic of the spheres. This
though the wrong is great and strong, God is our Mo-ther yet. She

is our Fa-ther's world; I rest me in the thought of
trusts us with her world, to keep it clean and fair, all

rocks and trees, of skies and seas; his hand the won - ders wrought.
earth and trees, all skies and seas; all crea - tures ev - ery - where.

GOD

The Great Creator of the Worlds

para. of Epistle to Diognetus, 3rd cent.?
F. Bland Tucker, 1939

TALLIS' ORDINAL   CM
Thomas Tallis, c. 1567

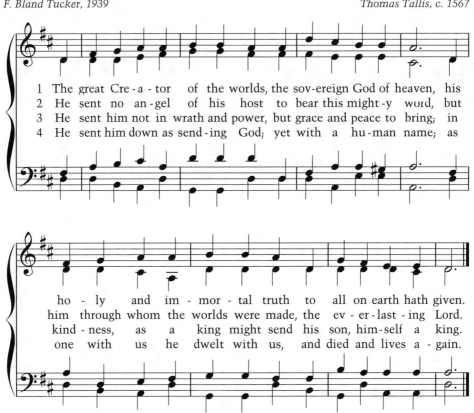

1 The great Cre-a-tor   of the worlds, the sov-ereign God of heaven, his
2 He sent no an-gel   of his   host to bear this might-y word, but
3 He sent him not in wrath and power, but grace and peace to bring;   in
4 He sent him down as send-ing God; yet with a   hu-man name;   as

ho - ly   and im - mor - tal truth to   all on earth hath given.
him through whom the worlds were made, the   ev - er - last - ing Lord.
kind - ness,   as   a   king might send his son, him-self a   king.
one with   us   he   dwelt with us,   and died and lives a - gain.

Another harmonization, 16.

When All Thy Mercies, O My God

Joseph Addison, 1712

SONG 67   CM
Llyfr y Psalmau, 1621
adapt. Orlando Gibbons, 1623

1 When all   thy mer-cies,   O my God, my ris-ing soul sur-veys, trans-
2 Un-num-bered com-forts   to my soul thy ten-der care be-stowed, be-
3 Ten thou-sand thou-sand pre-cious gifts my dai-ly thanks em-ploy;   nor
4 Through all   e - ter - ni - ty   to thee a joy-ful song I'll raise;   for,

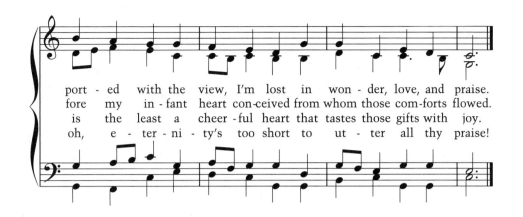

port - ed with the view, I'm lost in won - der, love, and praise.
fore my in - fant heart con-ceived from whom those com-forts flowed.
is the least a cheer -ful heart that tastes those gifts with joy.
oh, e - ter - ni - ty's too short to ut - ter all thy praise!

God Is Our Refuge and Our Strength 192

para. of Psalm 46
Scottish Psalter, 1650

YORK CM
Scottish Psalter, 1615
harm. John Milton, Sr., 1621

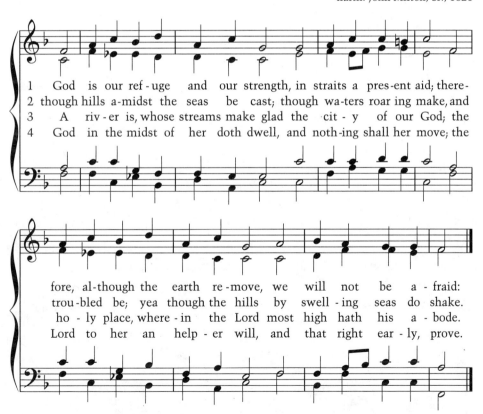

1 God is our ref - uge and our strength, in straits a pres-ent aid; there-
2 though hills a-midst the seas be cast; though wa-ters roar ing make, and
3 A riv - er is, whose streams make glad the cit - y of our God; the
4 God in the midst of her doth dwell, and noth-ing shall her move; the

fore, al-though the earth re -move, we will not be a - fraid:
trou-bled be; yea though the hills by swell -ing seas do shake.
ho - ly place, where -in the Lord most high hath his a - bode.
Lord to her an help - er will, and that right ear - ly, prove.

193   Lord of All Being, Throned Afar

Oliver Wendell Holmes, 1859

UFFINGHAM   LM
Jeremiah Clarke, 1701

1 Lord of all be - ing, throned a - far, thy glo - ry
2 Sun of our life, thy quick - ening ray sheds on our
3 Our mid -night is thy smile with - drawn; our noon -tide
4 Lord of all life, be - low, a - bove, whose light is
5 Grant us thy truth to make us free, and kin -dling

flames from sun and star; cen - ter and soul of
path the glow of day; star of our hope, thy
is thy gra - cious dawn; our rain -bow arch, thy
truth, whose warmth is love, be - fore thy ev - er -
hearts that burn for thee, till all thy liv - ing

ev - ery sphere, yet to each lov - ing heart how near!
sof - tened light cheers the long watch - es of the night.
mer - cy's sign; all, save the clouds of sin, are thine.
blaz - ing throne we ask no lus - ter of our own.
al - tars claim one ho - ly light, one heav - enly flame.

This music in F, 56.

GOD

God of the Earth, the Sky, the Sea

Samuel Longfellow, 1864

HERR JESU CHRIST, MEINS LEBENS LICHT LM
As hymnodus sacer, 1625
harm. Johann Sebastian Bach, 1724

194

1 God of the earth, the sky, the sea, mak - er of
2 Thy love is in the sun - shine's glow, thy life is
3 We feel thy calm at eve - ning's hour, thy gran - deur
4 But high - er far, and far more clear, thee in man's

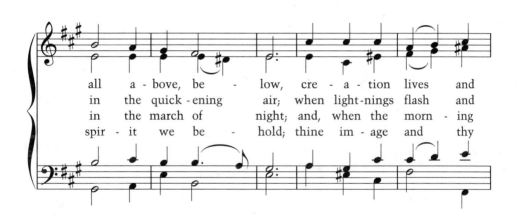

all a - bove, be - low, cre - a - tion lives and
in the quick - ening air; when light-nings flash and
in the march of night; and, when the morn - ing
spir - it we be - hold; thine im - age and thy

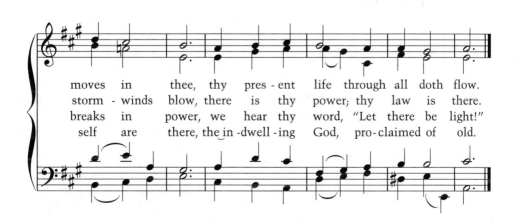

moves in thee, thy pres - ent life through all doth flow.
storm - winds blow, there is thy power; thy law is there.
breaks in power, we hear thy word, "Let there be light!"
self are there, the in-dwell-ing God, pro-claimed of old.

GOD

The King of Love My Shepherd Is

para. of Psalm 23
Henry W. Baker, 1868

DOMINUS REGIT ME 87 87
John Bacchus Dykes, 1868

1 The King of love my shep - herd is, whose
2 Where streams of liv - ing wa - ter flow, my
3 Per - verse and fool - ish oft I strayed, but
4 In death's dark vale I fear no ill, with

good - ness fail - eth nev - er; I noth - ing lack if
ran - somed soul he lead - eth, and where the ver - dant
yet in love he sought me, and on his shoul - der
thee, dear Lord, be - side me: thy rod and staff my

I am his, and he is mine for - ev - er.
pas - tures grow, with food ce - les - tial feed - eth.
gen - tly laid, and home re - joic - ing brought me.
com - fort still, thy cross be - fore to guide me.

5 Thou spreads't a table in my sight,
   thy unction grace bestoweth,
   and oh, what transport of delight
   from thy pure chalice floweth!

6 And so through all the length of days
   thy goodness faileth never;
   Good Shepherd, may I sing thy praise
   within thy house forever.

Alternative tune (ST. COLUMBA), 196.

GOD

The King of Love My Shepherd Is

para. of Psalm 23
Henry W. Baker, 1868

ST. COLUMBA 87 87
Irish melody
harm. Charles Villiers Stanford, 1905

1 The King of love my shep-herd is, whose good-ness
2 Where streams of liv-ing wa - ter flow, my ran-somed
3 Per - verse and fool-ish oft I strayed, but yet in
4 In death's dark vale I fear no ill, with thee, dear

fail - eth nev - er; I noth - ing lack if
soul he lead - eth, and where the ver - dant
love he sought me, and on his shoul - der
Lord, be - side me: thy rod and staff my

I am his, and he is mine for - ev - er.
pas - tures grow, with food ce - les - tial feed - eth.
gen - tly laid, and home re - joic - ing brought me.
com - fort still, thy cross be - fore to guide me.

5   Thou spreads't a table in my sight,
    thy unction grace bestoweth,
    and oh, what transport of delight
    from thy pure chalice floweth!

6   And so through all the length of days
    thy goodness faileth never;
    Good Shepherd, may I sing thy praise
    within thy house forever.

Alternative tune (DOMINUS REGIT ME), 195.

GOD

197   Unto the Hills Around Do I Lift Up

para. of Psalm 121
John Campbell, 1877

SANDON   10 4 10 4 10 10
Charles Henry Purday, 1857

1 Un - to the hills a -round do I lift up my long - ing
2 He will not suf - fer that thy foot be moved: safe shalt thou
3 Je - ho -vah is him - self thy keep -er true, thy change -less
4 From ev - ery e - vil shall he keep thy soul, from ev - ery

eyes;   O whence for me shall my sal - va -tion come, from
be.   No care - less slum - ber shall his eye -lids close, who
shade;   Je - ho -vah thy de - fense on thy right hand him -
sin;   Je - ho -vah shall pre -serve thy go -ing out, thy

whence a - rise? From God the Lord doth come my cer -tain
keep - eth thee. Be - hold, he sleep - eth not, he slum -bereth
self hath made. And thee no sun by day shall ev - er
com - ing in. A - bove thee watch -ing, he whom we a -

aid, from God the Lord who heaven and earth hath made.
ne'er, who keep -eth Is - rael in his ho -ly care.
smite; no moon shall harm thee in the si -lent night.
dore shall keep thee hence -forth, yea, for -ev -er -more.

GOD

The Lord's My Shepherd

198

para. of Psalm 23
Scottish Psalter, 1650

CRIMOND   CM
Jessie S. Irvine, 1872
harm. David Grant, 1872

1 The Lord's my shep - herd, I'll not want; he
2 My soul he doth re - store a - gain; and
3 Yea, though I walk in death's dark vale, yet
4 My ta - ble thou hast fur - nish - ed in
5 Good - ness and mer - cy all my life shall

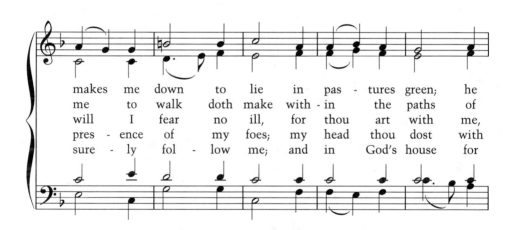

makes me down to lie in pas - tures green; he
me to walk doth make with - in the paths of
will I fear no ill, for thou art with me,
pres - ence of my foes; my head thou dost with
sure - ly fol - low me; and in God's house for

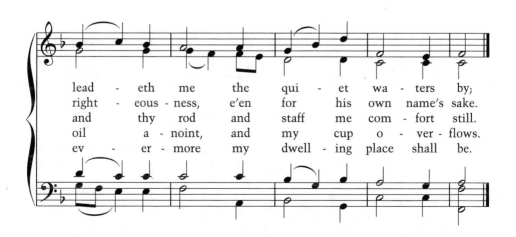

lead - eth me the qui - et wa - ters by;
right - eous - ness, e'en for his own name's sake.
and thy rod and staff me com - fort still.
oil a - noint, and my cup o - ver - flows.
ev - er - more my dwell - ing place shall be.

GOD

199   My God, How Wonderful Thou Art

Frederick W. Faber, 1849

WESTMINSTER   CM
James Turle, 1843

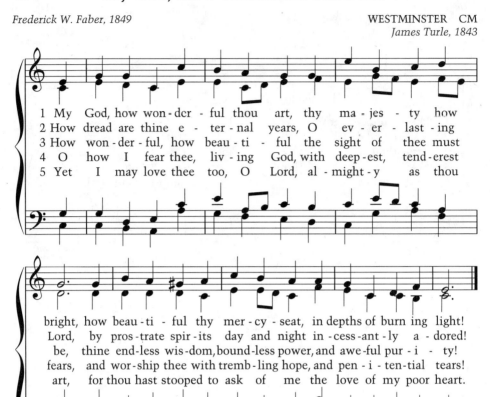

1 My God, how won-der-ful thou art, thy ma-jes-ty how
2 How dread are thine e-ter-nal years, O ev-er-last-ing
3 How won-der-ful, how beau-ti-ful the sight of thee must
4 O how I fear thee, liv-ing God, with deep-est, tend-erest
5 Yet I may love thee too, O Lord, al-might-y as thou

bright, how beau-ti-ful thy mer-cy-seat, in depths of burn-ing light!
Lord, by pros-trate spir-its day and night in-cess-ant-ly a-dored!
be, thine end-less wis-dom, bound-less power, and awe-ful pur-i-ty!
fears, and wor-ship thee with tremb-ling hope, and pen-i-ten-tial tears!
art, for thou hast stooped to ask of me the love of my poor heart.

200   I to the Hills Will Lift Mine Eyes

para. of Psalm 121
Scottish Psalter, 1650

DUNDEE   CM
Scottish Psalter, 1615
harm. Thomas Ravenscroft, 1621, alt.

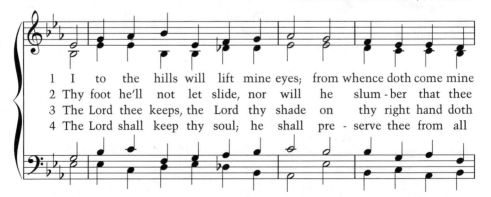

1 I to the hills will lift mine eyes; from whence doth come mine
2 Thy foot he'll not let slide, nor will he slum-ber that thee
3 The Lord thee keeps, the Lord thy shade on thy right hand doth
4 The Lord shall keep thy soul; he shall pre-serve thee from all

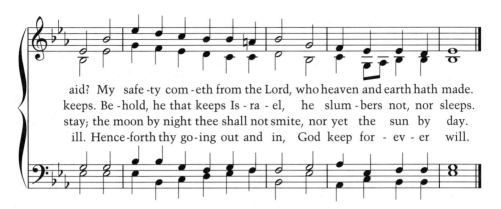

aid? My safe -ty com -eth from the Lord, who heaven and earth hath made.
keeps. Be -hold, he that keeps Is - ra - el, he slum -bers not, nor sleeps.
stay; the moon by night thee shall not smite, nor yet the sun by day.
ill. Hence-forth thy go-ing out and in, God keep for - ev - er will.

This music in D, 295.

God Moves in a Mysterious Way   201

William Cowper, 1774

LONDON NEW   CM
Scottish Psalter, 1635
adapt. Psalms and Hymns, 1671

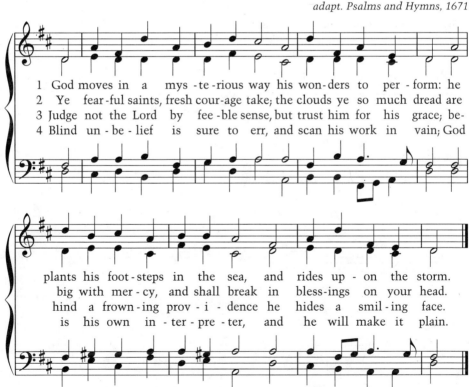

1 God moves in a   mys -te -rious way his won-ders to per - form: he
2 Ye fear-ful saints, fresh cour-age take; the clouds ye so much dread are
3 Judge not the Lord by fee -ble sense, but trust him for his grace; be-
4 Blind un - be - lief is sure to err, and scan his work in vain; God

plants his foot-steps in the sea, and rides up - on the storm.
big with mer - cy, and shall break in bless-ings on your head.
hind a frown-ing prov - i - dence he hides a smil -ing face.
is his own in - ter - pre -ter, and he will make it plain.

GOD

202 How Shall I Sing That Majesty

John Mason, 1683

COE FEN   CMD
Ken Naylor (1931–1991)

1 How shall I sing that maj-es-ty which an-gels do ad-mire? Let dust in dust and si-lence lie; sing, sing, ye heaven-ly choir. Thou-sands of thou-sands stand a-

2 Thy bright-ness un-to them ap-pears, whilst I thy foot-steps trace; a sound of God comes to my ears, but they be-hold thy face. En-light-en with faith's light my

3 How great a be-ing, Lord, is thine, which doth all be-ings keep! Thy knowl-edge is the on-ly line to sound so vast a deep. Thou art a sea with-out a

GOD

round thy throne, O God most high; ten thou-sand
heart, in-flame it with love's fire; then shall I
shore, a sun with-out a sphere; thy time is

times ten thou-sand sound thy praise; but who am I?
sing and bear a part with that ce - les - tial choir.
now and ev - er - more, thy place is ev - ery - where.

203 Immortal, Invisible, God Only Wise

Walter C. Smith, 1867, alt.

ST. DENIO 11 11 11 11
Welsh melody, c. 1810
adapt. John Roberts, 1839

1 Im - mor - tal, in - vis - i - ble, God on - ly wise, in
2 Un - rest - ing, un - hast - ing, and si - lent as light, nor
3 To all life thou giv - est, to both great and small; in
4 Great Fa - ther of glo - ry, pure Fa - ther of light, thine

light in - ac - ces - si - ble hid from our eyes, most
want - ing, nor wast - ing, thou rul - est in might; thy
all life thou liv - est, the true life of all; we
an - gels a - dore thee, all veil - ing their sight; all

bless - ed, most glo - rious, the An - cient of Days, al -
jus - tice like moun - tains high soar - ing a - bove thy
blos - som and flour - ish as leaves on the tree, and
praise we would ren - der; O help us to see 'tis

might - y, vic - to - rious, thy great name we praise.
clouds which are foun - tains of good - ness and love.
with - er and per - ish, but naught chang - eth thee.
on - ly the splen - dor of light hid - eth thee.

Dear Mother God

204

Janet Wootton (b. 1952)

WELWYN   11 10 11 10
Alfred Scott-Gatty (1847–1918)

1 Dear Moth-er God, your wings are warm a-round us,
2 You call to us, for we are in your im-age.
3 Let not our free-dom scorn the needs of oth-ers—

we are en-fold-ed in your love and care; safe
We wait on you, the nest is cold and bare; high
we climb the clouds un-til our strong heart sings; may

in the dark, your heart-beat's pulse sur-rounds us,
o-ver-head your wing-beats call us on-ward.
we en-fold our sis-ters and our broth-ers,

you call to us, for you are al-ways there.
Filled with your power, we ride the emp-ty air.
till all are strong, till all have ea-gles' wings.

GOD

Whate'er My God Ordains Is Right

Was Gott tut, das ist wohlgetan
Samuel Rodigast, 1674
trans. Catherine Winkworth, 1858, alt.

WAS GOTT TUT   87 87 44 77
Severus Gastorius, 1681
harm. Johann Sebastian Bach, 1724, alt.

1 What - e'er my God or - dains is right, his will a - bid - eth ho - ly. As he di - rects my life for me, I fol - low meek and low - ly. My God in - deed in ev - ery need doth well know how to shield me; to him, then, I will yield me.

2 What - e'er my God or - dains is right, he is my friend and fa - ther; he suf - fers naught to do me harm, though man - y storms may shak - en. Now I may know both joy and woe, some day I shall see clear - ly that he hath loved me dear - ly.

3 What - e'er my God or - dains is right, this truth re - mains un - shak - en. Though sor - row, need, or death be mine, I shall not be for - sak - en. I fear no harm, for with his arm he shall em - brace and shield me; so to my God I yield me.

GOD

O Bless the Lord, My Soul

para. of Psalm 103
James Montgomery, 1819

ST. THOMAS SM
Aaron Williams, 1763, rev. 1770

1 O bless the Lord, my soul! His grace to thee pro - claim! And
2 O bless the Lord, my soul! His mer - cies bear in mind! For -
3 He will not al - ways chide; he will with pa - tience wait; his
4 He par - dons all thy sins; pro - longs thy fee - ble breath; He

all that is with - in me join to bless his ho - ly name!
get not all his ben - e - fits! The Lord to thee is kind.
wrath is ev - er slow to rise, and read - y to a - bate.
heal - eth thine in - fir - mi - ties, and ran - soms thee from death.

5 He clothes thee with his love;
  upholds thee with his truth;
  and like the eagle he renews
  the vigor of thy youth.

6 Then bless his holy name,
  whose grace hath made thee whole,
  whose loving-kindness crowns thy days!
  O bless the Lord, my soul!

GOD

207 O God, the Rock of Ages

para. of Psalm 90
Edward Henry Bickersteth, 1860

MEIRIONYDD 76 76 D
William Lloyd, 1840

1 O God, the Rock of A - ges, who ev - er - more hast been, what
2 Our years are like the shad-ows on sun-ny hills that lie, or
3 O thou who canst not slum-ber, whose light grows nev-er pale, teach

time the tem-pest rag - es, our dwell-ing-place se - rene; be-
grass - es in the mead - ows that blos-som but to die; a
us a - right to num - ber our years be - fore they fail; on

fore thy first cre - a - tions, O Lord, the same as now, to
sleep, a dream, a sto - ry by strang-ers quick-ly told, an
us thy mer - cy light - en, on us thy good-ness rest, and

end - less gen - er - a - tions the ev - er - last - ing thou.
un - re - main - ing glo - ry of things that soon are old.
let thy spir - it bright - en the hearts thy - self hast blessed.

Eternal Light, Shine in My Heart

208

Christopher Idle, 1977

JACOB LM
Jane Manton Marshall, 1984

1 E - ter - nal light, shine in my heart; e - ter - nal hope, lift
2 E - ter - nal life, raise me from death; e - ter - nal bright - ness,
3 un - til by your most cost - ly grace, in - vit - ed by your

up my eyes; e - ter - nal power, be
help me see; e - ter - nal Spi - rit,
ho - ly Word, at last I come be -

my sup - port; e - ter - nal wis - dom, make me wise.
give me breath; e - ter - nal Sa - vior, come to me:
fore your face to know you, my e - ter - nal God.

GOD

209   Bright the Vision That Delighted

Richard Mant, 1837, alt.

LAUS DEO   87 87
Richard Redhead, 1853

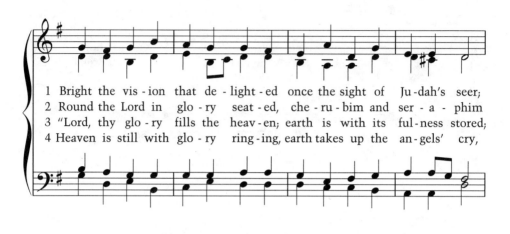

1 Bright the vis - ion that de - light - ed once the sight of Ju - dah's seer;
2 Round the Lord in glo - ry seat - ed, che - ru - bim and ser - a - phim
3 "Lord, thy glo - ry fills the heav - en; earth is with its ful - ness stored;
4 Heaven is still with glo - ry ring - ing, earth takes up the an - gels' cry,

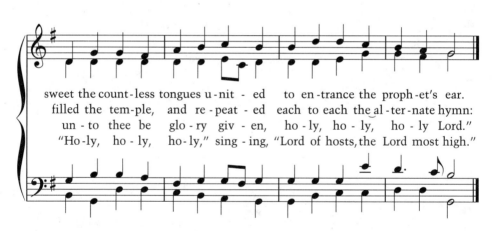

sweet the count - less tongues u - nit - ed to en - trance the proph - et's ear.
filled the tem - ple, and re - peat - ed each to each the al - ter - nate hymn:
un - to thee be glo - ry giv - en, ho - ly, ho - ly, ho - ly Lord."
"Ho - ly, ho - ly, ho - ly," sing - ing, "Lord of hosts, the Lord most high."

5   With the seraph train attending,
     with the holy Church below,
     now in worship without ending
     bid we thus our anthem flow:

6   "Lord, thy glory fills the heaven,
     earth is with its fulness stored;
     unto thee be glory given,
     holy, holy, holy Lord."

GOD

Our God, Our Help in Ages Past

para. of Psalm 90
Isaac Watts, 1719, alt.

ST. ANNE   CM
William Croft, 1708

210

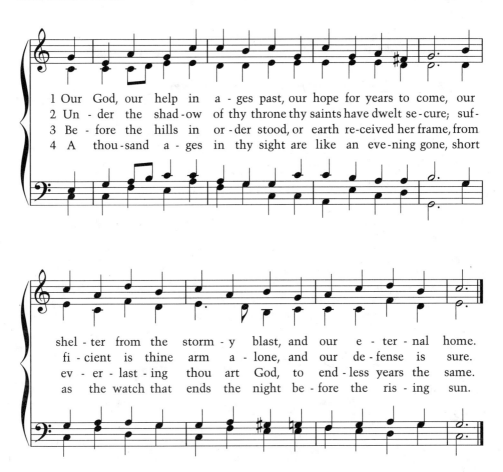

1 Our God, our help in a - ges past, our hope for years to come, our
2 Un - der the shad - ow of thy throne thy saints have dwelt se - cure; suf-
3 Be - fore the hills in or - der stood, or earth re - ceived her frame, from
4 A thou - sand a - ges in thy sight are like an eve - ning gone, short

shel - ter from the storm - y blast, and our e - ter - nal home.
fi - cient is thine arm a - lone, and our de - fense is sure.
ev - er - last - ing thou art God, to end - less years the same.
as the watch that ends the night be - fore the ris - ing sun.

5   Time, like an ever-rolling stream,
    bears all our years away;
    they fly, forgotten, as a dream
    dies at the opening day.

6   Our God, our help in ages past,
    our hope for years to come,
    be thou our guard while troubles last,
    and our eternal home.

GOD

211 Tell Out, My Soul, the Greatness of the Lord

para. of Magnificat
Timothy Dudley-Smith, 1962

WOODLANDS   10 10 10 10
Walter Greatorex, 1916, alt.

1 Tell out, my soul, the great-ness of the Lord! Un-
2 Tell out, my soul, the great-ness of his name! Make
3 Tell out, my soul, the great-ness of his might! Powers
4 Tell out, my soul, the glo-ries of his word! Firm

num-bered bless-ings give my spir-it voice; ten-der to
known his might, the deeds his arm has done; his mer-cy
and do-min-ions lay their glo-ry by. Proud hearts and
is his prom-ise, and his mer-cy sure. Tell out, my

me the prom-ise of his word; in
sure, from age to age the same; his
stub-born wills are put to flight, the
soul, the great-ness of the Lord to

God my Sa - vior shall my heart re - joice.
ho - ly name—the Lord, the might - y One.
hun - gry fed, the hum - ble lift - ed high.
chil - dren's chil - dren and for ev - er - more!

Lord Jesus, Think on Me 212

μνώεο Χριστέ
Synesius of Cyrene (c.370–414?)
trans. Allen W. Chatfield, 1876, alt.

SOUTHWELL SM
Psalmes of David, 1579

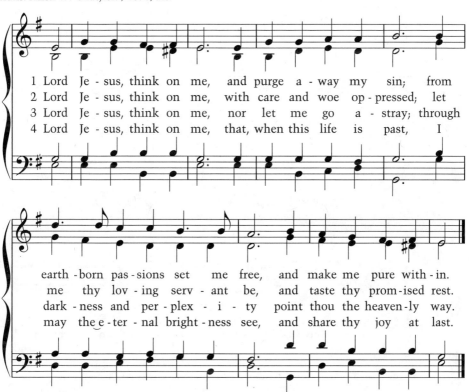

1 Lord Je - sus, think on me, and purge a - way my sin; from
2 Lord Je - sus, think on me, with care and woe op - pressed; let
3 Lord Je - sus, think on me, nor let me go a - stray; through
4 Lord Je - sus, think on me, that, when this life is past, I

earth - born pas - sions set me free, and make me pure with - in.
me thy lov - ing serv - ant be, and taste thy prom - ised rest.
dark - ness and per - plex - i - ty point thou the heaven - ly way.
may the e - ter - nal bright - ness see, and share thy joy at last.

JESUS CHRIST

213 Thou Didst Leave Thy Throne

Emily E. Elliott, 1864, alt.

MARGARET IRREGULAR
Thomas R. Matthews, 1876

1 Thou didst leave thy throne and thy king - ly crown, when thou cam - est to earth for me; but in Beth - le - hem's home was there found no room for thy ho - ly na - ti - vi - ty: O come to my heart, Lord

2 Heav - en's arch - es rang when the ang - els sang, pro - claim - ing thy roy - al de - gree; but in low - ly birth didst thou come to earth, and in great hu - mi - li - ty: O come to my heart, Lord

3 The fox - es found rest, and the birds their nest in the shade of the for - est tree; but thy couch was the sod, O thou Son of God, in the des - erts of Gal - i - lee: O come to my heart, Lord

4 Thou cam - est, O Lord, with the liv - ing word that should set thy peo - ple free; but with mock - ing scorn and with crown of thorn they bore thee to Cal - va - ry: O come to my heart, Lord

5 When the heav - ens shall ring, and the ang - els sing, at thy com - ing to vic - to - ry, let thy voice call me home, say - ing, "Yet there is room, there is room at my side for thee:" my heart shall re - joice, Lord

JESUS CHRIST

Je - sus; there is room in my heart for thee.
Je - sus; there is room in my heart for thee.
Je - sus; there is room in my heart for thee.
Je - sus; there is room in my heart for thee.
Je - sus; when thou com - est and call - est for me.

Jesus, the Very Thought of Thee 214

Jesu dulcis memoria
attrib. Bernard of Clairvaux (1090–1153)
trans. Edward Caswall, 1849, alt.

ST. AGNES CM
John Bacchus Dykes, 1866

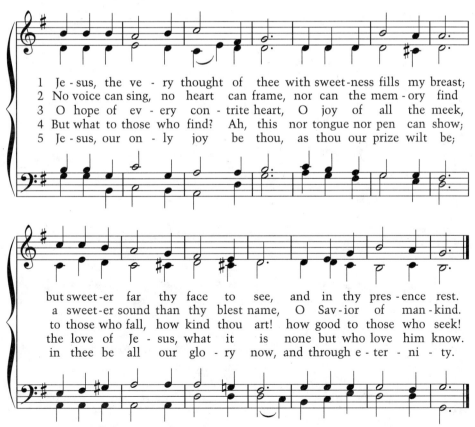

1 Je - sus, the ve - ry thought of thee with sweet-ness fills my breast;
2 No voice can sing, no heart can frame, nor can the mem - ory find
3 O hope of ev - ery con - trite heart, O joy of all the meek,
4 But what to those who find? Ah, this nor tongue nor pen can show;
5 Je - sus, our on - ly joy be thou, as thou our prize wilt be;

but sweet-er far thy face to see, and in thy pres - ence rest.
a sweet-er sound than thy blest name, O Sav - ior of man - kind.
to those who fall, how kind thou art! how good to those who seek!
the love of Je - sus, what it is none but who love him know.
in thee be all our glo - ry now, and through e - ter - ni - ty.

JESUS CHRIST

215

Sing We of the Blessed Mother

George B. Timms, 1975

RUSTINGTON   87 87 D
Charles Hubert Hastings Parry, 1897

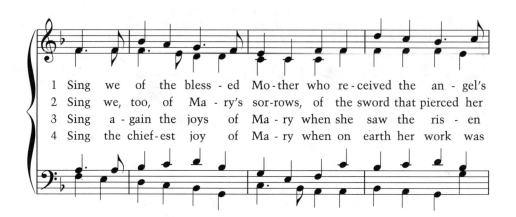

1 Sing we of the bless - ed Mo-ther who re - ceived the an - gel's
2 Sing we, too, of Ma - ry's sor-rows, of the sword that pierced her
3 Sing a - gain the joys of Ma - ry when she saw the ris - en
4 Sing the chief-est joy of Ma - ry when on earth her work was

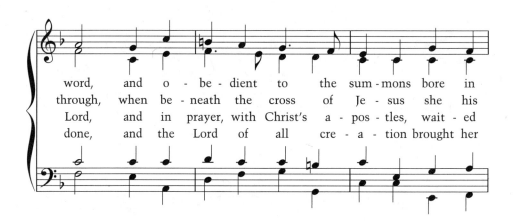

word, and o - be - dient to the sum - mons bore in
through, when be - neath the cross of Je - sus she his
Lord, and in prayer, with Christ's a - pos - tles, wait - ed
done, and the Lord of all cre - a - tion brought her

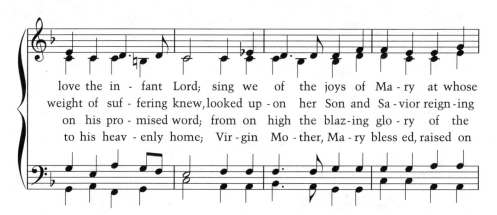

love the in - fant Lord; sing we of the joys of Ma - ry at whose
weight of suf - fering knew, looked up - on her Son and Sa - vior reign-ing
on his pro - mised word; from on high the blaz-ing glo - ry of the
to his heav - en - ly home; Vir - gin Mo - ther, Ma - ry bless ed, raised on

JESUS CHRIST

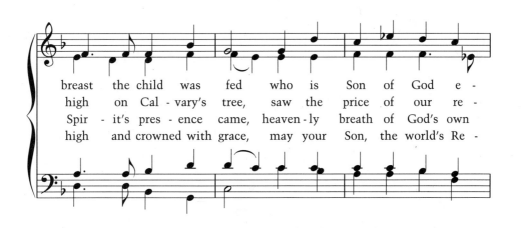

breast	the child	was	fed	who	is	Son	of	God	e -
high	on Cal - vary's	tree,	saw	the	price	of	our	re -
Spir - it's	pres - ence	came,	heaven - ly	breath	of	God's	own
high	and crowned with	grace,	may	your	Son,	the	world's	Re -

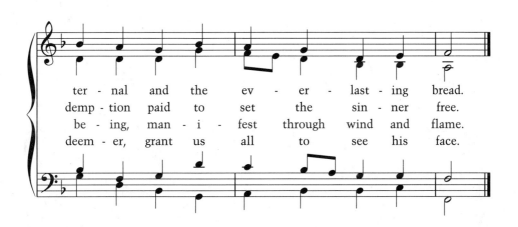

ter - nal	and	the	ev - er - last - ing	bread.
demp - tion	paid	to	set	the	sin - ner	free.
be - ing,	man - i - fest	through	wind	and	flame.
deem - er,	grant	us	all	to	see	his	face.

216   O Love, How Deep, How Broad, How High

O amor quam ecstaticus
Latin, 15th cent.
trans. Benjamin Webb, 1854

DEUS TUORUM MILITUM   LM
Grenoble Antiphoner, 1753

1 O love, how deep, how broad, how high, how pass - ing
2 For us bap - tized, for us he bore his ho - ly
3 For us he prayed, for us he taught, for us his
4 For us to wick - ed men be - trayed, scourged, mocked, in

thought and fan - ta - sy, that God, the Son of
fast, and hun - gered sore; for us temp - ta - tions
dai - ly works he wrought, by words and signs and
pur - ple robe ar - rayed, he bore the shame - ful

God, should take our mor - tal form for mor - tals' sake.
sharp he knew; for us the temp - ter o - ver - threw.
ac - tions, thus still seek - ing not him - self, but us.
cross and death; for us gave up his dy - ing breath.

5   For us he rose from death again,
     for us he went on high to reign;
     for us he sent his Spirit here
     to guide, to strengthen, and to cheer.

6   All glory to our Lord and God
     for love so deep, so high, so broad;
     the Trinity whom we adore
     for ever and forevermore.

JESUS CHRIST

Crown Him with Many Crowns

Matthew Bridges, 1851, alt.

DIADEMATA   SMD
George J. Elvey, 1868

1 Crown him with man-y crowns, the Lamb up-on his throne; hark!
2 Crown him the Lord of love; be-hold his hands and side, rich
3 Crown him the Lord of peace, whose power a scep-ter sways from
4 Crown him the Lord of years, the Po-ten-tate of time, Cre-

how the heaven-ly an-them drowns all mu-sic but its own; a-
wounds, yet vis-i-ble a-bove, in beau-ty glo-ri-fied; no
pole to pole, that wars may cease, and all be prayer and praise: his
a-tor of the roll-ing spheres, in-ef-fa-bly sub-lime. All

wake, my soul, and sing of him who died for thee, and
an-gel in the sky can ful-ly bear that sight, but
reign shall know no end; and round his pierc-ed feet fair
hail, Re-deem-er, hail! for thou hast died for me; thy

hail him as thy match-less King through all e-ter-ni-ty.
down-ward bends his burn-ing eye at mys-ter-ies so bright.
flowers of par-a-dise ex-tend their fra-grance ev-er sweet.
praise shall nev-er, nev-er fail through-out e-ter-ni-ty.

JESUS CHRIST

218   O Love of God, How Strong and True

Horatius Bonar, 1861

DE TAR LM
Calvin Hampton, 1970

1 O love of God, how strong and true,
(2 O wide-em-brac-ing, won-drous) Love,
(3 We read thee best in him who) came
(4 We read thy power to bless and) save

e - ter - nal and yet ev - er new;
we read thee in the sky a - bove;
to bear for us the cross of shame.
e'en in the dark-ness of the grave;

un - com - pre - hend - ed and un - bought,
we read thee in the earth be - low,
sent by the Fa - ther from on high,
still more in re - sur - rec - tion light

JESUS CHRIST

be - yond all knowl - edge and all
in seas that swell and streams and all that
our life to live, our death to
we read the full - ness of thy

thought.
flow.
die.
might.

1.2.3.

2 O wide - em - brac - ing, won - drous
3 We read thee best in him who
4 We read thy power to bless and

4.

JESUS CHRIST

219

Fairest Lord Jesus

Schönster Herr Jesu
Münster Gesangbuch, 1677
trans. Joseph August Seiss, 1873, alt.

ST. ELIZABETH   568 558
Silesian melody
Schlesische Volkslieder, 1842
harm. Richard Storrs Willis, 1850

1 Fair - est Lord Je - sus, rul - er of all na - ture,
2 Fair are the mea - dows, fair - er still the wood - lands,
3 Fair is the sun - shine, fair - er still the moon - light,
4 Beau - ti - ful Sav - ior! Lord of all the na - tions!

O thou of God and man the Son, thee will I cher - ish,
robed in the bloom - ing garb of spring: Je - sus is fair - er,
and all the twink - ling star - ry host: Je - sus shines bright - er,
Son of God and Son of Man! Glo - ry and hon - or,

thee will I hon - or, thou, my soul's glo - ry, joy, and crown.
Je - sus is pur - er who makes the woe - ful heart to sing.
Je - sus shines pur - er than all the an - gels heaven can boast.
praise, ad - o - ra - tion, now and for - ev - er - more be thine.

O for a Thousand Tongues to Sing

Charles Wesley, 1740, alt.

AZMON CM
Carl Gotthilf Gläser, 1828
adapt. Lowell Mason, 1839

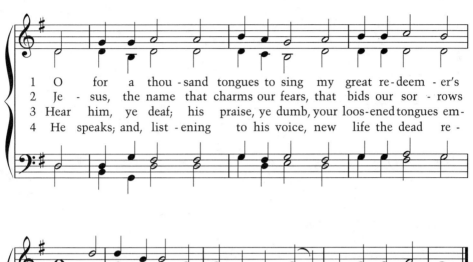

1 O for a thou-sand tongues to sing my great re-deem-er's
2 Je - sus, the name that charms our fears, that bids our sor - rows
3 Hear him, ye deaf; his praise, ye dumb, your loos-ened tongues em-
4 He speaks; and, list - ening to his voice, new life the dead re -

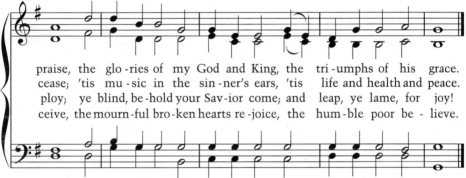

praise, the glo-ries of my God and King, the tri-umphs of his grace.
cease; 'tis mu - sic in the sin-ner's ears, 'tis life and health and peace.
ploy; ye blind, be-hold your Sav-ior come; and leap, ye lame, for joy!
ceive, the mourn-ful bro-ken hearts re-joice, the hum-ble poor be - lieve.

5   He breaks the power of cancelled sin,
    he sets the prisoner free:
    his blood can make the foulest clean;
    his blood availed for me.

6   My gracious master and my God,
    assist me to proclaim
    and spread through all the earth abroad
    the honors of thy name.

JESUS CHRIST

221   What Wondrous Love Is This, O My Soul

A General Selection of the Newest and Most
Admired Hymns and Spiritual Songs Now in Use, 1811, alt.

WONDROUS LOVE   12 9 12 12 9
The Southern Harmony, 1840
harm. Paul J. Christiansen, 1955

1 What won-drous love is this,   O my soul,   O my soul, what
2 What won-drous love is this,   O my soul,   O my soul, what
3 To God and to the Lamb   I will sing,   I will sing, to
4 And when from death I'm free,   I'll sing on,   I'll sing on, and

won-drous love is   this,   O my   soul! What   won-drous love is
won-drous love is   this,   O my   soul! What   won-drous love is
God and to the Lamb,   I will   sing;   to   God and to the
when from death I'm free,   I'll sing   on;   and   when from death I'm

this   that   caused the Lord of   bliss   to   bear the dread-ful
this,   that   caused the Lord of   life   to   lay a-side his
Lamb   who   is the great I   AM,   while   mil-lions join the
free,   I'll   sing and joy-ful   be,   and   through e-ter-ni-

JESUS CHRIST

curse   for   my   soul,   for   my   soul,   to
crown   for   my   soul,   for   my   soul,   to
theme   I   will   sing,   I   will   sing;   while
ty   I'll   sing   on,   I'll   sing   on,   and

bear   the   dread - ful   curse   for   my   soul.
lay   a - side   his   crown   for   my   soul.
mil - lions   join   the   theme   I   will   sing.
through   e - ter - ni - ty   I'll   sing   on.

222   We Have a Gospel to Proclaim

Edward J. Burns (b. 1938)

GARDINER LM
William Gardiner, 1815, alt.

1 We have a gos - pel to pro - claim, good news for
all through - out the earth; the gos - pel of a
Sav - ior's name: we sing his glo - ry, tell his worth.

2 Tell of his birth at Beth - le - hem not in a
roy - al house or hall but in a sta - ble
dark and dim, the Word made flesh, a light for all.

3 Tell of his death at Cal - va - ry, hat - ed by
those he came to save, in lone - ly suf - fering
on the cross; for all he loved his life he gave.

4 Tell of that glo - rious East - er morn: emp - ty the
tomb, for he was free. He broke the power of
death and hell that we might share his vic - to - ry.

5   Tell of his reign at God's right hand,
by all creation glorified.
He sends his Spirit on his church
to live for him, the Lamb who died.

6   Now we rejoice to name him King:
Jesus is Lord of all the earth.
This gospel-message we proclaim:
we sing his glory, tell his worth.

Words © Edward J. Burns.

Another harmonization (in A♭), 340.

JESUS CHRIST

Immortal Love, Forever Full

John Greenleaf Whittier, 1867

BISHOPTHORPE   CM
Jeremiah Clarke (c.1674–1707)

1 Im - mor - tal love, for - ev - er full, for -
2 Our out - ward lips con - fess the name, all
3 We may not climb the heaven - ly steeps to
4 but warm, sweet, ten - der, e - ven yet a
5 The heal - ing of his seam - less dress is

ev - er flow - ing free, for - ev - er shared, for -
oth - er names a - bove; love on - ly know - eth
bring the Lord Christ down; in vain we search the
pres - ent help is he; and faith has still its
by our beds of pain; we touch him in life's

ev - er whole, a nev - er ebb - ing sea!
whence it came, and com - pre - hend - eth love.
low - est deeps, for him no depths can drown:
Ol - i - vet, and love its Gal - i - lee.
throng and press, and we are whole a - gain.

JESUS CHRIST

224 He Leadeth Me, O Blessed Thought!

Joseph H. Gilmore, 1862

HE LEADETH ME   LM with Refrain
William B. Bradbury, 1864

1 He lead-eth me: O bless-ed thought! O words with heav-enly
2 Some-times 'mid scenes of deep-est gloom, some-times where E-den's
3 Lord, I would place my hand in thine, nor ev-er mur-mur
4 And when my task on earth is done, when, by thy grace, the

com-fort fraught! What-e'er I do, wher-e'er I be, still
bow-ers bloom, by wa-ters still, o'er trou-bled sea, still
nor re-pine; con-tent, what-ev-er lot I see, since
vic-tory's won, e'en death's cold wave I will not flee, since

'tis God's hand that lead-eth me.
'tis God's hand that lead-eth me.   He lead-eth me, he
'tis my God that lead-eth me.
God through Jor-dan lead-eth me.

lead-eth me, by his own hand he lead-eth me: his

faith-ful fol-lower I would be, for by his hand he lead-eth me.

Sing, My Soul, His Wondrous Love   225

Hymns and Spiritual Songs, 1801, alt.

ST. BEES   77 77
John Bacchus Dykes, 1862

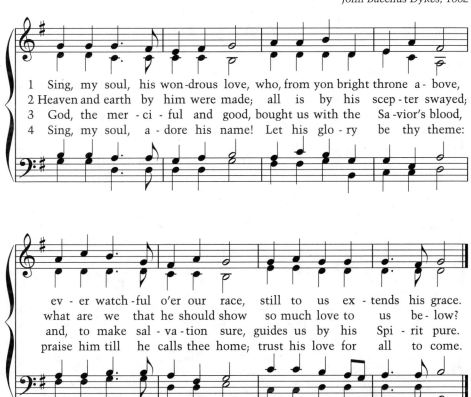

1 Sing, my soul, his won-drous love, who, from yon bright throne a-bove,
2 Heaven and earth by him were made; all is by his scep-ter swayed;
3 God, the mer-ci-ful and good, bought us with the Sa-vior's blood,
4 Sing, my soul, a-dore his name! Let his glo-ry be thy theme:

ev-er watch-ful o'er our race, still to us ex-tends his grace.
what are we that he should show so much love to us be-low?
and, to make sal-va-tion sure, guides us by his Spi-rit pure.
praise him till he calls thee home; trust his love for all to come.

226   Love Divine, All Loves Excelling

Charles Wesley, 1747, alt.

HYFRYDOL   87 87 D
Rowland Huw Prichard, 1830

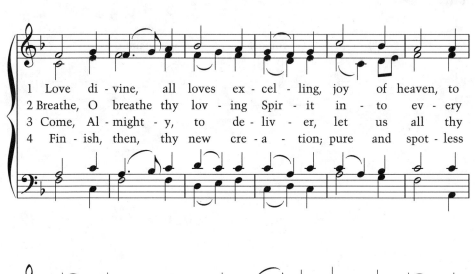

1 Love di - vine, all loves ex - cel - ling, joy of heaven, to
2 Breathe, O breathe thy lov - ing Spir - it in - to ev - ery
3 Come, Al - might - y, to de - liv - er, let us all thy
4 Fin - ish, then, thy new cre - a - tion; pure and spot - less

earth come down, fix in us thy hum - ble dwell - ing,
trou - bled breast; let us all in thee in - her - it,
life re - ceive; sud - den - ly re - turn, and nev - er,
let us be; let us see thy great sal - va - tion

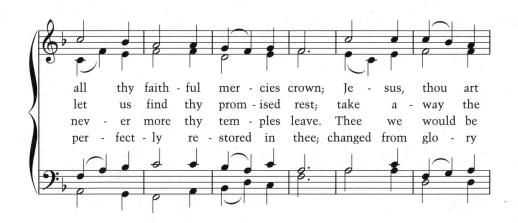

all thy faith - ful mer - cies crown; Je - sus, thou art
let us find thy prom - ised rest; take a - way the
nev - er more thy tem - ples leave. Thee we would be
per - fect - ly re - stored in thee; changed from glo - ry

JESUS CHRIST

all com - pas - sion, pure, un - bound - ed love thou art;
love of sin - ning, Al - pha and O - me - ga be;
al - ways bless - ing, serve thee as thy hosts a - bove,
in - to glo - ry, till in heaven we take our place,

vis - it us with thy sal - va - tion,
end of faith, as its be - gin - ning,
pray, and praise thee with - out ceas - ing,
till we cast our crowns be - fore thee,

en - ter ev - ery trem - bling heart.
set our hearts at lib - er - ty.
glo - ry in thy per - fect love.
lost in won - der, love, and praise.

JESUS CHRIST

227   **Hope of the World**

Georgia Elma Harkness, 1954, alt.   VICAR   11 10 11 10
                                                       V. Earle Copes, 1963

1 Hope   of the world,   thou Christ of great com - pas - sion,
2 Hope   of the world,   God's gift from high-est heav - en,
3 Hope   of the world,   a - foot on dust - y high - ways,
4 Hope   of the world,   who   by thy cross didst save   us
5 Hope   of the world,   O Christ o'er death vic - tor - ious,

speak to   our fear - ful   hearts by con - flict rent.
bring -ing to hun - gry   souls the bread of   life,
show -ing to wan - dering   souls the path of   light,
from death and dark   de - spair, from sin and guilt,
who by this sign didst   con -quer grief and pain,

Save us, thy peo - ple,   from con - sum - ing pas - sion,
still let thy Spir - it   un - to us be   giv - en,
walk thou be - side   us   lest the tempt-ing by - ways
we ren - der back   the   love thy mer - cy gave us;
we would be faith - ful   to thy gos - pel glo - rious;

JESUS CHRIST

who by our own false hopes and aims are spent.
to heal earth's wounds and end all bit - ter strife.
lure us a - way from thee to end - less night.
take thou our lives, and use them as thou wilt.
thou art our Lord! Thou dost for - ev - er reign.

Come, My Way, My Truth, My Life   228

George Herbert (1593–1632), alt.

OUNDLE   77 77
Orlando Gibbons (1583–1625)
adapt. Edward J. Hopkins (1818–1901)

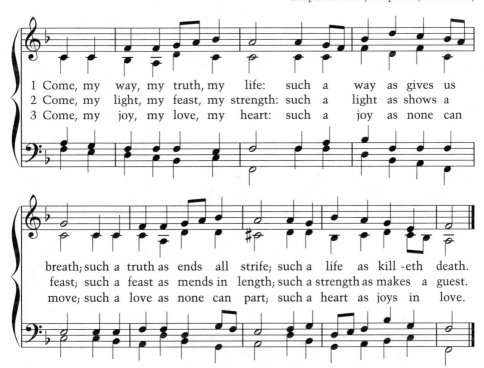

1 Come, my way, my truth, my life: such a way as gives us
2 Come, my light, my feast, my strength: such a light as shows a
3 Come, my joy, my love, my heart: such a joy as none can

breath; such a truth as ends all strife; such a life as kill -eth death.
feast; such a feast as mends in length; such a strength as makes a guest.
move; such a love as none can part; such a heart as joys in love.

JESUS CHRIST

229   He Comes to Us as One Unknown

Timothy Dudley-Smith, 1982

LOBT GOTT, IHR CHRISTEN   86 886
Nikolaus Hermann, 1554
harm. Johann Sebastian Bach, 1725

1 He comes to us as one un-known, a breath un-seen, un-
2 He comes when souls in si - lence lie and thoughts of day de-
3 He comes to us in sound of seas, the o - cean's fume and
4 He comes in love as once he came by flesh and blood and
5 He comes in truth when faith is grown; be - lieved, o - beyed, a-

heard; as though with - in a heart of stone, or
part; half - seen up - on the in - ward eye, a
foam; yet small and still up - on the breeze, a
birth; to bear with - in our mor - tal frame a
dored: the Christ in all the scrip - tures shown, as

shriv - eled seed in dark - ness sown, a pulse of be - ing stirred.
fall - ing star a - cross the sky of night with - in the heart.
wind that stirs the tops of trees, a voice to call us home.
life, a death, a sav - ing name for ev - ery child of earth.
yet un - seen, but not un-known, our Sa - vior and our Lord.

JESUS CHRIST

O Thou Great Friend to All of Us Below 230

Theodore Parker, 1846, alt.

TOULON 10 10 10 10
Genevan Psalter, 1551
harm. Claude Goudimel, 1565, alt.

1 O thou great friend to all of us be-low, who once ap-
2 Thee would I sing: thy truth is still the light which guides the
3 Yes, thou art still the life; thou art the way the ho-liest

peared in hum-blest guise on earth, sin to re-buke, to
na-tions grop-ing on their way, stum-bling and fall-ing
know– light, life, and way of heaven; and they who dear-est

call us from our woe, to break the cap-tive's chain and bring new birth.
in dis-as-trous night, yet hop-ing ev-er for the per-fect day.
hope and deep-est pray toil by the truth, life, way that thou hast given.

JESUS CHRIST

231 **There's a Wideness in God's Mercy**

Frederick W. Faber, 1861, alt.

BLAENWERN   87 87 D
William P. Rowlands, 1905

1 There's a wide-ness in God's mer-cy, like the
2 There is no place where earth's sor-rows are more
3 For the love of God is broad-er than the

wide-ness of the sea; there's a kind-ness in his
felt than up in heaven; there is no place where earth's
mea-sure of the mind; and the heart of the E-

jus-tice, which is more than lib-er-ty. There is
fail-ings have such kind-ly judg-ment given. There is
ter-nal is most won-der-ful-ly kind. If our

JESUS CHRIST

wel - come for the sin - ner, and more gra - ces
plen - ti - ful re - demp - tion in the blood that
love were but more faith - ful, we should take him

for the good; there is mer - cy with the
has been shed; there is joy for all the
at his word; and our life would be thanks -

Sa - vior; there is heal - ing in his blood.
mem - bers in the sor - rows of the Head.
giv - ing for the good - ness of the Lord.

Alternative tune (ST. HELENA), 232.

JESUS CHRIST

232 There's a Wideness in God's Mercy

Frederick W. Faber, 1861, alt.

ST. HELENA 87 87 D
Calvin Hampton, 1978

1 There's a wide-ness in God's mer - cy like the wide-ness
2 There is no place where earth's sor - rows are more felt than
3 For the love of God is broad - er than the mea - sure

of the sea; there's a kind -ness in his jus -
up in heaven; there is no place where earth's fail -
of the mind; and the heart of the E - ter -

* After final verse and interlude, stop on this E major chord to conclude.

JESUS CHRIST

tice, which is more than lib - er - ty.   There is wel - come
ings have such kind - ly judg - ment given.   There is plen - ti -
nal is most won - der - ful - ly kind.   If our love were

for the sin - ner,   and more gra - ces for the good; there is mer - cy
ful re - demp-tion   in the blood that has been shed; there is joy for
but more faith -ful,   we should take him at his word; and our life would

with the Sa - vior;   there is heal-ing in his blood.
all the mem -bers   in the sor-rows of the Head.
be thanks-giv - ing   for the good-ness of the Lord.

Alternative tune (BLAENWERN), 231.

JESUS CHRIST

233 Rejoice, the Lord Is King

Charles Wesley, 1746, alt.

GOPSAL   66 66 88
George Frideric Handel (1685–1759)
adapt. John Wilson, 1977, alt.

1 Re - joice, the Lord is King! Your Lord and King a - dore! Re -
2 The Lord, our Sav - ior, reigns, the God of truth and love; when
3 His king-dom can - not fail; he rules o'er earth and heaven; the

joice, give thanks, and sing, and tri - umph ev - er - more!
he had purged our stains, he took his seat a - bove.
keys of death and hell to Christ the Lord are given:

1.2.

Lift up your heart, lift up your voice!

Re - joice, a - gain I say re - joice!

3.

up your heart, lift up your voice!

Re - joice, a - gain I say re - joice!

Name of All Majesty

Timothy Dudley-Smith, 1979

MAJESTAS 66 55 66 64
Michael Baughen, 1982
adapt. Noël Tredinnick, 1984

1 Name of all ma-jes-ty, fath-om-less mys-ter-y,
2 Child of our des-ti-ny, God from e-ter-ni-ty,
3 Sa-vior of Cal-va-ry, cost-li-est vic-to-ry,
4 Source of all sove-reign-ty, light, im-mor-tal-i-ty,

King of the a-ges by ang-els a-dored;
love of the Fa-ther on sin-ners out-poured;
dark-ness de-feat-ed and E-den re-stored;
life ev-er-last-ing and heav-en as-sured;

power and auth-or-i-ty, splen-dor and dig-ni-ty,
see now what God has done send-ing his on-ly Son,
born as a man to die, nailed to a cross on high,
so with the ran-somed, we praise him e-ter-nal-ly,

bow to his mas-ter-y, Je-sus is Lord!
Christ the be-lov-ed one, Je-sus is Lord!
cold in the grave to lie, Je-sus is Lord!
Christ in his maj-es-ty, Je-sus is Lord!

JESUS CHRIST

Jesus Shall Reign Where'er the Sun 235

Isaac Watts, 1719, alt.

DUKE STREET LM
John Hatton, 1793

1 Je - sus shall reign wher - e'er the sun
2 For him shall end - less prayer be made,
3 Peo - ple and realms of ev - ery tongue
4 Bless - ings a - bound wher - e'er he reigns;
5 Let ev - ery crea - ture rise and bring

doth its suc - ces - sive jour - neys run;
and prais - es throng to crown his head;
dwell on his love with sweet - est song,
the pris - oner leaps to lose his chains,
pe - cul - iar hon - ors to our King;

his king - dom stretch from shore to shore
his name like sweet per - fume shall rise
and in - fant voic - es shall pro - claim
the wea - ry find e - ter - nal rest,
an - gels de - scend with songs a - gain,

till moons shall wax and wane no more.
with ev - ery morn - ing sac - ri - fice.
their ear - ly bless - ings on his name.
and all who suf - fer want are blest.
and earth re - peat the loud A - men.

JESUS CHRIST

At the Name of Jesus

Caroline Maria Noel, 1870, alt.

KING'S WESTON   65 65 D
Ralph Vaughan Williams, 1925

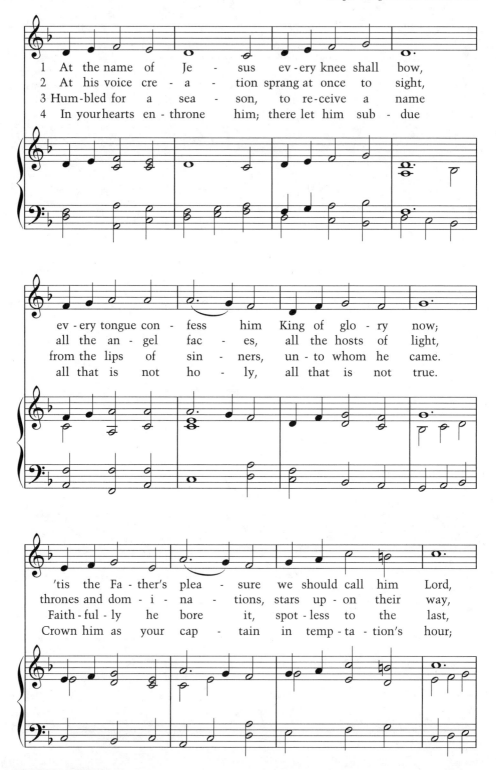

1 At the name of Je - sus ev - ery knee shall bow,
2 At his voice cre - a - tion sprang at once to sight,
3 Hum-bled for a sea - son, to re-ceive a name
4 In your hearts en - throne him; there let him sub - due

ev - ery tongue con - fess him King of glo - ry now;
all the an - gel fac - es, all the hosts of light,
from the lips of sin - ners, un - to whom he came.
all that is not ho - ly, all that is not true.

'tis the Fa - ther's plea - sure we should call him Lord,
thrones and dom - i - na - tions, stars up - on their way,
Faith-ful - ly he bore it, spot - less to the last,
Crown him as your cap - tain in temp - ta - tion's hour;

JESUS CHRIST

who from the be - gin - ning was the might - y Word.
all the heaven - ly or - ders, in their great ar - ray.
brought it back vic - to - rious, when from death he passed.
let his will en - fold you in its light and power.

Thou Art the Way; to Thee Alone   237

George Washington Doane, 1824

CONSOLATION CM
Ananias Davisson, 1812

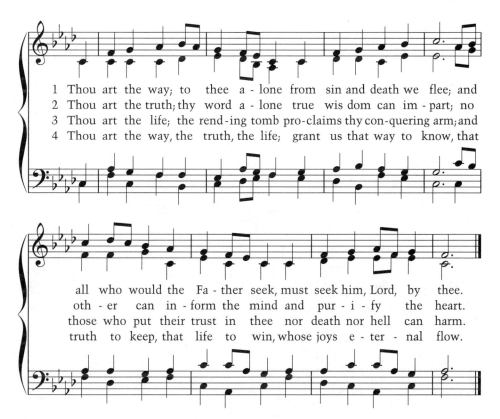

1 Thou art the way; to thee a - lone from sin and death we flee; and
2 Thou art the truth; thy word a - lone true wis dom can im - part; no
3 Thou art the life; the rend - ing tomb pro - claims thy con - quering arm; and
4 Thou art the way, the truth, the life; grant us that way to know, that

all who would the Fa - ther seek, must seek him, Lord, by thee.
oth - er can in - form the mind and pur - i - fy the heart.
those who put their trust in thee nor death nor hell can harm.
truth to keep, that life to win, whose joys e - ter - nal flow.

JESUS CHRIST

238   Ye Servants of God, Your Master Proclaim

Charles Wesley, 1744, alt.

PADERBORN   10 10 11 11
Catholisch-Paderbornisches Gesang-buch, 1765
harm. Sydney H. Nicholson, 1916

1. Ye serv-ants of God, your mas-ter pro-claim, and
2. God rul-eth on high, al-might-y to save, and
3. Sal-va-tion to God who sits on the throne! Let
4. Then let us a-dore and give him his right, all

pub-lish a-broad his won-der-ful name. The
still he is nigh, his pres-ence we have; the
all cry a-loud and hon-or the Son; the
glo-ry and power, all wis-dom and might, all

name, all vic-to-rious, of Je-sus ex-tol; his
great con-gre-ga-tion his tri-umph shall sing, as-
prais-es of Je-sus the an-gels pro-claim, fall
hon-or and bless-ing with an-gels a-bove, and

king-dom is glo-rious, he rules o-ver all.
crib-ing sal-va-tion to Je-sus, our King.
down on their fac-es and wor-ship the Lamb.
thanks nev-er ceas-ing and in-fi-nite love.

JESUS CHRIST

All Hail the Power of Jesus' Name

Edward Perronet, 1780, alt.

CORONATION 86 86 86
Oliver Holden, 1793

239

1 All hail the power of Je - sus' name! Let an-gels pros-trate fall; bring
2 Crown him, ye mar-tyrs of our God, who from his al - tar call; ex -
3 Ye seed of Is-rael's cho-sen race, ye ran-somed of the fall, hail
4 Let ev - ery kin-dred, ev - ery tribe, on this ter-res-trial ball, to
5 O that, with yon - der sa-cred throng, we at his feet may fall; we'll

forth the roy - al di - a - dem, and crown him Lord of all. Bring
tol the stem of Jes - se's rod, and crown him Lord of all. Ex -
him who saves you by his grace, and crown him Lord of all. Hail
him all maj - es - ty as - cribe, and crown him Lord of all. To
join the ev - er - last - ing song, and crown him Lord of all. We'll

forth the roy - al di - a - dem, and crown him Lord of all.
tol the stem of Jes - se's rod, and crown him Lord of all.
him who saves you by his grace, and crown him Lord of all.
him all maj - es - ty as - cribe, and crown him Lord of all.
join the ev - er - last - ing song, and crown him Lord of all.

JESUS CHRIST

240 Christ Triumphant, Ever Reigning

Michael Saward (b. 1932)

GUITING POWER 85 85 with Refrain
John Barnard (b. 1948)

1 Christ tri-um-phant, ev - er reign-ing, Sa-vior, Mas-ter, King,
2 Word in-car-nate, truth re-veal-ing Son of Man on earth!
3 Suf-fering Ser-vant, scorned, ill treat-ed, vic-tim cru-ci-fied!
4 Priest-ly King, en-throned for-ev-er high in heaven a-bove!
5 So, our hearts and voi-ces rais-ing through the a-ges long,

Lord of heaven, our lives sus-tain-ing, hear us as we sing:
Power and maj-es-ty con-ceal-ing by your hum-ble birth.
Death is through the cross de-feat-ed, sin-ners jus-ti-fied.
Sin and death and hell shall nev-er sti-fle hymns of love.
cease-less-ly up-on you gaz-ing, this shall be our song:

yours the glo-ry and the crown, the high re-known, the e-ter - nal name.

JESUS CHRIST

Come Down, O Love Divine 241

Descendi, Amor Santo
Bianco of Siena (c.1350–1434)
trans. Richard F. Littledale, 1867, alt.

DOWN AMPNEY 66 11 D
Ralph Vaughan Williams, 1906

1 Come down, O Love di - vine, seek thou this soul of
2 O let it free - ly burn, till earth - ly pas - sions
3 And so the yearn - ing strong with which the soul will

mine, and vis - it it with thine own ar - dor glow - ing;
turn to dust and ash - es in its heat con - sum - ing;
long, shall far out - pass the power of hu - man tell - ing;

O Com - fort - ter, draw near, with - in my heart ap -
and let thy glo - rious light shine ev - er on my
for none can guess its grace, till Love cre - ate a

pear, and kin - dle it, thy ho - ly flame be - stow - ing.
sight, and clothe me round, the while my path il - lum - ing.
place where - in the Ho - ly Spir - it makes his dwell - ing.

THE HOLY SPIRIT

242   Come, O Creator Spirit, Come

Veni Creator Spiritus
Latin, 9th cent.
trans. Robert Seymour Bridges, 1899

VENI CREATOR   LM
Plainsong, Mode 8
Sarum rite
harm. Charles Winfred Douglas, 1940

1 Come, O Cre - a - tor Spir - it, come,
2 O Com - fort - er, that name is thine,
3 Our sens - es with thy light in - flame,
4 May we by thee the Fa - ther learn,

and make with - in our hearts thy home;
of God most high the gift di - vine;
our hearts to heaven - ly love re - claim;
and know the Son, and thee dis - cern,

to us thy grace ce - les - tial give,
the well of life, the fire of love,
our bod - ies' poor in - fir - mi - ty
who art of both; and so a - dore

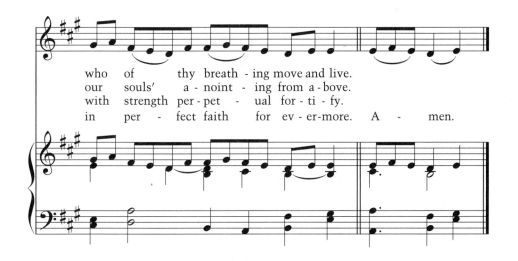

who   of   thy breath - ing move and live.
our   souls' a - noint - ing from a - bove.
with   strength per - pet - ual for - ti - fy.
in   per - fect faith   for ev - er-more. A - men.

Send Down Thy Truth, O God 243

Edward Rowland Sill, 1867

NOVA VITA   SM
Lister R. Peace, 1914

1 Send down thy truth,   O   God,   too long the   shad - ows frown!
2 Send down thy Spir - it   free   till   wil - der - ness   and   town
3 Send down thy love,   thy life,   our less - er   lives   to   crown,
4 Send down thy peace,   O   Lord,   earth's bit - ter   voic - es   drown

Too long the dark - ened way we've trod: thy truth, O Lord, send down!
one tem - ple   for   thy wor - ship be: thy Spir - it, O   send down!
and cleanse them of   their hate and strife: thy liv - ing love send down!
in   one deep o - cean of   ac - cord: thy peace, O God, send down!

244   Come, Holy Spirit, God and Lord

Komm, heiliger Geist, Herre Gott
Martin Luther, 1524
trans. Catherine Winkworth, 1855, alt.

DAS NEUGEBORNE KINDELEIN   LM
Melchior Vulpius, 1609
harm. Johann Sebastian Bach, 1724

1 Come, Ho-ly Spir-it, God and Lord! Be all thy
2 Lord, by the bright-ness of thy light, thou in the
3 Thou ho-ly light, our guide di-vine, O, cause the
4 From ev-ery er-ror keep us free; let none but

grac-es now out-poured on each be-liev-er's
faith dost all u-nite from ev-ery land and
Word of life to shine! Teach us to know our
Christ our mas-ter be that we in liv-ing

mind and heart; thy fer-vent love to us im-part.
ev-ery tongue; this to thy praise, O Lord, be sung.
God a-right and call him Fa-ther with de-light.
faith a-bide, in him with all our might con-fide.

5   Thou holy fire, our comfort true,
      grant us the will thy work to do
      and in thy service to abide;
      let trials turn us not aside.

6   Lord, by thy power prepare each heart
      and to our weakness strength impart
      that bravely here we may contend,
      through life and death to thee ascend.

THE HOLY SPIRIT

Like the Murmur of the Dove's Song 245

Carl P. Daw, Jr., 1982

BRIDEGROOM 87 87 6
Peter Cutts, 1969

1 Like the mur-mur of the dove's song, like the chal-lenge of her
2 To the mem-bers of Christ's bo-dy, to the branch-es of the
3 With the heal-ing of di-vi-sion, with the cease-less voice of

flight, like the vig-or of the wind's rush, like the
vine, to the Church in faith as-sem-bled, to her
prayer, with the power to love and wit-ness, with the

new flame's ea-ger might: come, Ho-ly Spi-rit, come.
midst as gift and sign: come, Ho-ly Spi-rit, come.
peace be-yond com-pare: come, Ho-ly Spi-rit, come.

THE HOLY SPIRIT

Praise the Spirit in Creation

Michael Hewlett (1916–2000), alt.

JULION 87 87 87
David Hurd, 1983

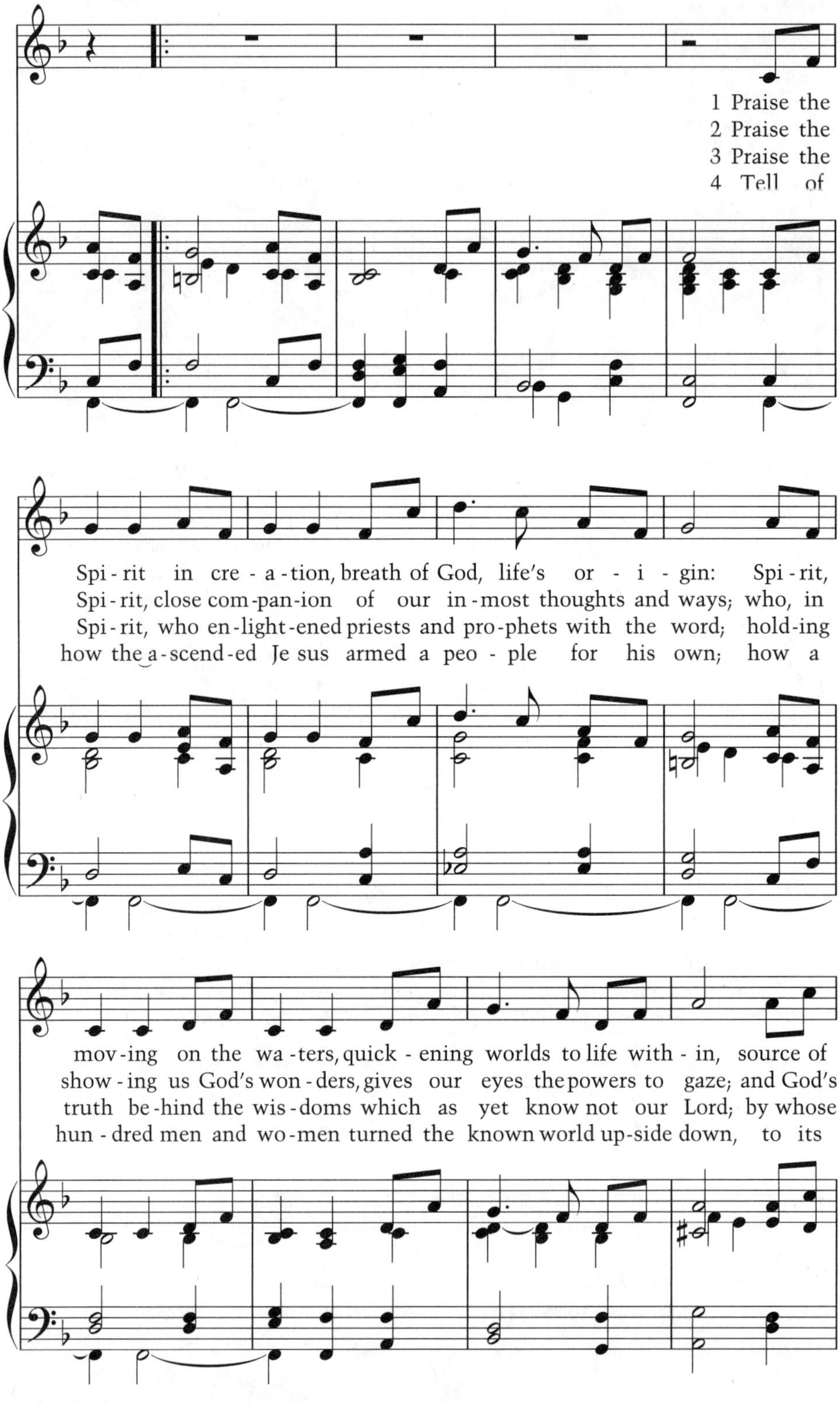

1 Praise the
2 Praise the
3 Praise the
4 Tell of

Spi-rit in cre-a-tion, breath of God, life's or-i-gin: Spi-rit,
Spi-rit, close com-pan-ion of our in-most thoughts and ways; who, in
Spi-rit, who en-light-ened priests and pro-phets with the word; hold-ing
how the a-scend-ed Je-sus armed a peo-ple for his own; how a

mov-ing on the wa-ters, quick-ening worlds to life with-in, source of
show-ing us God's won-ders, gives our eyes the powers to gaze; and God's
truth be-hind the wis-doms which as yet know not our Lord; by whose
hun-dred men and wo-men turned the known world up-side down, to its

THE HOLY SPIRIT

breath to all things breath-ing, life in whom   all lives be - gin.
will, to those who lis - ten, by a   still small voice con - veys.
love and power, in Je - sus God him-self   was seen and heard.
dark and fur-thest cor -ners by the wind   of hea-ven blown.

5   Pray we then, O Lord the Spirit,
    on our lives descend in might;
    let your flame break out within us,
    fire our hearts and clear our sight,
    till, white-hot in your possession,
    we, too, set the world alight.

6   Praise, O praise the Holy Spirit,
    praise the Father, praise the Word,
    Source, and Truth, and Inspiration,
    Trinity in deep accord:
    through your voice which speaks within us
    we, your creatures, call you Lord.

THE HOLY SPIRIT

Breathe on Me, Breath of God

Edwin Hatch, 1878, alt.

TRENTHAM SM
Robert Jackson, 1888

1 Breathe on me, breath of God, fill me with life a - new,
2 Breathe on me, breath of God, un - til my heart is pure,
3 Breathe on me, breath of God, till I am whol - ly thine,
4 Breathe on me, breath of God, so shall I nev - er die,

that I may love what thou dost love, and do what thou wouldst do.
un - til with thee I will one will, to do and to en - dure.
un - til this earth - ly part of me glows with thy fire di - vine.
but live with thee the per - fect life of thine e - ter - ni - ty.

Spirit Divine, Attend Our Prayers

Andrew Reed, 1829

NUN DANKET ALL' UND BRINGET EHR' CM
Johann Crüger, 1653

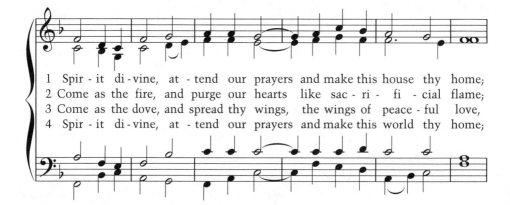

1 Spir - it di - vine, at - tend our prayers and make this house thy home;
2 Come as the fire, and purge our hearts like sac - ri - fi - cial flame;
3 Come as the dove, and spread thy wings, the wings of peace - ful love,
4 Spir - it di - vine, at - tend our prayers and make this world thy home;

THE HOLY SPIRIT

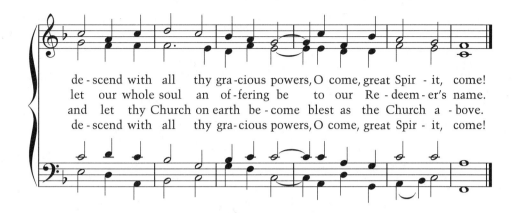

de - scend with all   thy gra-cious powers, O come, great Spir - it, come!
let   our whole soul   an of-fering be   to our Re - deem-er's name.
and   let thy Church on earth be - come blest as the Church a - bove.
de - scend with all   thy gra-cious powers, O come, great Spir - it, come!

Holy Spirit, Truth Divine   249

Samuel Longfellow, 1864

SONG 13   77 77
Orlando Gibbons, 1623
adapt. Charles Herbert Kitson (1874–1944)

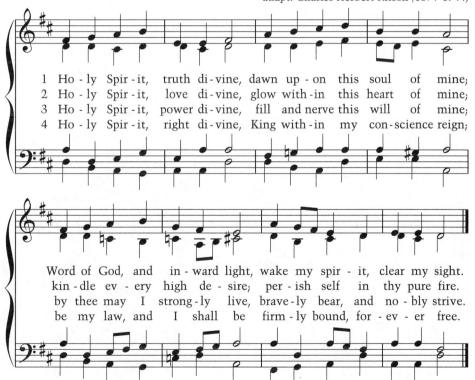

1 Ho - ly Spir - it,   truth di - vine, dawn up - on this soul   of   mine;
2 Ho - ly Spir - it,   love di - vine, glow with - in this heart of   mine;
3 Ho - ly Spir - it,   power di - vine, fill and nerve this will   of   mine;
4 Ho - ly Spir - it,   right di - vine, King with - in my con - science reign;

Word of God, and   in - ward light, wake my spir - it, clear my sight.
kin - dle ev - ery high de - sire; per - ish self   in   thy pure fire.
by thee may I   strong - ly live, brave - ly bear, and no - bly strive.
be my law,   and I shall be   firm - ly bound, for - ev - er free.

THE HOLY SPIRIT

250   There's a Spirit in the Air

Brian Wren, 1969, rev. 1995

LAUDS   77 77
John Wilson, 1969

1 There's a Spir - it in the air, tell - ing Chris - tians
2 Lose your shy - ness, find your tongue, tell the world what
3 When be - liev - ers break the bread, when a hun - gry
4 Still the Spir - it gives us light, see - ing wrong and
5 When a stran - ger's not a - lone, where the home - less

ev - ery-where: "Praise the love that Christ re-vealed,
God has done: God in Christ has come to stay.
child is fed, praise the love that Christ re-vealed,
set - ting right: God in Christ has come to stay.
find a home, praise the love that Christ re-vealed,

liv - ing, work - ing, in our world!"
Live to - mor - row's life to - day!
liv - ing, work - ing, in our world.
Live to - mor - row's life to - day!
liv - ing, work - ing, in our world.

6 May the Spirit fill our praise,
guide our thoughts and change our ways:
God in Christ has come to stay.
Live tomorrow's life today!

7 There's a Spirit in the air,
calling people everywhere:
praise the love that Christ revealed,
living, working, in our world.

THE HOLY SPIRIT

Holy, Holy, Holy! Lord God Almighty

Reginald Heber, 1826, alt.

NICAEA   11 12 12 10
John Bacchus Dykes, 1861

1 Ho - ly, ho - ly, ho - ly! Lord God al - might - y!
2 Ho - ly, ho - ly, ho - ly! all the saints a - dore thee,
3 Ho - ly, ho - ly, ho - ly! though the dark - ness hide thee,
4 Ho - ly, ho - ly, ho - ly! Lord God al - might - y!

Ear - ly in the morn - ing our song shall rise to thee;
cast - ing down their gold - en crowns a - round the glass - y sea;
though the sin - ful hu - man eye thy glo - ry may not see;
All thy works shall praise thy name in earth and sky and sea;

ho - ly, ho - ly, ho - ly! mer - ci - ful and might - y;
cher - u - bim and ser - a - phim fall - ing down be - fore thee,
on - ly thou art ho - ly; there is none be - side thee,
ho - ly, ho - ly, ho - ly! mer - ci - ful and might - y;

God in three per - sons, bless - ed Trin - i - ty!
which wert, and art, and ev - er - more shalt be.
per - fect in power, in love, and pur - i - ty.
God in three per - sons, bless - ed Trin - i - ty!

THE TRINITY

All Glory Be to God on High

Allein Gott in der Höh' sei Ehr'
Nikolaus Decius, 1525
trans. Catherine Winkworth, 1863, alt.

ALLEIN GOTT   87 87 887
Geistliche lieder, Leipzig, 1539
harm. Hieronymus Praetorius, 1604

1 All glo-ry be to God on high, and peace on earth from
2 O Lamb of God, Lord Je-sus Christ, whom God the Fa - ther
3 You on - ly are the Ho - ly One, who came for our sal-

hea - ven, and God's good will un - fail - ing - ly be
gave us, who for the world was sac - ri - ficed up -
va - tion, and on - ly you are God's true Son, who

to all peo - ple giv - en. We bless, we wor - ship
on the cross to save us; and, as you sit at
was be - fore cre - a - tion. You, on - ly, Christ, as

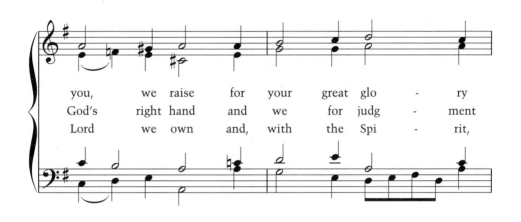

you,   we raise   for   your   great glo -   ry

God's   right hand   and   we   for   judg -   ment

Lord   we own   and,   with   the   Spi -   rit,

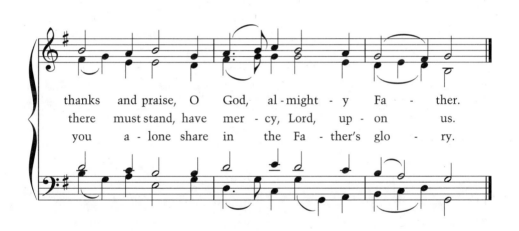

thanks   and praise,   O   God,   al - might - y   Fa -   ther.

there   must stand, have   mer - cy,   Lord,   up - on   us.

you   a - lone share   in   the   Fa - ther's   glo -   ry.

Come, Thou Almighty King

Anonymous English Tract, c. 1757, alt.

MOSCOW   664 6664
Felice de Giardini, 1769

1 Come, thou al-might-y King, help us thy name to sing;
help us to praise; Fa-ther, all glo-ri-ous, o'er all vic-
to-ri-ous, come, and reign o-ver us, An-cient of Days.

2 Come, thou in-car-nate Word, gird on thy might-y sword;
our prayer at-tend: come, and thy peo-ple bless, and give thy
word suc-cess; Spir-it of ho-li-ness, on us de-scend.

3 Come, ho-ly Com-fort-er, thy sa-cred wit-ness bear
in this glad hour! Thou who al-might-y art, now rule in
ev-ery heart, and ne'er from us de-part, Spir-it of power.

4 To the great One in Three e-ter-nal prais-es be
hence ev-er-more! His sov-ereign maj-es-ty may we in
glo-ry see, and to e-ter-ni-ty love and a-dore.

This music in F, 273.

THE TRINITY

Mothering God, You Gave Me Birth

254

Julian of Norwich (1342–c.1416)
adapt. Jean Wiebe Janzen, 1991

HESPERUS (QUÉBEC)   LM
Henry Baker, 1854

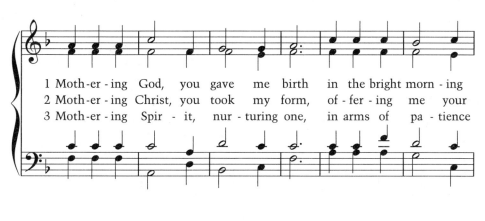

1 Moth-er-ing God, you gave me birth in the bright morn-ing
2 Moth-er-ing Christ, you took my form, of-fer-ing me your
3 Moth-er-ing Spir-it, nur-turing one, in arms of pa-tience

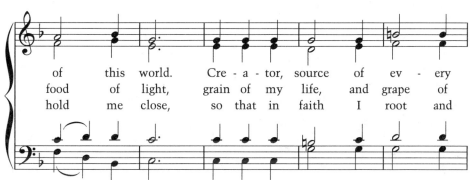

of this world. Cre-a-tor, source of ev-ery
food of light, grain of my life, and grape of
hold me close, so that in faith I root and

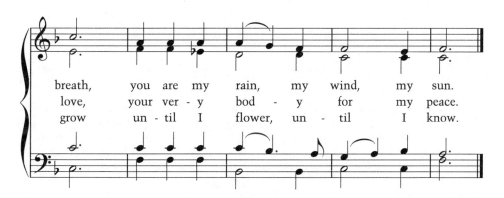

breath, you are my rain, my wind, my sun.
love, your ver-y bod-y for my peace.
grow un-til I flower, un-til I know.

THE TRINITY

255 Ancient of Days, Who Sittest Throned in Glory

William C. Doane, 1886, alt.

ALBANY 11 10 11 10
J. Albert Jeffery, 1886

1 An - cient of Days, who sit - test throned in glo - ry, to thee all knees are bent, all voic - es pray; thy love has blessed the

2 O ho - ly Fa - ther, who hast led thy chil - dren in all the a - ges with the fire and cloud, through seas dry - shod, through

3 O ho - ly Je - sus, Prince of Peace and Sa - vior, to thee we owe the peace that shall pre - vail, still - ing the rude wills

4 O Ho - ly Ghost, the Lord and the Life - giv - er, thine is the quick - ening power that gives in - crease: from thee have flowed, as

5 O Tri - une God, with heart and voice a - dor - ing, praise we the good - ness that doth crown our days; pray we that thou wilt

THE TRINITY

wide world's won - drous sto - ry
wea - ry wastes be - wil - dering,
of our wild be - ha - vior,
from a migh - ty riv - er,
hear us, still im - plor - ing

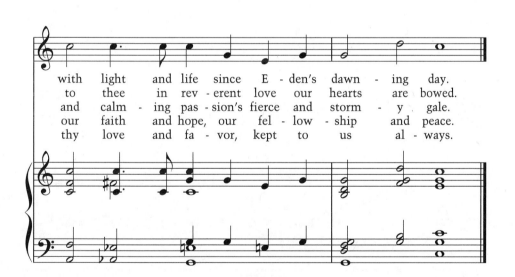

with light and life since E - den's dawn - ing day.
to thee in rev - erent love our hearts are bowed.
and calm - ing pas - sion's fierce and storm - y gale.
our faith and hope, our fel - low - ship and peace.
thy love and fa - vor, kept to us al - ways.

256

Eternal Father, Strong to Save

William Whiting, 1860, alt.

MELITA   88 88 88
John Bacchus Dykes, 1861

1 E - ter - nal Fa - ther, strong to save, whose arm hath bound the
2 O Christ, whose voice the wa - ters heard and hushed their ra - ging
3 Most Ho - ly Spi - rit, who didst brood up - on the cha - os
4 O Trin - i - ty of love and power, our breth-ren shield in

rest - less wave, who bidd'st the migh - ty o - cean deep its
at thy word, who walk - edst on the foam - ing deep, and
dark and rude, and bid its an - gry tu - mult cease, and
dan - ger's hour; from rock and temp - est, fire and foe, pro -

own ap - point - ed lim - its keep: O hear us when we
calm a - mid its rage didst sleep: O hear us when we
give, for wild con - fu - sion, peace; O hear us when we
tect them where - so - e'er they go; thus ev - er-more shall

cry to thee for those in per - il on the sea.
cry to thee for those in per - il on the sea.
cry to thee for those in per - il on the sea.
rise to thee glad hymns of praise from land and sea.

THE TRINITY

Blessed Jesus, at Thy Word

Liebster Jesu, wir sind hier
Tobias Clausnitzer, 1663
trans. Catherine Winkworth, 1858

LIEBSTER JESU   78 78 88
Johann Rudolph Ahle, 1664
harm. Johann Sebastian Bach (1685–1750)

1 Bless - ed Je - sus, at thy word we are gath -ered all to
2 All our knowl -edge, sense, and sight lie in deep - est dark -ness
3 Glo - rious Lord, thy - self im - part! Light of light, from God pro -

hear thee; let our hearts and souls be stirred
shroud - ed, till thy Spir - it breaks our night
ceed - ing, o - pen thou our ears and heart,

now to seek and love and fear thee; by thy teach -ings
with the beams of truth un - cloud - ed; thou a - lone to
help us by thy Spir - it's plead - ing; hear the cry thy

sweet and ho - ly, drawn from earth to love thee sole - ly.
God canst win us, thou must work all good with - in us.
peo - ple rais -es, hear, and bless our prayers and prais - es.

THE PEOPLE OF GOD

258   Glorious Things of Thee Are Spoken

John Newton, 1779, alt.

AUSTRIAN HYMN   87 87 D
Josef Haydn, 1797

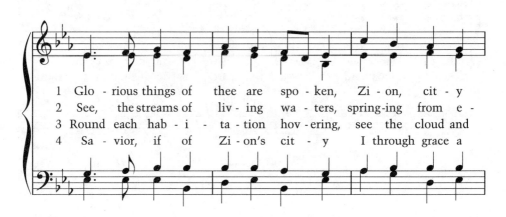

1 Glo - rious things of thee are spo - ken, Zi - on, cit - y
2 See, the streams of liv - ing wa - ters, spring-ing from e -
3 Round each hab - i - ta - tion hov - ering, see the cloud and
4 Sa - vior, if of Zi - on's cit - y I through grace a

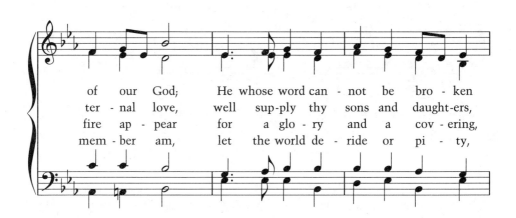

of our God; He whose word can - not be bro - ken
ter - nal love, well sup-ply thy sons and daught-ers,
fire ap - pear for a glo - ry and a cov - ering,
mem - ber am, let the world de - ride or pi - ty,

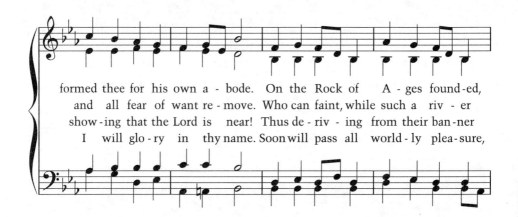

formed thee for his own a - bode. On the Rock of A - ges found-ed,
and all fear of want re - move. Who can faint, while such a riv - er
show-ing that the Lord is near! Thus de - riv - ing from their ban-ner
I will glo - ry in thy name. Soon will pass all world - ly plea-sure,

THE PEOPLE OF GOD

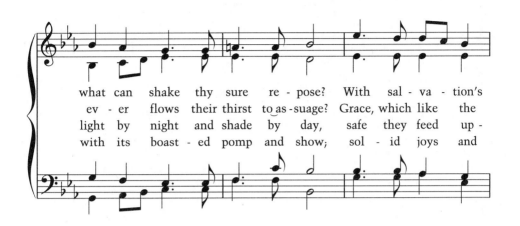

what can shake thy sure re - pose? With sal - va - tion's
ev - er flows their thirst to as -suage? Grace, which like the
light by night and shade by day, safe they feed up -
with its boast - ed pomp and show; sol - id joys and

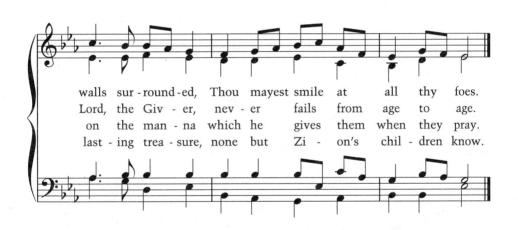

walls sur -round -ed, Thou mayest smile at all thy foes.
Lord, the Giv - er, nev - er fails from age to age.
on the man - na which he gives them when they pray.
last - ing trea -sure, none but Zi - on's chil - dren know.

259 The Church's One Foundation

Samuel John Stone, 1866

AURELIA 76 76 D
Samuel Sebastian Wesley, 1864

1 The Church's one foun-da-tion is Je-sus Christ her Lord; she
2 E-lect from ev-ery na-tion, yet one o'er all the earth, her
3 'Mid toil and trib-u-la-tion, and tu-mult of her war, she
4 Yet she on earth hath un-ion with God, the Three in One, and

is his new cre-a-tion by wa-ter and the word; from
char-ter of sal-va-tion, one Lord, one faith, one birth, one
waits the con-sum-ma-tion of peace for-ev-er-more; till
mys-tic sweet com-mun-ion with those whose rest is won. O

heaven he came and sought her to be his ho-ly bride; with
ho-ly name she bless-es, par-takes one ho-ly food, and
with the vi-sion glo-rious, her long-ing eyes are blest, and
hap-py ones and ho-ly! Lord, give us grace that we like

his own blood he bought her, and for her life he died.
to one hope she press-es, with ev-ery grace en-dued.
the great Church vic-to-rious shall be the Church at rest.
them, the meek and low-ly, on high may dwell with thee.

City of God, How Broad and Far

260

Samuel Johnson, 1864, alt.

RICHMOND CM
Thomas Haweis, 1792
adapt. Samuel Webbe, Jr., 1808
harm. Hymns Ancient and Modern, Revised, 1950

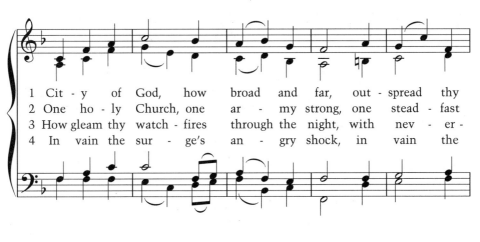

1 Cit - y of God, how broad and far, out - spread thy
2 One ho - ly Church, one ar - my strong, one stead - fast
3 How gleam thy watch - fires through the night, with nev - er -
4 In vain the sur - ge's an - gry shock, in vain the

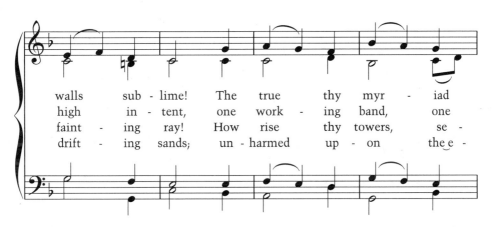

walls sub - lime! The true thy myr - iad
high in - tent, one work - ing band, one
faint - ing ray! How rise thy towers, se -
drift - ing sands; un - harmed up - on the e -

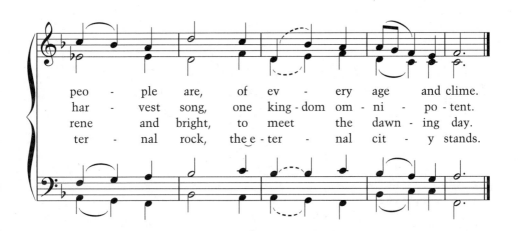

peo - ple are, of ev - ery age and clime.
har - vest song, one king - dom om - ni - po - tent.
rene and bright, to meet the dawn - ing day.
ter - nal rock, the e - ter - nal cit - y stands.

THE PEOPLE OF GOD

261 **Great God, the Followers of Thy Son**

Henry Ware, Jr., 1819

HEBRON   LM
Lowell Mason, 1830

1 Great God, the fol - lowers of thy Son, we
2 O grant thy bless - ing here to - day! O
3 We seek the truth which Je - sus brought; his
4 May faith and hope and love a - bound; our

bow be - fore thy mer - cy seat, to wor - ship thee, the
give thy peo - ple joy and peace! The to - kens of thy
path of light we long to tread: here be his ho - ly
sins and er - rors be for given; and we, in thy great

Ho - ly One, and pour our wish - es at thy feet.
love dis - play, and fa - vor that shall nev - er cease.
doc - trines taught, and here their pur - est in - fluence shed.
day, be found child - ren of God and heirs of heaven!

THE PEOPLE OF GOD

Christ Is Made the Sure Foundation

Angularis fundamentum
Latin, 8th cent.?
trans. John Mason Neale, 1851, alt.

WESTMINSTER ABBEY 87 87 87
Henry Purcell, c. 1680
adapt. Hymnal Supplement II, 1976

1 Christ is made the sure foun-da-tion, Christ the head and
2 All that ded-i-cat-ed cit - y, dear - ly loved of
3 To this tem-ple, where we call thee, come, O Lord of
4 Here vouch-safe to all thy serv-ants what they ask of

cor - ner - stone, cho - sen of the Lord, and pre-cious,
God on high, in ex-ul-tant ju - bi-la - tion
Hosts, to - day; with thy wont-ed lov - ing-kind-ness
thee to gain; what they gain from thee, for-ev - er

bind - ing all the Church in one; ho - ly Zi - on's
pours per - pet - ual mel-o - dy; God the One in
hear thy peo - ple as they pray, and thy full - est
with the bless - ed to re - tain, and here-af - ter

help for - ev - er, and her con - fi - dence a - lone.
Three a - dor - ing in glad hymns e - ter - nal - ly.
ben - e - dic - tion shed with - in its walls al - way.
in thy glo - ry ev - er - more with thee to reign.

THE PEOPLE OF GOD

263

Our Father, by Whose Servants

G. W. Briggs, 1920

NYLAND   76 76 D
Suomen Evankelis Luterilaisen Kirken Koraalikirja, 1909
harm. David Evans, 1927

1 Our   Fa - ther, by   whose ser - vants our house was built of
2 The change-ful years un - rest - ing their si - lent course have
3 They   reap not where they   la - bored; we   reap what they have
4 Be - fore us and be - side   us, still hold - en   in thine

old,   whose hand hath crowned her   chil - dren with
sped,   new com - rades ev - er   bring - ing in
sown;   our har - vest may be   gar - nered by
hand   a   cloud un - seen of   wit - ness, our

bless - ings man - i - fold,   for   thine un - fail - ing
com - rades' steps to   tread: and some are long for -
a - ges yet un - known. The days of   old   have
el - der com - rades stand: one fam - i - ly   un -

mer - cies far - strewn a - long our way,   with
got - ten, long   spent their hopes and fears;   safe
dowered us with gifts be - yond all praise: our
bro - ken, we   join, with one ac - claim,   one

THE PEOPLE OF GOD

all who passed be - fore us, we praise thy name to - day.
rest they in thy keep - ing, who chang - est not with years.
Fa - ther make us faith - ful to serve the com-ing days.
heart, one voice up - lift - ing, to glo - ri - fy thy name.

Spread, O Spread, Thou Mighty Word   264

Walte, walte nah und fern
Jonathan Friedrich Bahnmaier, 1827
trans. Arthur W. Farlander and
Charles Winfred Douglas, 1938, alt.

GOTT SEI DANK   77 77
Geistreiches Gesang-Buch, 1704
adapt. Johann Stötzel, 1744

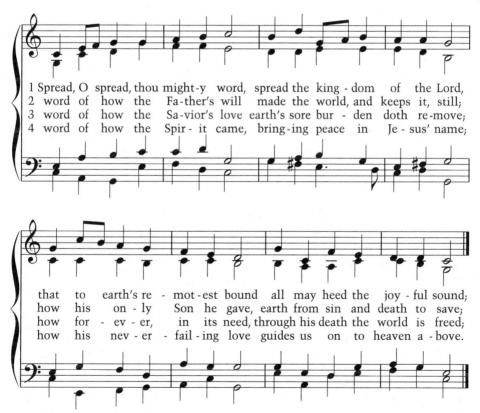

1 Spread, O spread, thou might-y word, spread the king - dom of the Lord,
2 word of how the Fa-ther's will made the world, and keeps it, still;
3 word of how the Sa-vior's love earth's sore bur - den doth re-move;
4 word of how the Spir - it came, bring-ing peace in Je - sus' name;

that to earth's re - mot-est bound all may heed the joy - ful sound;
how his on - ly Son he gave, earth from sin and death to save;
how for - ev - er, in its need, through his death the world is freed;
how his nev - er - fail-ing love guides us on to heaven a - bove.

THE PEOPLE OF GOD

We Come unto Our People's God

Thomas Hornblower Gill, 1868, alt.

NUN FREUT EUCH 87 87 887
Geistliche Lieder, Wittenberg, 1529

1 We come un-to our peo-ple's God; their rock is our sal-
2 Their joy un-to their Lord we bring; their song to us de-
3 Ye saints to come, take up the strain, the same sweet theme en-

va-tion; the e-ter-nal arms, their dear a-bode, we make our hab-i-
scend-eth; the Spir-it who in them did sing to us sweet mu-sic
deav-or; un-bro-ken be the gold-en chain! Keep on the song for-

ta-tion. We bring thee, Lord, the praise they brought, we
lend-eth: the song in them, in us, is one; we
ev-er! Safe in the same dear dwell-ing place, rich

seek thee as thy saints have sought in ev-ery gen-er-a-tion.
raise it high, we send it on, the song that nev-er end-eth.
with the same e-ter-nal grace, bless the same bound-less giv-er.

THE PEOPLE OF GOD

Rejoice, Ye Pure in Heart

266

Edward H. Plumptre, 1865

MARION   SM with Refrain
Arthur H. Messiter, 1883

1 Re - joice, ye   pure in heart!   Re - joice, give thanks, and sing!   Your
2 With   all   the   an - gel choirs,   with   all   the saints of   earth, pour
3 Your clear ho - san - nas raise,   and   al - le - lu - ias   loud; while
4 Yes,   on through life's long path,   still chant - ing   as   ye   go,   from
5 Still   lift   your stand - ard high,   still march in firm ar - ray,   as

glo - rious ban - ner   wave   on   high, the   cross of Christ your
out   the   strains of   joy   and bliss, true   rap - ture, no - blest
an - swering ech - oes   up - ward float, like wreaths of in - cense -
youth to   age,   by   night and   day,   in   glad - ness and   in
war - riors through the dark - ness toil, till dawns the gold - en

King.
mirth.
cloud.   Re - joice,   re - joice,   re - joice, give thanks and sing.
woe.
day.

re - joice,   re - joice,

6 At last the march shall end,
   the wearied ones shall rest;
   the pilgrims find their Father's house,
   Jerusalem the blest.
   Refrain

7 Then on, ye pure in heart!
   Rejoice, give thanks, and sing!
   Your glorious banner wave on high,
   the cross of Christ your King.
   Refrain

THE PEOPLE OF GOD

267   O Word of God Incarnate

William Walsham How, 1867

MUNICH 76 76 D
Neu-vermehrtes Gesangbuch, 1693
adapt. Felix Mendelssohn, 1847, alt.

1 O Word of God in-car-nate, O Wis-dom from on
2 The Church from her dear mas-ter re-ceived the gift di-
3 It float-eth like a ban-ner be-fore God's host un-
4 O make thy church, dear Sav-ior, a lamp of bur-nished

high, O Truth un-changed, un-chang-ing, O Light of our dark
vine, and still that light she lift-eth o'er all the earth to
furled; it shin-eth like a bea-con a-bove the dark-ling
gold, to bear a-mong the na-tions thy true light as of

sky, we praise thee for the ra-diance that from the hal-lowed
shine. It is the gol-den cas-ket where gems of truth are
world; it is the chart and com-pass that o'er life's surg-ing
old! O teach thy wan-dering pil-grims by this their path to

page, a lan-tern to our foot-steps, shines on from age to age.
stored; it is the heaven-drawn pic-ture of Christ, the liv-ing Word.
sea, 'mid mists, and rocks, and quick-sands still guides, O Christ, to thee.
trace, till, clouds and dark-ness end-ed, they see thee face to face.

THE PEOPLE OF GOD

Break Thou the Bread of Life

Mary A. Lathbury, 1877

BREAD OF LIFE   64 64 D
William F. Sherwin, 1877

1 Break thou the bread of life, dear Lord, to me,
2 Bless thou the truth, dear Lord, to me, to me,
3 Teach me to live, dear Lord, on - ly for thee,

as thou didst break the loaves be - side the sea;
as thou didst bless the bread by Gal - i - lee;
as thy dis - ci - ples lived in Gal - i - lee;

be - yond the sa - cred page I seek thee, Lord;
then shall all bond -age cease, all fet - ters fall,
then, all my strug-gles o'er, then, vic -tory won,

my spir - it pants for thee, O liv - ing Word!
and I shall find my peace, my all in all.
I shall be - hold thee, Lord, the liv - ing one.

THE PEOPLE OF GOD

269   O Zion, Haste, Thy Mission High Fulfilling

Mary Ann Thomson, 1868, alt.

TIDINGS   11 10 11 10 with Refrain
James Walch, 1875

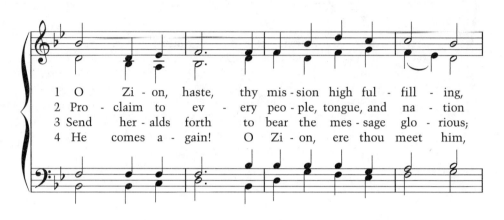

1 O   Zi - on, haste,   thy mis - sion high ful - fill - ing,
2 Pro - claim to   ev - ery peo - ple, tongue, and   na - tion
3 Send   her - alds forth   to bear the mes - sage glo - rious;
4 He   comes a - gain!   O   Zi - on, ere thou meet   him,

    to   tell   to   all   the   world that God   is   light;
    that   God, in   whom   they   live   and move, is   love;
    give   of   thy wealth   to   speed them on their   way;
    make   known to   ev - ery   heart   his   sav - ing   grace;

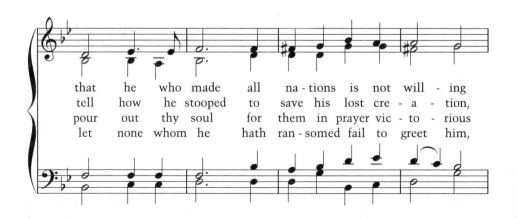

    that   he   who made   all   na - tions is   not will - ing
    tell   how   he stooped   to   save his   lost cre - a - tion,
    pour   out   thy soul   for   them in prayer vic - to - rious
    let   none whom he   hath ran - somed fail to   greet   him,

THE PEOPLE OF GOD

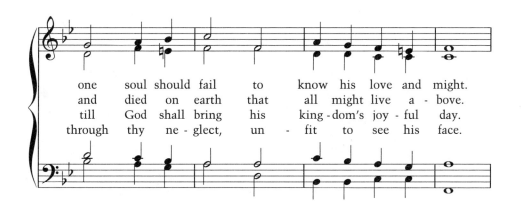

one soul should fail to know his love and might.
and died on earth that all might live a - bove.
till God shall bring his king - dom's joy - ful day.
through thy ne - glect, un - fit to see his face.

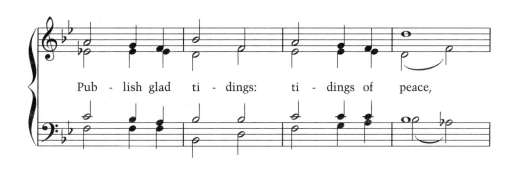

Pub - lish glad ti - dings: ti - dings of peace,

ti - dings of Je - sus, re - demp - tion, and re - lease.

270   Christ Is the King! O Friends Upraise

George Kennedy Allen Bell, 1933, alt.

CHRISTUS REX   888 888
David McKinley Williams, 1941

1 Christ is the King! O friends up-raise an-thems of
2 O Chris-tian wo - men, Chris-tian men, all the world
3 Let Love's un-con - quer - a - ble might your scat-tered

joy and ho - ly praise for his brave saints of an-cient days,
o - ver, seek a - gain the way dis - ci - ples fol-lowed then.
com - pa-nies u - nite in ser - vice to the Lord of light:

who with a faith for-ev - er new fol - lowed the King, and
Christ through all a - ges is the same: place the same hope in
so shall God's will on earth be done, new lamps be lit, new

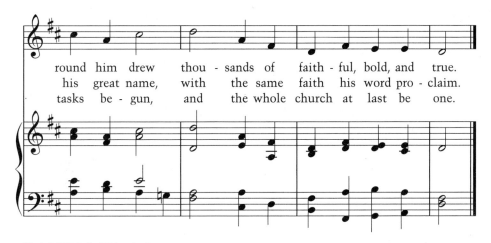

round him drew thou - sands of faith - ful, bold, and true.
his great name, with the same faith his word pro - claim.
tasks be - gun, and the whole church at last be one.

I Love Thy Kingdom, Lord 271

Timothy Dwight, 1801, alt.

ST. THOMAS SM
Aaron Williams, 1763, rev. 1770

1 I love thy king - dom Lord, the house of thine a - bode, the
2 I love thy Church, O God; her walls be - fore thee stand, dear
3 For her my tears shall fall, for her my prayers as - cend, to
4 Be - yond my high - est joy I prize her heaven - ly ways, her
5 Sure as thy truth shall last, to Zi - on shall be given the

church our blest re - deem - er saved with his own pre - cious blood.
as the ap - ple of thine eye, and grav - en on thy hand.
her my cares and toils be given till toils and cares shall end.
sweet com - mun - ion, sol - emn vows, her hymns of love and praise.
bright - est glo - ries earth can yield, and bright - er bliss of heaven.

THE PEOPLE OF GOD

272   Lift Every Voice and Sing

James Weldon Johnson, 1899, alt.

LIFT EVERY VOICE   IRREGULAR
John Rosamond Johnson, 1899

1 Lift ev-ery voice and
2 Ston -y the road we
3 God of our wea - ry

sing till earth and hea - ven ring, ring with the har - mon - ies of
trod, bit -ter the chas -tening rod, felt in the days when hope un -
years, God of our si - lent tears, thou who hast brought us thus far

lib - er - ty. Let our re - joic - ing rise high as the lis - tening
born had died; yet, with a stead - y beat, have not our wea - ry
on the way; thou who hast by thy might led us in - to the

skies; let it re - sound loud as the roll - ing sea. Sing a
feet come to the place for which our pa - rents sighed? We have
light; keep us for - ev - er in the path, we pray. Lest our

THE PEOPLE OF GOD

song full of the faith that the dark past has taught us;
come o-ver a way that with tears has been wa - tered;
feet stray from the plac-es, our God, where we met thee;

sing a song full of the hope that the pres-ent has brought
we have come, tread-ing our path through the blood of the slaugh -
lest, our hearts drunk with the wine of the world, we for-get

THE PEOPLE OF GOD

us; fac-ing the ris - ing sun of our new day be -
tered, out from the gloom - y past, till now we stand at
thee; shad-owed be-neath thy hand may we for - ev - er

gun, let us march on, till vic-to - ry is won.
last where the white gleam of our bright star is cast.
stand, true to our God, true to our na - tive land.

THE PEOPLE OF GOD

273   # Thou, Whose Almighty Word

John Marriott, c. 1813, alt.

MOSCOW   664 6664
Felice de Giardini, 1769

1 Thou, whose al - might - y word cha - os and dark - ness heard,
2 Thou, who didst come to bring, on thy re - deem - ing wing,
3 Spir - it of truth and love, life - giv - ing, ho - ly Dove,

and took their flight; hear us, we hum - bly pray, and where the
heal - ing and sight, health to the sick in mind, sight to the
speed forth thy flight; move on the wa - ters' face, bear - ing the

gos - pel's day sheds not its glo - rious ray let there be light!
in - ly blind; now to all hu - man-kind let there be light!
lamp of grace, and in earth's dark - est place let there be light!

This music in G, 253.

THE PEOPLE OF GOD

Thou Lord of Hosts, Whose Guiding Hand   274

Octavius Brooks Frothingham, 1846

ERHALT UNS, HERR   LM
Geistliche Lieder, Wittenberg, 1543
harm. Johann Sebastian Bach (1685–1750)

1 Thou Lord of hosts, whose guid - ing hand has
2 These spir - its lay their no - blest powers as
3 Send us wher - e'er thou wilt, O Lord, through
4 Send down thy con - stant aid, we pray; be

brought us here be - fore thy face, our spir - its wait for
of - ferings on thy ho - ly shrine; thine was the strength that
rug - ged toil and wea - rying fight; thy con - qu'ring love shall
thy pure an - gels with us still; thy truth, be that our

thy com - mand, our si - lent hearts im - plore thy peace.
nour - ished ours, the sol - diers of the cross are thine.
be our sword, and faith in thee our tru - est might.
firm - est stay, our on - ly rest to do thy will.

THE PEOPLE OF GOD

We Limit Not the Truth of God

John Robinson, 1620
adapt. George Rawson, 1853, alt.

OLD 137TH   CMD
Anglo-Genevan Psalter, 1556

1 We lim-it not the truth of God to our poor reach of
2 Who dares to bind to our dull sense the or-a-cles of
3 O Tri-ni-ty most ho-ly, send us in-crease from a-

mind, to no-tions of our time and place, crude, par-tial, and con-
heaven, for all the na-tions, tongues, and climes and all the a - ges
bove; en-large, ex-pand all liv-ing souls to com-pre-hend your

fined; no, let a new and bet-ter hope with-in our hearts be
given? The u-ni-verse, how much un-known! The o-cean un-ex-
love; and make us all go on to know, with no-bler powers con-

stirred;
plored! The Lord has yet more light and truth to break forth from his word.
ferred:

THE PEOPLE OF GOD

Go Forth for God

276

J. R. Peacey, 1970
adapt. New English Hymnal, 1986, alt.

MAGDA 11 10 10 10
Ralph Vaughan Williams, 1925

1 Go forth for God; go forth to the world in peace;
2 Go forth for God; go forth to the world in strength;
3 Go forth for God; go forth to the world in love;
4 Go forth for God; go forth to the world in joy,

be of good cour - age, armed with heaven - ly grace,
hold fast the good, be ur - gent for the right,
strength -en the faint, give cour - age to the weak,
to serve God's peo - ple ev - ery day and hour,

in God's good Spir - it dai - ly to in - crease, till
ren - der to no - one e - vil; Christ at length shall
help the af - flict - ed; rich - ly from a - bove his
and serv -ing Christ, his ev - ery gift em - ploy, re -

in the king - dom we be - hold God's face.
o - ver - come all dark - ness with true light.
love sup - plies the grace and power we seek.
joic - ing in the Ho - ly Spir - it's power.

THE PEOPLE OF GOD

277 All My Hope on God Is Founded

Meine Hoffnung stehet feste
Joachim Neander (1650–1680)
trans. Robert Seymour Bridges, 1899, alt.

MICHAEL   87 87 337
Herbert Howells, c. 1930

1 All my hope on God is found - ed; he doth still my
2 Mor - tal pride and earth - ly glo - ry, sword and crown be -
3 God's great good - ness aye en - dur - eth, deep his wis - dom,
4 Dai - ly doth the al - migh - ty giv - er boun - teous gifts on
5 Still from earth to God e - ter - nal sac - ri - fice of

trust re - new. Me through change and chance he guid - eth, on - ly
tray his trust; what with care and toil we build them, tower and
pass - ing thought: splen - dor, light, and life at - tend him, beau - ty
us be - stow; his de - sire our soul de - light - eth, plea - sure
praise be done, high a - bove all prais - es prais - ing for the

good and on - ly true. God un - known, he a -
tem - ple fall to dust. But God's power, hour by
spring - eth out of naught. Ev - er - more from his
leads us where we go. Love doth stand at his
gift of Christ his Son. Christ doth call one and

THE CHRISTIAN LIFE

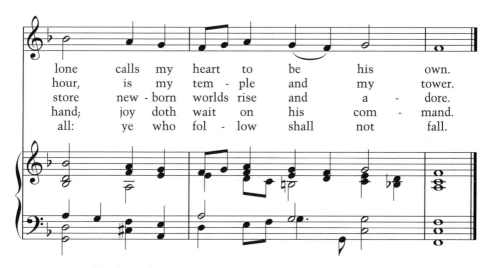

lone calls my heart to be his own.
hour, is my tem-ple and my tower.
store new-born worlds rise and a - dore.
hand; joy doth wait on his com - mand.
all: ye who fol-low shall not fall.

God Is My Strong Salvation   278

para. of Psalm 27   CHRISTUS, DER IST MEIN LEBEN   76 76
James Montgomery, 1822   Melchior Vulpius, 1609

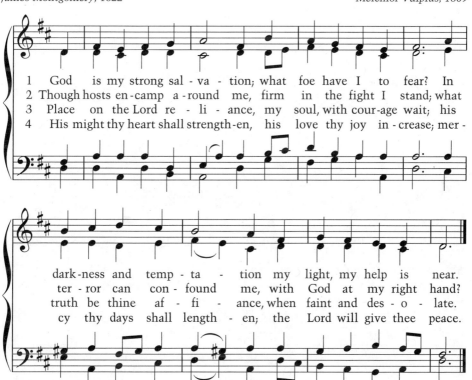

1 God is my strong sal - va - tion; what foe have I to fear? In
2 Though hosts en-camp a -round me, firm in the fight I stand; what
3 Place on the Lord re - li - ance, my soul, with cour-age wait; his
4 His might thy heart shall strength-en, his love thy joy in - crease; mer -

dark-ness and temp - ta - tion my light, my help is near.
ter - ror can con - found me, with God at my right hand?
truth be thine af - fi - ance, when faint and des - o - late.
cy thy days shall length - en; the Lord will give thee peace.

Another harmonization, 330.

279   **Awake, My Soul, Stretch Every Nerve**

Philip Doddridge (1702–1751), alt.

CHRISTMAS CM
George Frideric Handel, 1728
adapt. Melodia sacra, 1815

1 A - wake, my soul, stretch ev - ery nerve, and press with vig - or
2 A cloud of wit - ness - es a - round hold thee in full sur -
3 'Tis God's all - an - i - mat - ing voice that calls thee from on
4 Blest Sav - ior, in - tro - duced by thee, have I my race be -

on; a heaven - ly race de - mands thy zeal, and
vey; for - get the steps al - read - y trod, and
high; 'tis God's own hand pre - sents the prize to
gun; and crowned with vic - tory, at thy feet I'll

an im - mor - tal crown, and an im - mor - tal crown.
on - ward urge thy way, and on - ward urge thy way.
thine as - pir - ing eye, to thine as - pir - ing eye.
lay my hon - ors down, I'll lay my hon - ors down.

THE CHRISTIAN LIFE

O God, Thou Faithful God

O Gott, du frommer Gott
Johann Heermann, 1630
trans. Catherine Winkworth, 1858, alt.

O GOTT, DU FROMMER GOTT 67 67 66 66
Himmels-Lust, 1679
harm. Johann Sebastian Bach, 1726

1 O God, thou faith-ful God, thou foun-tain ev-er flow-ing, with
2 And grant me, Lord, to do, with read-y heart and will-ing, what
3 If dan-gers gath-er round, still keep me calm and fear-less; help

out whom noth-ing is, all per-fect gifts be-stow-ing. Grant
e'er thou shalt com-mand, my call-ing here ful-fill-ing; and
me to bear the cross when life is dark and cheer-less, to

me a health-y frame, and give me, Lord, with-in, a
do it when I ought, with zeal and joy-ful-ness; and
o-ver-come my foe with words and ac-tions kind; when

con-science free from blame, a soul un-hurt by sin.
bless the work I've wrought, for thou must give suc-cess.
coun-sel I would know, good coun-sel let me find.

THE CHRISTIAN LIFE

281 A Mighty Fortress Is Our God

Ein' feste Burg ist unser Gott
Martin Luther, 1528
trans. Frederic H. Hedge, 1852

EIN' FESTE BURG   87 87 66 66 7
Martin Luther, 1529

1 A might-y for-tress is our God, a bul-wark nev-er
2 Did we in our own strength con-fide, our striv-ing would be
3 And though this world, with dev-ils filled, should threat-en to un-
4 That word a-bove all earth-ly power, no thanks to them, a-

fail - ing; our help-er he a - mid the flood of
los - ing, were not the right man on our side, the
do us, we will not fear, for God hath willed his
bid - eth; the Spir-it and the gifts are ours through

mor-tal ills pre-vail - ing. For still our an - cient
man of God's own choos - ing. Dost ask who that may
truth to tri-umph through us. The prince of dark - ness
him who with us sid - eth. Let goods and kin - dred

foe doth seek to work us woe; his
be? Christ Je - sus, it is he; Lord
grim, we trem - ble not for him; his
go, this mor - tal life al - so; the

craft and power are great, and armed with cru - el
Sab - a - oth his name, from age to age the
rage we can en - dure, for lo, his doom is
bod - y they may kill; God's truth a - bid - eth

hate, on earth is not his e - qual.
same, and he must win the bat - tle.
sure: one lit - tle word shall fell him.
still, his king - dom is for - ev - er.

THE CHRISTIAN LIFE

How Firm a Foundation

Selection of Hymns, 1787, alt.

FOUNDATION 11 11 11 11
Genuine Church Music, 1832
harm. The Wesleyan Hymn and Tune Book, 1859

1 How firm a foun-da-tion, ye saints of the Lord, is
2 "Fear not, I am with thee, O, be not dis-mayed, for
3 "When through the deep wa-ters I call thee to go, the
4 "When through fi-er-y tri-als thy path-ways shall lie, my
5 The soul that on Je-sus has leaned for re-pose, I

laid for your faith in his ex-cel-lent word! What
I am thy God, and will still give thee aid. I'll
riv-ers of sor-row shall not thee o'er-flow; for
grace, all-suf-fi-cient, shall be thy sup-ply; the
will not, I will not de-sert to its foes; that

more can he say than to you he hath said, to
strength-en thee, help thee, and cause thee to stand, up-
I will be near thee, thy trou-bles to bless, and
flame shall not hurt thee; I on-ly de-sign thy
soul, though all hell should en-deav-or to shake, I'll

you who for ref-uge to Je-sus have fled?
held by my right-eous, om-nip-o-tent hand.
sanc-ti-fy to thee thy deep-est dis-tress.
dross to con-sume, and thy gold to re-fine.
nev-er, no, nev-er, no, nev-er for-sake."

THE CHRISTIAN LIFE

Through All the Changing Scenes of Life 283

para. of Psalm 34
A New Version of the Psalms, 1698

WILTSHIRE   CM
George Thomas Smart, 1795

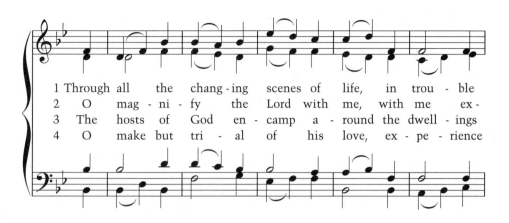

1 Through all   the   chang-ing scenes of   life,   in trou-ble
2 O   mag - ni - fy   the   Lord with   me,   with me   ex -
3 The hosts of   God   en - camp   a - round the dwell - ings
4 O   make but   tri - al   of   his   love,   ex - pe - rience

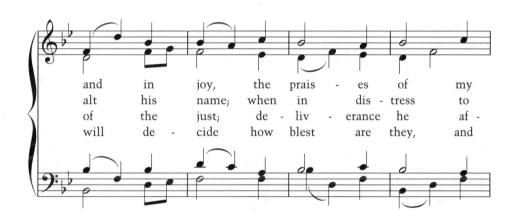

and   in   joy,   the   prais - es   of   my
alt   his   name; when in   dis - tress   to
of   the   just; de - liv - erance he   af -
will   de - cide how blest   are they,   and

God   shall still my   heart and   tongue em - ploy.
him   I   called, he   to   my   res - cue came.
fords to   all   who on   his   suc - cor trust.
on - ly   they, who in   his   truth con - fide.

THE CHRISTIAN LIFE

284   Out of the Depths I Cry to Thee

Aus tiefer Not schrei ich zu dir
Martin Luther, 1524
trans. Catherine Winkworth, 1863, alt.

AUS TIEFER NOT   87 87 887
attrib. Martin Luther, 1524
harm. Johann Sebastian Bach, 1724

1 Out of the depths I cry to thee, Lord,
2 Our par-don is thy gift, thy love and
3 And though it tar-ry till the night, and
4 Though great our sins and sore our woes, God's

hear me, I im-plore thee! Bend down thy
grace a-lone a-vail us; our works could
round till morn-ing wak-en, my heart shall
grace much more a-bound-eth; whose help-ing

gra-cious ear to me, let my prayer come be-
ne'er our guilt re-move, the strict-est life must
ne'er mis-trust his might, nor count it-self for-
love no lim-it knows, our ut-most need it

THE CHRISTIAN LIFE

fore thee! If thou re - mem - berest each mis -
fail us, That none may boast him - self of
sak - en. Do thus, O ye of Is - rael's
sound - eth; Our kind and faith - ful shep - herd,

deed, if each should have its right - ful meed,
aught, but own in fear thy grace hath wrought
seed, ye of the Spir - it born in - deed,
he, who shall at last set Is - rael free

who may a - bide thy pres - ence?
what in him seem - eth right - eous.
wait for our God's ap - pear - ing.
from all their sin and sor - row.

THE CHRISTIAN LIFE

285 Guide Me, O Thou Great Jehovah

Arglwydd, arwain trwy'r anialwch
William Williams, 1745
stanza 1: trans. Peter Williams, 1771
stanzas 2-3: trans. William Williams, c. 1774

CWM RHONDDA   87 87 87
John Hughes, 1905

1 Guide me, O thou great Je - ho - vah, pil - grim through this bar - ren land;
2 O - pen now the crys - tal foun - tain, whence the heal - ing stream doth flow;
3 When I tread the verge of Jor - dan, bid my anx - ious fears sub - side;

I am weak, but thou art might - y, hold me with thy power - ful hand;
let the fire and cloud - y pil - lar lead me all my jour - ney through;
death of death, and hell's de - struc - tion, land me safe on Ca - naan's side;

bread of heav - en, bread of heav - en, feed me till I want no
strong De - liv - erer, strong De - liv - erer, be thou still my strength and
songs of prais - es, songs of prais - es, I will ev - er give to

more, (want no more,) feed me till I want no more.
shield, (strength and shield,) be thou still my strength and shield.
thee, (give to thee,) I will ev - er give to thee.

THE CHRISTIAN LIFE

Dear Lord and Father of Mankind

John Greenleaf Whittier, 1872, alt.

REST 86 886
Frederick C. Maker, 1887

1 Dear Lord and Fa - ther of man - kind, for - give our fool - ish
2 In sim - ple trust like theirs who heard, be - side the Syr - ian
3 O Sab - bath rest by Gal - i - lee! O calm of hills a -
4 Drop thy still dews of qui - et - ness, till all our striv - ings
5 Breathe through the heats of our de - sire thy cool - ness and thy

ways! Re - clothe us in our right - ful mind, in
sea, the gra - cious call - ing of the Lord, let
bove, where Je - sus knelt to share with thee the
cease: take from our souls the strain and stress, and
balm; let sense be dumb, let flesh re - tire; speak

pur - er lives thy serv - ice find, in deep - er rev - erence, praise.
us, like them, with - out a word, rise up and fol - low thee.
si - lence of e - ter - ni - ty, in - ter - pret - ed by love!
let our or - dered lives con - fess the beau - ty of thy peace.
through the earth - quake, wind, and fire, O still, small voice of calm.

Alternative tune (REPTON), 287.

THE CHRISTIAN LIFE

Dear Lord and Father of Mankind

John Greenleaf Whittier, 1872, alt.

REPTON 86 886
Charles Hubert Hastings Parry, 1888, alt.

1 Dear Lord and Fa-ther of man-kind, for-give our fool-ish
2 In sim-ple trust like theirs who heard, be-side the Sy-rian
3 O Sab-bath rest by Gal-i-lee! O calm of hills a-
4 Drop thy still dews of qui-et-ness, till all our striv-ings
5 Breathe through the heats of our de-sire thy cool-ness and thy

ways! Re-clothe us in our right-ful mind, in
sea, the gra-cious call-ing of the Lord, let
bove, where Je-sus knelt to share with thee the
cease: take from our souls the strain and stress, and
balm; let sense be dumb, let flesh re-tire; speak

pur-er lives thy ser-vice find, in deep-er rev-erence,
us, like them, with-out a word, rise up and fol-low
si-lence of e-ter-ni-ty, in-ter-pret-ed by
let our or-dered lives con-fess the beau-ty of thy
through the earth-quake, wind, and fire, O still, small voice of

Alternative tune (REST), 286.

THE CHRISTIAN LIFE

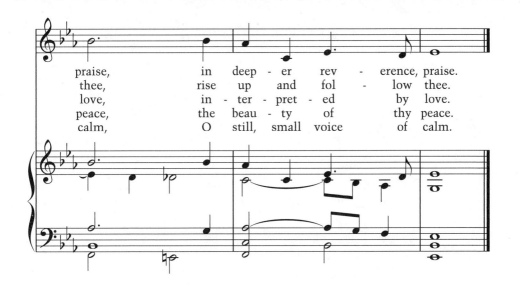

praise,   in deep - er rev - erence, praise.
thee,   rise up and fol - low thee.
love,   in - ter - pret - ed by love.
peace,   the beau - ty of thy peace.
calm,   O still, small voice of calm.

Forgive Our Sins as We Forgive   288

Rosamond E. Herklots, 1969, rev. 1983

DETROIT CM
Supplement to Kentucky Harmony, 1820
harm. Margaret W. Mealy, 1985

1 "For - give our sins as we for - give," you taught us, Lord, to pray, but
2 How can your par - don reach and bless the un - for - giv - ing heart that
3 In blaz - ing light your cross re - veals the truth we dim - ly knew: what
4 Lord, cleanse the depths with - in our souls and bid re - sent - ment cease. Then,

you a - lone can grant us grace to live the words we say.
broods on wrongs and will not let old bit - ter - ness de - part?
triv - ial debts are owed to us, how great our debt to you!
bound to all in bonds of love, our lives will spread your peace.

THE CHRISTIAN LIFE

289   Lead On, O King Eternal

Ernest W. Shurtleff, 1888

LANCASHIRE   76 76 D
Henry Thomas Smart, 1836

1 Lead on, O King e-ter-nal, the day of march has come; hence-
2 Lead on, O King e-ter-nal, till sin's fierce war shall cease, and
3 Lead on, O King e-ter-nal, we fol-low, not with fears, for

forth in fields of con-quest thy tents shall be our home. Through
ho-li-ness shall whis-per the sweet A-men of peace. For
glad-ness breaks like morn-ing wher-e'er thy face ap-pears. Thy

days of pre-pa-ra-tion thy grace has made us strong, and
not with swords loud clash-ing, nor roll of stir-ring drums, but
cross is lift-ed o'er us; we jour-ney in its light; the

now, O King e-ter-nal, we lift our bat-tle song.
deeds of love and mer-cy, the heaven-ly king-dom comes.
crown a-waits the con-quest; lead on, O God of might.

THE CHRISTIAN LIFE

Call Jehovah Thy Salvation

para. of Psalm 91
James Montgomery, 1822

TRUST 87 87
Felix Mendelssohn, 1840

1 Call Jehovah thy Salvation,
2 there no tumult shall alarm thee,
3 From the sword at noonday wasting,
4 he shall charge his angel legions

rest beneath the Almighty's shade, in his secret
thou shalt dread no hidden snare; guile nor vio-
from the noisome pestilence, in the depth of
watch and ward o'er thee to keep; though thou walk through

habitation dwell, and never be dismayed:
lence can harm thee, in eternal safeguard there.
midnight blasting, God shall be thy sure defense:
hostile regions, though in desert wilds thou sleep.

5   Since, with pure and firm affection,
    thou on God hast set thy love,
    with the wings of his protection
    he will shield thee from above:

6   thou shalt call on him in trouble,
    he will harken, he will save;
    here for grief reward thee double,
    crown with life beyond the grave.

THE CHRISTIAN LIFE

291   Be Thou My Vision, O Lord of My Heart

Rob tu mo bhoile, a Comedi cride
Irish, 8th cent.?
trans. Mary Byrne, 1905
adapt. Eleanor Hull, 1912, alt.

SLANE   10 10 9 10
Irish melody
harm. Harvard University Hymn Book, 1964

1 Be thou my vi - sion, O Lord of my heart;
2 Be thou my wis - dom, be thou my true word;
3 Be thou my buck - ler, my sword for the fight;
4 Rich - es I heed not, nor earth's emp - ty praise;
5 High King of heav - en, when vic - tory is won

naught be all else to me save that thou art—
I ev - er with thee, and thou with me, Lord;
be thou my dig - ni - ty, thou my de - light,
Thou mine in - her - it - ance, now and al - ways:
may I reach heav - en's joys, O bright heaven's Sun!

thou my best thought, by day or by night,
thou my great Fa - ther; thine own may I be;
thou my soul's shel - ter, thou my high tower;
thou and thou on - ly, first in my heart,
Heart of my heart, what - ev - er be - fall,

THE CHRISTIAN LIFE

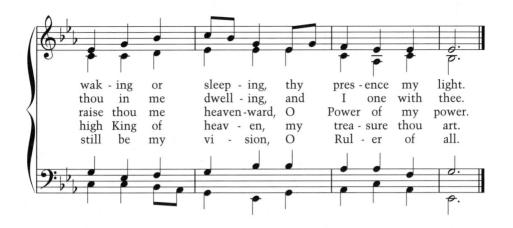

wak - ing   or   sleep - ing,   thy   pres - ence   my   light.
thou   in   me   dwell - ing,   and   I   one   with   thee.
raise thou   me   heaven-ward,   O   Power   of   my   power.
high   King   of   heav - en,   my   trea - sure   thou   art.
still   be   my   vi - sion,   O   Rul - er   of   all.

O for a Closer Walk with God   292

William Cowper, 1769

CAITHNESS   CM
Scottish Psalter, 1635

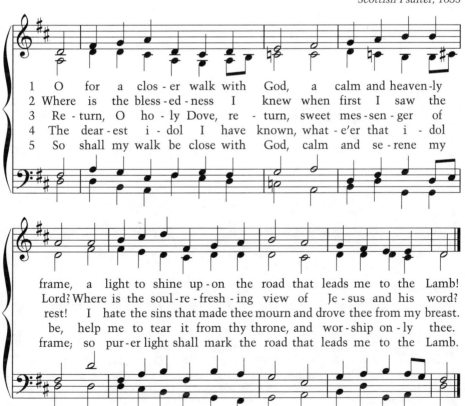

1 O   for   a   clos - er   walk with   God,   a   calm and heaven-ly
2 Where   is   the   bless - ed - ness   I   knew when first I   saw the
3 Re - turn,   O   ho - ly   Dove,   re - turn,   sweet mes - sen - ger   of
4 The   dear - est   i - dol   I   have   known, what - e'er that i - dol
5 So   shall my walk be close with   God,   calm   and se - rene   my

frame,   a   light to shine up-on   the   road that leads me to the Lamb!
Lord? Where is   the soul - re - fresh - ing view of   Je - sus and his   word?
rest!   I   hate the sins that made thee mourn and drove thee from my breast.
be,   help me to tear it   from thy throne, and wor - ship on - ly   thee.
frame; so pur - er light shall mark the road that leads me to the Lamb.

293   **Spirit of God, Descend upon My Heart**

George Croly, 1854

MORECOMBE   10 10 10 10
Frederick C. Atkinson, 1870

1 Spirit of God, descend upon my heart;
wean it from earth; through all its puls - es move;
stoop to my weak - ness might - y as thou art,
and make me love thee as I ought to love.

2 I ask no dream, no proph - et ec - sta - sies,
no sud - den rend - ing of the veil of clay,
no an - gel vis - it - ant, no o - pening skies;
but take the dim - ness of my soul a - way.

3 Hast thou not bid me love thee, God and King?
All, all thine own— soul, heart, and strength, and mind.
I see thy cross— there teach my heart to cling;
O let me seek thee, and O let me find!

4 Teach me to feel that thou art al - ways nigh;
teach me the strug - gles of the soul to bear,
to check the ris - ing doubt, the reb - el sigh;
teach me the pa - tience of un - an - swered prayer.

5 Teach me to love thee as thine an - gels love,
one ho - ly pas - sion fill - ing all my frame;
the kind - ling of the heaven - de - scend - ed Dove,
my heart an al - tar, and thy love the flame.

THE CHRISTIAN LIFE

How Sweet the Name of Jesus Sounds

John Newton, 1779, alt.

STRACATHRO CM
Charles Hutcheson, 1832

1 How sweet the name of Je - sus sounds in a be -
2 It makes the woun - ded spir - it whole, and calms the
3 Dear name! the rock on which I build, my shield and
4 Je - sus! my shep - herd, broth - er, friend, my proph - et,

liev - er's ear! It soothes all sor - rows,
trou - bled breast; 'tis man - na to the
hid - ing - place, my nev - er - fail - ing
priest, and King, my Lord, my life, my

heals all wounds, and drives a - way all fear.
hun - gry soul, and to the wear - y rest.
treas - ury filled with bound - less stores of grace.
way, my end, ac - cept the praise I bring.

5 Weak is the effort of my heart,
and cold my warmest thought;
but when I see thee as thou art,
I'll praise thee as I ought.

6 Till then I would thy love proclaim
with every fleeting breath;
and may the music of thy name
refresh my soul in death.

THE CHRISTIAN LIFE

295   O God of Bethel, by Whose Hand

Philip Doddridge, 1737
adapt. John Logan, 1781, alt.

DUNDEE CM
Scottish Psalter, 1615
harm. Thomas Ravenscroft, 1621, alt.

1   O God of Beth-el, by whose hand thy peo-ple still are fed, who
2   our vows, our prayers, we now pre-sent be-fore thy throne of grace; O
3 Through each per-plex-ing path of life our wan-dering foot-steps guide; give
4   O, spread thy cov-ering wings a-round till all our wan-derings cease, and

through this earth-ly pil-grim-age hast all thine Is-rael led,
God of Is-rael, be the God of this suc-ceed-ing race.
us each day our dai-ly bread, and rai-ment fit pro-vide.
at our Fa-ther's loved a-bode our souls ar-rive in peace.

This music in E♭, 200.

296   Put Thou Thy Trust in God

Befiehl du deine Wege
Paul Gerhardt, 1653
trans. John Wesley, 1739
adapt. Psalms and Hymns, 1836

AYLESBURY SM
Book of Psalmody, 1718
adapt. Psalm Tunes, 1724

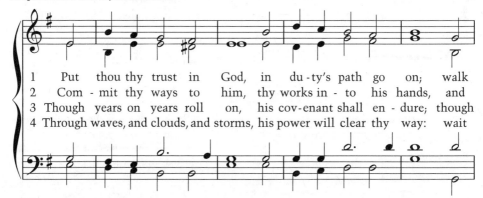

1   Put thou thy trust in God, in du-ty's path go on; walk
2   Com-mit thy ways to him, thy works in-to his hands, and
3 Though years on years roll on, his cov-enant shall en-dure; though
4 Through waves, and clouds, and storms, his power will clear thy way: wait

THE CHRISTIAN LIFE

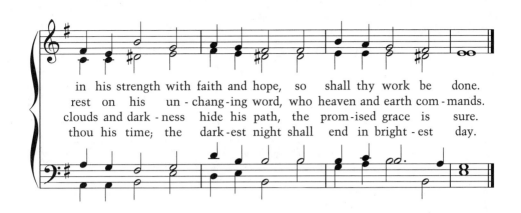

in his strength with faith and hope, so shall thy work be done.
rest on his un-chang-ing word, who heaven and earth com-mands.
clouds and dark-ness hide his path, the prom-ised grace is sure.
thou his time; the dark-est night shall end in bright-est day.

Prayer Is the Soul's Sincere Desire 297

James Montgomery, 1818, alt.

BEATITUDO CM
John Bacchus Dykes, 1875

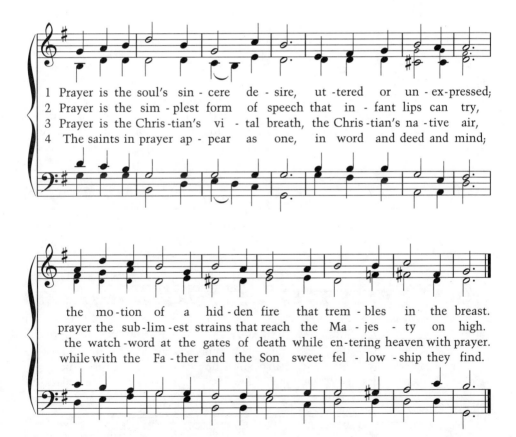

1 Prayer is the soul's sin-cere de-sire, ut-tered or un-ex-pressed;
2 Prayer is the sim-plest form of speech that in-fant lips can try,
3 Prayer is the Chris-tian's vi-tal breath, the Chris-tian's na-tive air,
4 The saints in prayer ap-pear as one, in word and deed and mind;

the mo-tion of a hid-den fire that trem-bles in the breast.
prayer the sub-lim-est strains that reach the Ma-jes-ty on high.
the watch-word at the gates of death while en-tering heaven with prayer.
while with the Fa-ther and the Son sweet fel-low-ship they find.

5 Nor prayer is made on earth alone:
the Holy Spirit pleads,
and Jesus on the eternal throne
for sinners intercedes.

6 O Thou by whom we come to God,
the life, the truth, the way,
the path of prayer thyself hast trod:
Lord, teach us how to pray!

THE CHRISTIAN LIFE

298   O Thou Who Camest from Above

Charles Wesley, 1762

HEREFORD   LM
Samuel Sebastian Wesley, 1872

1 O thou who cam - est from a - bove the fire ce -
2 There let it for thy glo - ry burn with in - ex -
3 Je - sus, con - firm my heart's de - sire to work, and
4 Read - y for all thy per - fect will, my acts of

les - tial to im - part, kin - dle a flame of
tin - guish - a - ble blaze, and trem - bling to its
speak, and think for thee; still let me guard the
faith and love re - peat; till death thy end - less

sa - cred love on the mean al - tar of my heart!
source re - turn in hum - ble prayer and ferv - ent praise.
ho - ly fire, and still stir up the gift in me.
mer - cies seal, and make the sac - ri - fice com - plete.

THE CHRISTIAN LIFE

Amazing Grace! How Sweet the Sound 299

stanzas 1-4: John Newton, 1779
stanza 5: A Collection of Sacred Ballads, 1790

NEW BRITAIN CM
Columbian Harmony, 1829
adapt. Edwin Othello Excel, 1910
harm. Austin C. Lovelace, 1964

1 A - maz - ing grace! how sweet the sound that saved a
2 'Twas grace that taught my heart to fear, and grace my
3 The Lord has prom - ised good to me, his word my
4 Through man - y dan - gers, toils, and snares, I have al -
5 When we've been there ten thou - sand years, bright shin - ing

wretch like me! I once was lost but
fears re - lieved; how pre - cious did that
hope se - cures; he will my shield and
rea - dy come; 'tis grace that brought me
as the sun, we've no less days to

now am found, was blind but now I see.
grace ap - pear the hour I first be - lieved!
por - tion be as long as life en - dures.
safe thus far, and grace will lead me home.
sing God's praise than when we'd first be - gun.

THE CHRISTIAN LIFE

300   Teach Me, My God and King

George Herbert (1593–1632), alt.

ST. MICHAEL SM
Genevan Psalter, 1551
harm. William Crotch, 1836

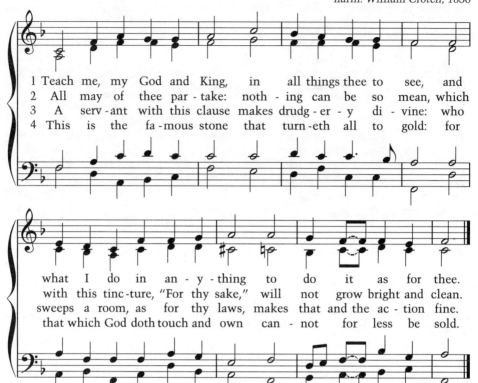

1 Teach me, my God and King, in all things thee to see, and
2 All may of thee par-take: noth-ing can be so mean, which
3 A serv-ant with this clause makes drudg-er-y di-vine: who
4 This is the fa-mous stone that turn-eth all to gold: for

what I do in an-y-thing to do it as for thee.
with this tinc-ture, "For thy sake," will not grow bright and clean.
sweeps a room, as for thy laws, makes that and the ac-tion fine.
that which God doth touch and own can-not for less be sold.

This music in G, 329.

301   Behold Us, Lord, a Little Space

John Ellerton, 1870

ABBEY CM
Scottish Psalter, 1615

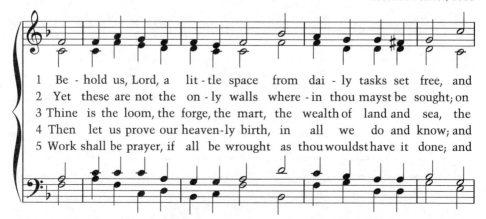

1 Be-hold us, Lord, a lit-tle space from dai-ly tasks set free, and
2 Yet these are not the on-ly walls where-in thou mayst be sought; on
3 Thine is the loom, the forge, the mart, the wealth of land and sea, the
4 Then let us prove our heaven-ly birth, in all we do and know; and
5 Work shall be prayer, if all be wrought as thou wouldst have it done; and

THE CHRISTIAN LIFE

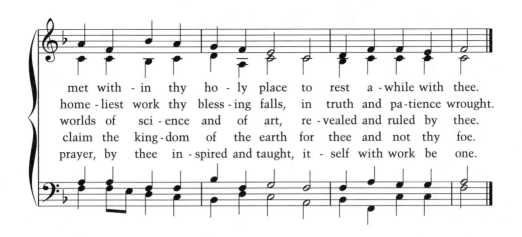

met with - in thy ho - ly place to rest a - while with thee.
home - liest work thy bless - ing falls, in truth and pa - tience wrought.
worlds of sci - ence and of art, re - vealed and ruled by thee.
claim the king - dom of the earth for thee and not thy foe.
prayer, by thee in - spired and taught, it - self with work be one.

My God, I Love Thee; Not Because 302

No me mueve, mi Dios, para quererte
Spanish, 16th cent.
trans. attrib. Francis Xavier (1506–1552)
trans. Edward Caswall, 1849

ST. FRANCIS XAVIER CM
John Stainer, 1875

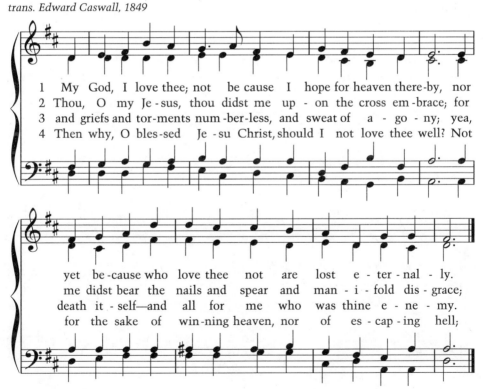

1 My God, I love thee; not be cause I hope for heaven there - by, nor
2 Thou, O my Je - sus, thou didst me up - on the cross em - brace; for
3 and griefs and tor - ments num - ber - less, and sweat of a - go - ny; yea,
4 Then why, O bles - sed Je - su Christ, should I not love thee well? Not

yet be - cause who love thee not are lost e - ter - nal - ly.
me didst bear the nails and spear and man - i - fold dis - grace;
death it - self—and all for me who was thine e - ne - my.
for the sake of win - ning heaven, nor of es - cap - ing hell;

5 not from the hope of gaining aught,
not seeking a reward;
but as thyself has lovèd me,
O ever-loving Lord.

6 So would I love thee, dearest Lord,
and in thy praise will sing;
solely because thou art my God,
and my most loving King.

303   As Pants the Hart for Cooling Streams

para. of Psalm 42
A New Version of Psalms, 1696, alt.

MARTYRDOM   CM
Hugh Wilson, 1800
adapt. Robert Smith, 1825

1 As pants the hart for cool - ing streams when
2 For thee, my God, the liv - ing God, my
3 Why rest - less, why cast down, my soul? Hope

heat - ed in the chase, so longs my soul, O
thirst - y soul doth pine. O when shall I be -
still, and thou shalt sing the praise of him who

God, for thee, and thy re - fresh - ing grace.
hold thy face, thou ma - jes - ty di - vine?
is thy God, thy health's e - ter - nal spring.

More Holiness Give Me

Philip P. Bliss, 1873

MY PRAYER 11 11 11 11
Philip P. Bliss, 1873

1 More ho-li-ness give me, more striv-ings with-in,
2 More gra-ti-tude give me, more trust in the Lord,
3 More pu-ri-ty give me, more strength to o'er-come,

more pa-tience in suf-ferings, more sor-row for sin,
more pride in his glo-ry, more hope in his word,
more free-dom from earth-stains, more long-ings for home;

more faith in my Sav-ior, more sense of his care,
more tears for his sor-rows, more pain at his grief,
more fit for the king-dom, more use-ful I'd be,

more joy in his serv-ice, more pur-pose in prayer.
more meek-ness in tri-al, more praise for re-lief.
more bless-ed and ho-ly, more, Sav-ior, like thee.

THE CHRISTIAN LIFE

305 Thine Arm, O Lord, in Days of Old

Edward H. Plumptre, 1864

ST. MATTHEW CMD
attrib. William Croft, 1708

1 Thine arm, O Lord, in days of old was strong to
2 And lo! thy touch brought life and health, gave speech, and
3 Be thou our great de-liv-erer still, thou Lord of

heal and save; it tri-umphed o'er dis-ease and
strength, and sight; and youth re-newed and fren-zy
life and death; re-store and quick-en, soothe and

death, o'er dark-ness and the grave; to thee they
calmed owned thee the Lord of light; and now, O
bless with thine al-might-y breath; to hands that

went, the blind, the dumb, the pal-sied and the
Lord, be near to bless, al-might-y as of
work, and eyes that see, give wis-dom's heaven-ly

THE CHRISTIAN LIFE

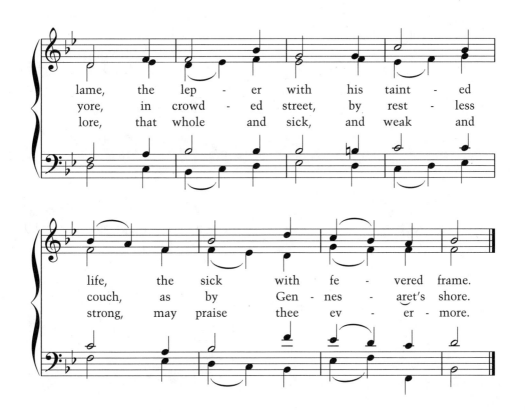

lame, the lep - er with his taint - ed
yore, in crowd - ed street, by rest - less
lore, that whole and sick, and weak and

life, the sick with fe - vered frame.
couch, as by Gen - nes - aret's shore.
strong, may praise thee ev - er - more.

There Is a Balm in Gilead

African American

BALM IN GILEAD   IRREGULAR with Refrain
African American melody
harm. Hymns of Truth and Light, 1998

Refrain

There is a balm in Gil-e-ad to make the wound-ed whole;

there is a balm in Gil-e-ad to heal the sin-sick soul.

1 Some-times I feel dis-cour-aged, and think my work's in vain, but
2 If you can-not preach like Pet-er, if you can-not pray like Paul, you can
3 Don't ev - er be dis-cour-aged for Je - sus is your friend, and

D.S.

then the Ho - ly Spi - rit re - vives my soul a - gain.
tell the love of Je - sus, and say he died for all. There is a
if you lack for knowl-edge, he'll ne'er re - fuse to lend.

Wer nur den lieben Gott lässt walten
Georg Neumark, 1641
trans. Catherine Winkworth, 1863, alt.

WER NUR DEN LIEBEN GOTT 98 98 88
Georg Neumark, 1657

1 If thou but suf - fer God to guide thee, and hope in him through all thy ways, he'll give thee strength, what-e'er be - tide thee, and bear thee through the e - vil days; who trusts in God's un - chang - ing love builds on the rock that nought can move.

2 On - ly be still, and wait his lei - sure in cheer - ful hope, with heart con - tent to take what-e'er thy Fa - ther's plea - sure and all de - serv - ing love have sent; nor doubt our in - most wants are known to him who chose us for his own.

3 Sing, pray, and keep his ways un - swerv - ing; so do thine own part faith - ful - ly, and trust his word, though un - de - serv - ing; thou yet shalt find it true for thee; God nev - er yet for - sook at need the soul that trust - ed him in - deed.

THE CHRISTIAN LIFE

308   Nearer, My God, to Thee

Sarah F. Adams, 1841

BETHANY   64 64 6 with Refrain
Lowell Mason, 1856

1 Near - er, my God, to thee, near - er to thee!
2 Though like the wan - der - er, the sun gone down,
3 There let the way ap - pear, steps un - to heaven;
4 Then, with my wak - ing thoughts bright with thy praise,
5 Or if, on joy - ful wing cleav - ing the sky,

E'en though it be a cross that rais - eth me;
dark - ness be o - ver me, my rest a stone;
all that thou send - est me, in mer - cy given;
out of my ston - y griefs Beth - el I'll raise;
sun, moon, and stars for - got, up - ward I fly,

still all my song shall be,
yet in my dreams I'd be
an - gels to beck - on me near - er my God, to thee,
so by my woes to be
still all my song shall be,

near - er, my God, to thee, near - er to thee!

THE CHRISTIAN LIFE

Samuel Johnson, 1846

INTERCESSOR   11 10 11 10
Charles Hubert Hastings Parry, 1904

1 Fa-ther, in thy mys-te-rious pres-ence kneel-ing, fain would our
2 Lord, we have wan-dered forth through doubt and sor - row, and thou hast
3 Now, Fa-ther, now, in thy dear pres-ence kneel-ing, our spir-its

souls feel all thy kin-dling love, for we are weak, and need some deep re-
made each step an on-ward one, and we will ev - er trust each un-known
yearn to feel thy kin-dling love; now make us strong, we need thy deep re-

veal - ing of trust and strength and calm-ness from a - bove.
mor - row; thou wilt sus - tain us till its work is done.
veal - ing of trust and strength and calm-ness from a - bove.

THE CHRISTIAN LIFE

310 Lead, Kindly Light, Amid th'Encircling Gloom

John Henry Newman, 1833

ALBERTA   10 4 10 4 10 10
William H. Harris, 1924

1 Lead, kind-ly Light, a-mid the en-cir-cling gloom, lead thou me
2 I was not ev - er thus, nor prayed that thou should lead me
3 So long thy power hath blest me, sure it still will lead me

unison

on; the night is dark, and I am far from home; lead thou me
on; I loved to choose and see my path; but now lead thou me
on, o'er moor and fen, o'er crag and tor-rent, till the night is

on. Keep thou my feet; I do not ask to see the
on. I loved the gar-ish day, and, spite of fears, pride
gone, and with the morn those an - gel fac - es smile, which

dis - tant scene; one step e - nough for me.
ruled my will: re - mem - ber not past years.
I have loved long since, and lost a - while.

THE CHRISTIAN LIFE

Lord, I Want to Be a Christian

African American

I WANT TO BE A CHRISTIAN   IRREGULAR
African American melody
harm. Carson P. Cooman, 2007

1 Lord, I want to be a Chris-tian in my heart, in my
2 Lord, I want to be more lov - ing in my heart, in my
3 Lord, I want to be more ho - ly in my heart, in my
4 Lord, I want to be like Je - sus in my heart, in my

heart; Lord, I want to be a Chris-tian in my heart.
heart; Lord, I want to be more lov -ing in my heart.
heart; Lord, I want to be more ho - ly in my heart.   (in my
heart; Lord, I want to be like Je - sus in my heart.

In my heart, in my heart;
heart,)   (in my heart,)   (in my

Lord, I want to be a Chris-tian in my heart.
heart;)   Lord, I want to be more lov - ing in my heart.
Lord, I want to be more ho - ly in my heart.
Lord, I want to be like Je - sus in my heart.

THE CHRISTIAN LIFE

312 Come, Thou Fount of Every Blessing

Robert Robinson, 1758

NETTLETON 87 87 D
A Repository of Sacred Music, Part II, 1813

1 Come, thou fount of ev-ery bless-ing, tune my heart to sing thy grace; streams of mer-cy nev-er ceas-ing, call for songs of loud-est praise. Teach me some me-lo-dious son-net sung by flam-ing tongues a-bove; praise the mount! I'm fixed up-on it, mount of thy re-deem-ing love.

2 Here I raise mine Eb-en-e-zer; hith-er by thy help I'm come; and I hope, by thy good plea-sure, safe-ly to ar-rive at home. Je-sus sought me when a stran-ger, wan-dering from the fold of God; he, to res-cue me from dan-ger, in-ter-posed his pre-cious blood.

3 O to grace how great a debt-or dai-ly I'm con-strained to be! Let thy good-ness, like a fet-ter, bind my wan-dering heart to thee: prone to wan-der, Lord, I feel it, prone to leave the God I love; here's my heart, O take and seal it, seal it for thy courts a-bove.

THE CHRISTIAN LIFE

Lord, Make Us Servants of Your Peace

Seigneur, faites de moi un instrument de votre paix
attrib. Francis of Assisi (1182–1226)
trans. James Quinn (b. 1919)

DICKINSON COLLEGE LM
Lee Hastings Bristol, Jr., 1960

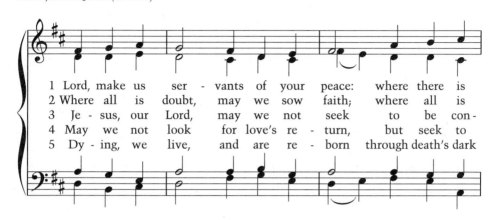

1 Lord, make us ser - vants of your peace: where there is
2 Where all is doubt, may we sow faith; where all is
3 Je - sus, our Lord, may we not seek to be con -
4 May we not look for love's re - turn, but seek to
5 Dy - ing, we live, and are re - born through death's dark

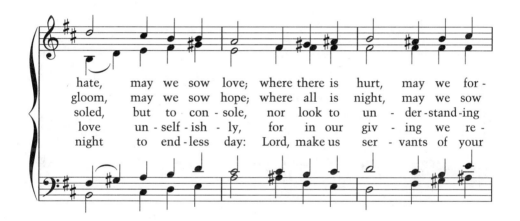

hate, may we sow love; where there is hurt, may we for -
gloom, may we sow hope; where all is night, may we sow
soled, but to con - sole, nor look to un - der -stand-ing
love un - self - ish - ly, for in our giv - ing we re -
night to end -less day: Lord, make us ser - vants of your

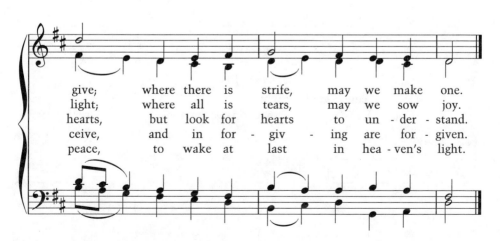

give; where there is strife, may we make one.
light; where all is tears, may we sow joy.
hearts, but look for hearts to un - der - stand.
ceive, and in for - giv - ing are for - given.
peace, to wake at last in hea - ven's light.

THE CHRISTIAN LIFE

314   O Master, Let Me Walk with Thee

Washington Gladden, 1879

MARYTON   LM
H. Percy Smith, 1874

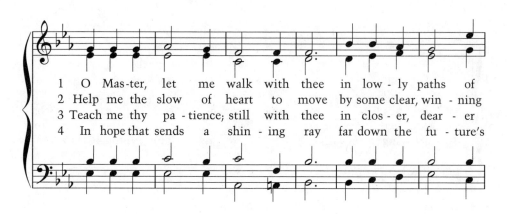

1 O Mas-ter, let me walk with thee in low - ly paths of
2 Help me the slow of heart to move by some clear, win - ning
3 Teach me thy pa - tience; still with thee in clos - er, dear - er
4 In hope that sends a shin - ing ray far down the fu - ture's

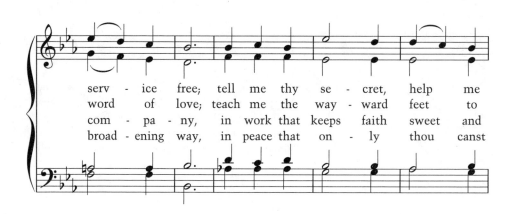

serv - ice free; tell me thy se - cret, help me
word of love; teach me the way - ward feet to
com - pa - ny, in work that keeps faith sweet and
broad - ening way, in peace that on - ly thou canst

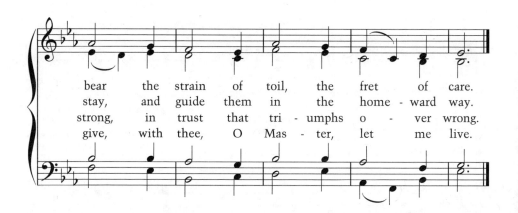

bear the strain of toil, the fret of care.
stay, and guide them in the home - ward way.
strong, in trust that tri - umphs o - ver wrong.
give, with thee, O Mas - ter, let me live.

THE CHRISTIAN LIFE

Lead Us, O Father, in the Paths of Peace 315

William Henry Burleigh, 1859

LANGRAN 10 10 10 10
James Langran, 1862

1 Lead us, O Father, in the paths of peace;
2 Lead us, O Father, in the paths of truth;
3 Lead us, O Father, in the paths of right;
4 Lead us, O Father, to thy heaven-ly rest,

with - out thy guid - ing hand we go a - stray,
un - helped by thee, in er - ror's maze we grope,
blind - ly we stum - ble when we walk a - lone,
how - ev - er rough and steep the path may be,

and doubts ap - pall, and sor - rows still in - crease;
while pas - sion stains and fol - ly dims our youth,
in - volved in shad - ows of a mor - tal night;
through joy or sor - row, as thou deem - est best,

lead us through Christ, the true and liv - ing way.
and age comes on un - cheered by faith and hope.
on - ly with thee we jour - ney safe - ly on.
un - til our lives are per - fect - ed in thee.

THE CHRISTIAN LIFE

316   Fight the Good Fight with All Thy Might

John S. B. Monsell, 1863, alt.

RUSHFORD   LM
Henry J. Ley, 1936

1 Fight the good fight with all thy might, Christ is thy
2 Run the straight race through God's good grace, lift up thine
3 Cast care a - side, lean on thy guide; his bound - less
4 Faint not nor fear, his arms are near; he chang - eth

strength and Christ thy right; lay hold on life, and it shall be thy
eyes and seek his face; life with its way be - fore us lies,
mer - cy will pro - vide; trust, and thy trust - ing soul shall prove
not, and thou art dear; on - ly be - lieve, and thou shalt see that

joy   and crown e - ter - nal - ly.
Christ is the path and Christ the prize.
Christ is its life and Christ its love.
Christ is all in all to thee.

THE CHRISTIAN LIFE

James Edmeston, 1821

MANNHEIM   87 87 87
Friedrich Filitz, 1847
harm. The English Hymnal, 1906

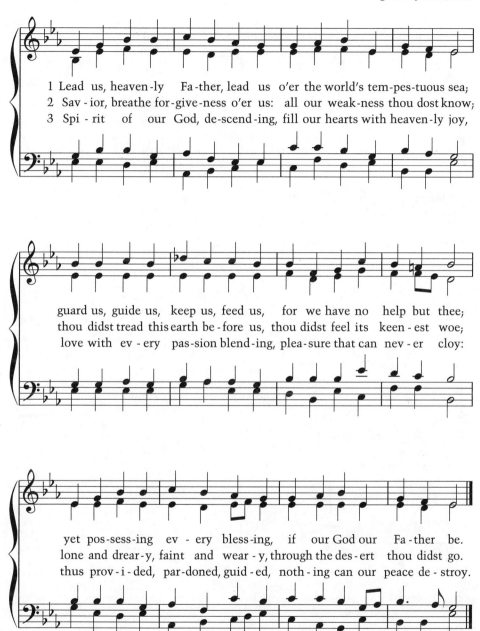

1 Lead us, heaven-ly Fa-ther, lead us o'er the world's tem-pes-tuous sea;
2 Sav - ior, breathe for-give-ness o'er us: all our weak-ness thou dost know;
3 Spi - rit of our God, de-scend-ing, fill our hearts with heaven-ly joy,

guard us, guide us, keep us, feed us, for we have no help but thee;
thou didst tread this earth be - fore us, thou didst feel its keen - est woe;
love with ev - ery pas-sion blend-ing, plea-sure that can nev - er cloy:

yet pos-sess-ing ev - ery bless-ing, if our God our Fa-ther be.
lone and drear-y, faint and wear - y, through the des - ert thou didst go.
thus prov-i - ded, par-doned, guid - ed, noth - ing can our peace de - stroy.

THE CHRISTIAN LIFE

318   O Jesus, I Have Promised

John E. Bode, 1868, alt.

WOLVERCOTE   76 76 D
William H. Ferguson, 1919, alt.

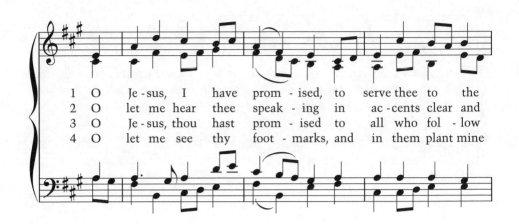

1 O Je-sus, I have prom-ised, to serve thee to the
2 O let me hear thee speak-ing in ac-cents clear and
3 O Je-sus, thou hast prom-ised to all who fol-low
4 O let me see thy foot-marks, and in them plant mine

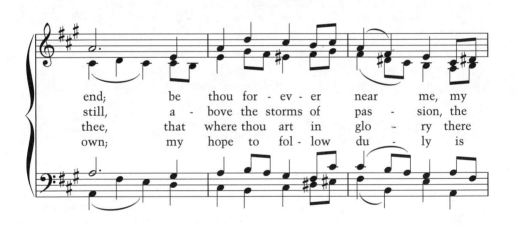

end;   be thou for-ev-er near me, my
still,   a-bove the storms of pas-sion, the
thee,   that where thou art in glo-ry there
own;   my hope to fol-low du-ly is

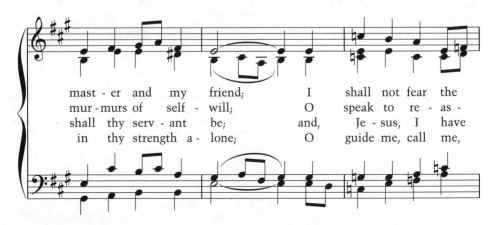

mast-er and my friend;   I shall not fear the
mur-murs of self-will;   O speak to re-as-
shall thy serv-ant be;   and, Je-sus, I have
in thy strength a-lone;   O guide me, call me,

THE CHRISTIAN LIFE

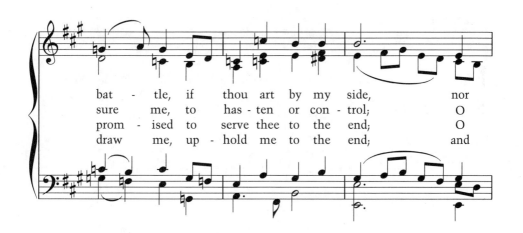

bat - tle, if thou art by my side, nor
sure me, to has - ten or con - trol; O
prom - ised to serve thee to the end; O
draw me, up - hold me to the end; and

wand - er from the path - way, if thou wilt be my guide.
speak, and make me lis - ten, thou guar - dian of my soul.
give me grace to fol - low, my mas - ter and my friend.
then in heaven re - ceive me, my sav - ior and my friend.

He Who Would Valiant Be

John Bunyan, 1684
adapt. Percy Dearmer, 1906, alt.

ST. DUNSTAN'S 65 65 66 65
Charles Winfred Douglas, 1917

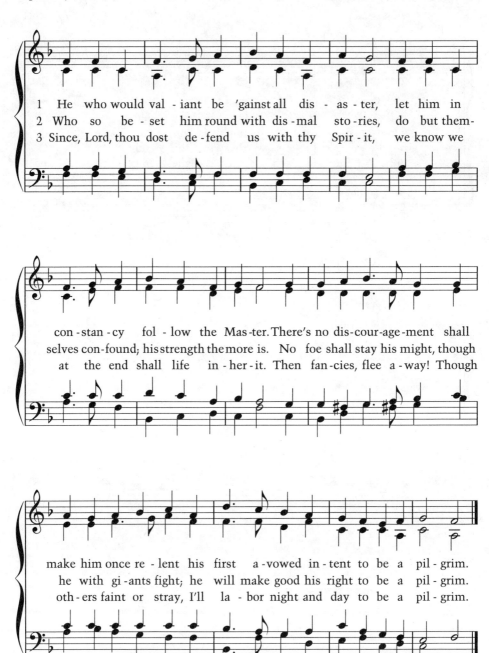

1 He who would val-iant be 'gainst all dis-as-ter, let him in
2 Who so be-set him round with dis-mal sto-ries, do but them-
3 Since, Lord, thou dost de-fend us with thy Spir-it, we know we

con-stan-cy fol-low the Mas-ter. There's no dis-cour-age-ment shall
selves con-found; his strength the more is. No foe shall stay his might, though
at the end shall life in-her-it. Then fan-cies, flee a-way! Though

make him once re-lent his first a-vowed in-tent to be a pil-grim.
he with gi-ants fight; he will make good his right to be a pil-grim.
oth-ers faint or stray, I'll la-bor night and day to be a pil-grim.

THE CHRISTIAN LIFE

I Heard the Voice of Jesus Say

Horatius Bonar, 1846

VOX DILECTI   CMD
John Bacchus Dykes, 1868

1 I heard the voice of Je-sus say, "Come un-to me and rest; lay
2 I heard the voice of Je-sus say, "Be-hold, I free-ly give the
3 I heard the voice of Je-sus say, "I am this dark world's light; look

down, thou wea-ry one, lay down thy head up-on my breast." I
liv-ing wa-ter; thirst-y one, stoop down and drink, and live." I
un-to me, thy morn shall rise, and all thy day be bright." I

came to Je-sus as I was, wea-ry, and worn, and sad; I
came to Je-sus and I drank of that life-giv-ing stream; my
looked to Je-sus and I found in him my star, my sun; and

found in him a rest-ing place, and he has made me glad.
thirst was quenched, my soul re-vived, and now I live in him.
in that light of life I'll walk, till trav-eling days are done.

THE CHRISTIAN LIFE

321   One Thought I Have, My Ample Creed

Frederick Lucian Hosmer, 1880

CORNHILL   CM
Harold Darke, 1931, alt.

1 One thought I have, my am - ple creed, so deep it
2 Each morn un - folds some fresh sur - prise, I feast at
3 At night my glad - ness is my prayer; I drop my
4 I ask not far be - fore to see, but take in

is and broad, and e - qual to my
life's full board; and ri - sing in my
dai - ly load, and ev - ery care is
trust my road; life, death, and im - mor -

ev - ery need: it is the thought of God.
in - ner skies shines forth the thought of God.
pil - lowed there u - pon the thought of God.
tal - i - ty are in my thought of God.

5 To this their secret strength they owed
the martyr's path who trod;
the fountains of their patience flowed
from out their thought of God.

6 Be still the light upon my way,
my pilgrim staff and rod,
my rest by night, my strength by day,
O blessèd thought of God.

THE CHRISTIAN LIFE

All Who Love and Serve Your City 322

Erik Routley, 1969, alt.

CHARLESTOWN 87 87
The Southern Harmony, 1835
harm. Edward Elwyn Jones, 2007

1 All who love and serve your ci - ty, all who
2 in your day of loss and sor - row, in your
3 In your day of wealth and plen - ty, wast - ed
4 For all days are days of judg - ment, and the
5 Ri - sen Lord! shall yet the ci - ty be the

bear its dai - ly stress, all who cry for peace and
day of help - less strife, hon - or, peace, and love re -
work and wast - ed play, call to mind the word of
Lord is wait - ing still, draw - ing near a world that
ci - ty of de - spair? Come to - day, our judge, our

jus - tice, all who curse and all who bless,
treat -ing, seek the Lord, who is your life.
Je - sus, "I must work while it is day."
spurns him, of - fering peace from Cal - vary's hill.
glo - ry; be its name, "The Lord is there!"

THE CHRISTIAN LIFE

323   Come, Labor On

Jane Laurie Borthwick, 1859, rev. 1863, alt.

ORA LABORA   4 10 10 10 4
T. Tertius Noble, 1918

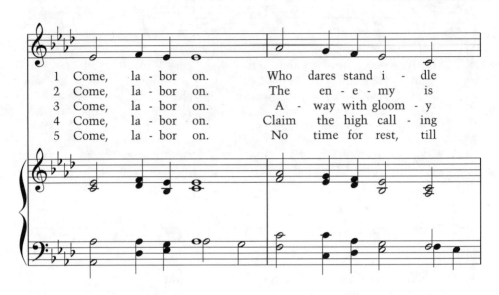

1 Come, la-bor on. Who dares stand i - dle
2 Come, la-bor on. The en - e - my is
3 Come, la-bor on. A - way with gloom - y
4 Come, la-bor on. Claim the high call - ing
5 Come, la-bor on. No time for rest, till

on the har - vest plain,   while all a - round us
watch-ing night and day,   to sow the tares, to
doubts and faith - less fear!   No arm so weak but
an - gels can - not share—   to young and old the
glows the west - ern sky,   till the long sha - dows

waves the gold-en grain? And to each ser - vant
snatch the seed a - way; while we in sleep our
may do ser -vice here: by feeb- lest a - gents
gos - pel glad -ness bear: re - deem the time; its
o'er our path -way lie, and a glad sound comes

does the mas -ter say, "Go work to - day."
du -ty have for-got, he slum - bered not.
may our God ful - fill his right - eous will.
hours too swift -ly fly. The night draws nigh.
with the set -ting sun, "Ser - vants, well done."

THE CHRISTIAN LIFE

324   Forth in Thy Name, O Lord, I Go

Charles Wesley, 1749, alt.

SONG 34   LM
Orlando Gibbons, 1623

1 Forth in thy name, O Lord, I go my dai - ly
2 The task thy wis - dom hath as - signed, O let me
3 Pre - serve me from my call - ing's snare, and hide my
4 Thee may I set at my right hand, whose eyes my
5 Give me to bear thy eas - y yoke, and ev - ery

la - bor to pur - sue, thee, on - ly thee re - solved to
cheer - ful - ly ful - fill; in all my works thy pres - ence
sim - ple heart a - bove, a - bove the thorns of chok - ing
in - most sub - stance see, and la - bor on at thy com-
mo - ment watch and pray, and still to things e - ter - nal

know in all I think, or speak, or do.
find, and prove thy good and per - fect will.
care, the gild - ed baits of world - ly love.
mand, and of - fer all my works to thee.
look, and has - ten to thy glo - rious day.

THE CHRISTIAN LIFE

Thy Kingdom Come! On Bended Knee

325

Frederick Lucian Hosmer, 1891

IRISH CM
Hymns and Sacred Poems, 1749

1 Thy king-dom come! on bend-ed knee the pass-ing a-ges pray; and faith-ful souls have yearned to see on earth that king-dom's day.

2 But the slow watch-es of the night not less to God be-long; and for the ev-er-last-ing right the si-lent stars are strong.

3 And lo, al-read-y on the hills the flags of dawn ap-pear; gird up your loins, ye proph-et souls, pro-claim the day is near.

4 The day in whose clear shin-ing light all wrong shall stand re-vealed; when jus-tice shall be throned in might, and ev-ery hurt be healed:

5 when knowl-edge, hand in hand with peace, shall walk the earth a-broad; the day of per-fect right-eous-ness, the prom-ised day of God.

THE KINGDOM OF GOD

326 Father Eternal, Ruler of Creation

Laurence Housman, 1919, alt.

LANGHAM 11 10 11 10
Geoffrey Turton Shaw, 1921

1 Fa - ther e - ter - nal, Ru - ler of cre -
2 Rac - es and peo - ples, lo, we stand di -
3 En - vious of heart, blind - eyed, with tongues con -
4 How shall we love thee, ho - ly hid - den

a - tion, Spi - rit of life, which moved ere form was
vid - ed, and, shar - ing not our griefs, no joy can
found - ed, na - tion by na - tion still goes un - for -
Be - ing, if we love not the world which thou hast

made, through the thick dark - ness
share; by wars and tu - mults
given, in wrath and fear, by
made? Bind us in thine own

cov - ering ev - ery na - tion, light to our
love is mocked, de - rid - ed; his sav - ing
jea - lous -ies sur - round - ed, build - ing proud
love for bet - ter see - ing thy Word made

blind - ness, O be thou our aid:
cross no na - tion yet will bear:
towers which shall not reach to heaven:
flesh, and in a man - ger laid:

thy king - dom come, O Lord, thy will be done.

327 God the Omnipotent! King, Who Ordainest

stanzas 1-2: Henry F. Chorley, 1842, alt.
stanzas 3-4: John Ellerton, 1870, alt.

RUSSIAN HYMN 11 10 11 9
Alexis F. Lvov, 1833

1 God the Om - nip - o - tent! King, who or - dain - est
2 God the All - mer - ci - ful! earth hath for - sak - en
3 God the all - right - eous One! earth hath de - fied thee;
4 God the All - prov - i - dent! earth by thy chas - tening

thun - der thy clar - ion, and light - ning thy sword,
thy ways all ho - ly, and slight - ed thy word;
yet to e - ter - ni - ty stand - eth thy word;
yet shall to free - dom and truth be re - stored;

show forth thy pit - y on high where thou reign - est:
bid not thy wrath in its ter - rors a - wak - en:
false - hood and wrong shall not tar - ry be - side thee:
through the thick dark - ness thy king - dom is has - tening:

give to us peace in our time, O Lord.
give to us peace in our time, O Lord.
give to us peace in our time, O Lord.
thou wilt give peace in thy time, O Lord.

Another harmonization (in C), 89.

THE KINGDOM OF GOD

Not Far Beyond the Sea, Nor High

George Bradford Caird, c. 1945

CORNWALL 886 886
Samuel Sebastian Wesley, 1872

328

1 Not far be-yond the sea, nor high a - bove the heavens, but
2 Root-ed and ground-ed in thy love, with saints on earth and
3 Help us to press to-ward that mark, and, though our vis-ion

ver - y nigh thy voice, O God, is heard. For
saints a - bove we join in full ac - cord, to
now is dark, to live by what we see. So,

each new step of faith we take thou hast more truth and
grasp the breadth, length, depth, and height, the cru - ci - fied and
when we see thee face to face, thy truth and light our

light to break forth from thy ho - ly word.
ris - en might of Christ, in - car - nate Word.
dwell - ing place for ev - er - more shall be.

THE KINGDOM OF GOD

329 O Day of God, Draw Nigh

Robert Balgarnie Young Scott, 1937

ST. MICHAEL SM
Genevan Psalter, 1551
harm. William Crotch, 1836

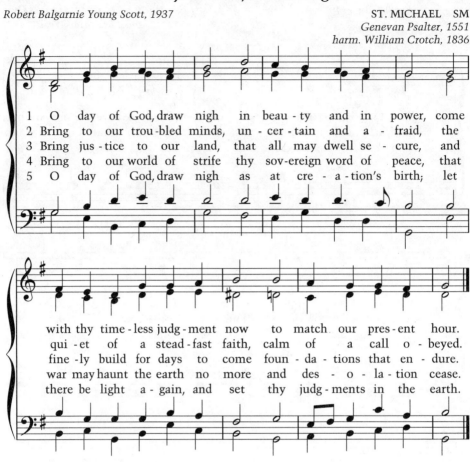

1 O day of God, draw nigh in beau - ty and in power, come
2 Bring to our trou - bled minds, un - cer - tain and a - fraid, the
3 Bring jus - tice to our land, that all may dwell se - cure, and
4 Bring to our world of strife thy sov - ereign word of peace, that
5 O day of God, draw nigh as at cre - a - tion's birth; let

with thy time - less judg - ment now to match our pres - ent hour.
qui - et of a stead - fast faith, calm of a call o - beyed.
fine - ly build for days to come foun - da - tions that en - dure.
war may haunt the earth no more and des - o - la - tion cease.
there be light a - gain, and set thy judg - ments in the earth.

This music in F, 300.

330 My Soul, There Is a Country

Henry Vaughan, 1650

CHRISTUS, DER IST MEIN LEBEN 76 76
Melchior Vulpius, 1609
harm. Johann Sebastian Bach (1685–1750)

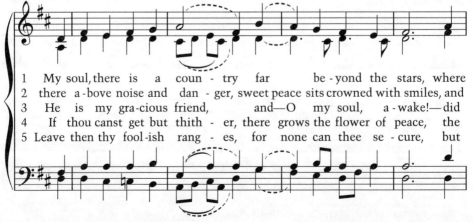

1 My soul, there is a coun - try far be - yond the stars, where
2 there a - bove noise and dan - ger, sweet peace sits crowned with smiles, and
3 He is my gra - cious friend, and—O my soul, a - wake!—did
4 If thou canst get but thith - er, there grows the flower of peace, the
5 Leave then thy fool - ish rang - es, for none can thee se - cure, but

THE KINGDOM OF GOD

stands a wing - ed sen - try all skill - ful in the wars:
one born in a man - ger com - mands the beau - teous files.
in pure love de - scend, to die here for thy sake.
Rose that can - not with - er, thy for - tress and thy ease.
one, who nev - er chang - es, thy God, thy life, thy cure.

Another harmonization, 278.

Love Is Kind and Suffers Long 331

Christopher Wordsworth, 1862

CAPE TOWN 77 75
Friedrich Filitz, 1847

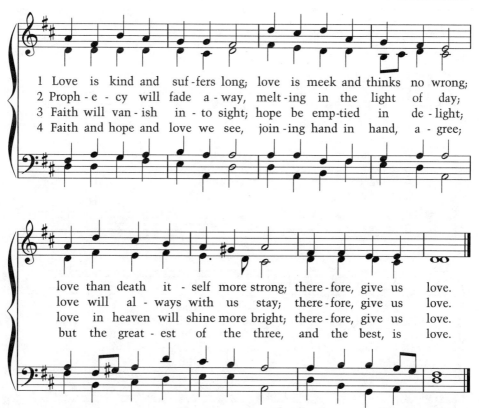

1 Love is kind and suf - fers long; love is meek and thinks no wrong;
2 Proph - e - cy will fade a - way, melt - ing in the light of day;
3 Faith will van - ish in - to sight; hope be emp - tied in de - light;
4 Faith and hope and love we see, join - ing hand in hand, a - gree;

love than death it - self more strong; there - fore, give us love.
love will al - ways with us stay; there - fore, give us love.
love in heaven will shine more bright; there - fore, give us love.
but the great - est of the three, and the best, is love.

THE KINGDOM OF GOD

332   O What Their Joy and Their Glory Must Be

O quanta qualia sunt illa sabbata
Peter Abelard (1079–1142)
trans. John Mason Neale, 1854, alt.

O QUANTA QUALIA   10 10 10 10
Paris Antiphoner, 1681
harm. Harvard University Hymn Book, 1964

1 O what their joy and their glo - ry must be,
2 Tru - ly Je - ru - sa - lem name we that shore,
3 There, where no trou - ble dis - trac - tion can bring,
4 Low - ly be - fore him with prais - es we fall,

those end - less sab - baths the bless - ed ones see:
vi - sion of peace, that brings joy ev - er - more;
we the sweet an - thems of Zi - on shall sing,
of whom, and in whom, and through whom are all:

crown for the val - iant, to wea - ry ones rest;
wish and ful - fill - ment can sev - ered be ne'er,
while for thy grace, Lord, their voic - es of praise
of whom, the Fa - ther; and in whom, the Son;

God shall be all, and in all ev - er blest.
nor the thing prayed for come short of the prayer.
thy bless - ed peo - ple shall ev - er - more raise.
through whom, the Spir - it, with these ev - er One.

THE KINGDOM OF GOD

God of Grace and God of Glory

Harry Emerson Fosdick, 1930, alt.

REGENT SQUARE 87 87 87
Henry Thomas Smart, 1867

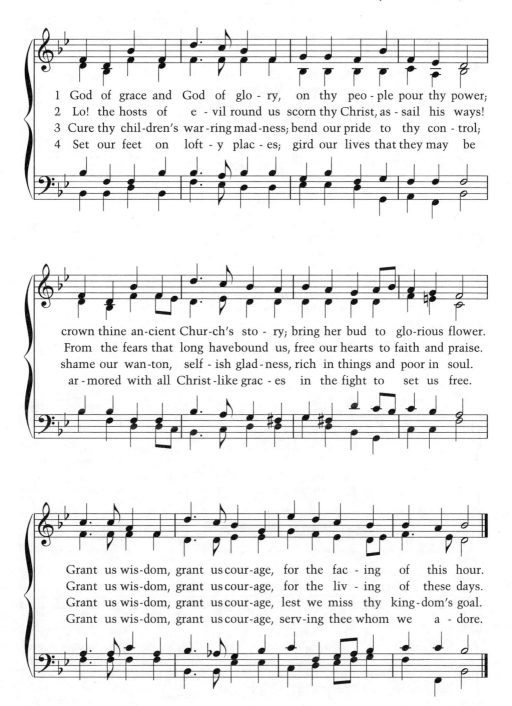

1 God of grace and God of glo - ry, on thy peo - ple pour thy power;
2 Lo! the hosts of e - vil round us scorn thy Christ, as - sail his ways!
3 Cure thy chil-dren's war - ring mad-ness; bend our pride to thy con - trol;
4 Set our feet on loft - y plac - es; gird our lives that they may be

crown thine an-cient Chur-ch's sto - ry; bring her bud to glo-rious flower.
From the fears that long have bound us, free our hearts to faith and praise.
shame our wan-ton, self - ish glad-ness, rich in things and poor in soul.
ar - mored with all Christ-like grac - es in the fight to set us free.

Grant us wis-dom, grant us cour-age, for the fac - ing of this hour.
Grant us wis-dom, grant us cour-age, for the liv - ing of these days.
Grant us wis-dom, grant us cour-age, lest we miss thy king-dom's goal.
Grant us wis-dom, grant us cour-age, serv-ing thee whom we a - dore.

THE KINGDOM OF GOD

334 Jerusalem the Golden

Urbs Sion aurea
Bernard of Cluny (c.1100–c.1150)
trans. John Mason Neale, 1858, alt.

EWING 76 76 D
Alexander Ewing, 1853

1 Je - ru - sa - lem the gold - en, with milk and ho - ney blest, be-
2 They stand, those halls of Zi - on, all ju - bi - lant with song, and
3 There is the throne of Da - vid; and there, from care re - leased, the
4 Oh, sweet and bless - ed coun - try, the home of God's e - lect! Oh,

neath thy con - tem - pla - tion sink heart and voice op - pressed: I
bright with man - y an an - gel, and all the mar - tyr throng: the
shout of them that tri - umph, the song of them that feast; and
sweet and bless - ed coun - try that ea - ger hearts ex - pect! Je-

know not, oh, I know not, what joys a - wait us there; what
Prince is ev - er in them, the day - light is se - rene; the
they who with their lead - er have con - quered in the fight, for
sus, in mer - cy bring us to that dear land of rest, who

ra - dian - cy of glo - ry, what bliss be - yond com - pare.
pas - tures of the bless - ed are decked in glo - rious sheen.
ev - er and for ev - er are clad in robes of white.
art, with God the Fa - ther, and Spi - rit, ev - er blest.

THE KINGDOM OF GOD

Walter Russell Bowie, 1910, alt.

SANCTA CIVITAS   86 86 86
Herbert Howells, 1964, alt.

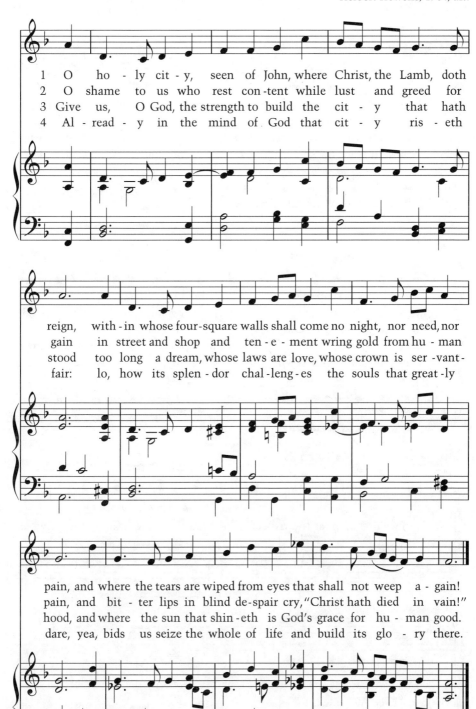

1 O ho - ly cit - y, seen of John, where Christ, the Lamb, doth
2 O shame to us who rest con -tent while lust and greed for
3 Give us, O God, the strength to build the cit - y that hath
4 Al - read - y in the mind of God that cit - y ris - eth

reign, with - in whose four-square walls shall come no night, nor need, nor
gain in street and shop and ten - e - ment wring gold from hu - man
stood too long a dream, whose laws are love, whose crown is ser -vant-
fair: lo, how its splen - dor chal -leng-es the souls that great -ly

pain, and where the tears are wiped from eyes that shall not weep a - gain!
pain, and bit - ter lips in blind de-spair cry, "Christ hath died in vain!"
hood, and where the sun that shin -eth is God's grace for hu - man good.
dare, yea, bids us seize the whole of life and build its glo - ry there.

THE KINGDOM OF GOD

Shall We Gather at the River

Robert Lowry, 1864

HANSON PLACE   87 87 with Refrain
Robert Lowry, 1864

1 Shall we gath-er at the riv-er, where bright an-gel feet have trod,
2 On the mar-gin of the riv-er, wash-ing up its sil-ver spray,
3 Ere we reach the shin-ing riv-er, lay we ev-ery bur-den down;
4 Soon we'll reach the shin-ing riv-er, soon our pil-grim-age will cease;

with its crys-tal tide for-ev-er flow-ing by the throne of   God?
we will walk and wor-ship ev-er, all the hap-py gol-den   day.
grace our spir-its will de-liv-er, and pro-vide a robe and   crown.
soon our hap-py hearts will quiv-er with the mel-o-dy of   peace.

Yes, we'll gath-er at the riv-er, the beau-ti-ful, the beau-ti-ful   riv-er;

gath-er with the saints at the riv-er that flows by the throne of   God.

THE KINGDOM OF GOD

English, 16th cent.?

LAND OF REST   CM
Appendix to The Christian Harp, 1836
adapt. Annabel Morris Buchanan, 1938
harm. Charles Haizlip Webb, 1988

1 Je - ru - sa - lem, my hap - py home, when
2 Thy saints are crowned with glo - ry great; they
3 There Da - vid stands with harp in hand as
4 Our La - dy sings *Mag - ni - fi - cat* with
5 Je - ru - sa - lem, Je - ru - sa - lem, God

shall I come to thee? When shall my sor - rows
see God face to face; they tri - umph still, they
mas - ter of the choir: ten thou - sand times would
tune sur - pass - ing sweet, and bless - ed mar - tyrs'
grant that I may see thine end - less joy, and

have an end? Thy joys when shall I see?
still re - joice in that most hap - py place.
one be blest who might this mu - sic hear.
har - mo - ny doth ring in ev - ery street.
of the same par - ta - ker ev - er be.

Music © 1989 The United Methodist Publishing House.

THE KINGDOM OF GOD

High o'er the Lonely Hills

Jan Struther, 1931, alt.

DAWN   64 64 6664
T. H. Ingham, 1931

1 High o'er the lone - ly hills black turns to gray, bird - song the
2 So, o'er the hills of life, storm - y, for - lorn, out of the
3 Hear we no beat of drums, fan - fare nor cry, when Christ the
4 Bid then fare - well to sleep: rise up and run! What though the

val - ley fills, mists fold a - way; gray wakes to green a - gain,
cloud and strife sun - rise is born; swift grows the light for us;
her - ald comes qui - et - ly nigh; splen - dor he makes on earth;
hill be steep? Strength's in the sun. Now shall you find at last

beau - ty is seen a - gain, gold and se - rene a - gain dawn - eth the day.
end - ed is night for us; sound - less and bright for us break - eth God's morn.
col - or a - wakes on earth; sud - den - ly breaks on earth light from the sky.
night's left be - hind at last; for hu - man - kind at last day has be - gun!

THE KINGDOM OF GOD

Behold a Sower! From Afar

Washington Gladden, 1897

WEYMOUTH CMD
Theodore Parker Ferris, 1941

1 Be-hold a sow-er! From a-far he go-eth forth with might; the
2 O Lord of life, to thee we lift our hearts in praise for those, thy
3 Shine forth, O Light, that we may see, with hearts all un-a-fraid, the
4 Light up thy word; the fet-tered page from kill-ing bond-age free: light

roll-ing years his fur-rows are, his seed the grow-ing light; for
proph-ets, who have shown thy gift of grace that ev-er grows, of
mean-ing and the mys-ter-y of things that thou hast made: shine
up our way; lead forth this age in love's large lib-er-ty. O

all the just his word is sown, it spring-eth up al-way; the
truth that spreads from shore to shore, of wis-dom's wid-en-ing ray, of
forth, and let the dark-ling past be-neath thy beam grow bright; shine
Light of light! With-in us dwell, through us thy ra-diance pour, that

ten-der blade is hope's young dawn, the har-vest, love's new day.
light that shin-eth more and more un-to thy per-fect day.
forth, and touch the fu-ture vast with thine un-troub-led light.
word and life thy truths may tell, and praise thee ev-er-more.

THE KINGDOM OF GOD

340   Where Cross the Crowded Ways of Life

Frank Mason North, 1903

GARDINER LM
William Gardiner, 1815

1 Where cross the crowd - ed ways of life, where sound the
2 In haunts of wretch - ed - ness and need, on sha - dowed
3 The cup of wa - ter given for thee still holds the
4 O Mas - ter, from the moun - tain side, make haste to
5 till all the world shall learn thy love, and fol - low

cries of race and clan, a - bove the noise of
tresh - olds dark with fears, from paths where hide the
fresh - ness of thy grace; yet long these mul - ti -
heal these hearts of pain; a - mong these rest - less
where thy feet have trod; till glo - rious from thy

self - ish strife, we hear thy voice, O Son of Man.
lures of greed, we catch the vi - sion of thy tears.
tudes to see the true com - pas - sion of thy face.
throngs a - bide, O tread the ci - ty's streets a - gain;
heaven a - bove, shall come the ci - ty of our God.

Another harmonization (in B♭), 222.

THE KINGDOM OF GOD

In Christ There Is No East or West

John Oxenham, 1908, alt.

MCKEE CM
African American melody
harm. Harry T. Burleigh (1866–1949)

341

1 In Christ there is no east or west, in
2 In him shall true hearts ev - ery - where their
3 Join hands, dis - ci - ples of the faith, what -
4 In Christ now meet both east and west, in

him no south or north, but one great fel - low -
high com - mun - ion find; his serv - ice is the
e'er your race may be! Who serves my Fa - ther
him meet south and north; all Christ - ly souls are

ship of love through - out the whole wide earth.
gold - en cord close bind - ing hu - man - kind.
as a child is sure - ly kin to me.
one in him through - out the whole wide earth.

THE KINGDOM OF GOD

How Great Thou Art

Stuart K. Hine, 1953

HOW GREAT THOU ART   11 10 11 10 with Refrain
Swedish melody
harm. Stuart K. Hine, 1953

1 O Lord my God, when I in awe - some
2 When through the woods and for - est glades I
3 And when I think that God, his Son not
4 When Christ shall come with shout of ac - cla -

won - der con - si - der all the worlds thy hand hath
wan - der, and hear the birds sing sweet - ly in the
spar - ing, sent him to die— I scarce can take it
ma - tion and take me home— what joy shall fill my

made, I see the stars, I hear the roll - ing
trees; when I look down from loft - y moun - tain
in: that on the cross, my bur - den glad - ly
heart! Then shall I bow in hum - ble a - dor -

THE KINGDOM OF GOD

thun - der, thy power through-out the un - i - verse dis -
gran - deur, and hear the brook, and feel the gen - tle
bear - ing, he bled and died to take a - way my
a - tion, and there pro - claim, my God, how great thou

played;
breeze;
sin;
art!

Then sings my soul, my Sav - ior God, to

thee, how great thou art! how great thou art! Then sings my

soul, my Sav-ior God, to thee, how great thou art! how great thou art!

343 Seek Not Afar for Beauty

Minot Judson Savage (1841–1918)

COOLINGE 10 10 10 10
Cyril Vincent Taylor, 1951

1 Seek not a - far for beau - ty; lo, it glows in dew-wet
2 Go not a - broad for hap - pi - ness; be - hold it is a
3 In won - der - work - ings or some bush a - flame, we look for

grass - es all a - bout your feet, in birds, in
flow - er bloom - ing at your door. Bring love and
truth and fan - cy it con - cealed; but in earth's

sun - shine, child - ish fac - es sweet, in stars and
laugh - ter home, and ev - er - more joy shall be
com - mon things it stands re - vealed, while grass and

moun - tain sum - mits topped with snows.
yours as chang - ing years un - fold.
flowers and stars spell out the name.

THE KINGDOM OF GOD

Precious Lord, Take My Hand

344

Thomas A. Dorsey, 1932

PRECIOUS LORD IRREGULAR with Refrain
George N. Allen (1812–1877)
adapt. Thomas A. Dorsey, 1932, alt.

1 Pre - cious Lord, take my hand, lead me on, let me
2 When my way grows drear, pre - cious Lord, lin - ger
3 When the dark - ness ap - pears and the night draws

stand, I am tired, I am weak, I am worn;
near, when my life is al - most gone;
near, and the day is past and gone;

through the storm, through the night, lead me on to the
hear my cry, head my call, hold my hand, lest I
at the riv - er I stand, guide my feet, hold my

light, take my hand, pre - cious Lord, lead me on.
fall, take my hand, pre - cious Lord, lead me on.
hand, take my hand, pre - cious Lord, lead me on.

THE KINGDOM OF GOD

345 Morning Glory, Starlit Sky

W. H. Vanstone, 1978, alt.

MEMORIAL CHURCH 77 77 D
Carson P. Cooman, 2002

1 Morn - ing glo - ry, star - lit sky, soar - ing mu - sic,
2 Love that gives, gives ev - er more, gives with zeal, with
3 There - fore he who shows us God help - less hangs up -

schol - ar's truth, flight of swal - lows, au - tumn leaves,
eag - er hands, spares not, keeps not, all out - pours,
on the tree; and the nails and crown of thorns

mem - ory's trea - sure, grace of youth:
ven - tures all, its all ex - pends.
tell of what God's love must be.

THE KINGDOM OF GOD

o - pen are the gifts of God, gifts of love to
Drained is love in mak - ing full, bound in set - ting
Here is God: no mon - arch he, throned in eas - y

mind and sense; hid - den is love's a - go - ny,
o - thers free, poor in mak - ing ma - ny rich,
state to reign; here is God, whose arms of love

love's en - dea - vor, love's ex - pense.
weak in giv - ing power to be.
ach - ing, spent, the world sus - tain.

THE KINGDOM OF GOD

346
From Thee All Skill and Science Flow

Charles Kingsley, 1871

MARSH CHAPEL CM
Max Miller, 1984

1 From thee all skill and sci-ence flow, all pi - ty,
2 Im - part them, Lord, to each and all, as each and
3 And has - ten, Lord, that per - fect day when pain and

care, and love, all calm and cour - age, faith and
all shall need, to rise, like in - cense, each to
death shall cease, and thy just rule shall fill the

hope: O pour them from a - bove.
thee, in no - ble thought and deed.
earth with health and light and peace.

THE KINGDOM OF GOD

I Sought God's Love in Sun and Stars 347

Thomas Curtis Clark (1877–1953)

HARVARD 86 86 88
Arthur Berridge (1855–1932)

1 I sought God's love in sun and stars, and where the wild seas roll,
2 I sought God's love in lore of books, in charts of sci-ence's skill;

I found it not. As mute I stood, fear o-ver-whelmed my soul; but
they left me or-phaned as be-fore—his love e-lud-ed still; then

when I gave to one in need, I found the Lord of lords in-deed.
in de-spair I breathed a prayer; the Lord of Love was stand-ing there!

348   Praise the Source of Faith and Learning

Thomas H. Troeger, 1987, rev. 1989

RUSTINGTON   87 87 D
Charles Hubert Hastings Parry, 1897

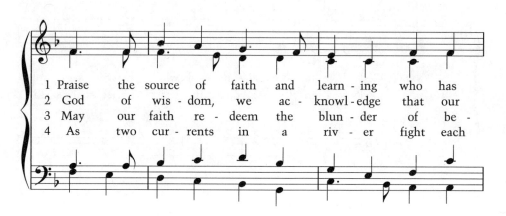

1 Praise the source of faith and learn - ing who has
2 God of wis - dom, we ac - knowl - edge that our
3 May our faith re - deem the blun - der of be -
4 As two cur - rents in a riv - er fight each

sparked and stoked the mind with a pas - sion for dis -
sci - ence and our art and the breadth of hu - man
liev - ing that our thought has dis - placed the grounds for
oth - er's un - der - tow till con - verg - ing they de -

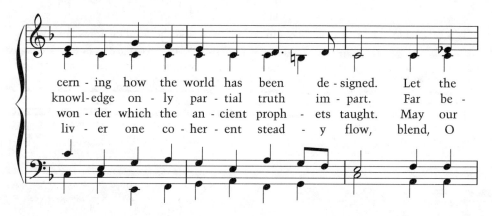

cern - ing how the world has been de - signed. Let the
knowl - edge on - ly par - tial truth im - part. Far be -
won - der which the an - cient proph - ets taught. May our
liv - er one co - her - ent stead - y flow, blend, O

UNIVERSITY AND NATION

sense of won - der flow - ing from the won - ders we sur -
yond our cal - cu - la - tion lies a depth we can - not
learn - ing curb the er - ror which un - think - ing faith can
God, our faith and learn - ing till they carve a sin - gle

vey keep our faith for - ev - er
sound where your pur - pose for cre -
breed lest we jus - ti - fy some
course, till they join as one, re -

grow - ing and re - new our need to pray.
a - tion and the pulse of life are found.
ter - ror with an an - ti - quat - ed creed.
turn - ing praise and thanks to you, their source.

349 · At the Dawning of Creation

Jeffery Rowthorn, 2005

UNION SEMINARY 87 87 44 7
Harold W. Friedell, 1957

1 At the dawn-ing of cre-a - tion stars and an - gels sang for
2 In the shap-ing of each na - tion mus-ic clothes a peo-ple's
3 In this in - sti-tute of learn-ing trea-sured be each mind and

joy; earth and sky in a-do - ra - tion all of
dream; when they long for li - be - ra - tion songs of
heart and, the spi - rit's gifts dis - cern - ing, God be

time for praise em - ploy, Al-le-lu - ia! Al-le-
hope be - come their theme. Al-le-lu - ia! Al-le-
thanked for ev - ery art. Al-le-lu - ia! Al-le-

lu - ia! As God's wond - ers they de - ploy.
lu - ia! Praise to God, our hope su - preme.
lu - ia! Praise re - sounds and all have part.

UNIVERSITY AND NATION

Father of All, We Lift to Thee Our Praise   350

Lionel de Jersey Harvard, 1915

OLD FIRST   10 10 10 10
Genevan Psalter, 1542, alt.

1 Fa - ther of all, we lift to thee our praise,
2 Oft have we fol - lowed oth - er steps than thine,
3 For - ward we go from out these hal - lowed walls,
4 Out of the depths our cry is e - ver heard,

bowed here be - fore thee ere we go our ways.
dimmed in our hearts the sa - cred fire di - vine;
fear - less with thee wher - e'er our du - ty calls;
doubt or temp - ta - tion e'er thy love hath stirred.

Rich has thy dower of bless - ings on us been,
grant we may seek and find thee as thou art,
sun - dered in bo - dy, make us one in thee,
Fa - ther, for - sake not thou our fal - tering way,

rich as re - flec - tion of thy life se - rene.
then send thy strength on ev - ery will - ing heart.
one in the truth that makes thy chil - dren free.
God of our found - ers, be thou ours to - day.

UNIVERSITY AND NATION

351 **For the Splendor of Creation**

Carl P. Daw, Jr., 1989

THAXTED   14 14 15 14 14 14
Gustav Holst, 1921, alt.

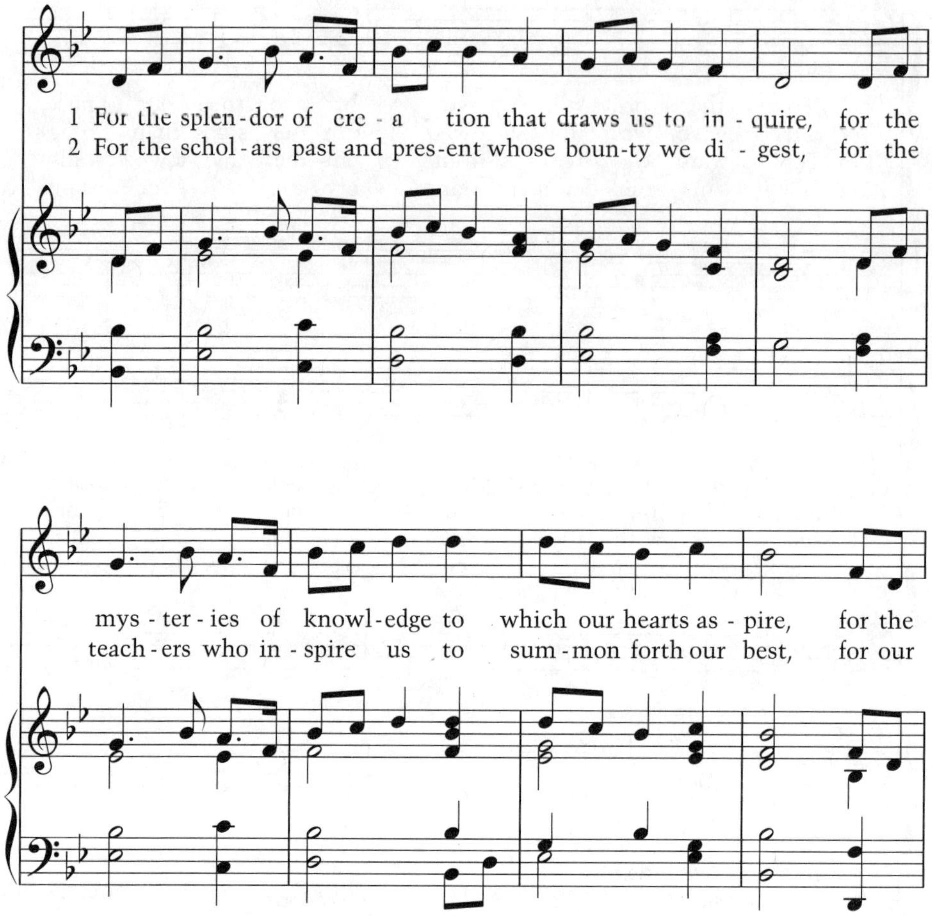

1 For the splen-dor of cre-a tion that draws us to in-quire, for the
2 For the schol-ars past and pres-ent whose boun-ty we di-gest, for the

mys-ter-ies of knowl-edge to which our hearts as-pire, for the
teach-ers who in-spire us to sum-mon forth our best, for our

deep and sub-tle beau-ties which de-light the eye and ear, for the
ri-vals and com pan-ions, some-times fool-ish, some-times wise, for the

UNIVERSITY AND NATION

dis - ci - pline of log - ic, the strug - gle to be clear, for the
hu - man web up - hold - ing this no - ble en - ter - prise, for the

un - ex - plained re - main - der, the puz - zling and the odd: for the
com - mon life that binds us through days that soar or plod: for this

joy and pain of learn - ing, we give you thanks, O God.
place and for these peo - ple, we give you thanks, O God.

352 O Gracious God, Your Servants First

G. W. Briggs, 1920, alt.

THORNBURY 76 76 D
Basil Harwood, 1898

1 O gra-cious God, your ser - vants first built this school of
2 The change-ful years un-rest - ing their si - lent course have
3 They reap not where they la - bored; we reap what they have

old; your hand has crowned their chil-dren with bless ings man-i-
sped, new stu-dents ev - er bring-ing in stu-dents' steps to
sown: our har-vest will be gath-ered by a - ges yet un-

fold. For your un - fail - ing mer - cies, far
tread: and some are long for - got - ten, long
known. The days of old have showered us with

unison

strewn a - long our way, with all who passed be - fore us, we
spent their hopes and fears; safe rest they in your keep - ing, un-
gifts be - yond all praise; O make us ev - er faith - ful to

UNIVERSITY AND NATION

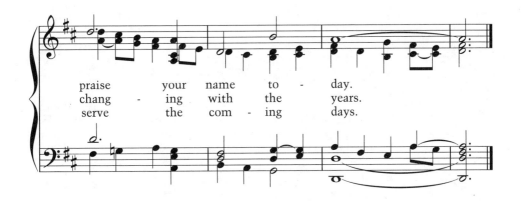

praise   your   name   to - day.
chang - ing   with   the   years.
serve   the   com - ing days.

Life of Ages, Richly Poured   353

Samuel Johnson, 1864

CULBACH   77 77
Heilige Seelenlust, 1657

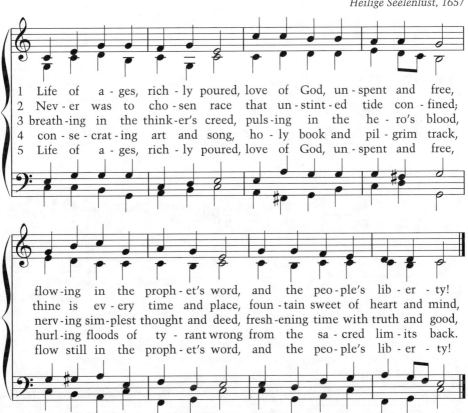

1 Life of a - ges, rich - ly poured, love of God, un - spent and free,
2 Nev - er was to cho - sen race that un - stint - ed tide con - fined;
3 breath-ing in the think-er's creed, puls-ing in the he - ro's blood,
4 con - se - crat-ing art and song, ho - ly book and pil - grim track,
5 Life of a - ges, rich - ly poured, love of God, un - spent and free,

flow-ing in the proph - et's word, and the peo-ple's lib - er - ty!
thine is ev - er - y time and place, foun - tain sweet of heart and mind,
nerv-ing sim-plest thought and deed, fresh-ening time with truth and good,
hurl-ing floods of ty - rant wrong from the sa - cred lim - its back.
flow still in the proph - et's word, and the peo-ple's lib - er - ty!

354 **Lord, You Have Brought Us**

Cyril A. Alington, 1936

SHELDONIAN 10 10 10 10
Cyril Vincent Taylor, 1949

1 Lord, you have brought us to our journey's end: once more to
2 If we have learned to feel our neighbor's need, to fight for
3 If from your paths, by judgment un-dis-mayed, and for your
4 For all the joys which you have deigned to share, for all the

you our grate-ful prayers as-cend; once more we
truth in thought and word and deed; if these are
gifts un-grate-ful, we have strayed, if day by
pains which you have helped to bear, for all our

stand to praise you for the past; grant prayer and
les-sons which the years have taught, con-firm then,
day our prayers were faint and few, for-give, O
friends, in life and death the same, we thank you,

praise be hon-est to the last.
Lord, what you in us have wrought.
Lord, and build our hearts a-new.
Lord, and praise your glo-rious name.

UNIVERSITY AND NATION

Give Ear, Ye Children, to My Law   355

para. of Psalm 78
stanzas 1-3: A New Version of the Psalms, 1696
stanzas 4-5: Isaac Watts, 1719
adapt. Jeremy Belknap, 1795

ST. MARTIN'S   CM
William Tans'ur, 1755

1 Give ear, ye chil - dren, to my law de -
2 My tongue, by in - spi - ra - tion taught, shall
3 which we from sa - cred reg - is - ters of
4 Let chil - dren learn the might - y deeds which
5 Our lips shall tell them to our sons, and

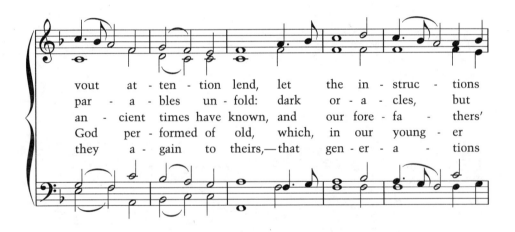

vout at - ten - tion lend, let the in - struc - tions
par - a - bles un - fold: dark or - a - cles, but
an - cient times have known, and our fore - fa - thers'
God per - formed of old, which, in our young - er
they a - gain to theirs,—that gen - er - a - tions

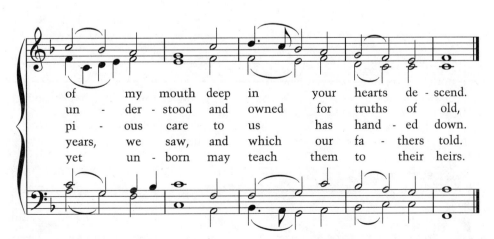

of my mouth deep in your hearts de - scend.
un - der - stood and owned for truths of old,
pi - ous care to us has hand - ed down.
years, we saw, and which our fa - thers told.
yet un - born may teach them to their heirs.

UNIVERSITY AND NATION

356 Deus omnium Creator

James Bradstreet Greenough, 1894

HARVARD HYMN   888 7 D
John Knowles Paine, 1883

1 De - us om - ni - um Cre - a - tor, re - rum mun - di
2 Pa - tres nos - tri huc per - la - ti, tu - o mo - ni -
3 Qua de spe fac te pre - ca - mur in e - ven - tu -
4 Sic dum ci - vi - tas ma - ne - bit, cla - rum lu - men

mo - de - ra - tor, cres - cat cu - ius es fun - da - tor,
tu, per - gra - ti, de - di - ca - runt ve - ri - ta - ti
ne fal - la - mur, sed ma - ior - a dum co - na - mur
hic lu - ce - bit, lu - ce an - gu - los re - ple - bit,

nos - tra U - ni - ver - si - tas, in - te - gri sint
par - vum tum Con - le - gi - um, id - que tu - o
fa - ve - as la - bor - i - bus, si - mul gra - ti -
fu - ge - rit ob - scu - ri - tas, er - ror ter - ri -

UNIVERSITY AND NATION

cu - ra - to - res, e - ru - di - ti pro - fes - so - res,
post fa - vo - re auc - tum sem - per et a - mo - re
as ha - be - mus quod tam di - u iam flo - re - mus
tus la - te - bit, vir - tus vi - vi - da va - le - bit,

lar - gi - an - tur do - na - to - res
bo - nam spem os - ten - tat fo - re
nec au - di - re re - mit - te - mus
et in - sig - ni - or flo - re - bit

be - ne par - tas co - pi - as.
tem - plum qua - si re - gi - um.
ve - ri - ta - tis mo - ni - tus.
nos - tra U - ni - ver - si - tas.

UNIVERSITY AND NATION

357   Thy Book Falls Open, Lord: We Read

David McCord, 1964

NISI DOMINUS   88 88 10 8
Randall Thompson, 1964

1 Thy book falls o - pen, Lord: we read, who shear the land to
2 A - gainst the wind to morn - ing tide we came in col - o -
3 Vouch - safe us, Lord this In - dian ground where men of won - drous
4 The pat - terns of the web con - spire, the se - crets of the
5 John Har - vard's Har - vard: an - cient clan, de - lib - er - ate in

fleece the sky, strike in - ward to the cen - tral seed, sail
ny, be - got this Col - lege in the light de - nied a
mind and tongue, un - wea - ried in pri - va - tion, found thy
void in - vite; di - vid - ing at - om, quench - ing fire, we
peace and war, hu - mane in wis - dom, man for man as

out - ward when the reefs are dry— di -
god - ly but be - lea - guered lot, twice
serv - ice, tes - ti - fied the young; and
kill the snake to keep the bite; build
men for men who went be - fore through

UNIVERSITY AND NATION

358   **Fair Harvard**

Samuel Gilman, 1836, alt.

FAIR HARVARD   IRREGULAR
Vocal Music, 1775
adapt. Karl Pomeroy Harrington, 1922

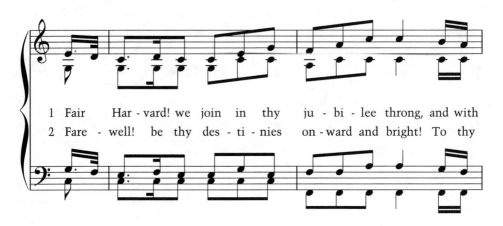

1 Fair Har-vard! we join in thy ju-bi-lee throng, and with
2 Fare-well! be thy des-ti-nies on-ward and bright! To thy

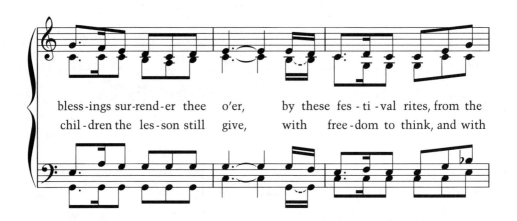

bless-ings sur-rend-er thee o'er, by these fes-ti-val rites, from the
chil-dren the les-son still give, with free-dom to think, and with

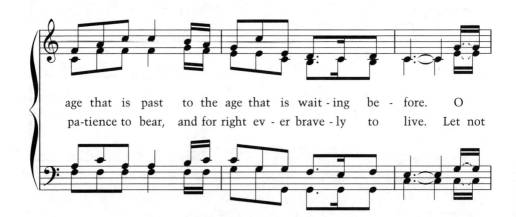

age that is past to the age that is wait-ing be - fore. O
pa-tience to bear, and for right ev - er brave-ly to live. Let not

rel - ic and type of our an - ces - tors' worth, that hast
moss - cov - ered er - ror moor thee at its side, as the

long kept their mem - o - ry warm, first flower of their wil - der - ness!
world on truth's cur - rent glides by; be the her - ald of light, and the

star of their night! Calm ris - ing through change and through storm.
bear - er of love, till the stock of the Pur - i - tans die.

Now Praise We Great and Famous Men

para. of Ecclesiasticus 44:1-7
William George Tarrant, 1912, alt.

ACH GOTT UND HERR   87 87
As hymnodus sacer, 1625
harm. Johann Sebastian Bach (1685–1750)

1 Now praise we great and fa - mous men, the
2 Praise ho - ly wom - en, bea - cons too of
3 Praise we the wise and brave and strong, who
4 Praise we the great of heart and mind, the
5 Praise we the peace - ful, those of skill, who

fa - thers named in sto - ry; and praise the Lord, who
God's e - ter - nal splen - dor. Like then, great wom - en
graced their gen - er - a - tion, who helped the right, and
sing - ers sweet - ly gift - ed, whose mu - sic like a
build - ed homes of beau - ty. And, rich in art, made

now as then re - veals in men his glo - ry.
tried and true to - day their praise do ren - der.
fought the wrong, and hon - ored thus their na - tion.
might - y wind the souls of all up - lift - ed.
rich - er still our liv - ing through their du - ty.

UNIVERSITY AND NATION

O Valiant Hearts, Who to Your Glory Came   360

John Stanhope Arkwright, 1919, alt.

VALIANT HEARTS   10 10 10 10
Gustav Holst, 1925

1 O val - iant hearts, who to your glo - ry came
2 Proud - ly you gath - ered, rank on rank, to war,
3 Splen - did you passed, the great sur - ren - der made,
4 O ris - en Lord, O Shep - herd of our dead,

through dust of con - flict and through bat - tle flame,
as who had heard God's mes - sage from a - far;
in - to the light that nev - er more shall fade;
whose cross has bought them and whose staff has led,

tran - quil you lie, your knight - ly vir - tue proved,
all you had hoped for, all you had, you gave
deep your con - tent - ment in that blest a - bode,
in glo - rious hope their proud and sor - rowing land

your mem - ory hal - lowed in the land you loved.
to save us, yet your - selves you scorned to save.
who wait the last clear trum - pet - call of God.
com - mits her chil - dren to thy gra - cious hand.

UNIVERSITY AND NATION

361   Not Alone for Mighty Empire

William Pierson Merrill, 1909
adapt. Matthew F. Burt, 2007

GENEVA   87 87 D
George Henry Day, 1940

1 Not a-lone for migh-ty em-pire stretch-ing far o'er land and sea, not a-lone for boun-teous harv-ests lift we up our hearts to thee:

2 Not for bat-tle-ship and for-tress, not for con-quests, of the sword, but for con-quests of the spir-it, give we thanks to thee, O Lord;

3 For the arm-ies of the faith-ful, souls that passed and left no name; for the glo-ry that il-lu-mines pa-triot lives of death-less fame;

4 God of jus-tice, save the peo-ple from the clash of race and creed, from the strife of class and fac-tion, make our na-tion free in-deed;

UNIVERSITY AND NATION

stand - ing in the liv - ing pre - sent,
for the her - i - tage of free - dom,
for our pro - phets and a - pos - tles,
keep our faith in your re - demp - tion

mem - o - ry and hope be - tween, Lord, we would with
for the home, the church, the school, for the tasks that
loy - al to the liv - ing Word, for all he - roes
strong as when the pil - grims trod through this land to

deep thanks-giv - ing praise thee most for things un -seen.
bring us near - er to the joys of heav -en's rule.
of the Spir - it, give we thanks to thee, O Lord.
find its boun - ty in the fel - low - ship of God.

UNIVERSITY AND NATION

O God of Earth and Altar

G. K. Chesterton, 1906, alt.

KING'S LYNN   76 76 D
English melody
harm. Ralph Vaughan Williams, 1906

1 O God of earth and al - tar, bow down and hear our
2 From all that ter - ror teach - es, from lies of pen and
3 Tie in a liv - ing teth - er the prince and priest and

cry, our earth - ly ru - lers fal - ter, our
page, from all the ea - sy speech - es that
thrall, bind all our lives to - geth - er, smite

peo - ple drift and die; the walls of gold en -
mas - quer - ade as sage, from sale and prof - a -
us and save us all; in ire and ex - ul -

UNIVERSITY AND NATION

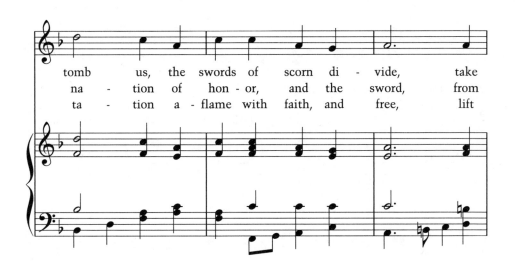

tomb us, the swords of scorn di - vide, take
na - tion of hon - or, and the sword, from
ta - tion a - flame with faith, and free, lift

not thy thun - der from us, but take a - way our pride.
sleep and from dam - na - tion, de - liv - er us, good Lord!
up a liv - ing na - tion, a sin - gle sword to thee.

UNIVERSITY AND NATION

363   Judge Eternal, Throned in Splendor

Henry Scott Holland, 1902, alt.

ZEUCH MICH, ZEUCH MICH   87 87 87
Geistreiches Gesang-Buch, Darmstadt, 1698
harm. William Henry Monk, 1861

1 Judge e - ter - nal, throned in splen - dor, Lord of lords and
2 Still the wea - ry folk are pin - ing for the hour that
3 Crown, O God, thine own en - deav - or; cleave our dark - ness

King of kings, with thy liv - ing fire of judg - ment
brings re - lease, and the cit - y's crowd - ed clang - or
with thy sword; feed the faint and hun - gry peo - ples

purge this land of bit - ter things: sol - ace all its
cries a - loud for sin to cease, and the home - steads
with the rich - ness of thy word; cleanse the bod - y

wide do - min - ion with the heal - ing of thy wings.
and the wood - lands plead in si - lence for their peace.
of this na - tion through the glo - ry of the Lord.

UNIVERSITY AND NATION

God of the Nations, Whose Almighty Hand 364

Daniel Crane Roberts, 1876, alt.

NATIONAL HYMN 10 10 10 10
George William Warren, 1888

1 God of the na - tions, whose al - might - y
2 Thy love di - vine hath led us in the
3 From war's a - larms, from dead - ly pes - ti -
4 Re - fresh thy peo - ple on their pil - grim

hand   leads forth in beau - ty all the star - ry band
past,   in this free land by thee our lot is cast;
lence,   be thy strong arm our ev - er sure de - fense;
way,   lead us from night to nev - er - end - ing day;

of   shin - ing worlds   in splen - dor through the skies,
be   thou   our   ru -   ler, guard - ian, guide, and stay,
thy true   re - li -   gion in our hearts in - crease,
fill all   our lives   with love and grace di - vine,

our   grate - ful songs   be - fore thy throne a - rise.
thy   word our law,   thy paths our cho - sen way.
thy   boun - teous good - ness nour - ish us in peace.
and   glo - ry, laud,   and praise be   ev - er thine.

UNIVERSITY AND NATION

365   And Did Those Feet in Ancient Time

William Blake, 1804

JERUSALEM   LMD
Charles Hubert Hastings Parry, 1916

1 And did those feet in an-cient time, walk up-on England's moun-tains green? And was the ho - ly Lamb of

God on Eng-land's plea-sant pas - tures seen? And did the coun - te-nance di - vine shine forth up - on our cloud-ed hills? And was Je - ru - sa-lem build-ed here a - mong those

green and plea-sant land.

My Country, 'Tis of Thee

366

Samuel Francis Smith, 1831

AMERICA   664 6664
Harmonia Anglicana, London, c. 1744, alt.

1 My coun-try, 'tis of thee, sweet land of lib - er - ty,
2 My na - tive coun - try, thee, land of the no - ble free,
3 Let mu - sic swell the breeze, and ring from all the trees
4 Our fa - thers' God, to thee, au - thor of lib - er - ty,

of thee I sing; land where my fa - thers died, land of the
thy name I love; I love thy rocks and rills, thy woods and
sweet free-dom's song; let mor - tal tongues a - wake; let all that
to thee we sing; long may our land be bright with free-dom's

pil - grims' pride, from ev - ery moun -tain side let free - dom ring.
tem - pled hills; my heart with rap -ture thrills like that a - bove.
breathe par - take; let rocks their si - lence break; the sound pro - long.
ho - ly light; pro - tect us by thy might, great God, our King.

367   Battle Hymn of the Republic

Julia W. Howe, 1861, alt.   BATTLE HYMN OF THE REPUBLIC   15 15 15 6 with Refrain

American, 19th cent.

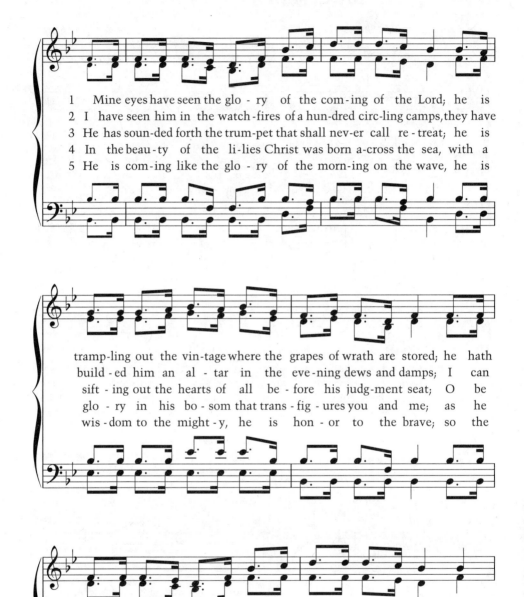

1. Mine eyes have seen the glo - ry of the com-ing of the Lord; he is
2. I have seen him in the watch-fires of a hun-dred circ-ling camps, they have
3. He has soun-ded forth the trum-pet that shall nev-er call re - treat; he is
4. In the beau-ty of the li-lies Christ was born a-cross the sea, with a
5. He is com-ing like the glo - ry of the morn-ing on the wave, he is

tramp-ling out the vin-tage where the grapes of wrath are stored; he hath
build-ed him an al-tar in the eve-ning dews and damps; I can
sift-ing out the hearts of all be-fore his judg-ment seat; O be
glo - ry in his bo-som that trans-fig-ures you and me; as he
wis-dom to the might-y, he is hon-or to the brave; so the

loosed the fate-ful light-ning of his ter-ri-ble swift sword; his
read his right-eous sen-tence by the dim and flar-ing lamps; his
swift, my soul, to an-swer him; be ju-bi-lant, my feet! Our
died to make men ho-ly, let us work till all are free, while
world shall be his foot-stool, and the soul of wrong his slave. Our

UNIVERSITY AND NATION

truth is march-ing on.
day is march-ing on.
God is march-ing on.   Glo - ry, glo-ry, Hal-le-lu - jah!
God is march-ing on.
God is march-ing on.

Glo - ry, glo-ry, Hal-le-lu - jah!   Glo - ry, glo-ry, Hal-le-

lu - jah! His truth is march - ing on.

The Star-Spangled Banner

Francis Scott Key, 1814

NATIONAL ANTHEM   IRREGULAR
John Stafford Smith, c. 1777, alt.

1 O   say, can you   see,   by the dawn's ear - ly   light,   what so
2 O   thus be   it   ev - er, when free-men shall stand   be -

proud - ly   we hailed   at the twi-light's last gleam-ing, whose broad
tween their loved homes   and the war's des - o - la - tion! Blest with

stripes and bright stars, through the per - il - lous fight, o'er the ram-parts we
vic - tory and peace, may the heaven-res-cued land praise the power that hath

watched, were so gal-lant-ly stream - ing? And the rock-ets' red glare, the bombs
made and pre-served us a   na - tion! Then con-quer we must, when our

UNIVERSITY AND NATION

burst-ing in air, gave proof through the night that our flag was still
cause it is just, and this be our mot-to, "In God is our

there. O say does that star-span-gled ban-ner yet
trust." And the star-span-gled ban-ner in tri-umph shall

wave o'er the land of the free and the home of the brave?
wave o'er the land of the free and the home of the brave!

369   O Beautiful for Spacious Skies

Katherine Lee Bates, 1904, alt.

MATERNA CMD
Samuel Augustus Ward, 1882

1 O beau-ti-ful for spa-cious skies, for am-ber waves of grain, for
2 O beau-ti-ful for he-roes proved in lib-er-at-ing strife, who
3 O beau-ti-ful for pa-triot dream that sees be-yond the years thine
4 O beau-ti-ful for glo-ry-tale of lib-er-a-ting strife when

pur-ple moun-tain ma-jes-ties a-bove the fruit-ed plain! A-
more than self their coun-try loved, and mer-cy more than life! A-
al-a-bas-ter ci-ties gleam, un-dimmed by hu-man tears! A-
once and twice, for man's a-vail, men lav-ished pre-cious life! A-

mer-i-ca! A-mer-i-ca! God shed his grace on thee, and
mer-i-ca! A-mer-i-ca! God mend thine ev-ery flaw, con-
mer-i-ca! A-mer-i-ca! God shed his grace on thee, and
mer-i-ca! A-mer-i-ca! God shed his grace on thee, till

crown thy good with bro-ther-hood from sea to shin-ing sea.
firm thy soul in self-con-trol, thy lib-er-ty in law.
crown thy good with bro-ther-hood from sea to shin-ing sea.
self-ish gain no long-er stain the ban-ner of the free!

UNIVERSITY AND NATION

Glory to You, Our Faithful God

370

para. of Benedictus es, Domine
Carl P. Daw, Jr., 1990

O JESU CHRISTE, WAHRES LICHT LM
Nürnbergisches Gesang-Buch, 1676

1 Glo-ry to you, our faith-ful God, for you are
2 Glo-ry to you in splen-dor shrined, re-splend-ent
3 Glo-ry to you, in heav-en's height, guard-ing the

wor-thy of all praise; blest be the ra-diance
on your roy-al throne, dwell-ing be-tween the
deep with watch-ful care. Glo-ry to you, our

of your name: we will ex-alt you ev-er-more.
cher-u-bim: we will ex-alt you ev-er-more.
Tri-une God; we will ex-alt you ev-er-more.

DOXOLOGY

371   **Glory Be to the Father**

Gloria Patri

EHR' SEI DEM VATER   746 876
Plainsong, Tone 5
adapt. Regina H. Fryxell, 1958

Glo - ry be to the Fa - ther, and to the Son,

and to the Ho - ly Ghost: as it was in the be - gin - ning,

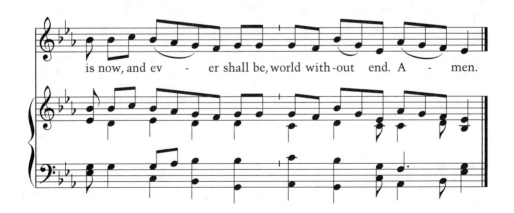

is now, and ev - er shall be, world with-out end. A - men.

DOXOLOGY

Notes on the Hymns

1   All People That on Earth Do Dwell

OLD HUNDREDTH first appeared as the setting for Psalm 134 in the Genevan Psalter of 1551, but was used as the proper tune for William Kethe's paraphrase of Psalm 100 in the early English psalters. It soon became associated with the "Old Version" psalter of Sternhold and Hopkins first published 1562, hence the present name. This hymn has traditionally been sung each week as the opening hymn in Sunday morning worship services in The Memorial Church.

2   All Creatures of Our God and King

Based on the "Cantico delle creature," better known as the "Cantico di fratre sole" ("Canticle of brother sun") attributed to Francis of Assisi, the founder of the Franciscan Order, this paraphrase was originally written for a children's musical festival, but has found wide use as one of the best-known paraphrases of this text.

3   Let the Whole Creation Cry

The author of this text, Stopford Brooke, a Famous London preacher, resigned his Church of England orders in 1880 in protest against "ecclesiastical dogmatism." This text was written in 1881 and prepared for his independent congregation at Bedford Chapel, London, England.

4   For the Beauty of the Earth

The inspiration for this text by Folliot Sandford Pierpoint allegedly came from frequent walks he took near his home in Bath, England. It was originally written as a Eucharistic hymn, but has found wide use in many other circumstances, particularly with children. Information on the tune can be found in the note about no. 135.

5   Now Thank We All Our God

The translator of this text, English poet Catherine Winkworth, is one of the most significant figures in the history of hymnody, as many of her more than two hundred translations of German chorales are still in widespread use. Although both she and her sister had been active translators of German prose, it was upon being presented with copies of German chorale collections by the German ambassador to England that Winkworth's intense engagement with translating the German chorale tradition began.

6   When the Morning Stars Together

Drawing on both his commitment to working-class people and his love of the Hebrew prophets, the British clergyman and poet Alfred Bayly wrote many hymns, such as "What does the Lord require for praise and offering?" whose focus on social justice and contemporary concerns helped to spark the "Hymn Renaissance" of the 1960s and 1970s.

7   O Be Joyful in the Lord

Curtis Beach was a 1935 graduate of Harvard who served as a Congregational minister in Pittsburgh, Pennsylvania. Both text and tune for this hymn were composed for the Congregational *Pilgrim Hymnal* of 1958. Pilgrim Press, the publishers of that book, were responsible for the physical production of the 1964 edition of *The Harvard University Hymn Book*.

8   Let Us with a Gladsome Mind

This paraphrase of Psalm 136 by John Milton was written when he was only fifteen years old and originally contained 24 verses. The source of the tune MONKLAND proved a hymnological riddle for many years before discoveries in the late 20th century revealed the myriad Moravian connections to the original tune and its adaptation.

9   Praise, My Soul, the King of Heaven

This hymn is one of the most popular hymns in Great Britain and has been sung at many state occasions, including the 1947 wedding in Westminster Abbey of the then-Princess Elizabeth and Prince Philip. The printed harmonization appeared with the second stanza of John Goss's original, which provided a different accompaniment for each verse.

10   We Sing of God, the Mighty Source

Although he was one of the most important and visionary poets of his era, Christopher Smart spent parts of his adult life committed to an asylum because of manifestations of severe, delusional religious mania. This hymn is an extensive adaptation from verses in his *magnum opus*, the epic "A Song to David," written during one of his periods of confinement.

11   Sing Praise to God Who Reigns Above

The author of the German language original of this text, Johann Schütz, was a lawyer by profession, but was heavily involved in the German Pietistic movement of the late 17th and early 18th centuries, which combined a Lutheran focus on the primacy of scripture with Calvinist and Puritan values of piety in individual living.

12   The God of Abraham Praise

This hymn is one of the few examples in modern hymnody of a translation from a non-biblical Hebrew source poem. Although first translated in England in 1763, the version here used is of American origin. Matching the Jewish origins of the text, the tune was adapted from a traditional synagogue melody by English cantor Meyer Lyon.

13   Come, O Come, in Pious Lays

George Wither supported the Parliamentary cause during the English Civil War and first published this text in a collection of hymns that he dedicated to the members of the Long Parliament (1640–1649). J. S. Bach's harmonization of this tune comes not from a cantata, but from a collection of harmonized chorale melodies published posthumously in 1769.

14   God is Love, Let Heaven Adore Him

This text was discovered posthumously among the papers of Timothy Rees, Bishop of Llandaff, Wales. The tune was composed by a Church of England priest, Cyril Vincent Taylor, on a Sunday morning in 1941 in the BBC's wartime headquarters. Taylor was then working in the division of religious broadcasting, in Abbot's Leigh, near Bristol, England.

15   Praise Our Great and Gracious Lord

The tune MAOZ TSUR is traditionally sung at Chanukah, during the lighting of the lights in home and synagogue. Although it was believed for years to be entirely of Jewish origin, musicologists in the early 20th century traced its first sources to a hymn of Martin Luther based upon a German folk song.

16   O God, We Praise Thee and Confess

The tune TALLIS' ORDINAL was originally composed for a translation of the Pentecost hymn "Veni Creator Spiritus." In the original 1549 edition of the English *Book of Common Prayer*, the hymn was prescribed for use at ordination services, hence the tune name.

17   Ye Holy Angels Bright

John Darwall served as the vicar of Walsall in Staffordshire, England and composed tunes for all 150 psalms. However, this tune, originally written for a paraphrase of Psalm 148, is the only one that survives today. This text was first published in Richard Baxter's *The Poor Man's Family Book*, which provided "forms of prayer, praise, and catechism for the use of ignorant families that need them."

18   King of Glory, King of Peace

The entire poetic corpus of English metaphysical poet George Herbert was first published in the year following his death. John Wesley adapted this text in a wordier version that he published in 1737, and it was only in 20th century hymnals that this text began to appear in its concise, original form.

19   O Praise Ye the Lord! Sing Praise in the Height

Henry W. Baker, author of this paraphrase of Psalms 148 and 150, served as the chairman of the committee that prepared *Hymns Ancient and Modern*, the most popular and influential English hymnal of the nineteenth century. Charles Hubert Hastings Parry's tune was extracted from the end of his choral anthem *Hear My Words* of 1894.

20   Angel-Voices Ever Singing

Both text and tune of this hymn were originally written to celebrate an 1861 organ dedication at the Church of St. John the Evangelist at Wingate in Lancashire, England. Though popular with British congregations, it has rarely appeared in American hymnals.

21   Holy God, We Praise Thy Name

The text of this hymn is a translation into English of a German metrical version of the "Te Deum laudamus." This text, one of the best-known hymns of the early church, was traditionally ascribed to Saints Ambrose and Augustine on the occasion of Augustine's baptism by Ambrose in 387. Modern scholarship dates the text to the 4th or 5th centuries and believes it likely to be an assemblage of older material.

22   O Worship the King, All Glorious Above

This text is the best-known hymn by English poet Robert Grant, who served as a Member of Parliament. Born in India, he returned there after schooling in England to become Governor of Bombay in 1834. In addition to volumes of sacred poetry, he also published several books on the economics and trade dynamics of the colonial Indian government.

23   Joyful, Joyful, We Adore Thee

American Presbyterian minister Henry van Dyke presented this text in 1907 to the president of Williams College of Williamstown, Massachusetts claiming that it had been inspired by the Berkshire Mountains near the college campus. He wrote it specifically for this melody, taken from the finale of Ludwig van Beethoven's *Symphony No. 9*, op. 125.

24   Praise to the Holiest in the Height

The text of this hymn is an excerpt from the 1875 extended poem "The Dream of Gerontius" written by John Henry Newman. English musician and clergyman John Bacchus Dykes was one of the most frequently commissioned hymn tune composers of his era. It is believed that he adapted material from one of his previous hymn tunes to create the tune GERONTIUS, specifically for this poem.

25   When in Our Music God Is Glorified

English Methodist clergyman and poet Fred Pratt Green was one of the prime movers in the "Hymn Renaissance" of the 1960s, sparking a widespread interest in the creation of new hymn texts and tunes. This text is among Green's best-known works. Charles Villiers Stanford's tune ENGELBERG was originally written for the text "For All the Saints," but is now more commonly associated with the present text.

26   Before Jehovah's Aweful Throne

This adaptation of an Isaac Watts text was prepared by John Wesley while he was serving as a missionary in the state of Georgia. It was first published in Charleston, South Carolina in 1737, in the first hymnal (as distinct from a psalter) to be printed within the American colonies.

27   We Gather Together to Ask the Lord's Blessing

This anonymous hymn, which celebrated the winning of Dutch independence from Spain at the end of the sixteenth century, was first published in 1626. The translator, Theodore Baker, served for many years as literary editor for G. Schirmer music publishers in New York; he also edited the seminal *Biographical Dictionary of Musicians*.

28   To God Be the Glory

Although composed by Americans Fanny Crosby and William Doane, this hymn first gained popularity in Great Britain, where it featured in the Moody and Sankey revival meetings of the late 19th century. The hymn finally entered widespread use in America after it appeared in the 1954 crusades of the American evangelist Billy Graham, following his 1952 crusades in Great Britain.

29   This Is My Song, O God of All the Nations

This hymn tune originally appears as the quiet middle section of Finnish composer Jean Sibelius's nationalistic symphonic poem entitled *Finlandia*, op. 26. Once the tune became popular, Sibelius arranged it as a stand-alone hymn, in which version it has become associated with the patriotic words by Veikko Antero Koskenniemi: "Oi, Suomi, katso, sinun päiväs' koittaa" (O, Finland, behold thy day is dawning.) Lloyd Stone's text is an international adaptation of the original Finnish poem.

30   To God with Gladness Sing

James Quinn is a Scottish Jesuit priest and poet best known for his influential text collection *New Hymns for All Seasons*, published in 1969. In the years following, his texts and paraphrases have been included in most English-language hymnals. Samuel Sebastian Wesley's tune HAREWOOD is named for a village in West Yorkshire, England.

31   Ye Watchers and Ye Holy Ones

Athelstan Laurie Riley wrote this text specifically for *The English Hymnal* of 1906. The text displays Riley's enthusiasm for the rites of the Eastern Orthodox Church: the second stanza of the text is a paraphrase of the "Theotokion." Ralph Vaughan Williams adapted the hymn tune LASST UNS ERFREUEN from a 15th century German church melody specifically for this text.

32   God Beyond All Human Praises

Charles P. Price, an Episcopal priest, served Harvard University as Plummer Professor of Christian Morals and Preacher to the University from 1963 to 1972. Both text and tune of this hymn were written for the investiture of Mary Adelia McLeod as Episcopal Bishop of Vermont in 1993. The original version of this text had eight verses, suitable for use in festival procession.

33   Praise to the Lord, the Almighty

Although this hymn is well-known to most congregations, the tune, as it appeared in the third edition of *The Harvard University Hymn Book* and again here, displays a number of differences from the more commonly-known form. This more florid version uses J. S. Bach's harmonization and adaptation of the melody as it appears in Cantata No. 57, *"Selig ist der Mann,"* originally written for the second day of the Christmas festival in 1725.

34   Let All the World in Every Corner Sing

The unusual metrical demands of George Herbert's poetry have provided interesting challenges for composers. English organist and composer Basil Harwood's tune LUCKINGTON is most commonly associated with this text, one of Herbert's shortest and most straight-forward poems, originally entitled "Antiphon."

35   God of the Morning, at Whose Voice

William Billings is often considered the most significant American composer of the 18th century. A native of Boston and a tanner by trade, he provided a great impetus to the development of choral music in New England by organizing many singing schools and publishing numerous volumes of hymn tunes and anthems. His idiosyncratic musical style developed largely independently of European influences and possesses rough-hewn harmonies and textures.

36   My Soul, Awake and Render

German composer and organist Nicolas Selnecker served as pastor of St. Thomas' Church in Leipzig, Germany, where he founded the choir that J. S. Bach would direct two centuries later. Bach's vibrant harmonization of this chorale is taken from Cantata No. 194, "*Höchsterwünschtes Freudenfest*," originally composed for the dedication of a church.

37   Father, We Praise Thee, Now the Night Is Over

The original Latin hymn from which this text is derived has been ascribed to Pope Gregory the Great, who did much to shape the musical tradition of the medieval church by encouraging the codification of the many chants used in the Roman church and the standardization of their liturgical use. In France during the 16th and 17th centuries, traditional unmeasured plainsong melodies were often replaced with metrical tunes founded on plainsong, such as CHRISTE SANCTORUM.

38   Once More the Daylight Shines Abroad

Under the influence of Martin Luther's teaching, author Michael Weisse left his monastery and joined the Bohemian Brethren, descendants of the followers of 15th century reformer Jan Hus, and the ancestors of the Moravians (or United Brethren). As well as authoring original hymn texts, he translated many Czech hymns into German.

39   Lord God of Morning and of Night

American composer M. Lee Suitor composed the tune CORNISH for a festival of young people in Atlanta in 1975. The tune was originally named ST. DAVID, but the composer renamed in honor of a friend whose name was Cornish. It was first published in the Episcopal *Hymnal 1982* and has since appeared in a number of books.

40   Morning Has Broken

For the Anglican hymnal *Songs of Praise* of 1931, editor Percy Dearmer asked poet Eleanor Farjeon to write a text for the Irish folk melody BUNESSAN. He specifically requested a text of "thanksgiving for each day as it comes." The tune gained its name from the town in Scotland that was the birthplace of Mary Macdonald, author of the tune's original text, "Christ in the manger."

41   Christ Whose Glory Fills the Skies

The tune RATISBON is a composite of many difference sources. Originally stemming from a 15th century German folk hymn, many divergent versions were published through the years before William Henry Havergal dramatically adapted it into its current form. Since the first publication of his version in 1847, it has been associated with this text by Charles Wesley.

42   Each Morning Brings Us Fresh Outpoured

The author of this text, Johannes Zwick, was a minister and leader of the Swiss Reformation. Active in religious musical circles, he served as the chief editor of the first two editions, in 1536 and 1540, of the Swiss hymnal *Nüw gsangbüchle*.

43   Awake, My Soul, and with the Sun

Thomas Ken wrote hymns for use at morning, evening, and midnight for the students at Winchester College, where he was a fellow. He later served as canon of Winchester Cathedral. The most famous of the dissenting bishops during the Glorious Revolution, he was imprisoned and then removed from his See.

44   When Morning Gilds the Skies

Although Joseph Barnby composed nearly 250 hymn tunes during his musical career, he is remembered primarily for LAUDES DOMINI, which draws upon the style of the 19th century partsong, a genre in which he was also proficient. As a conductor and musicologist, he is best remembered for popularizing the music of French composer Charles Gounod in England.

45   Heaven and Earth, and Sea and Air

German theologican and poet Joachim Neander wrote over sixty hymn texts and composed music for nearly all of them, though he is remembered today primarily as a poet. The inspiration for many of his poems was the Düssel valley, which was re-named "Neanderthal" ("Neander valley") in his honor during the 19th century. It was in this valley that the skeletal remains of *Homo neanderthalensis* were discovered in 1856, thus linking Neander's name to one of the most important discoveries in paleoanthropology.

46   Awake, Awake to Love and Work

English clergyman and poet Geoffrey A. Studdert-Kennedy served as a military chaplain during World War I, during which he earned the nickname "Woodbine Willie" for his habit of distributing cigarettes to soldiers. Studdert-Kennedy published many volumes of poems and hymns, including such striking texts as "When through the whirl of wheels and engines humming," which celebrates God's grace even in an era of mechanized warfare.

47   New Every Morning Is the Love

John Keble, professor of poetry at Oxford, was one of the leaders of the Oxford Movement in the Church of England. His famous sermon of 1833 on "national apostasy" was a major inspiration for this effort to reassert the catholicity of the Anglican church.

48   Come, My Soul, Thou Must Be Waking

The tune RICHTER gained its name from its original text by Christian Friedrich Richter. It first appeared in the *Gestreiches Gesang-Buch* of 1704, which was edited by Johann Anastasius Freylinghausen, the leading hymnodist of the German Pietist movement. This book became the most popular German hymnal of the 18th century.

49   Abide with Me, Fast Falls the Eventide

The creation of the tune EVENTIDE by William Henry Monk is told in two different stories—either of which may be true. In the first, Monk left a committee meeting of the editorial board of *Hymns Ancient and Modern* and, realizing that no tune had yet been selected for this text, composed the tune in ten minutes. In the other, more maudlin, story, Monk wrote the tune at twilight, while seated with his wife watching the setting of the evening sun.

50   O Gladsome Light, O Grace

The text of this hymn is a translation and paraphrase of the "Phos hilaron," widely considered to be the earliest known non-biblical Christian hymn still used today. The hymn is used in the Vespers liturgy of the Byzantine church, and appears in the Episcopal *Book of Common Prayer* as the invitatory at Evening Prayer.

51   The Duteous Day Now Closeth

The tune O WELT, ICH MUSS DICH LASSEN is first found in a harmonization by Heinrich Isaac, composer to Emperor Maximilian I, in a collection published in 1539. It appears there to the traveling artisan's song, "Innsbruck, ich muss dich lassen." The tune name derives from its use for Johann Hesse's funeral hymn, which is a sacred adaptation of the original Innsbruck text.

52   Christ, Mighty Savior, Light of All Creation

The original Latin text of this hymn appears in the Mozarabic liturgy for Vespers on the Third Sunday after Epiphany. Anne K. LeCroy's translation reduced the original nine stanzas of the hymn to five and cast it in contemporary language. The melody is drawn from a breviary of an Augustinian house in Freiburg, Switzerland.

53   Again, as Evening's Shadow Falls

Poet Samuel Longfellow, younger brother of Henry Wadsworth Longfellow, graduated from Harvard College in 1838, and from Harvard Divinity School in 1846. He served Unitarian congregations in Massachusetts, New York, and Pennsylvania, and, together with Samuel Johnson, published two Unitarian hymnals.

54   O Strength and Stay Upholding All Creation

English musician and clergyman John Bacchus Dykes was one of the most frequently commissioned hymn tune composers of his era. He composed over 300 tunes and, although an Anglican cleric, accepted many commissions for hymns from non-Anglican sources. A large number of his hymn tunes have remained in active use.

55   The Day Thou Gavest, Lord, Is Ended

The inspiration for this text came to John Ellerton when an anonymous author wrote two weak stanzas for the journal *Church Poetry*, beginning with the first line of this hymn. Ellerton used that line as the starting point for his own superior text. The tune ST. CLEMENT was written expressly for this text, though it originally appeared in the key of A major.

56   Creator of the Earth and Sky

The text of this hymn is one of the few that can be conclusively attributed to Ambrose of Milan, one of the most important bishops of the early church. He became Bishop of Milan in 374 by acclamation, though at the time was unbaptized and possessed no theological training. The tune was originally named UFFINGTON but was changed, perhaps unintentionally, in 1789 to UFFINGHAM.

57   All Praise to Thee, My God, This Night

Thomas Tallis composed nine tunes to accompany the 1567 publication *The Whole Psalter translated into English Metre*; each tune is referred to by its number. TALLIS'

CANON is a shortened form of "The Eighth Tune." In the original form, each line was repeated to make an eight line melody. As the tune name implies, the tune can be sung as a canon, and Tallis's original harmonization contains the canon itself embedded in the harmony.

58   Savior, Again to Thy Dear Name We Raise

This tune by Edward J. Hopkins was not named in its original publication. In later hymnals, the tune was given the name ELLERS, a nickname for the author of the text, John Ellerton, a noted English hymnologist and editor. The four-part harmony, which first appeared in 1874, is widely thought to have been written by Arthur Sullivan.

59   To You Before the Close of Day

This text of this hymn has traditionally been used during the office of Compline and was intended for general use throughout the year. The Sarum plainchant associated with it is the only tune ever found matched with this text in medieval manuscripts. In its earliest printing it is accompanied by a rubric reading, "The following melody is used on both feasts and ferial days."

60   God, That Madest Earth and Heaven

The title of this traditional Welsh lullaby AR HYD Y NOS means "All Through the Night," a recurring phrase found in the original Welsh text. The music was first notated in 1784 by Edward Jones in his influential treatise *Musical and Poetical Relicks of the Welsh Bards*.

61   From Glory to Glory Advancing

This text of this hymn is a paraphrase of the concluding prayer in the Liturgy of St. James, which exists in both Greek and Syriac forms and is the primary liturgy used by the Syriac Orthodox Church. It is named for "James the Just," called the brother of Jesus, who is considered the first Patriarch of Jerusalem and the author of the Epistle of James.

62   And Now, O Father, Mindful of the Love

The text of this hymn by William Bright is a paraphrase of a section from the mass which begins with the phrase "Unde et memores, Domini" ("and now, mindful of the Lord"). This Latin phrase provided the name for William Henry Monk's tune, which was composed specifically for this text in the 1875 edition of *Hymns Ancient and Modern*.

63   Draw Night and Take the Body of the Lord

Peter J. Gomes is Plummer Professor of Christian Morals and Pusey Minister in The Memorial Church, Harvard University. He composed the tune EDINGTON in honor of Mark D. W. Edington on the occasion of his ordination to the Episcopal priesthood in 2001. Edington served variously as Epps Fellow, Chaplain to Harvard College, and Associate Minister in The Memorial Church from 2000 to 2007.

64   All for Jesus, All for Jesus

Both text and tune of this hymn were written for inclusion in the Holy Week oratorio *The Crucifixion* by composer John Stainer and poet William J. Sparrow-Simpson. In the manner of the Bach passions, which served as an inspiration for Stainer's classic work, congregational hymns are an important component.

65 Let Us Break Bread Together

This African American spiritual unusually addresses the subject of Holy Communion; scholars believe that it reflected the experience of slaves who attended Episcopal worship services. This new harmonization was written by Harry Lyn Huff, Assistant University Organist and Choirmaster in The Memorial Church, Harvard University.

66 Here, O My Lord, I See Thee Face to Face

The tune NYACK, by American composer Warren Michel Swenson, was the prize-winning hymn in a 1977 competition of the Episcopal Diocese of New York for performance at the first New York Diocesan Festival of Music and Worship. The tune is named for Nyack, New York, where the composer then lived.

67 Just As I Am, without One Plea

English poet Charlotte Elliott lived a reclusive life as an invalid; indeed, she published a number of hymns in an 1836 collection entitled *Invalid's Hymn Book*. The text first appeared in America in 1865, where it has always since been associated with William B. Bradbury's tune WOODWORTH.

68 Lord, Enthroned in Heavenly Splendor

George H. Bourne's text first appeared in a collection of seven post-communion hymns which he self-published for distribution at St. Edmund's College, Salisbury, England, where he served as warden. As this hymn began to be anthologized, the author approved this five stanza version, reduced from his original ten.

69 Deck Thyself, My Soul, with Gladness

Johann Franck was one of the most active German hymn poets of the 17th century; he titled this hymn "Preparation for Holy Communion." This harmonization of SCHMÜCKE DICH by J. S. Bach appears in his *Cantata No. 180*, originally composed for the Twentieth Sunday of Trinity in 1724.

70 Thou, Who at Thy First Eucharist Didst Pray

SONG I was written by Orlando Gibbons as the first tune for George Wither's *Hymnes and Songs of the Church of 1623*. It was one of Gibbons's tunes specifically intended for congregational and not choral use. As was common with English tunes of its era, it was first published with simply a melody and bass line.

71 O Day of Rest and Gladness

Christopher Wordsworth was Bishop of Lincoln, England; he also served as literary executor for his uncle, poet William Wordsworth. His publications consist primarily of commentaries on the Greek Old and New Testaments, a biography of his uncle, and a single book of religious poetry published in 1862, in which this text appears.

72 We the Lord's People, Heart and Voice Uniting

Richard Wayne Dirksen served on the musical staff of the National Cathedral in Washington, D.C. from 1942 through 1988, first as Assistant Organist and then as

Organist and Choirmaster. He was the first lay person in the Anglican communion to be named a Canon Precentor, in which role he administered all the cathedral's worship services until 1991. He composed the tune DECATUR PLACE for *Hymnal 1982* as a metrical adaptation of his tune INNISFREE FARM.

73 Great God, We Sing That Mighty Hand

Philip Doddridge was an English clergyman whose three hundred hymns are considered, along with the work of Isaac Watts, to be the most important contributions of English Congregationalist hymnody from their era. Composer William Knapp served as the parish clerk of St. John's Church in Poole, England for over four decades, during which time he published two volumes of original hymn tunes and anthems.

74 Praise to God, Immortal Praise

English poet Anna Laetitia A. Barbauld was a Presbyterian dissenter who published numerous books on the education of young children. The tune ORIENTIS PARTIBUS originally appeared in a liturgy for the Feast of the Circumcision written by French composer Pierre de Corbeil. The carol-like character of the tune suggests it may have been used in a pageant or procession before the service itself.

75 Lord, for the Years

Peter J. Gomes is Plummer Professor of Christian Morals and Pusey Minister in The Memorial Church, Harvard University. He composed the tune RUNCIE in memory of his good friend Robert Alexander Kennedy Runcie, who was the 102nd Archbishop of Canterbury, serving from 1980 to 1991. Runcie was married to a concert pianist and maintained a life-long interest in music.

76 Great Is Thy Faithfulness

In 1923, American Methodist minister Thomas O. Chisholm sent a sampling of his poems to his friend and fellow minister William M. Runyan. Runyan wrote the tune FAITHFULNESS for the text and published it in a collection of his work that year. In America, it became particularly associated with the Moody Bible Institute in Chicago, with which Runyan was affiliated for many years.

77 Come, Ye Thankful People, Come

English clergyman Henry Alford's text was originally written during a period in which he served a rural parish where the yearly "Harvest Home" festival, referred to in the text's first line, was of great importance. The tune ST. GEORGE'S WINDSOR gained its name from composer George J. Elvey's forty-seven-year tenure as organist of St. George's Chapel, Windsor, England.

78 For the Fruit of All Creation

Francis Jackson composed the tune EAST ACKLAM in 1957, naming it after the English village where he lived. The tune did not gain widespread use until 1970, when hymnologist John Wilson suggested to poet Fred Pratt Green that he write a Thanksgiving-themed text specifically for the tune. The rhythmic pattern of the text's repetitions at the end of the first, second, and fourth lines is carefully tied to the contours of the tune.

79   We Plow the Fields and Scatter

The text of this hymn was adapted from the writings of German philosopher Matthias Claudius, who wrote many spiritual poems. Although he did not intend them to be set to music, some have found appeal as hymn texts in translation. This particular poem was originally titled "Peasants' Song."

80   Sing to the Lord of Harvest

The author of this text, John S. B. Monsell, was an English clergyman who published eleven volumes of devotional poetry and hymns. At the end of his life, he served as rector of St. Nicholas' Church in Guildford, England, where he was killed when he fell from the church's roof during a rebuilding project.

81   Lord of All Hopefulness, Lord of All Joy

Jan Struther was the literary pseudonym of the English author Joyce Anstruther, the author of this text. She is best remembered for the creation of the famed fictional character "Mrs. Miniver" in a series of newspaper columns in *The Times*. Near the end of her life, Anstruther frequently appeared on American radio quiz shows as a panelist.

82   In Our Day of Thanksgiving

English banker and stockbroker Richard Strutt named his tune ST. CATHERINE'S COURT after the large estate in Bath, England that he inherited from his aunt. Strutt was a man of many interests, working in the fields of music (as choirmaster of St. John's Church, Wilton Road, London), theology, horticulture, and zoology, in addition to his work in finance.

83   For All the Saints

William Walsham How was an active English hymnwriter and hymnal editor. As Suffragan Bishop in East London, he became known as "the poor man's bishop." Ralph Vaughan Williams composed the tune SINE NOMINE for this text in *The English Hymnal* of 1906, for which he served as musical editor.

84   Give Us the Wings of Faith to Rise

This All Saints text of Isaac Watts is well-known in British hymnals, but has been less frequently used America. Derek Williams composed the tune SAN ROCCO for this text for an anniversary service at Selwyn College, Cambridge. It is named for the church of San Rocco in Venice.

85   We Sing for All the Unsung Saints

American poet Carl P. Daw, Jr. wrote this text as "a simpler and non-militaristic alternative to W. W. How's text 'For all the saints'." Ralph Vaughan Williams gave this folk tune the name KINGSFOLD when he first created his arrangement in *The English Hymnal* of 1906. It was named for the village in Sussex in which he first heard the melody sung.

86   Who Are These Like Stars Appearing

For an 1844 publication, translator Frances Elizabeth Cox adapted five stanzas from Theobald Heinrich Schenck's German original twenty-stanza text, which had been inspired by verses from Revelation 7. Like her contemporary Catherine Winkworth, Cox was an active translator of German hymns into English.

87 I Sing a Song of the Saints of God

Poet Lesbia Scott originally created her hymn texts for private use in "our own nursery, as an expression of the faith we were trying to give the children." Although not originally intending them for publication, she subsequently released a collection of her children's hymns in 1929 containing poetry, music, and artwork. The tune GRAND ISLE gained its name from the retirement community in Vermont where its composer lived.

88 O Lord of Life, Whose Power Sustains

Peter J. Gomes is Plummer Professor of Christian Morals and Pusey Minister in The Memorial Church, Harvard University. The tune ARMISTICE was written for use at the yearly Veterans Day celebrations in November, which also commemorate the anniversary of the dedication of The Memorial Church, built as a World War I memorial.

89 Christ the Victorious, Give to Your Servants

This text by Carl P. Daw, Jr. is a paraphrase of the Kontakion for the Departed as used in the memorial and burial liturgies of the Eastern Orthodox Church. Daw wrote this paraphrase "specifically for the tune RUSSIAN HYMN in order to preserve some of the flavor of the original text for congregations unable to sing the traditional Kiev melody for the Kontakion."

90 God Be with You Till We Meet Again

This familiar text by Jeremiah Rankin was inspired by the etymology of the phrase "good-bye," which evolved from the phrase "God be with you." The tune RANDOLPH, written by Ralph Vaughan Williams for *The English Hymnal* of 1906 alternates phrases in unison and harmony, representing the sense of unity and separateness implied at parting.

91 O Come, O Come, Emmanuel

This hymn is based on the seven Greater Antiphons for Vespers in the week before Christmas. These antiphons are often called the "O Antiphons," because each one begins with the word "O." For many years this tune was considered to be an editorial conglomerate of various phrases from plainsong melodies. However, a discovery in 1966 revealed a 15th century French volume in which the entire tune appears.

92 Creator of the Stars of Night

John Mason Neale was a leader of the 19th century liturgical revival in the Church of England. His research into hymnody yielded over two hundred translations of Greek and Latin texts, bringing many early hymns back into common usage. This Advent hymn appears in the first part of his collection *Hymnal Noted* of 1851, one of his most influential books.

93 Wake, Awake, for Night is Flying

Lutheran minister Philipp Nicolai published a collection in 1599 of meditations on death and eternal life, inspired by the serious plague of 1597 in Unna, Germany. J. S.

Bach's harmonization of WACHET AUF appears in his *Cantata No. 140*, composed for the Twenty-seventh Sunday after Trinity in 1731.

94   Comfort, Comfort Ye My People

GENEVA 42 gained its name from its original publication as the tune for a French paraphrase of Psalm 42 in the Genevan Psalter of 1551. Due to its inclusion in contemporary German collections, it has become one of the best-known Genevan psalm tunes.

95   Watchman, Tell Us of the Night

John Bowring, editor of the *Westminster Review*, Member of Parliament, and later governor of Hong Kong, published this text in a collection of his hymns in 1825. The tune ABERYSTWYTH was named for the Welsh town and college at which its composer, Joseph Parry, was professor of music.

96   On Jordan's Bank the Baptist's Cry

Charles Coffin published the original Latin text of this hymn in the Paris Breviary of 1736, to which he contributed many neo-Latin texts, intending to improve upon the literary quality of the original medieval hymns. English clergyman John Chandler subsequently translated many of these hymns for an 1837 publication, mistakenly believing them to be of ancient origin.

97   The Angel Gabriel from Heaven Came

This carol was collected by Sabine Baring-Gould, an English clergyman who traveled in the Basque territories and authored a book on the regions near the Pyrenees. All of Baring-Gould's work papers were destroyed, but comparison with other sources reveals that his translation is a very free adaptation of the original.

98   The Lord Will Come and Not Be Slow

In 1648, the noted English poet John Milton wrote paraphrases of Psalms 80 through 88 in an effort to provide English versions that were closer to the original Hebrew text. This hymn's text is a combination of phrases and stanzas from those paraphrases. The harmonization of this tune from the Scottish Psalter of 1615 was created by John Milton, Sr., the poet's father, for a 1621 publication.

99   Hark, a Thrilling Voice Is Sounding

The original Latin text of this hymn is notable in that a specific scriptural reference can be found in nearly every line. Edward Caswall's translation of the Latin originally began with the phrase "Hark, an awful voice is sounding"; it has understandably been modernized by 20th century editors.

100   Lo! He Comes, with Clouds Descending

Charles Wesley's text originally appeared under the title "Thy Kingdom Come" in a 1758 collection that he published anonymously. The tune name HELMSLEY was intended as an homage to Wesley, named after a Yorkshire town whose vicar was a friend of his.

101   Lift Up Your Heads, Ye Mighty Gates

The author of the original German text of this hymn, Georg Weissel, was a Lutheran minister and a member of the "Poetical Union" in Königsberg. This group of writers led by Simon Dach brought about a revival of Germany poetry near the end of the Thirty Years' War. In some hymnals this text, loosely based on Psalm 24, appears in the "Ascension" section.

102   Savior of the Nations, Come

When Martin Luther created his German translation of the original Latin text of this hymn, he adapted the melody from plainsong sources. By making small changes to the melody line and rhythm, Luther turned the original tune into a sturdy German chorale. This chorale tune was one of the most popular among German organ composers of the 17th and 18th centuries, who composed numerous preludes based upon it.

103   Let All Mortal Flesh Keep Silence

The text of this hymn is a paraphrase of the prayer of the Cherubic Hymn in the Liturgy of St. James of the Orthodox Church. The tune PICARDY gained its name from the province in northern France, where it was originally associated with a French folk ballad.

104   Hark, What a Sound, and Too Divine for Hearing

English composer Richard Runciman Terry was one of the primary figures in the revival of Tudor era church music, inspired by the renaissance of Gregorian chant in France. Terry's own compositions, however, utilized the rich harmonic style of his own era, represented here by HIGHWOOD, one of his most stirring and majestic hymn tunes.

105   Lord Christ, When First Thou Cam'st to Earth

American author Walter Russell Bowie published only two hymns in his lifetime (this text and "O Holy City Seen of John"), but both remain in active use and are included in this hymnal. This text was written at the request of the Dean of Liverpool Cathedral, England, who sought an Advent hymn with a darker spirit.

106   Come, Thou Long-Expected Jesus

This text by Charles Wesley was originally published in his anonymous collection of nativity hymns in 1745. In its original form, Christian F. Witt's melody contained a number of bouncing dotted rhythms at the ends of phrases. Hymnal editors "smoothed out" these rhythmic elements to create the more placid version known today.

107   I Want to Walk as a Child of the Light

This hymn gained its tune name HOUSTON from Church of the Redeemer, Houston, Texas, a congregation with which the author/composer Kathleen Thomerson has many ties. Noted for the breadth of musical styles employed in its worship, Church of the Redeemer did much to popularize this hymn, which draws on both traditional hymn styles and those of gospel songs.

108   Hail to the Lord's Anointed

Author James Montgomery was an outspoken newspaper editor in Sheffield, England, who was twice imprisoned for advocating liberal ideas. He is considered one of the great figures of English Nonconformist hymnody and wrote more than four-hundred hymns. J. S. Bach's harmonization of this tune comes not from a cantata, but from his collection of harmonized chorale melodies published in 1787.

109   People, Look East, the Time Is Near

English poet Eleanor Farjeon's original carol was written for the 1928 edition of *The Oxford Book of Carols*. Farjeon received wide acclaim as an author of children's stories and nursery rhymes. In addition, she published over thirty volumes of fiction, poetry, and translations. Today she is remembered almost exclusively for this text and "Morning Has Broken."

110   Joy to the World! The Lord Is Come

Composer Lowell Mason, one-time president of the Handel and Haydn Society in Boston, originally published the tune ANTIOCH with the claim that it was "arranged from Handel." Because no direct Handelian source could be found, it was thought for many years to be Mason's original composition, until hymnologist John Wilson discovered that Mason's version of the tune was obliquely arranged from earlier anonymous tunes containing phrases quoting various portions of Handel works.

111   It Came Upon a Midnight Clear

This hymn is one of the earliest Christmas hymns still in use for which both text and music were created in America. The text by minister Edmund Hamilton Sears notably does not contain any reference to Jesus' birth, focusing instead on the message of the angels and the issues of social justice that were particularly important to American Unitarians.

112   All My Heart This Night Rejoices

Composer Johann Georg Ebeling was the successor of Johann Crüger as director of music at St. Nicholas' Church in Berlin, Germany. Poet Paul Gerhardt was on the clerical staff of the church and collaborated with Ebeling on the creation of over one hundred hymns, including this one.

113   O Little Town of Bethlehem

Phillips Brooks, a graduate of Harvard College in 1855, was one of the greatest preachers of his generation. From 1869 until 1891 he served as rector of Trinity Episcopal Church, Boston; he was also a founding member of the Board of Preachers at Harvard University in 1886, before becoming Episcopal Bishop of Massachusetts in 1891. It is believed that this text was inspired by his visit to Bethlehem in 1865.

114   Stille Nacht! Heilige Nacht!
115   Silent Night, Holy Night

This familiar German carol was written in 1818 for a Christmas Eve service at St. Nicholas' Church in Oberndorf, Austria, where an organ malfunction necessitated last-minute changes in the music. Joseph Mohr, the assistant priest, and Franz Gruber, the local organist, hastily wrote the hymn for performance with guitar accompaniment.

116   Calm, on the Listening Ear of Night

Edmund Hamilton Sears, author of this text, was a graduate of Union College and Harvard Divinity School. As a Unitarian minister, he served churches in Wayland, Lancaster, and Weston, Massachusetts. His published works include several volumes of theological commentary and one volume of sacred poetry and hymns.

117   See, Amid the Winter's Snow

Composer John Goss, who wrote this tune, served as the organist of St. Paul's Cathedral in London, England. His compositions were almost exclusively written within the genres of Anglican liturgical music and secular glees. During his tenure at St. Paul's, he served as professor at the Royal Academy of Music, where his most famous student was Arthur Sullivan.

118   Christians, Awake, Salute the Happy Morn

Author John Byrom wrote this text as a Christmas present for his daughter Dolly, who had requested a poem as a gift. She awoke on Christmas morning 1749 to find the poem, entitled "Christmas Day for Dolly," on her breakfast plate. John Wainwright's tune YORKSHIRE was composed specifically for the text; despite neither composer nor poet having any known connection to Yorkshire, this was the name that stuck with the tune after earlier publications used a variety of alternatives.

119   Adeste fideles
120   O Come, All Ye Faithful

Both the text and tune of this famous hymn are probably the work of John Francis Wade, who made his living copying and selling church music at Douay, a center for English Catholic refugees in France. The English translation was created by John Frederick Oakeley, an early supporter of the Oxford Movement and a Roman Catholic convert, who translated Latin hymns into English to offset the influence of evangelical hymnody.

121   Hark! The Herald Angels Sing

The original lines of this Christmas text of Charles Wesley read "Hark how all the welkin rings, / Glory to the King of Kings." The tune MENDELSSOHN was adapted by William H. Cummings from the second movement of Felix Mendelssohn's cantata *Festgesang an die Künstler*, op. 68, for male chorus and orchestra, composed in 1840 for a festival at Leipzig commemorating the invention of printing.

122   Shepherds Came, Their Praises Bringing

The translation of this medieval Latin carol was created by George Bradford Caird, an English Congregational minister who held posts in theology at McGill University in Montreal, Quebec, Canada and the University of Oxford, England. This tune was a particular favorite of John Raymond Ferris, University Organist and Choirmaster from 1958–1990, who chose it as the subject for an organ improvisation by Anton Heiller at the 1967 dedication of the C. B. Fisk organ in The Memorial Church, Harvard University.

123   Angels We Have Heard on High

The tune GLORIA is one of the most popular French carol melodies. Its exact origin is in doubt, though it is surmised that it arose in the 18th century, although the version used here is adapted from an English source from 1875. In England, the tune often appears with the text "Angels from the realms of glory."

124 While Shepherds Watched Their Flocks

Although this tune is of unknown authorship, its most likely origin is an adaptation from the work of English Reformation composer Christopher Tye. The first significant printing of the tune was in a psalter published by Thomas Ravenscroft in 1621. Ravenscroft gave each tune in the collection the name of cathedrals and choral societies, hence this one gained the name WINCHESTER. The appellation "OLD" was added in the 19th century to distinguish it from the tune WINCHESTER NEW. This paraphrase of Luke 2:8–15, which appeared in a 1700 supplement, is one of the enduring legacies of Nahum Tate's and Nicholas Brady's "New Version" of the Psalter, first published in 1696.

125 Personent hodie

The text and tune of this hymn are likely parodies of an older Latin song, "Intonent hodie voces ecclesiae." In Theodoric Petri's *Piæ Cantiones* of 1582, many older hymns were adapted and edited theologically, and in this way the text gained its current form. Traditionally, this hymn has been sung during the yearly Harvard Christmas Carol Services, accompanied by the ringing of bells.

126 Once in Royal David's City

This hymn was not widely known until it gained great visibility as a yearly part of the radio broadcasts of the service of Nine Lessons and Carols from King's College, Cambridge, England, beginning in the mid-20th century. The author of the text, Cecil Frances ("Fanny") Alexander, originally wrote the poem as a children's hymn. Later revisions, including an entirely new third stanza by James Waring McCrady, gave the hymn wider appeal.

127 In dulci jubilo

The original version of this macaronic carol (a text consisting of a mix of Latin and vernacular) alternated the Latin phrases with German. Although many American hymn books have printed an entirely English version, Percy Dearmer's translation better maintains the original character of the text. According to tradition, the carol was said to have been inspired by a band of angels who sang it to the German mystic Heinrich Suss.

128 Lo, How a Rose E'er Blooming

When first published, the original German text of this carol contained twenty-three stanzas. The current version is a composite of two verses from the original German 15th century text with a final verse by Friedrich Layritz. The harmonization is by the German composer Michael Praetorius, whose chorale harmonizations were published in a collection entitled *Musæ Sioniae*.

129 Of the Father's Love Begotten

After a brilliant career as a lawyer in the imperial administration, the Spaniard Marcus Aurelius Prudentius Clemens retired from the active world to lead an ascetic life and to write the religious lyrics which have established his reputation as the first great poet of the Latin church. The tune DIVINUM MYSTERIUM had its origins as a Sanctus trope—musical interpolations inserted into liturgical chants.

130   Angels, from the Realms of Glory

This text by James Montgomery was originally published in the newspaper he edited for Christmas Eve in 1916. When it later began to be set with music, the final stanza (beginning "Sinners, wrung with true repentance, / Doomed for guilt to endless pain") was omitted. The tune by Henry Smart gained its name from the location of St. Philip's Presbyterian Church in London, England, where he was organist.

131   Jesus, the Light of the World

Although George Elderkin was active as a publisher and editor of many gospel hymns, this adaptation and setting of Charles Wesley's famous Christmas text, appearing in its better-known form at no. 121, has proved to be his most enduring composition. In some ways the interpolated phrase "Jesus, the Light of the world" is reminiscent of the "Alleluia" added to each line of Wesley's Easter hymn, but the gospel song tradition emerges as the primary influence through the prominence of the refrain sung after every stanza.

132   The First Nowell

The tune for this hymn was transcribed by William Sandys in Cornwall, England for a book of Christmas carols he published in 1833. It has been the subject of much research and conjecture over the years due to some of the unusual characteristics in the tune. It is believed by some that Sandys may have heard the singing of a composite of the original melody and a harmony part, which he then combined to form the basis of the tune known today.

133   How Brightly Shines the Morning Star!

German Lutheran minister Philipp Nicolai composed both the original text and tune of this very famous chorale, which was first published in 1599. In the years that followed, many changes and revisions were made, and by the time William Mercer created his English translation, it shared only basic features with Nicolai's original; it is thus speculated that Mercer felt the tune was the most significant part of Nicolai's composition.

134   What Star Is This, with Beams So Bright

Charles Coffin published the original Latin text of this hymn in the Paris Breviary of 1736, to which he contributed many neo-Latin texts, intending to improve upon the literary quality of the original medieval hymns. English clergyman John Chandler translated many of these hymns for an 1837 publication, mistakenly believing them to be of ancient origin.

135   As with Gladness Men of Old

William Chatterton Dix wrote this text while suffering from illness for a private collection published in about 1860. The text has long been paired with the tune DIX, adapted and named by William Henry Monk from German composer Conrad Kocher's original melody. Dix himself, however, did not approve of this combination of text and tune.

136   We Three Kings

John Henry Hopkins, Jr. originally intended this hymn to be performed with alternating groups of voices: the inner verses were to be sung by three different male soloists, portraying the kings, the outer verses by the men's trio together, and the chorus by the congregation. His original version also contained organ interludes between the verses.

137   Brightest and Best

English clergyman Reginald Heber composed his hymn texts for his own congregation in Hodnet, Shropshire, England with the intent of using them to inspire better singing among his parishioners. He originally wrote this text to be used with a Scottish folk tune entitled WANDERING WILLIE. The musical setting is adapted from a choral anthem written by James Proctor Harding for the Gifford Hall Mission in Islington, London, England.

138   Worship the Lord in the Beauty of Holiness

The author of this text, John S. B. Monsell, was an English clergyman who published eleven volumes of devotional poetry and hymns. At the end of his life, he served as rector of St. Nicholas' Church in Guildford, England, where he was killed when he fell from the church's roof during a rebuilding project.

139   Jesus, on the Mountain Peak

This hymn by English-American author Brian Wren was the second text he wrote, yet has become one of his best-known. Originally bearing the title "Christ upon the Mountain Peak," Wren revised it in 1995 to incorporate changes in his theological thinking. The tune MOWSLEY is named for the village in Leicestershire, England, where the composer Cyril Vincent Taylor spent his childhood.

140   Songs of Thankfulness and Praise

Christopher Wordsworth was Bishop of Lincoln, England; he also served as literary executor for his uncle, poet William Wordsworth. His publications consist primarily of commentaries on the Greek Old and New Testaments, a biography of his uncle, and a single book of religious poetry published in 1862, in which this text appears. J. S. Bach's harmonization of this tune comes not from a cantata, but from a collection of harmonized chorale melodies published posthumously in 1769.

141   The Glory of These Forty Days

Although the earliest source of this anonymous Latin text dates from the 10th century, it is suspected that it may be much older. In the earliest extant sources, it is appointed for Matins of the Third Sunday in Lent. Despite this tune's modern association with this text and the Lenten season, the chorale's harmonization comes from J. S. Bach's Cantata No. 6, "*Bleib bei uns,*" written for performance on Easter Monday of 1725.

142   Eternal Lord of Love, Behold Your Church

This text by Thomas H. Cain was commissioned for the Episcopal *Hymnal 1982.* Cain commented that he intended the hymn specifically to address those who would be renewing their baptismal covenants at the Easter Vigil. The tune OLD 124TH is, along with GENEVAN 42, one of the best-known psalm tunes of that era, in spite of its uncommon meter.

143   Forty Days and Forty Nights

The original text of this hymn, consisting of nine stanzas filled with florid language, has been adapted by several different authors. The first publication of the tune AUS DER TIEFE in 1676 attributed it simply to "M. H." It is suspected that this is Martin Herbst, although it has also been attributed to M. Heinlein, hence the tune name HEINLEIN under which it sometimes appears.

144   Now Let Us All with One Accord

This tune by English composer Percy Carter Buck was originally intended for the Latin Holy Week text "Vexilla Regis proderunt." It was because of this connection that he named it GONFALON ROYAL, as "gonfalon" is an Old English word (from the Norman period) that means "banner." The first three notes of Buck's tune also quote the "Vexilla Regis" plainchant.

145   Lord, Who Throughout These Forty Days

Claudia F. Hernaman wrote her hymns originally for children and first published them in an 1873 collection entitled *A Child's Book of Praise*. This text bears a number of similarities to "Forty Days and Forty Nights." The tune name ST. FLAVIAN (after St. Flavian of Antioch) is a curiosity, since all publications and adaptations of this hymn were within Anglican circles, yet Flavian is not memorialized in the Anglican calendar of saints.

146   Jesus, Who This Our Lententide

When editor Edward Miller first published the tune ROCKINGHAM in 1790, he claimed that "part of the melody" had been taken from an earlier hymn, apparently TUNBRIDGE, which appeared in an obscure collection from 1778. This popular tune quickly entered widespread use, first appearing in a published collection in the United States in 1805.

147   Ride On, Ride On in Majesty

Henry Hart Milman was Professor of Poetry at the University of Oxford, England and published a number of plays and poems before changing fields to write on ecclesiastical history and perform clerical duties. English-born composer Graham George composed THE KING'S MAJESTY for the Episcopal *Hymnal 1940*. He later served as professor of music at Queen's University in Kingston, Ontario, Canada.

148   All Glory Laud and Honor

Theodulph, Bishop of Orleans, is said to have written this text while imprisoned in the early 9th century for an alleged role (which he denied) in a plot to overthrow King Louis I of France. Popular legend has stated that he was inspired to write the hymn as a Palm Sunday procession passed in front of his jail cell's window; upon hearing Theodulph's singing of the hymn to the assembled congregation, the king freed him at once. Later evidence has shown, however, that Theodulph was almost certainly not freed and died in prison.

149   Alone Thou Goest Forth, O Lord

Medieval cleric and theologian Peter Abelard's Good Friday hymn was written for the Convent of the Paraclete, founded at Nogent-sur-Seine, France, and presided over by his wife Héloise after she had taken the veil. The doomed love story of "Abelard and Héloise" has been the subject of many musical dramas.

150   My Song Is Love Unknown

Samuel Crossman was an English minister who sympathized with the Puritans in the mid-17th century, and was expelled from the Church of England in 1662 with a number of other like-minded clergy. English composer John Ireland wrote his tune LOVE UNKNOWN after receiving a request from fellow composer Geoffrey Shaw for a setting of Samuel Crossman's text.

151   Go to Dark Gethsemane

This hymn by James Montgomery originally contained a final stanza about Easter morning. To increase its usefulness during Holy Week, the stanza was omitted from subsequent publications. The tune PETRA by Richard Redhead gained its name from its original association with the text "Rock of Ages, cleft for me," after the Latin word for "rock."

152   To Mock Your Reign

Composer Francis Westbrook, planning to write a choral anthem arrangement, asked poet Fred Pratt Green to write a text specifically for Thomas Tallis's THE THIRD TUNE. He requested a text that would be "virile yet wistful." Of the nine tunes that Tallis composed for *The Whole Psalter translated into English Metre* of 1567, this one is the most complicated, with its combination of duple and triple meters.

153   Ah, Holy Jesus, How Hast Thou Offended

Johann Heermann, a noted German hymnwriter of the 17th century, spent most of his life as pastor of the small town of Köben in Silesia, during the troubled period of the Thirty Years' War. This text is inspired by a passage from the writings of Jean de Fécamp, though it was sometimes attributed to Augustine. The translation by the British poet Robert Bridges was created for *The Yattendon Hymnal* of 1899.

154   Cross of Jesus, Cross of Sorrow

Both text and tune of this hymn were written for inclusion in the Holy Week oratorio The Crucifixion by composer John Stainer and poet William J. Sparrow-Simpson. In the manner of the Bach passions, which served as an inspiration for Stainer's classic work, congregational hymns are an important component.

155   My Faith Looks up to Thee

American poet and Yale graduate Ray Palmer wrote this text, his first, when he was twenty-one years old. Shortly afterwards, he met the composer and editor Lowell Mason on the streets of Boston. Mason was seeking new texts and tunes for his hymnal publications and soon set Palmer's text to music, as one of over 1,500 hymn tunes he wrote during his active career as a composer, conductor, and editor. Although responsible for the introduction of much European music to America, Mason is often criticized for his suppression of colonial American hymns, which he believed to be rough and uncultured.

156   Sing, My Tongue the Glorious Battle

Venantius Honorius Fortunatus' text was likely written in 569 for the reception at the convent of St. Croix in Poitiers, France, of some holy relics sent by the Byzantine Emperor Justin II to Queen Rhadegund of the Franks. Fortunatus, though born in Italy, spent most of his life in Poitiers under the patronage of the Queen, and became bishop of the diocese shortly before his death.

157   Beneath the Cross of Jesus

Elizabeth C. Clephane wrote eight hymn texts that were published in volumes of *The Family Treasury*, appearing between 1872 through 1874. These hymns originally appeared under the title "Breathings on the Border." Frederick C. Maker wrote his tune ST. CHRISTOPHER specifically for this text.

158   Were You There When They Crucified My Lord?

When this African American spiritual was published in the Episcopal *Hymnal 1940*, it represented the first time a spiritual had been included in a hymnal intended for a general audience, rather than for black American congregations. Harmonizer Melva Wilson Costen is a noted expert on African American sacred music and served as Professor of Music and Worship at Interdenominational Theological Center in Atlanta, Georgia.

159   There Is a Green Hill Far Away

Cecil Frances ("Fanny") Alexander published this text in 1848 as one of a series of children's hymns inspired by articles of the Apostles' Creed. The notion of the "green hill" seems perhaps at odds with the actual landscape of the Holy Land; indeed, Alexander never visited this part of the world, but claimed that the hill that had inspired her was actually in Londonderry, Northern Ireland.

160   When I Survey the Wondrous Cross

This text by Isaac Watts is widely regarded as one of his greatest achievements as a hymnwriter. It appeared among the hymns for the Lord's Supper in his *Hymns and Spiritual Songs* of 1707, where it is identified as based on Galatians 6:14. The strong visual element of this meditation on the crucified Christ makes it remarkably comparable to medieval Latin hymns on the same subject.

161   We Sing the Praise of Him Who Died

Thomas Kelly's text first appeared in a collection of his hymns in 1815 with an epigraph of Galatians 6:14. This is the first hymnal to pair this text with William Henry Hall's tune. The tune's name, ONEONTA, is an Iroquois word thought to mean "mountain" and also the name of a number of locales in the United States.

162   In the Cross of Christ I Glory

Hymnologist Erik Routley notes that John Bowring's well-known text was inspired by the approach by boat to Macau, China. As one draws near, the white church building of Our Lady of Fatima becomes visible upon the island's highest hill. Most of the church was destroyed in a political revolution, but one wall, with a large smoke-blackened metal cross, remains undamaged.

163   O Sacred Head, Now Wounded

Paul Gerhardt's original German text of this hymn was a free adaptation from "Salve caput cruentatum," a medieval devotional poem that has been attributed to various authors. J. S. Bach's harmonization of Hans Leo Hassler's tune is one of several that appear in his *St. Matthew Passion*, BWV 244, of 1729.

164   Come, Ye Faithful, Raise the Strain

The Greek original of this text is an ode to be used on "Low Sunday" (the first Sunday after Easter) in the Greek Orthodox Liturgy. John Mason Neale's translation uses the first half of the original ode. It is nowadays often sung at the Easter Vigil, due to its textual reference to the crossing of the Red Sea "with unmoistened foot." Arthur Sullivan composed his tune ST. KEVIN for this text, naming it in honor of the Irish saint.

165   Christ the Lord Is Risen Again

The melody of LLANFAIR was written by Robert Williams, a blind basket-maker in Mynydd Ithel, on the island of Anglesey, Wales. John Roberts collected and harmonized a number of Welsh folk melodies, which he then published in 1839. The tune entered wide circulation because of its inclusion as an official hymn at the Llangollen International Eisteddfod.

166   We Know That Christ Is Raised

English Congregationalist minister and author John Brownlow Geyer wrote this text while serving as a tutor at Chestnut College in Cambridge, England. Geyer is quoted as writing: "At that time a good deal of work was going on round the corner... producing living cells ('the baby in the test tube'). The hymn attempted to illustrate the Christian doctrine of baptism in relation to those experiments. Originally intended as a hymn for the Sacrament of baptism, it has become popular as an Easter hymn."

167   Love's Redeeming Work Is Done

The original first stanza of this Easter text by Charles Wesley was the well-known "Christ the Lord is risen today, / Songs of men and angels say!" By omitting that stanza, the text can be used during the entire the Easter season. The tune was named SAVANNAH because John Wesley, one of whose texts was originally used with this tune, served as an Anglican clergyman there in 1736–37.

168   O Sons and Daughters, Let Us Sing

Jean Tisserand, a Franciscan based in Paris, France, is thought to have written the original version of this text, which he titled "L'aleluya du jour de Pasques." Other stanzas by unknown authors were added in later collections. The tune likely originated as a French air contemporary with the text.

169   Christ Is Alive! Let Christians Sing

In his 1983 collection *Faith Looking Forward*, poet Brian Wren provides the following commentary on the origins of this text in 1968: "Ten days after the assassination of Dr. Martin Luther King, I and my congregation at Hockley, Essex, met to celebrate Easter. The hymn tried to say [that Christ is alive] with truth and integrity in words that would be more widely applied."

170   A Brighter Dawn Is Breaking

The author of this text, Percy Dearmer, was an English priest and one of the most noted Anglo-Catholic liturgists of the early 20th century. He authored an 1899 volume entitled *The Parson's Handbook*, which was a significant and influential document of Anglican "high church" practice. As a hymnologist, Dearmer is most famous for his work as co-editor with Ralph Vaughan Williams of *The English Hymnal* of 1906.

171 Alleluia! Alleluia! Hearts to Heaven

Christopher Wordsworth was Bishop of Lincoln, England; he also served as literary executor for his uncle, poet William Wordsworth. Arthur Sullivan originally composed his tune LUX EOI for the text "Hark! A thrilling voice is sounding," but it has been associated with Wordsworth's Easter text since the 1892 edition of the Episcopal *Hymnal.*

172 Christ the Lord Is Risen Today

The tune EASTER HYMN first appeared in the anonymous collection *Lyra Davidica* in 1707. Of the twenty-five tunes in the collection, this is one of the nine of English origin. Throughout its history it has been known by many other names including WORGAN, THE RESURRECTION, and SALISBURY.

173 The Strife Is O'er, the Battle Done

William Henry Monk adapted the tune VICTORY from the "Gloria Patria" in the third tone *Magnificat* of the Renaissance composer Giovanni Perluigi da Palestrina. The "Alleluias" that begin and end the tune are Monk's own composition, while the internal phrases are taken almost exactly from Palestrina's choral work.

174 Thine Be the Glory, Risen, Conquering Son

The music for this hymn is adapted from George Frideric Handel's oratorio *Judas Maccabaeus,* HWV 54, written in 1746 to celebrate the Jacobite Rising of the year prior. An extract from the chorus "See, the Conqu'ring hero comes" was taken by the Swiss theologian and cleric Edmond Louis Budry as the basis for his Easter text that is widely known today in Richard B. Hoyle's English translation.

175 Jesus Lives! Thy Terrors Now

Christian Fürchtegott Gellert was one of the most popular poets of the German Enlightenment, whose works at one point had a sales popularity second only to the Bible (though many scholars today feel they enjoyed an inflated position relative to their actual literary value). Some of his texts were set to music by Ludwig van Beethoven. The original first line of Cox's English translation began "Jesus lives! no longer now" and was wisely revised by her in the following years.

176 The Day of Resurrection

This hymn is based on the first ode of the "Golden Canon" of John of Damascus, sung at the ante-communion in the Easter midnight service of the Greek Orthodox Church. The publication in 1862 of John Mason Neale's *Hymns of the Eastern Church,* in which this hymn appears, indicates Neale's interest in both Latin and Greek sources in the quest for Anglican liturgical renewal.

177 Now Is Eternal Life

English composer Charles Steggall named his tune CHRISTCHURCH in honor of Christ Church, Lancaster Gate in London, England, where he served as organist. He also served as a professor at the Royal Academy of Music, where he became an influential and well-loved teacher. Although its author was an Anglican clergyman, this text first appeared in another denomination's hymnal, *Congregational Praise* of 1951.

178   Ye Choirs of New Jerusalem

The text of this hymn is attributed to Fulbert of Chartres, a French bishop and scholar of canon law, who wrote a variety of poems during his lifetime. The translator, Robert Campbell, a Scottish lawyer and scholar of classical languages, translated Latin hymns into English in his spare time.

179   Christ Jesus Lay in Death's Strong Bands

This hymn, a German version of the Latin Easter sequence "Victimae Paschali laudes," is the most famous Easter hymn of Martin Luther. Many of Luther's texts were adaptations of medieval vernacular German hymns. In this case, he used "Christ ist erstanden" as the source for a new hymn in a different meter.

180   Now the Green Blade Riseth

John MacLeod Campbell Crum wrote this Easter carol specifically for the French melody NOËL NOUVELET for the 1928 edition of the *Oxford Book of Carols*. The French tune had its origins as a Christmas hymn, and its tune name is adapted from the words of the original text, which celebrated singing "new carols" for Christmastide.

181   God Is Gone Up on High

Charles Wesley published this text in a 1746 collection of his Ascension hymns. John Darwall served as the vicar of Walsall, Staffordshire in England, and composed tunes for all 150 psalms. However, this tune, originally written for paraphrase of Psalm 148, is the only one that survives today.

182   Hail Thee, Festival Day!

This hymn is a translation of the Ascension section of the Sarum and York processional versions of a poem by Venantius Honorius Fortunatus, originally written in honor of the baptism of conquered Saxons in the mid-6th century. The tune by Ralph Vaughan Williams gained its name from the opening words of the original Latin text.

183   Christ, Above All Glory Seated

This Ascension text has a complex history both in its original Latin and in various English translations. The version used here was compiled by a 19th-century Anglican priest, later bishop, for his collection of Sunday and holy day hymns. The tune IN BABILONE is a traditional Dutch melody that first appeared in a collection of "peasant songs and country dances" in 1710. It is presented in an arrangement by Dutch composer Julius Röntgen, an active figure in the musical life of late-19th and early-20th century Amsterdam, and a good friend of the composer Johannes Brahms.

184   Hail the Day That Sees Him Rise

The original first two lines of Charles Wesley's text began "Hail the day that sees him rise / ravished from our wishful eyes!" The tune ORIENTIS PARTIBUS originally appeared in a liturgy for the Feast of the Circumcision written by French composer Pierre de Corbeil. Its carol-like character suggests it may have been used in a pageant or procession before the service itself.

185   The Head That Once Was Crowned with Thorns

Thomas Kelly's text was inspired by a poem of John Bunyan entitled "One Thing is Needful, or Serious Meditations upon the Four Last Things," which began with the same opening line as Kelly's text. The tune was named ST. MAGNUS in a 1762 publication, in honor of the church of St. Magnus the Martyr, London Bridge, England.

186   And Have the Bright Immensities

The musical editor of the Episcopal *Hymnal 1940*, Charles Winfred Douglas, adapted this tune from George Frideric Handel's oratorio *Susanna*, HWV 66, of 1748. The music comes from a passage with the text "Ask if yon damask rose be sweet." This tune had also been adapted for sacred use prior to Douglas's version; such versions appeared in American psalm books of the early 19th century.

187   The Spacious Firmament on High

Two weeks after the text of hymn no. 191, this celebrated paraphrase of Psalm 19:1–4 appeared in *The Spectator* of August 23, 1712, at the conclusion of Joseph Addison's essay on the means by which faith may be strengthened by observation of the natural world. The tune CREATION is an adaptation of the chorus "The heavens are telling" from Josef Haydn's oratorio *The Creation*, Hob. XXI:2, of 1798. It is thought that the arrangement is likely the work of Isaac Baker Woodbury, a magazine editor who published the journal *The Choral*, in which this adaptation first appeared in 1845.

188   I Sing the Mighty Power of God

Isaac Watts, author of this hymn, was one of the most significant hymn writers of his era, serving as pastor to the Independent congregation in Mark Lane, London, England before he went into semi-retirement due to poor health. He wrote more than 600 hymns with the intent of providing more variety than the commonly used psalm paraphrases allowed; for these efforts, he is often termed "the father of modern English hymnody."

189   This Is Our Father's World

The original text of this hymn was authored by Maltbie D. Babcock and first published posthumously in a book entitled *Thoughts for Everyday Living*. His niece, Mary Babcock Crawford, prompted by ecological concerns, wrote an additional stanza for a search sponsored by the Hymn Society of America. The adaptation of the second stanza to use feminine imagery for God is the work of the present editors.

190   The Great Creator of the Worlds

Written for the Episcopal *Hymnal 1940*, this hymn is a paraphrase by F. Bland Tucker of a passage in an anonymous apology for the Christian religion, the "Epistle to Diognetus," probably written during the 3rd century. The harmonization presented here is Tallis's original. Further comment on the tune may be found at no. 16.

191   When All Thy Mercies, O My God

Joseph Addison, English government official, essayist, and Fellow of Magdalen College, Oxford, published this hymn in *The Spectator* of August 9, 1712, at the end of an essay on "Gratitude." Orlando Gibbons wrote the tune SONG 67 for a hymn celebrating St. Matthias' Day in George Wither's *Hymnes and Songs of the Church* of 1623.

192 God Is Our Refuge and Our Strength

Both text and tune for this hymn come from the Scottish Psalter, which the Church of Scotland began producing in 1564 as an expansion of the Anglo-Genevan Psalter of 1561. The harmonization of YORK was provided for Thomas Ravenscroft's psalter of 1621 by John Milton, Sr., an amateur composer and father of the noted English poet.

193 Lord of All Being, Throned Afar

Oliver Wendell Holmes, Sr., a graduate of Harvard College in 1829, taught medicine at Dartmouth College from 1839 to 1847, and at Harvard Medical School from 1847 to 1882, serving as dean there from 1847 to 1852. Also a poet and essayist of note, he contributed a column to *The Atlantic Monthly* entitled "The Professor at the Breakfast Table." This hymn was first published in his column in December 1859. The tune is discussed at no. 56.

194 God of the Earth, the Sky, the Sea

Poet Samuel Longfellow, younger brother of Henry Wadsworth Longfellow, graduated from Harvard College in 1838, and from Harvard Divinity School in 1846. He served Unitarian congregations in Massachusetts, New York, and Pennsylvania, and, together with Samuel Johnson, published two Unitarian hymnals; this text appears in the second, *Hymns of the Spirit* of 1864.

195 The King of Love My Shepherd Is

It was reported that the dying words of author Henry W. Baker in 1877 were those of the third verse of this hymn: "Perverse and foolish oft I strayed...." Baker asked John Bacchus Dykes to compose the tune DOMINUS REGIT ME (which takes its name from the Latin opening of the psalm) for his paraphrase. The text and tune made their first appearance together in the 1868 Appendix to *Hymns Ancient and Modern* of 1861, for which Baker served as principal editor.

196 The King of Love My Shepherd Is

George Petri collected the Irish folk tune ST. COLUMBA in the mid-19th century; it was later edited with all of Petri's transcriptions by Charles Villiers Stanford for the Irish Literary Society in the early 20th century. The memorable "triplet" figuration in the second phrase of the hymn is almost certainly the work of Ralph Vaughan Williams, when he used Stanford's harmonization nearly verbatim in the *English Hymnal* of 1906.

197 Unto the Hills Around Do I Lift Up

Charles Henry Purday originally composed the tune SANDON for the text "Lead, kindly light." Purday was an English vocalist, conductor, and musical activist, who published a book in 1877 on proposed attempts to reform musical copyright laws.

198 The Lord's My Shepherd

This paraphrase of Psalm 23 is one of the most famous texts from the Scottish Psalter of 1650, which is still the authorized version of the Church of Scotland. The tune CRIMOND was named by Jessie S. Irvine for one of the locations in Scotland where she lived while growing up. The popularity of this pairing owes much to its use at the 1947 wedding in Westminster Abbey of the then-Princess Elizabeth and Prince Philip, as well as in St. Paul's Cathedral in 1948 for the silver wedding anniversary of King George VI and Queen Elizabeth.

199   My God, How Wonderful Thou Art

Frederick W. Faber published the original version of this text in a book entitled *Jesus and Mary: Or Catholic Hymns* in 1849. Faber was a founding member of the Brompton Oratory in London, England, and intended this topical collection to be useful in teaching and instructing new converts to the faith. The tune name WESTMINSTER probably reflects the composer James Turle's long association with Westminster Abbey, where he was organist and master of the choristers from 1831 to 1875.

200   I to the Hills Will Lift Mine Eyes

The Scottish Psalter of 1650, from which this paraphrase of Psalm 121 is taken, was intended to be a psalter for all Presbyterians (including English ones) in competition with the 1562 "Old Version" psalter of Sternhold and Hopkins. The harmonization for this tune from the Scottish Psalter of 1615 was written by English composer and editor Thomas Ravenscroft for his collection *The Whole Booke of Psalmes* of 1621. This anthology contained harmonizations by many leading composers of the day and was the greatest product of the English psalm-tune tradition in the period before the English Civil War.

201   God Moves in a Mysterious Way

William Cowper spent most of his life in Olney, Buckinghamshire, England, writing religious poetry and assisting his friend John Newton, the curate there, in his evangelistic work. A collection of their joint hymnic work was published in 1779 as *Olney Hymns* in which this already-popular text appeared.

202   How Shall I Sing That Majesty

English cleric John Mason, author of this text, wrote a series of hymns and poems, including a full paraphrase of the Song of Solomon. Just before his death, Mason reported a vision of a visit from Jesus which he interpreted to mean that Christ's return was nigh. After preaching a series of memorable sermons, crowds gathered in his town of Water Stratford, England expecting the Second Coming. Ken Naylor's tune COE FEN is named for an area of public marshland in Cambridge, England. Although it is greatly admired in the British Isles, this may be its first appearance in a North American hymnal.

203   Immortal, Invisible, God Only Wise

Walter Chalmers Smith, a minister and for a time moderator of the Free Church of Scotland, included this text based on 1 Timothy 1:17 in a collection he published in 1867. John Roberts harmonized a number of Welsh folk melodies, among them ST. DENIO, which he published in 1839,

204   Dear Mother God

Janet Wootton, an English Greek scholar and professor, wrote this text as part of an effort to increase the use of feminine imagery of God in hymnody. With composer June Boyce-Tillman, Wootton edited *Reflecting Praise*, a 1993 collection of hymns celebrating the work and contributions of women.

205   Whate'er My God Ordains Is Right

German composer Severus Gastorus composed the tune WAS GOTT TUT for the German text of this hymn, written by his friend Samuel Rodigast. The harmonization by J. S. Bach appears in his *Cantata No. 12, "Weinen, Klagen, Sorgen, Zagen,"* originally composed for the Third Sunday after Easter in 1724.

206   O Bless the Lord, My Soul

Author James Montgomery was an outspoken newspaper editor in Sheffield, England who was twice imprisoned for advocating liberal ideas. He is considered one of the great figures of English Nonconformist hymnody and wrote more than four-hundred hymns, of which this is one of the best-known. Composer Aaron Williams was a London music teacher and publisher who produced several widely-used collections of hymn and psalm tunes.

207   O God, the Rock of Ages

English clergyman Edward Henry Bickersteth, the author of this text, served as Bishop of Exeter and wrote many religious poems and hymns; he also served as editor of several hymnals. The tune MEIRIONYDD was written by William Lloyd, a Welsh farmer and amateur musician who published a collection of his tunes in 1840.

208   Eternal Light, Shine in My Heart

The inspiration for this text of English poet Christopher Idle came from a prayer of Alcuin appearing in a 1941 publication entitled *Daily Prayer*. American composer Jane Manton Marshall's tune JACOB was commissioned by the parents of Sarah Jacob to be sung at her confirmation at First Methodist Church in Richardson, Texas.

209   Bright the Vision That Delighted

Isaiah's vision found in chapter 6, on which this text of Richard Mant is based, has served as the inspiration for numerous hymns and anthems over the years. Composer Richard Redhead was an active figure in the Oxford Movement in England. He served for over thirty years as organist of Margaret Chapel, London and was co-editor for the first modern English Gregorian psalter, *Laudes Diurnæ* of 1843.

210   Our God, Our Help in Ages Past

This text is one of the most famous psalm paraphrases written by Isaac Watts. He titled it "Man Frail and God Eternal" in its original publication. Although the tune ST. ANNE was originally published anonymously in 1708, it was attributed conclusively to William Croft, organist of St. Anne's Church, Soho in London, England, from 1700 to 1711, by a number of his contemporaries.

211   Tell Out, My Soul, the Greatness of the Lord

This text by English poet and bishop Timothy Dudley-Smith is both one of his earliest poems and one of his best-known. His inspiration came from a review copy he had received of *The New English Bible*, in which the opening line of the hymn appears as the first words of the Magnificat text in Luke. The tune WOODLANDS is named after a house at Gresham's School in Norfolk, England, where the composer Walter Greatorex served as director of music.

212   Lord Jesus, Think on Me

The original Greek text of this hymn is the epilogue to a series of ten odes on Christian doctrine by Synesius, Bishop of Cyrene. The tune SOUTHWELL first appeared in a psalter of 1579 edited by William Damon, organist of the Chapel Royal during the reign of Queen Elizabeth I.

213   Thou Didst Leave Thy Throne

The author of this hymn, English poet Emily E. Elliott, was the niece of hymn writer Charlotte Elliott (see no. 67) and served as the editor of the *Church Missionary Juvenile Instructor*. Though trained as a minister, Thomas R. Matthews was very active in sacred music circles, editing several publications and writing more than 100 hymn tunes; he was renowned for his great compositional speed.

214   Jesus, the Very Thought of Thee

The original text of this hymn is a cento from the opening stanzas of the "Jubilus rhythmicus de nomine Jesu," one of the greatest poems in medieval Latin literature. Though often ascribed to Bernard of Clairvaux, it is thought more likely to be the work of an English Cistercian monk writing near the end of the 12th century.

215   Sing We of the Blessed Mother

English archdeacon George B. Timms wrote this text to fill a perceived need for Marian hymns in British parishes. Its content resembles biographically apocryphal carol texts such as "The Seven Joys of Mary." The tune RUSTINGTON is named for the village in Sussex, England, in which composer Charles Hubert Hastings Parry spent the final years of his life.

216   O Love, How Deep, How Broad, How High

The translator of this text, Benjamin Webb, was a close friend and associate of John Mason Neale, with whom he was active in the Anglican liturgical revival. In France during the 16th and 17th centuries, traditional unmeasured plainsong melodies were often replaced with metrical tunes founded on plainsong, such as DEUS TUORUM MILITUM.

217   Crown Him with Many Crowns

Matthew Bridges was an Englishman who entered the Roman Catholic Church under the influence of the Oxford Movement; he is best remembered today for a small handful of hymn texts, of which this is one. George J. Elvey wrote the tune DIADEMATA for this text for the 1868 Appendix to *Hymns Ancient and Modern*.

218   O Love of God, How Strong and True

This hymn brings together the work of a 19th century Free Church of Scotland minister and a 20th century American musician. Composer Calvin Hampton named nearly all of his tunes after close personal friends. DE TAR honored Vernon de Tar, organist and choirmaster for many years of the Church of the Ascension in New York City. This tune brought Hampton international prominence upon its first publication in 1973, particularly for its creative use of rock-influenced textures.

219   Fairest Lord Jesus

Although this hymn has often been called the "Crusader's Hymn," there is no historical justification for this practice. The tune gained its name ST. ELIZABETH because of its use in composer Franz Liszt's 1862 oratorio *The Legend of St. Elizabeth*, based on the life of the Hungarian saint whose basket of bread was turned into flowers.

220   O for a Thousand Tongues to Sing

One of the most famous texts by Charles Wesley, this hymn was originally headed "For the Anniversary of One's Conversion," which celebrates Wesley's "conversion" on May 21, 1738. The versions in common use today are centos of Wesley's original, beginning with his seventh stanza. This was the opening hymn in the Wesleys' 1780 *Collection of Hymns for the Use of the People called Methodists* and has continued to open most Methodist hymnals ever since.

221   What Wondrous Love Is This, O My Soul

The unusual meter and stanza structure of this anonymous text is sometimes known as the "Captain Kidd" meter (after the famous pirate), because of its connection with an 18th century ballad beginning "My name was Robert Kidd, when I sailed, when I sailed." The rich harmonization used here is by Paul J. Christiansen, who was director of the Concordia Choir in Minnesota for over fifty years.

222   We Have a Gospel to Proclaim

Englishman William Gardiner was a stocking manufacturer and amateur musician whose enthusiastic support for the works of Ludwig van Beethoven led to the first performances of Beethoven's music in England in 1794. Gardiner published a collection entitled *Sacred Melodies, from Haydn, Mozart, and Beethoven, Adapted to the Best English Poets, and appropriate to the Use of the British Church* in 1812. In the second volume of 1815, he published the tune GARDINER claiming "subject Beethoven." However, a lack of any known source in Beethoven's work has implied to hymnologists that Gardiner was the sole author.

223   Immortal Love, Forever Full

This text is a composite from John Greenleaf Whittier's poem, "Our Master," which appeared in an 1867 collection of his poems. Whittier, a native of Massachusetts of Quaker background, was one of the foremost 19th century American poets and an ardent abolitionist.

224   He Leadeth Me, O Blessed Thought!

Joseph H. Gilmore was a Baptist minister and head of the department of English at the University of Rochester, New York. Gilmore tells that the creation of this text occurred while guest preaching in Philadelphia in 1862; he was struck by the words "he leadeth me" during a reading of Psalm 23. His wife submitted the text to a Boston magazine, and he did not know that William B. Bradbury had created a musical setting until a few years later when he appeared as a job candidate at a church in Rochester and found the hymn scheduled for that morning's service.

225   Sing, My Soul, His Wondrous Love

This anonymous text is of American origin, appearing in a collection published in Baltimore, Maryland in 1801. John Bacchus Dykes's tunes ST. BEES is named for St.

Bees Theological College in Cumbria, England, the first theological college outside of Oxford and Cambridge designed for the training of Church of England clergy.

226   Love Divine, All Loves Excelling

The inspiration for Charles Wesley's famed text seems to be an aria from John Dryden's masque *King Arthur*, set to music by Henry Purcell: "Fairest Isle, all isles excelling." Originally, this text was sung to a hymn adaptation of Purcell's tune; it was first matched to the stirring Welsh tune HYFRYDOL in the Episcopal *Hymnal 1940*.

227   Hope of the World

This text by Georgia Elma Harkness was the winning entry in a competition sponsored by the Hymn Society of America for use at the Second Assembly of the World Council of Churches in 1954; the theme of the conference was "Jesus Christ, hope of the world." The tune VICAR by V. Earle Copes takes its name from Copes's first name and the name of his father.

228   Come, My Way, My Truth, My Life

The entire poetic corpus of English metaphysical poet George Herbert, including this text, was first published in the year following his death. The tune OUNDLE was adapted by Edward J. Hopkins from Orlando Gibbons's choral anthem for Ascensiontide, *O Clap Your Hands*.

229   He Comes to Us as One Unknown

The first line of this text by English poet and bishop Timothy Dudley-Smith is a quotation from Albert Schweitzer's *The Quest of the Historical Jesus* of 1906. A polymath with exceptionally broad interests, Schweitzer was active as an organist, biographer, liberal theologian, philosopher, and medical doctor.

230   O Thou Great Friend to All of Us Below

Author of this hymn, Theodore Parker, a graduate of Harvard College and Harvard Divinity School, was ordained as a Unitarian minister but subsequently broke with Unitarianism, preaching a simpler and more rationalistic Christianity to a congregation that met in Boston Music Hall. The tune TOULON is a shortened form of the hymn tune GENEVAN 124.

231   There's a Wideness in God's Mercy

Since its initial publication appearance in 1861, Frederick W. Faber's original text of this hymn has been heavily edited and adapted. Many different centos have been created from Faber's original thirteen stanzas to the point where almost no two books have exactly the same combination. The tune BLAENWERN is named for a small farm near Tufton, Dyfed, where the Welsh composer William P. Rowlands recuperated from a serious childhood illness.

232   There's a Wideness in God's Mercy

Calvin Hampton's tune ST. HELENA was named after the Sisters of the Order of St. Helena who were in residence at Calvary Church, New York City, where Hampton served as director of music. After Hampton's early death from AIDS in 1984, this hymn took on significance as an unofficial anthem for the many American musicians who died of AIDS during the 1980s.

233   Rejoice, the Lord Is King

Late in his life, composer George Frideric Handel wrote a few tunes, of which this is one, for hymn texts of Charles Wesley. They were not published until 1826, some eighty years after their creation. The name GOPSAL is that of a small village in Leicestershire, England, which was the home of Charles Jennens, librettist for Handel's *Messiah*, HWV 56.

234   Name of All Majesty

English bishop Timothy Dudley-Smith reports that this hymn was modeled on the metrical form of a poem by Walter de la Mare, whose *Collected Poems* he was reading in early 1979. The final line of each stanza ("Jesus is Lord") is regarded as one of the earliest Christian credal affirmations. The text was created with no known tune in mind. MAJESTAS was composed for the hymn's first publication in *Hymns for Today's Church*.

235   Jesus Shall Reign Where'er the Sun

This paraphrase of the latter part of Psalm 72 demonstrates how Isaac Watts adapted the psalms, fulfilling his announced intention to make David "speak like a Christian." The tune DUKE STREET was published anonymously in a Scottish collection of 1793. The attribution to John Hatton appeared in later publications; next to nothing is known about him. The tune's name derives from a district of St. Helens, Windle in Lancashire, England.

236   At the Name of Jesus

Like her contemporary Charlotte Elliott, Caroline Maria Noel was an invalid whose hymns were written from the perspective of years of quiet suffering. She published a collection in 1861 entitled *Name of Jesus, and other Verses for the Sick and Lonely*. Ralph Vaughan Williams composed the tune KING'S WESTON in 1925 for *Songs of Praise*, naming it for a village near Bristol, England.

237   Thou Art the Way; to Thee Alone

This text is one of the most noted of American 19th century origin. Author George Washington Doane was the Episcopal bishop of New Jersey and published one volume of poems in 1824. The tune CONSOLATION first appeared in *Sixteen Tune Settings*, published in Philadelphia in 1812, in which Andrew Law introduced an idiosyncratic shape-note system.

238   Ye Servants of God, Your Master Proclaim

The original version of this text by Charles Wesley was filled with maritime imagery, which has been omitted in later appearances to allow for wider use. The German folk melody PADERBORN was harmonized by Sydney H. Nicholson, an English conductor and composer best known as the founder of the Royal School of Church Music.

239   All Hail the Power of Jesus' Name

The first stanza of this text was published in *Gospel Magazine* in 1779, with the remainder following in an issue in 1780. The tune CORONATION, the earliest American hymn tune in continuous use, was written by Oliver Holden, a carpenter in Charlestown, Massachusetts, who also kept a music store and taught music, preached in his own "Puritan Church," and served in the Massachusetts legislature.

240   Christ Triumphant, Ever Reigning

This hymn is one of the best-known to come out of England during the second half of the 20th century. The text is the most popular of the hundred hymns written by Anglican clergyman Michael Saward, whose last appointment before retiring in 2000 was as Canon Treasurer of St. Paul's Cathedral in London. The tune is similarly the best-known creation of John Barnard, an active composer, arranger, choir director, and organist in northwest London, England. It gains its name from Guiting Power, a village in Gloucestershire, England.

241   Come Down, O Love Divine

This text comes from the *laudi* of Bianco of Siena, a member of the Order of the Jesuates, lay followers of the Augustinian rule. The *laudi* were sacred poems in the vernacular, inspired by the Italian hymns attributed to Francis of Assisi. The tune DOWN AMPNEY is named for the birthplace in Gloucestershire, England of its composer Ralph Vaughan Williams.

242   Come, O Creator Spirit, Come

This Pentecost hymn is one of the most famous of the plainchant hymns and was the only non-biblical hymn included in the first English *Book of Common Prayer* of 1549, where it was prescribed for the Ordering of Priests. The plainchant tune is thought to be of earlier origin than the text, perhaps dating as early as the 4th century.

243   Send Down Thy Truth, O God

Edward Rowland Sill was a graduate of Yale College and Harvard Divinity School; he later became a professor of English at the University of California. This text appears in an 1867 collection of his poetry entitled *The Hermitage*. Lister R. Peace composed the tune NOVA VITA for *The Church Hymnal for the Christian Year*, which he co-edited in 1917.

244   Come, Holy Spirit, God and Lord

The original source of this hymn's text is the medieval Latin antiphon "Veni Sancte Spiritus." The tune by Melchior Vulpius was originally intended for a Christmas hymn, hence its German tune name. This harmonization by J. S. Bach appears in his *Cantata No. 122*, originally composed for the Sunday after Christmas in 1724.

245   Like the Murmur of the Dove's Song

Carl P. Daw, Jr. wrote his text specifically for Peter Cutts's tune BRIDGEGROOM during the editorial process of the Episcopal *Hymnal 1982*. It has since gone on to become the best-known hymn of both poet and composer. After serving for many years in British colleges, composer Peter Cutts emigrated to America where he became director of music at Andover Newton Theological School in Andover, Massachusetts. In 2005, he retired and returned to his native country.

246   Praise the Spirit in Creation

American organist and composer David Hurd, who has served for many years as professor of music at General Seminary, New York City, wrote his tune JULION as what he terms "a generic tune" intended for use with any fitting text. The first pairing of this text of Michael Hewlett with Hurd's tune was in the Episcopal *Hymnal 1982*.

247 Breathe on Me, Breath of God

In addition to his work as a poet, Edwin Hatch was an English theologian best known for his research on the influence of early Greek ideas on later Christianity and for the creation of a concordance to the Septuagint. This text was originally intended as an ordination hymn.

248 Spirit Divine, Attend Our Prayers

Andrew Reed was a Congregational lay preacher in London and an ardent philanthropist who founded numerous hospitals and orphanages. He wrote this hymn for a service on Good Friday in 1829 sponsored by the London Board of Congregational Ministers, promoting "a revival of religion in the British churches."

249 Holy Spirit, Truth Divine

This text by Samuel Longfellow was marked as a "Prayer for Inspiration" in its original publication. Longfellow, younger brother of Henry Wadsworth Longfellow, graduated from Harvard College in 1838, and from Harvard Divinity School in 1846.

250 There's a Spirit in the Air

Composer John Wilson, one of the most active hymnologists of the 20th century, wrote his tune LAUDS for this text by poet Brian Wren, who immigrated to America from England in 1983. The tune is named for the monastic office read nearest dawn.

251 Holy, Holy, Holy! Lord God Almighty

English clergyman and poet Reginald Heber, the author of this text, began writing a collection of hymn texts while he was vicar of Hodnet, Shropshire, England. He intended to create a set of hymns for the entire church year drawing upon both his own work and that of other poets. His appointment as Bishop of Calcutta in 1823, however, prevented the collection from being published until a version appeared posthumously in 1827. It is because of this collection that Heber is credited as the driving force behind the acceptance of hymns alongside psalm settings in Anglican worship. The joining of Heber's text with John Bacchus Dykes' tune NICAEA began in *Hymns Ancient and Modern* in 1861 and has been indissoluble. The tune name recalls the site of the Ecumenical Council of 325 that formulated an important credal affirmation of the doctrine of the Trinity.

252 All Glory Be to God on High

Nikolaus Decius, a north German monk, who text appears here in Winkworth's translation, was an early adherent to the teachings of Martin Luther. In about 1521, Decius had written the earliest hymns of the Reformation, three Low German texts replacing the Latin Gloria, Sanctus, and Agnus Dei. The original version of the tune ALLEIN GOTT is thought to be an adaptation by Decius himself of a plainsong Gloria.

253 Come, Thou Almighty King

The tune MOSCOW was composed by Felice de Giardini, a distinguished Italian violinist who led the orchestra at the Italian opera in London. The tune is named for the place of the composer's death. Both text and tune of this hymn are a parody of the British national anthem, "God save the King."

254   Mothering God, You Gave Me Birth

Julian of Norwich is considered one of the most significant English mystics, who in her visions saw many maternal and feminine images of God. Her *Sixteen Revelations of Divine Love*, appearing c. 1393, is thought to be the first English language book by a female author. This text is a poetic adaptation of some of the more famous sections of her writings.

255   Ancient of Days, Who Sittest Throned in Glory

This text by William C. Doane, first bishop of the Episcopal Diocese of Albany, New York was written for the bicentennial of Albany's charter in 1886. The original first stanza of the hymn specifically reflected that anniversary. The tune ALBANY was composed for the occasion by J. Albert Jeffery, the organist of the Episcopal Cathedral of All Saints in Albany.

256   Eternal Father, Strong to Save

William Whiting's text was substantially revised by the editors of the 1861 edition of *Hymns Ancient and Modern*, including changing the opening words from "O Thou Who bidd'st the ocean deep." John Bacchus Dykes's tune MELITA was commissioned for this text. The hymn is known throughout the English speaking world as the "Navy hymn" and has been widely used on national and military ceremonial occasions.

257   Blessed Jesus, at Thy Word

This text was written by Tobias Clausnitzer, a Lutheran pastor in Weiden, Germany; he intended it for use as a Sunday hymn before the sermon. J. S. Bach's harmonization of this tune comes not from a cantata, but from his collection of harmonized chorale melodies published posthumously in 1769.

258   Glorious Things of Thee Are Spoken

At some times and places, this text celebrating "Zion, or the City of God" has proved more popular than John Newton's now-better-known "Amazing Grace." The tune of this hymn was composed, after many drafts, by Josef Haydn in response to a commission for the national anthem of Austria; it was inspired by his visits to London and the fervor and power of the British national anthem. It became one of Haydn's favorites of his own work, and he continued to make varied arrangements of it and played it on the piano almost daily near the end of his life.

259   The Church's One Foundation

English curate Samuel John Stone wrote this text for his own parish for the purpose of teaching basic doctrine. He wrote a series of twelve hymns on the articles of the Apostles' Creed. The tune name came about through a mistaken belief that AURELIA was the Latin world for gold, because it was sung originally to the words "Jerusalem the Golden" by composer Samuel Sebastian Wesley's mother.

260   City of God, How Broad and Far

Poet Samuel Johnson edited a hymnal in 1846, while he and his collaborator Samuel Longfellow were in their final year at Harvard Divinity School. The collection was a landmark of Unitarian hymnody and noted for the high quality of its included poetry. Johnson wrote this hymn text while serving as minister of the Free Church in Lynn, Massachusetts.

261 Great God, the Followers of Thy Son

Henry Ware, Jr., the author of this text, was one of the first faculty members of Harvard Divinity School and an influential Unitarian theologian. He also served as the first president of the Harvard Musical Association. Ware was a significant mentor to Ralph Waldo Emerson in Emerson's student years; but in later life he began distancing himself from Emerson's ideology, culminating in the publication of his rebuttal of his writings.

262 Christ Is Made the Sure Foundation

This text is a translation of the second half of the Latin hymn "Urbs beata Jerusalem," one of the first hymns inspired by the apocalyptic vision of the heavenly Jerusalem. WESTMINSTER ABBEY is adapted from the closing "Alleluias" of Henry Purcell's choral anthem *O God, Thou Art My God*, z. 35. The tune's name reflects Purcell's service as organist of Westminster Abbey in London, England.

263 Our Father, by Whose Servants

G. W. Briggs wrote this text while serving as Rector of Loughborough in Leicestershire, England for use at the grammar school there. The original second verse of the hymn reflected the four hundred year history of the school, but was later adapted by the author to be of more general use. The tune NYLAND is a Finnish folk melody and is named for a province in Finland.

264 Spread, O Spread, Thou Mighty Word

Jonathan Friedrich Bahnmaier was briefly a professor of education and homiletics at the University of Tübingen, Germany, and later town preacher at Kircheim-unter-Teck, in Württemberg. An active participant in educational and missionary work, he privately published this hymn text, which reflects his personal evangelical beliefs.

265 We Come unto Our People's God

Thomas Hornblower Gill wrote this text inspired by Psalm 90 and published it in a personal collection entitled *Golden Chain of Praise Hymns*. As a Unitarian, he was denied admission to Oxford University because he refused to assent to the Articles of the Church of England. Later, however, he abandoned his Unitarian roots and became associated with an Evangelical branch of the Church.

266 Rejoice, Ye Pure in Heart

This text was written for a choir festival in Peterborough Cathedral, England in 1865. The original version contained a number of stanzas of dated diction that have been dropped by later publications. Arthur H. Messiter wrote the tune specifically for the text, naming it MARION after his mother.

267 O Word of God Incarnate

The tune MUNICH is an adaptation of a German melody created by Felix Mendelssohn for the quartet "Cast thy burden upon the Lord" in his oratorio *Elijah*, op. 70 of 1847. Mendelssohn's use of traditional chorale melodies in his oratorios and organ works reflects the influence of J. S. Bach, whose large-scale compositions Mendelssohn reintroduced to the German and English concert public.

268   Break Thou the Bread of Life

This hymn was commissioned by the Chautauqua Institute in New York State for use in its Bible study and literary discussion groups; the Chautauqua movement was designed to provide continuing education and reinvigoration for Sunday School teachers in American churches. The poet, Mary A. Lathbury, was known as the "poet laureate of Chautauqua;" composer William F. Sherwin was Chautauqua's director of music at the time.

269   O Zion, Haste, Thy Mission High Fulfilling

Mary Ann Thomson wrote this hymn text while awake one night with one of her children who was sick with typhoid fever. Though James Walch's tune was originally written for Frederick Faber's text "Hark, hark, my soul! Angelic songs are swelling," it gained its common name TIDINGS from its association with Thomson's text.

270   Christ Is the King! O Friends Upraise

Although born in Wales, composer David McKinley Williams spent most of his career in the United States, where he was an active member of the committee that produced the Episcopal *Hymnal 1940*. His tune CHRISTUS REX was written specifically for George Kennedy Allen Bell's text, hence its tune name.

271   I Love Thy Kingdom, Lord

Timothy Dwight wrote this text inspired by Psalm 137 for an edition of the psalms published in Connecticut in 1801. Dwight was a graduate of Yale and son-in-law of the great preacher Jonathan Edwards; he was a Congregationalist minister and served as a chaplain during the Revolutionary War. He later became president of Yale College. Composer Aaron Williams was a London music teacher and publisher who produced several widely-used collections of hymn and psalm tunes.

272   Lift Every Voice and Sing

Brothers James Weldon and John Rosamond Johnson wrote this hymn for a concert in Jacksonville, Florida in 1900 to celebrate the birthday of Abraham Lincoln. This hymn quickly became symbolic for African Americans and was later adopted as the "Negro National Anthem" by the NAACP.

273   Thou, Whose Almighty Word

Due to the modesty of the author, John Marriott, this text was not published or quoted during his lifetime. After his death in 1825, the text made its first appearance in a speech by Thomas Mortimer to the London Missionary Society. The tune MOSCOW was composed by Felice de Giardini, a distinguished Italian violinist who led the orchestra at the Italian opera in London. The tune is named for the place of the composer's death.

274   Thou Lord of Hosts, Whose Guiding Hand

Octavius Brooks Frothingham wrote this hymn in 1846 for the Commencement exercises of his class at Harvard Divinity School. The text was first published that same year in a Unitarian hymnal edited by Samuel Longfellow and Samuel Johnson. A Harvard College graduate, Frothingham served Unitarian congregations in Salem, Massachusetts, and New York City.

275   We Limit Not the Truth of God

This text by George Rawson was adapted from a speech given by John Robinson to the Pilgrims before they left Leyden, England on their voyage to the New World in 1620. This is the first hymnal to pair the text with the Genevan psalm tune OLD 137TH, perhaps appropriate since psalm tunes would have been the genre of sacred music known to the Pilgrims.

276   Go Forth for God

J. R. Peacey's text was inspired by the dismissal in the Anglican/Episcopal liturgy: "Go in peace to love and serve the Lord." Peacey, an Anglican clergyman, served as headmaster of a school in Calcutta, India before his tenure at Bristol Cathedral, England, after World War II. He wrote only eighteen hymn texts.

277   All My Hope on God Is Founded

English composer Herbert Howells wrote the hymn tune MICHAEL after receiving a request from the director of music of Charterhouse School, England for a setting of this text. Howells claims he wrote the entire tune immediately at the breakfast table upon opening the mail and finding the request. The tune is named for the composer's son, who died at a young age of meningitis. The English text by poet Robert Bridges is, by his own admission, "a free version" of a hymn by Joachim Neander (see the note at no. 45).

278   God Is My Strong Salvation

Author James Montgomery was an outspoken newspaper editor in Sheffield, England, who was twice imprisoned for advocating liberal ideas. He is considered one of the great figures of English Nonconformist hymnody and wrote more than four-hundred hymns. This original harmonization of the tune by Melchior Vulpius is simpler than J. S. Bach's more florid version.

279   Awake, My Soul, Stretch Every Nerve

This text by Nonconformist English hymnwriter Philip Doddridge was originally titled "Pressing on in the Christian Race." The tune CHRISTMAS is adapted from the soprano aria "Non vi piacque ingiusti Dei" from the second act of George Frideric Handel's opera *Siroe*, HWV 24, of 1728.

280   O God, Thou Faithful God

Johann Heerman published this "Daily Prayer" in a collection of musical devotions in 1630. The tune's harmonization by J. S. Bach appears in his *Cantata No. 45*, "Es ist dir gesagt, Mensch, was gut ist," originally composed for the Eighth Sunday after Trinity in 1726.

281   A Mighty Fortress Is Our God

This translation of Martin Luther's classic hymn of the Reformation was written by Frederic H. Hedge, a graduate of Harvard College and Harvard Divinity School, and co-editor of a hymnal published in 1853. After service as a Unitarian minister in New England, Hedge became professor of ecclesiastical history, and later German literature, at Harvard.

282   How Firm a Foundation

This hymn was attributed to "K" in its original publication *A Selection of Hymns from the best authors*, compiled by John Rippon. "K" has been tentatively identified as Richard Keen, the precentor of the London Baptist congregation that Rippon served as minister. The anonymous pentatonic American folk-hymn tune now firmly associated with this text dates from the first half of the 19th century.

283   Through All the Changing Scenes of Life

This text is selected from the 18 stanzas that made up the Tate and Brady revision of Psalm 34 in the 1698 edition of their *New Version of the Psalms of David*. Composer and conductor George Thomas Smart was one of the founders of the London Philharmonic Society and an editor of publications of early music. As a major musical figure on the London scene he was a close friend of many leading figures of the day including Ludwig van Beethoven and especially Carl Maria von Weber, who died in Smart's house.

284   Out of the Depths I Cry to Thee

Martin Luther's great paraphrase of Psalm 130 is found in the first three hymnals of the German Reformation. Although the accompanying tune has often been ascribed to Luther, it may well be the work of his musical assistant Johann Walther. The harmonization by J. S. Bach appears in his *Cantata No. 38*, originally composed for the Twenty-first Sunday after Trinity in 1724.

285   Guide Me, O Thou Great Jehovah

Poet William Williams was called the "Sweet Singer of Wales" and was the chief hymnodist of the Welsh Methodist Revival; he wrote more than eight hundred Welsh and one hundred English hymns, of which this is probably the most popular. The tune CWM RHONDDA was composed for the annual Welsh Cymanfa Ganu (Singing Festival) by John Hughes, a railway employee.

286   Dear Lord and Father of Mankind

In his poem "The Brewing of Soma," John Greenleaf Whitter describes the efforts of certain East Indian tribes to commune with their gods by drinking intoxicating soma. The poet suggests that in certain forms of devotion we "brew... the heathen Soma still" and prays that God "will forgive our foolish ways." Whittier, a native of Massachusetts of Quaker background, was one of the foremost 19th century American poets and an ardent abolitionist. The tune REST was written for this text by Frederick C. Maker, an organist who spent his entire life in Bristol, England.

287   Dear Lord and Father of Mankind

The tune REPTON is extracted from an aria sung by the title character in Charles Hubert Hastings Parry's oratorio *Judith* of 1888. The tune gained its name from its first use as a hymn at Repton School, Derbyshire, England, whose director of music was a close friend of Parry's.

288   Forgive Our Sins as We Forgive

English hymnwriter Rosamond Herklots was inspired to write this hymn while digging for weeds in a garden. She felt there was a parallel between the way that weeds choke desired flowers and the way that long-carried sins and grievances choke people's ability to grow and love.

289 Lead On, O King Eternal

This text by Ernest W. Shurtleff was written for his graduation from Andover Theological Seminary, Andover, Massachusetts. The tune LANCASHIRE was written originally for the missionary hymn "From Greenland's icy mountain." Though written in England, the tune gained far greater popularity in the United States than it had in Great Britain.

290 Call Jehovah Thy Salvation

Author James Montgomery was an outspoken newspaper editor in Sheffield, England who was twice imprisoned for advocating liberal ideas. He is considered one of the great figures of English Nonconformist hymnody, authoring more than four hundred hymns, including this one. The tune TRUST is derived from the opening theme of the second movement of a composition for mezzo-soprano solo and chorus that Mendelssohn wrote in 1840 for Charles Bayles Broadley's version of Psalm 13. The tune name reflects the musical theme's text, "On thy love my heart reposes."

291 Be Thou My Vision, O Lord of My Heart

Both translator and versifier of this poem were associated with the study of the Irish language in England: Mary Byrne was a linguistic researcher for the Board of Intermediate Education, and Eleanor Hull was founder and secretary of the Irish Text Society. The text as a hymn first appeared in her collection of Irish poems in 1912. The hymn tune SLANE is derived from an Irish ballad melody, and the tune name recalls the Hill of Slane, where Easter fires are still lit every year in memory of the bonfire kindled there by St. Patrick in defiance of the pagan kings reigning on the nearby Hill of Tara.

292 O for a Closer Walk with God

Based on Genesis 5:24 and entitled "Walking with God," this hymn by English poet William Cowper was written during the serious illness of a close friend. CAITHNESS is one of the "Common Tunes" from the Scottish Psalter.

293 Spirit of God, Descend upon My Heart

The tune MORECOMBE was intended by its composer Frederick C. Atkinson for the text "Abide with me." Though that pairing never became popular, it has been frequently linked with this text by Irish poet George Croly.

294 How Sweet the Name of Jesus Sounds

This text by John Newton was inspired by Song of Solomon 1:3 – "Thy name is as an ointment poured forth." In his original version, the fourth verse began: "Jesus! my shepherd, husband, friend," which Christianizes the poetic imagery from the Song of Solomon. Charles Hutcheson, composer of the tune STRACATHRO, was a Scottish merchant and avid amateur composer.

295 O God of Bethel, by Whose Hand

Philip Doddridge's text was entitled "Jacob's Vow: from Genesis 28:20,22" and included in a posthumous collection of his work. DUNDEE is one of the "Common Tunes" from the Scottish Psalter, where it was originally entitled FRENCH TUNE.

296 Put Thou Thy Trust in God

Paul Gerhardt's hymn was inspired by Psalm 37:5 and altered considerably by John Wesley in his first translation and by later editors. The tune AYLESBURY first appeared in the *Book of Psalmody* of 1718, a very popular collection edited by John Chetham, curate and schoolmaster at Skipton, Yorkshire, England.

297 Praise Is the Soul's Sincere Desire

Author James Montgomery was an outspoken newspaper editor in Sheffield, England, who was twice imprisoned for advocating liberal ideas. This text was written at the request of Edward Bickersteth for inclusion in his *Treatise on Prayer* of 1819. John Bacchus Dykes was commissioned to write the tune BEATITUDO for the text "How bright those glorious spirits shine" in the second edition of *Hymns Ancient and Modern* in 1875. Dykes received £100 for his tunes written for that edition.

298 O Thou Who Camest from Above

Charles Wesley based this hymn on Leviticus 6:13: "The fire shall ever be burning upon the altar; it shall never go out." His grandson, the English composer Samuel Sebastian Wesley, was one of the most noted contributors to church music of the mid-19th century, and one of the last composers of "verse anthems" in the traditional English form. Many of his hymn tunes were adapted from sections of his anthems; this one, however, was written as an original hymn for the Three Choirs Festival at Hereford, hence its tune name.

299 Amazing Grace! How Sweet the Sound

This is one of the most famous hymns ever written, known in every country of the world. John Newton wrote this hymn after his conversion to Christianity, reflecting on his past life as a captain of a slave-ship. Written to be used with a sermon at his parish in Olney for New Year's Day 1773, it was entitled "Faith's Review and Expectation" in *Olney Hymns* of 1779. The text was not joined to the American folk-hymn tune NEW BRITAIN until they appeared together in William Walker's *Southern Harmony* of 1835.

300 Teach Me, My God and King

When this hymn of George Herbert was published in the posthumous collection of his work, it was entitled "The Elixir." This reference to the preparation by which alchemists hoped to change base metals into gold may also be found in the second and fourth stanzas of the text.

301 Behold Us, Lord, a Little Space

John Ellerton wrote this hymn in 1870 for a midday service in a London church and published it in *Church Hymns* in 1871 for which he served as editor. ABBEY is one of the "Common Tunes" from the Scottish Psalter.

302 My God, I Love Thee; Not Because

The original Spanish text of this hymn is a sonnet attributed to Francis Xavier, one of the most significant Roman Catholic missionaries and a co-founder of the Jesuit Order. His ministry took him to India and Asia, and he is thought by the Catholic Church to have converted more to Christianity than any single person other than Paul.

303   As Pants the Hart for Cooling Streams

This paraphrase of Psalm 42 is likely the work of either Irishman Nahum Tate, who became Poet Laureate of Great Britain in 1692, or Nicholas Brady, a royal chaplain; together, they were the primary editors of the *New Version* of the Psalter of 1696, in which this hymn appears.

304   More Holiness Give Me

The author of both text and tune of this hymn, Philip P. Bliss, was a noted American gospel hymn composer of the 19th century. He was killed in a train wreck in Ashtabula, Ohio when a bridge collapsed. Though he survived the initial plunge, he went back into the fire to rescue his wife, and both perished.

305   Thine Arm, O Lord, in Days of Old

This hymn on the subject of healing was authored by Edward H. Plumptre for publication in a leaflet produced by the chapel of King's College Hospital in London, England. It is not known how the tune got its name: in *A Supplement to the New Version of Psalms* in which it first appeared in 1708, tunes without names were named after saints.

306   There Is a Balm in Gilead

The chorus of this spiritual is based on two verses passages from Jeremiah—8:22 and 46:11. As with some other spirituals, the verses have little textual connection to the chorus. The hymn was first introduced to American congregations in a 1907 collection published by John and Frederick Work.

307   If Thou But Suffer God to Guide Thee

In 1641, on the way from his home in Thuringia to the University of Königsberg, Georg Neumark was robbed by highwaymen and left destitute. After a fruitless search for employment, he finally obtained a position as a tutor to a wealthy family in Kiel. This hymn, based on Psalm 55:22 and entitled "A Song of Comfort: God will care for and help every one in His own time," was inspired by his change of fortune.

308   Nearer, My God, to Thee

This hymn has been surrounded by several unverified anecdotes about its use in the 20th century. It was thought to be the final hymn played the band as the R.M.S. Titanic sank in 1912. It is also asserted that phrases from this text were the final words of the assassinated American president William McKinley in 1901.

309   Father, in Thy Mysterious Presence

This text was written by Samuel Johnson for a hymnal he co-edited in 1846, when he and his collaborator Samuel Longfellow were in their final year at Harvard Divinity School. The collection was a landmark of Unitarian hymnody and noted for the high quality of its included poetry.

310   Lead, Kindly Light, Amid th'Encircling Gloom

English clergyman John Henry Newman traveled as a young man in Italy. Becoming sick, he was forced to delay his journey for three weeks while he recovered. Anxious to return to his work in England, he wrote this text while on a ship in the Straits of Bonifacio.

311   Lord, I Want to Be a Christian

This spiritual's emphasis on an interior "religion of the heart" suggests both the emotional depth of African American Christianity and the limitations that people of color faced in trying to put their faith into action. Historically, it was often difficult for them to assemble for worship, and—whether slave or freed—they also faced the challenge of trying to maintain a Christian spirit in the face of oppression by a nominally Christian dominant society.

312   Come, Thou Fount of Every Blessing

Robert Robinson wrote this text as a hymn for Pentecost. This book uses Robinson's original version with its vivid reference from 1 Samuel 7:12 in the second verse to an "Ebenezer." The folk-hymn tune NETTLETON has had many names and carried many texts since its first appearance in 1813, but it is now firmly associated with this text.

313   Lord, Make Us Servants of Your Peace

Though probably not actually written by Francis of Assisi, this prayer has long been attributed to him and concisely expresses his teachings and ideology. The tune name refers to the composer Lee Hastings Bristol's *alma mater*, Dickinson College, in Carlisle, Pennsylvania. He adapted the tune from his anthem "Lord of all being throned afar."

314   O Master, Let Me Walk with Thee

Washington Gladden was minister of the First Congregational Church in Columbus, Ohio and a leading exponent of the "social gospel." He wrote this hymn in 1879 for a devotional column he edited in the magazine *Sunday Afternoon*. Although it was written and first published in England for a text by John Keble, the association of the tune MARYTON with Gladden's text has made it more popular on this side of the Atlantic than it is there.

315   Lead Us, O Father, in the Paths of Peace

William Henry Burleigh, a lecturer and editor for the abolitionist movement and later Harbormaster of New York City, wrote numerous hymns. Several, including this hymn, were published in Charles Dexter Cleveland's 1868 collection *Gems from American Sacred Poetry*. Published in both London and New York, this volume was a source of American hymnody frequently drawn upon by English hymnal editors, hence Burleigh's hymns are probably better known in England than in his own country.

316   Fight the Good Fight with All Thy Might

John S. B. Monsell composed this hymn for the Nineteenth Sunday after Trinity and based it on 1 Timothy 6:12. Henry Ley, composer of RUSHFORD, was professor of organ at the Royal College of Music and organist of Eton College, Windsor, England.

317   Lead Us, Heavenly Father, Lead Us

This text by James Edmeston was first published under the title "Hymn, Written for the Children of the London Orphan Asylum." Edmeston was an English architect who was a prolific avocational writer of hymns, said to have written a hymn each Sunday for most of his life, resulting in a corpus of over 2,000 texts.

318   O Jesus, I Have Promised

Anglican priest and poet John Ernest Bode wrote this text for his daughter and two sons, who were all confirmed on the same occasion. William H. Ferguson's tune WOLVERCOTE was originally written for this text for use at Lancing College in West Sussex, England, where he was on the teaching staff. The tune was named for a village close to Oxford, where Ferguson studied.

319   He Who Would Valiant Be

This text by Percy Dearmer is based on the poem "Who would true valor see" from a chapter of John Bunyan's *Pilgrim's Progress* of 1684. Composer Charles Winfred Douglas was one of the most distinguished American church musicians of the 20th century. As a major figure in the musical history of the Episcopal Church, he strongly influenced American sacred music in his work as an editor, arranger, and composer.

320   I Heard the Voice of Jesus Say

Horatius Bonar was one of the founders of the Free Church of Scotland and served as a minister in Edinburgh. His text was originally titled "The Voice from Galilee" and is based on John 1:16. John Bacchus Dykes's tune VOX DILECTI mirrors the bipartite nature of the text with its key change from minor to major at the halfway point.

321   One Thought I have, My Ample Creed

Frederick Lucian Hosmer, author of this text, was a graduate of Harvard College and Harvard Divinity School who served as a Unitarian minister in Massachusetts, Illinois, and California. A recognized authority on hymnody through his work as an editor, he taught courses on the subject at Harvard Divinity School. Harold Darke's tune CORNHILL gained its name from the church of St. Michael's, Cornhill, England, where he served as organist for over fifty years.

322   All Who Love and Serve Your City

Erik Routley was one of the most significant figures in hymnody in the second half of the 20th century. Although known chiefly as an editor and scholar, Routley produced both hymn texts and tunes when the need arose. This text, his first, was written during a workshop during in which he had been assigned to write a hymn tune. In the next room, poet and minister Alan Luff was humming while writing a text, and Routley was so annoyed with this musical distraction that he decided to write this text, rather than a tune. It is set here to the folk-hymn tune now known as CHARLESTOWN; among such tunes, it was the one most frequently reprinted in the 19th century.

323   Come, Labor On

English-born organist and composer T. Tertius Noble spent much of his career in the United States at St. Thomas Episcopal Church, Fifth Avenue, New York City, where he began its influential choir school for boys. Though Noble, like his colleagues Stanford and Parry, composed music in all genres, he is remembered today exclusively for church music.

324   Forth in Thy Name, O Lord, I Go

This text by Charles Wesley was originally titled "For Believers Before Work." SONG 34 by Orlando Gibbons was originally intended for George Wither's paraphrase of Luke

2:13–14, "The Angels sang, and thus sing we," but has subsequently been associated with many texts.

325 Thy Kingdom Come! On Bended Knee

Frederick Lucian Hosmer was a graduate of Harvard College and Harvard Divinity School who served as a Unitarian minister in Massachusetts, Illinois, and California. A recognized authority on hymnody through his work as an editor, he taught courses on the subject at Harvard Divinity School. He wrote this text for the 1891 Commencement exercises of Meadville Theological School, Pennsylvania.

326 Father Eternal, Ruler of Creation

Laurence Housman was an English illustrator, art critic, and playwright, best known for his play Victoria Regina of 1934. He wrote this text in 1919 for the Life and Liberty Movement, an organization formed at the end of World War I to promote international peace. Composer Geoffrey Shaw set the text to music for a 1921 meeting of the Movement.

327 God the Omnipotent! King, Who Ordainest

The first two stanzas of this hymn are from a text, "In Time of War," written by Henry F. Chorley, a music critic for the London *Times*. The remaining stanzas were written by John Ellerton, inspired by Chorley's work. The tune RUSSIAN HYMN was written by Alexis Lvov, a Russian government official, at the command of Tsar Nicholas I, who intended it to be a new national anthem.

328 Not Far Beyond the Sea, Nor High

George Bradford Caird, an English Congregational minister, held posts in theology at McGill University in Montreal, Quebec, Canada and the University of Oxford. He wrote this text for the use of Mansfield College, Oxford, inspired by John Robinson's address to the Pilgrims before they left on their voyage to the New World in 1620. Samuel Sebastian Wesley composed his tune CORNHILL for his grandfather Charles's text "Thou God of glorious majesty."

329 O Day of God, Draw Nigh

Reginald Balgarnie Young Scott was professor of Old Testament and religion at United Theological College in Montreal, Quebec, Canada and Princeton Seminary. He wrote this text for a hymn sheet of the Fellowship for a Christian Social Order.

330 My Soul, There Is a Country

Henry Vaughan, a physician in his native south Wales, was a staunch Royalist during the English Civil War. His mystical verse established him as one of the leading poets of 17th century England. This text, entitled "Peace," appeared in his 1650 collection *Silex Scintillans [The Sparkling Flint] or Sacred Poems and Private Ejaculations*.

331 Love Is Kind and Suffers Long

Christopher Wordsworth was Bishop of Lincoln, England; he also served as literary executor for his uncle, poet William Wordsworth. His publications consist primarily of commentaries on the Greek Old and New Testaments, a biography of his uncle, and a single book of religious poetry published in 1862, in which this text appears.

332   O What Their Joy and Their Glory Must Be

Medieval cleric and theologian Peter Abelard's hymn was written for the Convent of the Paraclete, founded at Nogent-sur-Seine, France, and presided over by his wife Héloise after she had taken the veil. In France during the 16th and 17th centuries, traditional unmeasured plainsong melodies were often replaced with metrical tunes founded on plainsong, such as O QUANTA QUALIA.

333   God of Grace and God of Glory

Harry Emerson Fosdick, first pastor of Riverside Church in New York City, wrote this hymn for the opening service of the church in 1930. One of the most noted religious authors and radio preachers of his time, Fosdick also served as Professor of Practical Theology at Union Seminary, New York City. Although it has most often appeared with other tunes, Fosdick intended this text for Henry Thomas Smart's tune REGENT SQUARE.

334   Jerusalem the Golden

The original Latin text for this hymn is an extract from the extended poem *De contemptu mundi* by Bernard of Cluny, a Benedictine monk. Although John Mason Neale created a number of hymns from sections of Bernard's poem, this is the only one still in common use. The tune now called EWING was originally named ST. BEDE by its composer, Alexander Ewing, a member of the Aberdeen Harmonic Choir. It was joined to this text in *Hymns Ancient and Modern* of 1861 after some adjustments by W. H. Monk. Because Ewing was out of the country at the time, he was not consulted about the changes, about which he later commented, "It now seems to me a good deal like a polka."

335   O Holy City, Seen of John

American author Walter Russell Bowie published only two hymns in his lifetime (this text and "Lord Christ, When First Thou Cam'st to Earth"), but both remain in active use. Herbert Howells composed the tune SANCTA CIVITAS, named for the text, for a 1964 publication.

336   Shall We Gather at the River

Robert Lowry's hymn is named for Hanson Place Baptist Church, Brooklyn, New York, where he was pastor at the time of its composition. During an oppressively hot July, Lowry was lying about in "a state of physical exhaustion" when he began to imagine a vision of the "river of life" as described in the book of Revelation.

337   Jerusalem, My Happy Home

This text is attributed to "F. B. P." in its manuscript. Despite many research attempts over the years, the author has not been able to be identified. The American folk hymn LAND OF REST gained its original name from its association with the text "O, land of rest, for thee I sigh!"

338   High o'er the Lonely Hills

Jan Struther was the literary pseudonym of the English author Joyce Anstruther, the author of this text. She is best remembered for the creation of the famed fictional character "Mrs. Miniver" in a series of newspaper columns in *The Times*. Near the end of her life, Anstruther frequently appeared on American radio quiz shows as a panelist.

Nothing is known of the 20th century composer T. H. Ingham; the companion to the Episcopal *Hymnal 1940* (in which his tune DAWN appears) does not even grant him an entry in the biography section.

339 Behold a Sower! From Afar

Washington Gladden was minister of First Congregational Church in Columbus, Ohio and a leading exponent of the "social gospel." Theodore Parker Ferris was rector of Trinity Episcopal Church in Boston, Massachusetts from 1942 to 1972; he was one of the most influential preachers and authors of his time.

340 Where Cross the Crowded Ways of Life

During the editorial process of the 1905 *Methodist Hymnal*, it was suggested to author Frank Mason North, a prominent figure in Methodist mission activities, that a new missionary hymn was necessary. English composer William Gardiner was a stocking manufacturer and amateur musician whose enthusiastic support for the works of Ludwig van Beethoven led to the first performances of Beethoven's music in England in 1794.

341 In Christ There Is No East or West

Harry T. Burleigh was an African American baritone, composer, and editor well-known for his arrangements and editions of spirituals. Although it was believed that the tune MCKEE was adapted from a spiritual entitled "I know the angel's done changed my name," research conducted by Charles Stanford into Irish music revealed that the tune was actually an Irish folk melody that came to America through immigrants.

342 How Great Thou Art

Stuart K. Hine, a missionary in Russia, based the tune of this hymn on a Swedish folk melody he overheard in a Russian variation while on a missionary journey in western Ukraine. This hymn gained great popularity in America due to its use in the Billy Graham Crusades of the mid-20th century.

343 Seek Not Afar for Beauty

Minot Judson Savage, author of this text, was an American Unitarian clergyman who served congregations in California, Missouri, Illinois, Massachusetts, and New York City. He received an honorary Doctorate of Divinity from Harvard in 1896 and published many books on the subject of the intersection of science and religion.

344 Precious Lord, Take My Hand

Thomas A. Dorsey is a crucial figure in the history of American gospel music and served as director of music at the Pilgrim Baptist Church in Chicago, Illinois, for over forty years. Drawing on his early years as "Georgia Tom," a jazz pianist, he wrote music that combined elements of Christian hymnody with jazz and the blues. This hymn is his best known composition, having been performed and recorded by many American popular musicians such as Mahalia Jackson and Elvis Presley, and as a personal favorite hymn of Martin Luther King, Jr.

345 Morning Glory, Starlit Sky

In the tradition of new music brought about by past editions of *The Harvard University Hymn Book*, the tune MEMORIAL CHURCH was commissioned from composer Carson

P. Cooman, a 2004 graduate of Harvard College, specifically for V. H. Vanstone's text, for which the hymnal committee wished a new setting.

346   From Thee All Skill and Science Flow

English novelist Charles Kingsley, author of *The Water-babies*, is noted for a famous literary argument he entertained with John Henry Newman. This is the first appearance of Kingsley's text with the tune MARSH CHAPEL by American organist Max Miller, who has long been associated with Boston University as University Organist and Professor of Organ. The tune takes it name from the university's chapel.

347   I Sought God's Love in Sun and Stars

English organist Arthur Berridge served for many years as the Secretary of the Free Church Choir Union in England and organist of the Westgrove Baptist Church. He composed a number of hymns and part songs, although it is not known why he entitled this particular tune HARVARD.

348   Praise the Source of Faith and Learning

Thomas Troeger, an active American religious poet, has been associated with many academic institutions, including the Iliff School of Theology and Yale Divinity School, as both a professor of homiletics and dean. This text, in particular, reflects on the inspiration of his experience in academic communities. It was commissioned by Duke University in Durham, North Carolina, and reflects the school's motto, "Faith and Learning."

349   At the Dawning of Creation

American priest and poet Jeffery Rowthorn served as Episcopal Bishop of Europe. He has been affiliated with Yale University and was co-editor of Yale's *New Hymnal for Colleges and Schools* in 1992. Harold W. Friedell's tune UNION SEMINARY, for which this text was written, is extracted from his most famous composition, the choral anthem *Draw Us in the Spirit's Tether*.

350   Father of All, We Lift to Thee Our Praise

The text of this hymn is by Lionel de Jersey Harvard, the only relative of John Harvard to attend the university, authoring this text in 1915, the year of his graduation. Harvard was killed while serving in the British army during World War I and is memorialized in The Memorial Church, where his named is inscribed upon the wall of the Memorial Room.

351   For the Splendor of Creation

The tune THAXTED was adapted by English composer Gustav Holst from the "Jupiter" movement of his symphonic work *The Planets*, op. 32, written between 1914 and 1916, but not premiered until 1920 because of World War I. The tune is named for the English village in which Holst resided for most of his life. Author Carl P. Daw, Jr. wrote this text celebrating academic communities specifically for Holst's tune, not only because of its grandeur, but also because it is not associated with any particular religious tradition.

352 O Gracious God, Your Servants

English composer Basil Harwood is best remembered today for his hymn tunes, of which THORNBURY is one of the most famous and stirring. The tune's name comes from a town in Wiltshire, England, the county where Harwood was born.

353 Life of Ages, Richly Poured

This text, titled "Inspiration," comes from a hymnal that Samuel Johnson edited in 1846, while he and his collaborator Samuel Longfellow were in their final year at Harvard Divinity School. The collection was a landmark of Unitarian hymnody and was noted for the high quality of its included poetry.

354 Lord, You Have Brought Us

The tune SHELDONIAN was composed by a Church of England priest, Cyril Vincent Taylor, who is best remembered for his role as editor for *Hymns Ancient and Modern*. The tune gained its name from the Sheldonian Theatre at the University of Oxford, England, where Taylor studied.

355 Give Ear, Ye Children, to My Law

The text of this hymn was adapted by Jeremy Belknap, a graduate of Harvard College in 1762 and later an Overseer of the University. He served as a Congregational minister in New Hampshire and in Boston. This text and tune have been sung at Harvard commencements at least since 1806, and are now also traditionally used at the Baccalaureate Service.

356 Deus omnium creator

This text was written in 1894 and published in the 1895 edition of *The University Hymn Book for use in the Chapel of Harvard University* by James Bradstreet Greenough, professor of Latin at Harvard. The tune HARVARD HYMN was written by John Knowles Paine in 1883 for use at the Harvard commencement dinner. First set to another text of Greenough's, it became associated with this text in the 1895 book. Paine was the first University Organist and Choirmaster, becoming the first professor of music in America upon his promotion in 1875.

357 Thy Book Falls Open, Lord: We Read

This text was written for the 1964 edition of *The Harvard University Hymn Book* by poet David McCord, a 1921 graduate of Harvard College who served for many years as the Executive Director of the Harvard Fund Council (now the Harvard College Fund). The tune was composed for the text by the author's close friend Randall Thompson, a Harvard graduate in 1920 and a distinguished American composer who was for many years a faculty member of the Department of Music.

358 Fair Harvard

The lyrics to Harvard's *alma mater* were written by Samuel Gilman, a member of the class of 1811 and a Unitarian minister in Massachusetts. An article from 1919 by W. H. Grattan Flood established that the tune was adapted from an Irish air with the original lyric of "My lodging it is on the cold ground."

359 Now Praise We Great and Famous Men

This hymn based on Ecclesiasticus 44:1–7 was written by William George Tarrant, a Unitarian minister and hymnal editor in London. A verse celebrating the contributions of women has been added in this publication. J. S. Bach's harmonization of this tune comes not from a cantata, but from his collection of harmonized chorale melodies published posthumously in 1765.

360 O Valiant Hearts, Who to Your Glory Came

This hymn, entitled "The Supreme Sacrifice," was published in a book of wartime poems in 1919 by John Stanhope Arkwright, an English barrister and Member of Parliament. The tune VALIANT HEARTS was composed for the text by English composer Gustav Holst.

361 Not Alone for Mighty Empire

William Pierson Merrill wrote this text in 1909 when he was minister of the Sixth Presbyterian Church in Chicago, Illinois. The tune GENEVA, written for this text, was composed by George Henry Day, organist of Trinity Episcopal Church in Geneva, New York, hence the tune name.

362 O God of Earth and Altar

The author of this text, G. K. Chesterton, was a noted English poet, essayist, and writer of popular detective stories. A deeply religious man, he became a Roman Catholic in his later years, and published essays and books on Christian apologetics. Ralph Vaughan Williams collected the original folk melody in King's Lynn, Norfolk, England in 1905, hence the tune name.

363 Judge Eternal, Throned in Splendor

Henry Scott Holland was an English clergyman deeply concerned about the Christian response to contemporary social and economic problems. He was one of the founders of the Christian Social Union and served as editor of its magazine, *The Commonwealth*, in which he published this hymn text.

364 God of the Nations, Whose Almighty Hand

This text was written by Daniel Crane Roberts, an Episcopal priest in Vermont, to celebrate the national centennial on July 4, 1876. George W. Warren composed the tune NATIONAL HYMN for the centennial celebrations in 1892 of the adoption of the United States Constitution.

365 And Did Those Feet in Ancient Times

Charles Hubert Hastings Parry composed this tune for William Blake's nationalistic poem entitled "Milton." Because of the text's English fanaticism and Parry's rousing tune, the hymn has become a "second national anthem" in England and curiously popular in the United States, even with its original text.

366 My Country, 'Tis of Thee

Samuel Francis Smith, an American Baptist minister, wrote this hymn while a student at Andover Theological Seminary in Andover, Massachusetts. The hymn was first performed on July 4, 1831 at the Park Street Congregational Church in Boston, with a choir directed by Lowell Mason.

367   Battle Hymn of the Republic

Julia Ward Howe wrote the text of this patriotic song during the American Civil War at the suggestion of a friend for new lyrics to the song "John Brown's Body", a commonly-sung marching song of the Union soldiers.

368   The Star-Spangled Banner

Francis Scott Key wrote the text of the national anthem of the United States of America during the War of 1812 in the midst of the bombing of Fort McHenry by British forces in September 1814. Key set his lyrics to the tune "To Anacreon in Heaven," from a collection of glees published in London by John Stafford Smith.

369   O Beautiful for Spacious Skies

Katharine Lee Bates's text was inspired by a summer visit to the state of Colorado and a day trip climbing Pike's Peak. She later wrote that the opening lines of the text came to her as she stood on the peak and looked out at "the sea-like expanse of fertile country spreading away so far under those ample skies." Samuel Augustus Ward's tune MATERNA gained its name from its original text "O mother dear, Jerusalem."

370   Glory to You, Our Faithful God

The text of this canticle, "Benedictus es, Domine," comes from the Apocryphal "Song of the Three Young Men" ascribed to Shadrach, Meshach, and Abednego (or Daniel-Ananiah, Misael, and Azariah) while in the Babylonian King Nebuchadnezzar's fiery furnace.

371   Glory Be to the Father

The doxology "Gloria Patria" is of great antiquity. The first clause may date from the end of the first century, and the second was in use at least by the sixth century. This hymn is traditionally sung each week in Sunday morning worship services in The Memorial Church.

Index of Original First Lines of Translated Hymns

ORIGINAL FIRST LINES OF TRANSLATED HYMNS

GREEK

HEBREW

IRISH

ITALIAN

LATIN

SPANISH

WELSH

Index of Authors, Translators, and Textual Sources

Index of Composers, Arrangers, and Musical Sources

Metrical Index of Tunes

Alphabetical Index of Tunes

Index of First Lines and Titles